LEGITIMATE EXPECTATIONS IN THE COMMON LAW WORLD

The recognition and enforcement of legitimate expectations by courts has been a striking feature of English law since *R v North and East Devon Health Authority*; *ex parte Coughlan* [2001] 3 QB 213. Although the substantive form of legitimate expectation adopted in *Coughlan* was quickly accepted by English courts and received a generally favourable response from public law scholars, the doctrine of that case has largely been rejected in other common law jurisdictions. The central principles of *Coughlan* have been rejected by courts in common law jurisdictions outside the UK for a range of reasons, such as incompatibility with local constitutional doctrine, or because they mark an undesirable drift towards merits review. The sceptical and critical reception to *Coughlan* outside England is a striking contrast to the reception the case received within the UK. This book provides a detailed scholarly analysis of these issues and considers the doctrine of legitimate expectations both in England and elsewhere in the common law world.

Volume 12 in the series Hart Studies in Comparative Public Law

Hart Studies in Comparative Public Law

Recent titles in this series:

The Use of Foreign Precedents by Constitutional Judges
Edited by Tania Groppi and Marie-Claire Ponthoreau

Israeli Constitutional Law in the Making
Edited by Gideon Sapir, Daphne Barak-Erez and Aharon Barak

Judicial Decision-Making in a Globalised World
A Comparative Analysis of the Changing Practices
of Western Highest Courts
Elaine Mak

Constitutionalising Secession
David Haljan

Parliaments and Human Rights
Redressing the Democratic Deficit
Edited by Murray Hunt, Hayley Hooper and Paul Yowell

The Right to Freedom of Assembly
A Comparative Study
Orsolya Salát

An Inquiry into the Existence of Global Values
Through the Lens of Comparative Constitutional Law
Edited by Dennis Davis, Alan Richter and Cheryl Saunders

The Scope and Intensity of Substantive Review
Traversing Taggart's Rainbow
Edited by Hanna Wilberg and Mark Elliott

Entick v Carrington
250 Years of the Rule of Law
Edited by Adam Tomkins and Paul Scott

Administrative Law and Judicial Deference
Matthew Lewans

Soft Law and Public Authorities
Remedies and Reform
Greg Weeks

Legitimate Expectations in the Common Law World

Edited by
Matthew Groves and Greg Weeks

•HART•
OXFORD • LONDON • NEW YORK • NEW DELHI • SYDNEY

HART PUBLISHING
Bloomsbury Publishing Plc
Kemp House, Chawley Park, Cumnor Hill, Oxford, OX2 9PH, UK

HART PUBLISHING, the Hart/Stag logo, BLOOMSBURY and the Diana logo are trademarks of Bloomsbury Publishing Plc
First published in Great Britain 2017

First published in hardback, 2017
Paperback edition, 2019

A catalogue record for this book is available from the British Library.

Library of Congress Cataloging-in-Publication Data

Names: Groves, Matthew, editor. | Weeks, Greg (Law teacher), editor.

Title: Legitimate expectations in the common law world / edited by Matthew Groves and Greg Weeks.

Description: Oxford [UK] ; Portland, Oregon : Hart Publishing, 2016. | Series: Hart studies in comparative public law ; volume 12 | Includes bibliographical references and index.

Identifiers: LCCN 2016037626 (print) | LCCN 2016038121 (ebook) | ISBN 9781849467780 (hardback) | ISBN 9781509909506 (Epub) Subjects: LCSH: Common law. | Jurisprudence.

Classification: LCC K588 .L44 2017 (print) | LCC K588 (ebook) | DDC 340.5/7—dc23

LC record available at https://lccn.loc.gov/2016037626

ISBN: HB: 978-1-84946-778-0
PB: 978-1-50992-973-3
ePDF: 978-1-50990-949-0
ePub: 978-1-50990-950-6

Series: Hart Studies in Comparative Public Law, volume 12

Typeset by Compuscript Ltd, Shannon

To find out more about our authors and books visit www.hartpublishing.co.uk. Here you will find extracts, author information, details of forthcoming events and the option to sign up for our newsletters.

Foreword

Comparative common law research is not easy, especially in public law. Not long ago, it was not easy for logistical reasons. It was difficult to get access to the law in other jurisdictions in a timely way. Months would pass before decisions were published and reached law libraries around the world. The problem today is the opposite. Law is available from the highest courts of most countries more or less instantly. There is far too much law for anyone to keep up with

And there are traps for the unwary. Legal concepts that share similar names and histories may operate in quite different ways. The concept of legitimate expectation is a good example. From its modest origins, the concept has come to mean very different things in different common law jurisdictions—everything from an aspect of procedural fairness to a substantive check on the exercise of government power—and one of the interesting questions posed by this collection is whether the law is likely to converge or continue to evolve along different paths.

In Canada, a cautious approach to legitimate expectation taken from the outset has continued, and as a result to have a legitimate expectation may result in no more than a right to notice before a public authority acts in a manner that affects an individual who holds the expectation. In England, by contrast, to have a legitimate expectation is to have a means of holding a public authority to its word, on substantive as well as procedural matters. Australia, which flirted with the most expansive conception of the doctrine, has since resiled from it.

Despite these differences, as the essays in this collection demonstrate, common doctrinal issues arise in every jurisdiction. What is required in order to give rise to an expectation? Is a policy or past practice sufficient, or must there be a promise or undertaking? What makes an expectation 'legitimate' and so entitled to protection? Is knowledge of a particular policy or practice required in order for an expectation to be created? Is reliance on that policy or practice required? Is detriment necessary?

The answers to these sorts of questions ultimately determine how easy or difficult it is to establish a legitimate expectation, but the more important issue is normative in nature: What does it mean to hold a legitimate expectation?

The questions here go to the heart of the relationship between the judiciary and the executive. To what extent, if any, can courts assume responsibility for holding governments to their policies and undertakings? To what extent should they? What distinguishes legitimate expectation from estoppel, which traditionally was not available against public authorities? Is legitimate expectation designed to promote good public administration, to protect the dignity of those subject to state action, or both?

These are just some of the questions addressed by the articles in this collection, which features in-depth consideration of English, Canadian, Australian, New Zealand, Hong Kong, Singapore and Indian law by a distinguished group of contributors. The editors describe their collection as a 'celebration of the common law mosaic', but the contributions do much more than simply address the doctrine and its operation in different jurisdictions. They engage with the profound questions that make administrative law so interesting and challenging.

This is an outstanding collection and a great contribution to administrative law scholarship.

Grant Huscroft
Court of Appeal for Ontario

Table of Contents

List of Contributors

Sas Ansari is a PhD candidate at Osgoode Hall Law School in York University, Canada.

Janina Boughey is a Lecturer in the Faculty of Law at Monash University, Australia.

Chintan Chandrachud is a PhD candidate at Sidney Sussex College, University of Cambridge.

Paul Daly is Senior Lecturer in Public Law, University of Cambridge and the Derek Bowett Fellow in Law at Queens' College, Cambridge.

Joanna Davidson is a barrister at the Sydney bar, practising mainly in public and administrative law.

Mark Elliott is a Professor of Public Law at the University of Cambridge and a Fellow of St Catharine's College, Cambridge.

Matthew Groves is a Professor in the Faculty of Law at Monash University, Australia.

Cora Hoexter is a Professor of Law at the University of the Witwatersrand, Johannesburg.

Swati Jhaveri is an Assistant Professor in the Faculty of Law at the National University of Singapore.

Philip A Joseph is a Professor Law at the University of Canterbury, New Zealand.

Lorne Sossin is Dean of the Osgoode Hall Law School in York University, Canada.

Kristina Stern SC is a leading silk at the Sydney bar, with an extensive practice in public and administrative law.

Robert Thomas is a Professor of Public Law in the School of Law, University of Manchester.

Jason NE Varuhas is an Associate Professor in the Melbourne Law School at the University of Melbourne and an Associate Fellow at the Centre for Public Law, University of Cambridge.

Greg Weeks is a Senior Lecturer in the Faculty of Law at the University of New South Wales, Australia.

1

The Legitimate Expectation as an Instrument and Illustration of Common Law Change

MATTHEW GROVES AND GREG WEEKS

THIS BOOK MIGHT be understood as an extended essay in family relations. After all, the countries within the common law world are united to a significant extent by their shared heritage of English legal principles. As with all families, the younger members grow up and change but do so in different ways. Some stay close to their parents. Some do not. If the common law is placed within this analogy, it would be cast as a parent whose influence is imprinted deeply and hard to let go of. But as with all parents, the common law knew its children would leave home and change during that time.

Not long before it lost appellate jurisdiction over the courts of New Zealand, the Privy Council conceded that 'the common law is no longer monolithic'.[1] The Law Lords accepted that one consequence of this change was that courts of other jurisdictions could 'make a deliberate policy decision to depart from the English approach' as part of the development of the common law of their own jurisdictions.[2] The distinguished New Zealand jurist Lord Cooke was not a judge in the just quoted Privy Council decision but, in a speech delivered around the same time, he approached the very same issue from a very different perspective. Lord Cooke suggested that the common law was becoming less English.[3] The important subtlety of this

[1] *B v Auckland District Law Society (New Zealand)* [2003] 2 AC 736, 759 [55]. The same point was acknowledged by Lord Robert Walker, 'Developing the Common Law: How Far is Too Far?' (2013) 37 *Melbourne University Law Review* 232, 234.

[2] *Auckland District Law Society*, ibid. In the case at hand, the Lords deftly enforced English law by finding that the New Zealand courts had purported to apply rather than change English law. Since that law had been misunderstood, the decision of the New Zealand Court of Appeal was overturned.

[3] Sir Robin Cooke, 'The Road Ahead for the Common Law' (2004) 53 *International and Comparative Law Quarterly* 273, 274.

point was not that Commonwealth courts could depart from principles of English common law, as the Privy Council suggested, but rather that the English courts might be losing control of the common law itself. One can easily understand why the Privy Council did not express the point in such terms. After all, it is one thing to lose territory acquired by an empire. It is quite another to accept that former colonies may have seized a cherished part of the old country. While the Privy Council's admission anticipates that different common law jurisdictions may adopt differing principles, that possibility typically comes into sharpest focus when jurisdictions outside the UK decide to reject or change principles developed by courts within the UK.

The emergence of different approaches within the common law is not limited to variations to common law principles and can sometimes identify the UK as a recipient rather than originator of change. In an influential article, Gardbaum explained the different paths taken by some of the common law countries which had adopted bills or charters of rights in recent times.[4] He examined the different such instruments adopted by Canada, New Zealand and the UK, all of which had deliberately departed from the model of rights protection, adopted in the US, that allows courts to invalidate legislation. He noted that different common law jurisdictions had incorporated different means within their new human rights instruments to enable courts to deal with legislation that contravened those instruments. A common theme of these instruments was that they had 'decoupled judicial review from judicial supremacy by empowering legislatures to have the last word'.[5] A little noticed aspect of Gardbaum's analysis was the idea that the UK was only one of several nations that was following and adjusting the earlier model adopted in the US.[6] That occurrence has a long history, not limited to UK legislation that draws from innovations elsewhere in the common law world. Recent empirical research on the Privy Council has found that it did not simply influence the law through much of the common law world but also provided a means by which English doctrines could be tested and sometimes adjusted by reference to the colonial variations that came before the Judicial Committee in its appellate jurisdiction.[7] The key question about legitimate expectations therefore cannot focus simply on the departure of various jurisdictions from the English approach. Instead, the key questions

[4] Stephen Gardbaum, 'The New Commonwealth Model of Constitutionalism' (2001) 49 *American Journal of Comparative Law* 102.

[5] Ibid, 709. This analysis is also consistent with the human rights instruments that were adopted in some Australian jurisdictions after Gardbaum's article.

[6] Gardbaum extended this theory beyond those bills and charters of rights to constitutional doctrine more generally in Stephen Gardbaum, *The New Model of Constitutionalism: Theory and Practice* (Cambridge University Press, 2013).

[7] Paul Mitchell, 'The Privy Council and the Difficulty of Distance' (2016) 36 *Oxford Journal of Legal Studies* 26.

are the more open ones of what different approaches to legitimate expectations have arisen in the common law world and why.

Much of the previous paragraph is at odds with a decision the Privy Council delivered shortly before this book was sent for copy editing. The case was yet another messy criminal prosecution that came to the Judicial Committee with much political baggage. In this instance, dispute arose about legislation that sought to repeal a legislative prohibition on criminal prosecutions for conduct alleged to have occurred more than 10 years earlier. The prohibition was repealed only two weeks after it commenced and seemed only to serve the purpose of giving those who stood to benefit from it a reason to launch further litigation to forestall their prosecution. The Privy Council dismissed every one of a swathe of objections, including a claim of legitimate expectations—the expectation being that those who benefitted from the legislative prohibition expected to continue to enjoy that benefit. Delivering judgment on behalf of the Judicial Committee, Lord Sumption accepted that parliaments could repeal legislation that they were empowered to enact. He explained:

> The Constitution does not protect legitimate expectations as such, and there must be some doubt whether, and if so when, breach of a legitimate expectation can ever, in itself, be the basis of a constitutional challenge to the validity of an otherwise regular law.[8]

That reasoning was ostensibly directed to the Constitution of Trinidad and Tobago but also appeared to confirm the constitutional position of legitimate expectations more generally. The Privy Council seemed anxious to make clear that legitimate expectations sit below higher constitutional questions and, by implication, within constitutional fundamentals. That last point is made clear by the examination of different jurisdictions in this book and their common concern that legitimate expectations, especially their substantive enforcement, must sit within constitutional boundaries. It is, however, notable that the Privy Council felt the need to reiterate a basic limit on the legitimate expectation. The doctrine cannot provide a restraint on an otherwise plenary legislative power. The message is two-fold. First, to the extent that legitimate expectations restrain official power, they do so against executive or bureaucratic rather than legislative power. Second, legitimate expectations will not provide a form of bottom up reasoning in which a restraint on official power at one level of our constitutional arrangements may travel upwards to influence higher level constitutional doctrine.[9]

[8] *Ferguson v Attorney-General of Trinidad and Tobago* [2016] UKPC 2 [36].

[9] We take this from Richard Posner, 'Legal Reasoning from the Top Down and from the Bottom Up: The Question of Unenumerated Constitutional Rights' (1992) 59 *University of Chicago Law Review* 433. We also note that the top down/bottom up metaphor has long since moved beyond public law: Keith Mason, 'Do Top-down and Bottom-up Reasoning Ever

The Privy Council addressed the constitutional basis of legitimate expectations about a year earlier, when it located the doctrine within the common law constitutionalism. In *Rainbow Insurance Company Ltd v Financial Services Commission (Mauritius)*,[10] the Council rejected a claimed legitimate expectation in great detail. The expectation was claimed on so many different bases that it appeared to provoke the Council to explain what it regarded as the first principle of the doctrine. The Privy Council explained:

> The courts have developed the principle of legitimate expectation as part of administrative law to protect persons from gross unfairness or abuse of power by a public authority. The constitutional principle of the rule of law underpins the protection of legitimate expectations as it prohibits the arbitrary use of power by public authorities.[11]

This reasoning locates legitimate expectations firmly within the realm of the common law and in the particular realm of common law constitutionalism and all of its associated questions. The most obvious problem is the circular and self-reinforcing nature of principles of common law constitutionalism. They are defined by the courts, justified by the courts and protected by the courts.[12] The executive is subject to legitimate expectations but has little say in their content or application.

The role of the courts in legitimate expectations is controversial for another reason related to constitutional law at the higher level because it provides yet another example of the 'last word' debate that has always dogged constitutional law. A perpetual question in constitutional law, particularly constitutional judicial review, is who should have the last word on issues, the legislature or the courts? This question divides constitutional lawyers largely into opposing camps, so that one favours the last word on the legality and legitimacy of legislation being exercised by either the courts or parliaments.[13] It is only more recently that some authors have accepted that the better approach might be a middle ground, in which all of the different institutions might serve distinct and complementary

Meet?' in Elise Bant and Matthew Harding (eds), *Exploring Private Law* (Cambridge University Press, 2010) 19; Carmine Conte, 'From Only the "Bottom Up"? Legitimate Forms of Reasoning in Private Law' (2015) 35 *Oxford Journal of Legal Studies* 1.

[10] *Rainbow Insurance Company Ltd v Financial Services Commission (Mauritius)* [2015] UKPC 15.

[11] Ibid, [51] (Lord Hodge, delivering judgment for the Council).

[12] The true problem is not the judicial origin of such principles but their ad hoc nature, which makes the search for coherence principle a deep problem. See eg, Tom Poole, 'Back to the Future? Unearthing the Theory of Common Law Constitutionalism' (2003) 23 *Oxford Journal of Legal Studies* 435.

[13] Aileen Kavanagh, 'Constitutional Review, the Courts and Democratic Scepticism' (2009) 62 *Current Legal Problems* 102, 134–35.

roles.[14] That possibility aligns with recent suggestions that the age of a rigid approach to the separation of powers has passed, or should pass, into history.[15] To the extent that the separation of powers is viewed as explicit within a written constitution, as is the case in Australia, history shows that its rigidity is not easily tempered.[16]

The legitimate expectation raises a similar problem but with a slight change, so that the question of who should have the final say involves the courts and the executive. That question is the administrative law equivalent of the perpetual question in constitutional law but is acutely felt in legitimate expectations because the traditional settlement of administrative law does not unfold as expected. That settlement accords the last word on the law to the courts and the last word on the facts to the executive. There will always be a hazy dividing line between the two but in itself does not mean the basic segmentation in this division and allocation of functions is not real or workable. As a former Chief Justice of Australia explained when he acknowledged that judicial review on the ground of unreasonableness can often edge close to a form of factual or merits review, the blur between judicial and other review 'is not always clear cut; but neither is the difference between night and day; and twilight does not invalidate the distinction between night and day…'[17] The enforcement of legitimate expectations, or principles that make actions contrary to legitimate expectations overly difficult, may still contradict this doctrinal fundamental. This is because, even though courts do not formally exercise the power vested in administrative officials, it is often argued that they nonetheless do so in a practical sense. Thomas contradicts that longstanding objection with two key arguments. First, that the steps of judicial reasoning taken in the more controversial legitimate expectations cases are actually modest in a doctrinal sense. His second and closely related point is that the few instances where substantive enforcement occurred can be entirely justified.

Weeks extends these possibilities by posing a question that is surprisingly neglected in the legitimate expectation cases, namely are the courts the best

[14] A valuable recent example, made by reference to rights protection, is Murray Hunt, 'Introduction' in Murray Hunt, Hayley Hooper and Paul Yowell (eds), *Parliament and Human Rights* (Hart Publishing, 2015).

[15] Eoin Carolan, *The New Separation of Powers* (Oxford University Press, 2009).

[16] The *Boilermakers' Case* has a virtually unassailable place in Australian constitutional thought, belying the narrowness of the result in the case itself: *R v Kirby; ex parte Boilermakers' Society of Australia* (1956) 94 CLR 254. That its strict separation of judicial functions from non-judicial bodies, and vice versa, remained contentious was illustrated by the fact that two High Court justices invited, without undue subtlety, argument that *Boilermakers'* should be overruled: *Re Joske; ex parte Australian Building Construction Employees & Builders Labourers Federation* (1974) 130 CLR 87, 90 (Barwick CJ); 102 (Mason J). That challenge never transpired and it is now extremely unlikely that it ever will.

[17] Murray Gleeson, 'Judicial Legitimacy' (2000) 20 *Australian Bar Review* 4, 11.

placed to provide the remedies that these cases typically require? Legal scholars typically approach this question from entirely the opposite direction, by arguing that courts can and should extend their form of adjudication (and, it follows, develop suitable legal principles) for those disputes which have traditionally been thought to be better determined by the executive. The classic example is the polycentric dispute, which raises a multitude of complex and often interrelated issues. *Coughlan*[18] can be labelled as a prime example of polycentricity if the case is placed in the wider perspective of all of the many funding decisions the respondent authority had to make. What had to be allocated for Ms Coughlan's home (Mardon House) would have to be taken from, or not allocated in the future to, another health programme or perhaps another area of the authority's work. The authority's capacity to develop its own policy, or to follow government policy more generally for the delivery of health services, was compromised. When these possibilities come into play, the continued operation of Mardon House can be seen to have affected many programmes and people other than the parties to *Coughlan's* case. Many now argue that polycentric disputes are neither unique to public law disputes nor ones that the political process can invariably resolve in a better way than the courts,[19] though such arguments have some notable unbelievers.[20] If the courts are able to undertake a context-sensitive balancing of finely weighed issues, or seemingly veer closer to deciding the factual merits of a decision, as arguably occurred in *Coughlan*, one can ask why the traffic should be all one way. Is the executive perhaps better suited to crafting remedies in many of the disputes that are currently argued as legitimate expectation cases?

At first glance, this book may be understood as providing competing narratives about the growing differences between the law of England and other common law jurisdictions. That is correct because, at one level, the book examines whether and why different jurisdictions have adopted the substantive legitimate expectation that was given effect in *Coughlan's* case, or taken quite different approaches to the recognition and enforcement of legitimate expectations. But closer analysis of the legitimate expectation reveals that *Coughlan* and the many other equivalent landmark cases of other common law jurisdictions are more about the balanced and evolving relations between the courts, governments and citizens. That is because the recognition and enforcement expectations serve as an expression variously

[18] *R v North and East Devon Health Authority; ex parte Coughlan* [2001] 1 QB 213.

[19] Jeff King has developed these arguments with clarity in 'The Pervasiveness of Polycentricity' [2008] *Public Law* 101 and 'The Justiciability of Resource Allocation' (2007) 70 *Modern Law Review* 197.

[20] See, eg, Tom Poole, 'Questioning Common Law Constitutionalism' (2005) 25 *Legal Studies* 142.

of when and why officials should be held to legal account, what people who deal with government may rightly expect in those dealings and, finally, just how far courts may devise legal principles that reflect and direct the administrative process. These issues are as much moral as they are legal because how they are approached and resolved reflects interwoven questions of morality, expectation, fairness and reasonableness. The solution posed in one paper written prior to this volume is to use 'a clear and unequivocal promise' as 'the gateway for a legitimate expectation arising because it is the point at which a public authority assumes moral and legal obligation for the individual'.[21]

Perhaps the most important moral issue underlying the enforcement of legitimate expectations is their very recognition. The notion that governments and their agencies and individual bureaucrats can create expectations on the part of people who are affected by the exercise of official power presumes a level of responsibility for the expectations so created. It follows that accountability, transparency and consistency for expectations created by public entities or their officers either do or should exist. Elliott argues that the evolution of legitimate expectations has helped this presumption to become part of orthodoxy in English law. In England, people can now expect as a matter of law that public officials will be held to their word by the courts. That does not seem to be the case in the other particular jurisdictions examined by other articles in this volume. The emergence of distinct approaches to similar issues within the common law world is hardly surprising in light of the quite different constitutional structures of many former British colonies. Those differences have led to quite different constitutional structures, even if they are located within the same central elements of liberal democracy, ministerial responsibility, cabinet government and a rule of law system that incorporates some form of the separation of powers. There are enough differences in these constituent elements of governance that developments in British public law often cannot now translate easily throughout the Commonwealth.

The most striking example comes from Australia. The relatively strict Australian conception of the separation of judicial power has led the High Court of Australia to reject both *Coughlan* and its normative principles as incompatible with the limits placed upon the constitutionally entrenched role of the courts. The analysis of Groves suggests that this position is explicable as much to the allocation of providing fuller rights of merits review to administrative tribunals as to constitutional doctrine. However, he also makes clear that any significant changes to the principles governing judicial

[21] Jack Watson, 'Clarity and Ambiguity: A New Approach to the Test of Legitimacy in the Law of Legitimate Expectations' (2010) 30 *Legal Studies* 633, 651.

power could easily bring wider constitutional principles undone. The weight of too much constitutional doctrine now sits on the separation (and protection) of judicial power for it to be brought undone by the acceptance of a substantive approach to legitimate expectations.

Stern and Davidson take a more pragmatic approach to change in Australia which, at one level, appears to identify the path of least resistance. They acknowledge the constitutional obstacles to substantive enforcement of expectations identified in Australia but note that the growing focus on an 'outcome focussed' form of unreasonableness review may be evolving in a form that can give effect to the underlying values of an otherwise prohibited doctrine. This approach would be limited and heavily dependent on the statutory context of each case. Those elements of expanding unreasonableness review avoid the recourse to normative considerations that is common in England but still go some way to using an approach not so far away from the forbidden English one.[22] That assessment aligns with that of Elliott, who locates *Coughlan* within a wider journey of substantive review in English law. The substantive legitimate expectation has served as both a cause and effect of this journey and can be used to map changes to orthodoxy in English law.

One key assumption of Australian law—which is that notions of substantive justice or fairness form part of the merits and thus lie beyond the reach of judicial review in any formal sense—is completely alien to South Africa's constitutional structure. Hoexter explains how South African courts rejected historical distinctions between 'quasi-judicial' and 'purely administrative' traces and other technical distinctions during a time when South Africa's new constitutional structure largely excised such formalities. This contrasts with Joseph's analysis of how New Zealand shed formalism from its administrative law through adopting legitimate expectations as a common law doctrine. Hoexter notes the subtle but crucial point that, while the South African Constitution grants people a clear right to administrative action that is 'lawful, reasonable and procedurally fair',[23] neither this clause nor the legislation enacted pursuant to it clearly adopt the language or concepts of legitimate expectations.[24] Hoexter nonetheless traces how the legitimate

[22] We feel compelled to point out that this may be the only known instance where Australians are offended by the frank language of the English, rather than the reverse.

[23] Constitution of the Republic of South Africa, 1996 s 33(b).

[24] Hoexter usefully traces the causative effect of a single confusing reference to legitimate expectations that was included in the Promotion of Administrative Justice Act 3 of 2000 (SA). The effect of this point is especially counterintuitive in legitimate expectations, where so many cases are founded on attempts to use the doctrine to resolve claims of unfairness or uncertainty due to administrative conduct. The South African experience in part shows how similar issues elided with what arguably should have been an unremarkable question of statutory interpretation.

expectation has gained traction in modern South African law, initially as a device to free notions of fairness and natural justice from a narrow range of deprivation cases, releasing them into a wider range of public entitlements. According to Hoexter, South African law now stands at the edge of the divide between procedural and substantive expectations. The contrast to Australia could not be more striking. Legitimate expectations have fallen prey to wider constitutional doctrines in Australia but in South Africa they are being enlivened, and may even be extended, by constitutional change. This reinforces the point that a country's constitutional arrangements are paramount to the treatment of legitimate expectations in that country's administrative law jurisprudence.

Constitutional considerations of a different kind are revealed by the analysis of Hong Kong and Singapore by Jhaveri, and also the Australian experience recounted by Groves. These chapters examine three jurisdictions with quite different constitutional frameworks. All have the common quality of rejecting much of the core reasoning used of *Coughlan*, though to quite different effect. In Australia, both acceptance of *Coughlan* specifically and a substantive legitimate expectations doctrine generally remain impossible on constitutional grounds. The doctrine simply cannot stand with the quite rigid conception of the separation of powers that has evolved in Australia. The obstacle presented by the separation of powers is not self-evident in Hong Kong and Singapore. Jhaveri makes clear that separation of powers considerations have influenced but not precluded the adoption of forms of the substantive legitimate expectation in those jurisdictions. The clear lesson seems to be that constitutional issues in general, and separation of powers doctrines in particular, can greatly influence whether a substantive version of legitimate expectations may be adopted and what form it may take. The reasons in each instance were largely anchored in domestic constitutional considerations and the wider legal balance that courts in each jurisdiction have reached as they fashion constitutional doctrines.

The Indian experience documented by Chandrachud is entirely different. Indian courts have accepted the legitimate expectation in many forms, including the notion that expectations can sometime be given or deserve substantive effect. That possibility is at odds with the Australian position noted by Groves and is all the more curious because Chandrachud notes that Indian courts make frequent reference to the key Australian case that ultimately doomed any substantive enforcement of legitimate expectations.[25] At the same time, Indian courts also make regular reference to *Coughlan*

[25] *Attorney-General (NSW) v Quin* (1990) 170 CLR 1. This decision is an exemplar of top down reasoning because Brennan J explained the constitutional allocation of powers and functions at a high level of abstraction, so much so that he did not refer to a single provision of the Australian Constitution during several key pages of his judgment.

which adopts a position entirely at odds with the Australian one. Chandrachud's ironic conclusion is that Indian courts have accepted the legitimate expectation but in name only. Their purported adoption of the doctrine simply does not survive close scrutiny. The reason is surely that the underlying issue of *Coughlan* is more about the nature of the review it embodied rather than the particular doctrine by which it was done.

To an outside observer, *Coughlan* may be best explained as an important stepping stone in the longer English journey from estoppel to a more substantive form of judicial review of administrative action.[26] The case clearly marked a 'giant step', to quote from one of the leading works on judicial review outside of England, because it added a 'third basis for attack' on decisions by allowing a court to 'conduct its own evaluation of the authority's policy decision in terms of its fairness'.[27] The longstanding criticism of this new basis for judicial attack on administrative decisions is that its intrusion into the executive realm lacks a coherent underlying basis. Varuhas and Daly offer solutions which are similar in their rationale but entirely different in their approach. Each argues for greater clarity and internal consistency within legitimate expectations but takes an entirely different path. Varuhas essentially strips away the accumulated complexity and detail of layers of cases to reveal the apparent core of the legitimate expectation—a promise made by an authority. The pluralist focus of Daly is complementary because it argues that the differing purposes or underlying values of the legitimate expectation cases can be reconciled but should not be somehow compressed into a single overarching moral or normative goal. Each of these approaches proceeds on the twin assumptions that the overall doctrine of legitimate expectations lacks coherence but can become coherent if properly refined and revised. This recognises that current judicial methodologies are not always successful.

In her analysis of proportionality and legitimate expectations, Boughey notes that the Court of Appeal objected to a rationality standard in *Coughlan* because such a principle would allow public authorities to be a judge of their own cause. She notes that Laws LJ addressed that same issue in *Nadarajah*[28] and concluded that 'the court is the judge, or the last judge' of the question of whether any asserted public interest justified a public agency in departing from a promise.[29] Boughey rightly questions the value

[26] The case has also been explained as a key driver in the movement of English public law towards the adoption of a 'rights focus': Tom Poole, 'The Reformation of English Administrative Law' (2009) 68 *Cambridge Law Journal* 142. The case was also given a clear (and very favourable) human rights analysis in Jeffrey Jowell, 'Beyond the Rule of Law: Towards Constitutional Judicial Review' [2000] *Public Law* 671, 677–78.

[27] Mark Aronson and Matthew Groves, *Judicial Review of Administrative Action*, 5th edn (Lexis Nexis, 2013) 385.

[28] *R (Nadarajah) v Secretary of State for the Home Department* [2005] EWCA Civ 1363.

[29] Ibid, [68].

of the proportionality approach suggested by Laws LJ. The problem may be due in part to the obvious contradiction when courts identify the danger of public authorities acting as a 'judge in their own cause' about legitimate expectations. In one sense, such cautions simply express the enduring concern that judges in public law cases express against the possibly untrammelled power of public agencies.

Lawyers are understandably attuned to the dangers of unfettered power in the hands of public agencies and typically deploy separation of powers in their response. Public agencies should not be able to decide those legal elements of the problem because that function is allocated to the courts, which usefully prevents those agencies from deciding matters of policy and also law. The difficulty with any use of this justification in the legitimate expectation cases is that the courts assert their jurisdiction over those legal elements of the dispute but fail to grapple with the extent to which their assumption of that power inevitably draws in questions of both law and public interest. It is not clear why the courts are simultaneously uneasy with the possibility of public agencies making decisions about matters of public interest which are tied to legal principles, while also developing legal principles that allow courts the final say over many public interest issues. If the courts rightly believe that law and public interest can and should be blended, they need also to explain why we should be assumed to know all of the issues that should be blended, let alone do the blending. Put simply, are judges better suited to assessing the public interest consequences of their decisions than bureaucrats are to deciding the legal implications of the expectations they may create? Boughey leaves no doubt that the question of how this balance should be struck cannot be decided by proportionality, at least not as proportionality is currently known.

The UK Supreme Court appeared to recognise this difficulty in *Mandalia v Secretary of State for the Home Department*,[30] a decision delivered in the months before the chapters in this book were finalised. In that case, illegality was claimed after English authorities refused the applicant an extension on his visa without first providing him a chance to submit information in support of an extension. The failure to provide that chance was all the more striking because the authorities' own policy provided that such a chance should be given, particularly where applications appeared to contain a minor error or be missing the sort of documents this applicant's document omitted.[31] The UK Supreme Court essentially required that the policy be

[30] *Mandalia v Secretary of State for the Home Department* [2015] 1 WLR 4546.

[31] The information was copies of bank statements confirming the funds available to the applicant. Such information was crucial to satisfying the very prescriptive criteria for a visa extension. The document allowing applicants a chance to provide information for this criteria was described as a 'process instruction', which seems an apt label because it was an internal administrative guidance document for those who administered the relevant legislation.

enforced by use of principles that were 'no doubt related to the doctrine of legitimate expectations but free-standing'.[32] That independent principle, the Supreme Court made clear, was 'best articulated' in *Nadarajah* as one that required a promise or practice adopted by a government agency to be honoured unless there was a good reason to the contrary. The Supreme Court also cited the explanation for this legal requirement for governments and their agencies to adhere to promises and policies as clearly 'grounded in fairness' but resting in the wider proposition of a 'requirement of good administration, by which public bodies ought to deal straightforwardly and consistently with the public'.[33]

Interestingly, the Supreme Court drew support from other decisions for the questionable assertion of Laws LJ in *Nadarajah* that the court should have the final and binding word on whether any asserted public interest was sufficient for departing from a policy.[34] We say 'questionable' because it is one thing to accept that the courts should have the final word over legal issues. This is largely uncontroversial in those issues where the courts have particular expertise, such as statutory interpretation and matters affecting the evolution of the common law. While theories about the rule of law vary almost infinitely, few would disagree that the courts can and should exercise the last word on such issues when discharging their function in a society governed by the rule of law. However, it is another matter entirely to take a step further, as Laws LJ did in *Nadarajah* and the Court of Appeal did in *Coughlan*, by asserting that the court should undertake a balancing exercise. Such a function could easily be done by another arm of government and is arguably unsuited in any case to the judiciary.

One subsequent English case suggested that *Mandalia* had the virtue of providing a 'rather less technical approach to the [Migration] Rules than had previously been the case'.[35] Lord Wilson made a similar point in *Mandalia* when he noted that the guidance in issue may have been difficult for applicants to understand but it almost certainly made life easier for the officials required to administer the law. That was because those officials 'have to a substantial extent been relieved of the obligation to consider whether to exercise discretion in their processing of applications'.[36] The Supreme Court was able to insist on observance of the policy without attracting such loud disapproval as that which met *Coughlan* because in *Mandalia* it was the

[32] *Mandalia* (n 30) [29].
[33] *Mandalia* (n 30) [29], citing *Nadarajah* (n 28) [68].
[34] Authority for this proposition was taken from *R (SK (Zimbabwe)) v Secretary of State for the Home Department (Bail for Immigration Detainees Intervening)* [2011] 1 WLR 1299 [36].
[35] *MH (Bangladesh) v Secretary of State for the Home Department* [2015] EWCA Civ 1442 [17].
[36] *Mandalia* (n 30) [2].

government rather than the court that trimmed the discretion of the decision maker. The role of policy and other forms of soft law in both creating expectations and regulating the decision-making processes of administrators is adroitly covered by Ansari and Sossin.

A book which attempts to knit together views on a single doctrine from common law countries whose legal systems developed from England's legal influence embarks to some extent on a fool's errand. These are not countries which share an overarching, shared legal structure, as is the case in the EU. The countries whose approaches to legitimate expectations are addressed in this book do not belong to a monolithic legal tradition but one which is fragmented. Importantly, the common law is subject in every one of these countries to the constitutional arrangements that they have adopted, whether they are unwritten or written, include a bill or charter of rights or not. It follows that one country's approach to dealing with legitimate expectations, whether recognised procedurally or enforced substantively, will always be different to the approach of other countries. What does not follow is that these differences are never susceptible to change or that one country's approach is right and the others' are wrong.

We have pointed out elsewhere that:

> There are compelling constitutional reasons for courts in each jurisdiction to decide matters regarding legitimate expectations as they do and UK courts can scarcely avoid applying a rights-based analysis any more than Australian courts can ignore the Australian Constitution. However, the dialogue between the two countries remains and has been beneficial to developing the law. It is noteworthy and oddly pleasing that the High Court devoted so much of its judgment in Lam to refuting Coughlan even though the applicant had not mentioned Coughlan at all. While the Court of Appeal did not directly influence the result in Lam, the thinking of the High Court had certainly been affected by developments in the United Kingdom. Nobody need feel defensive about this, since it proves that neither Australia nor the United Kingdom is truly isolated from each other or the rest of the common law world.[37]

What is true of Australia and the UK is also true of Canada and New Zealand, Hong Kong and South Africa, India and Singapore. The common law world may not be legally unified in the manner of the EU but this book demonstrates that the countries in it still have much to say to one another. Within the acceptance that common law doctrines and innovations must fit within constitutional structures, rather than the reverse, there remains much that each jurisdiction can learn from its common law family. This book is not only a sustained analysis of legitimate expectations but a

[37] Matthew Groves and Greg Weeks, 'The Legitimacy of Expectations about Fairness: Can Process and Substance be Untangled?' in John Bell et al (eds), *Public Law Adjudication in Common Law Systems: Process and Substance* (Hart Publishing, 2016) 165, 187.

celebration of the common law mosaic of which the countries represented herein form part.

The most recent word on legitimate expectations from the most senior UK judges suggests that this common law mosaic is continuing and that the UK law is now taking account of developments from other common law jurisdictions in this area. The decision in question came not from the Supreme Court but the Privy Council, which perhaps gave the Supreme Court judges sitting in that jurisdiction a useful means to consider developments outside the UK. The case was *United Policyholders Group v Attorney-General of Trinidad and Tobago*,[38] which turned on the question of whether statements made by officials from the government of Trinidad and Tobago during the global financial crisis of 2009 had created a legitimate expectation among policy holders of an insurance company that the government had assumed control of a large insurance company during the crisis. After a national election, a newly elected government did not honour the statements of the previous one. The Privy Council held that no legitimate expectation has arisen in the circumstances and, even if one had, the government was justified in breaking the promises that underpinned the expectation. Lords Neuberger, Mance, Clarke and Sumption were able to reach these findings after reciting the key, settled principles governing the legitimate expectation in the UK.[39]

Lord Carnwath agreed with the other Lords but made several important points about the uncertain and perhaps narrowing focus of the legitimate expectation. He conceded that the many cases and academic commentary that followed *Coughlan* had not clarified the uncertainties surrounding legitimate expectations. Although that point appears obvious from the papers in this book, it was still surprising that Lord Carnwath suggested that many of these problems were perhaps because 'the court in *Coughlan* may have been unnecessarily ambitious in seeking a grand unifying theory for all the authorities loosely grouped under the heading of legitimate expectation'.[40] Lord Carnwath also questioned whether the courts should continue that search when the underlying basis of *Coughlan* could be justified on the more narrow idea from a view founded in the 'basic rule of law and human conduct that promises relied on by others should be kept.'[41] Lord Carnwath drew support for this proposition from the chapter of Elliott in this volume but also accepted that attempts to give substantive enforcement of expectations had not gained traction outside the UK.[42]

[38] *United Policyholders Group v Attorney-General of Trinidad and Tobago* [2016] UKPC 17.
[39] *United Policyholders* (n 38) [37]–[39].
[40] *United Policyholders* (n 38) [112].
[41] *United Policyholders* (n 38) [117].
[42] *United Policyholders* (n 38) [119].

If courts were to hold otherwise, this would ossify public administration and utterly undermine administrative pursuit of the public good. If government wished to change policy X it could nonetheless be bound to continue to apply policy X to everyone who was subject to that policy rather than policy Y (or at least everyone who is left worse off by the policy change). An exception 'could not be made without making it for all'.[23] Consider an administrative decision to depart from a policy that all prisoners shall have access to television on the basis that television access has been observed to undermine prison discipline; assume the new policy erects a presumption against access to television. If the prior policy gave rise to enforceable expectations among all prisoners that they would continue to have television access, despite a change in policy, then any policy change would be utterly ineffective, as all of those in prison at the time of the policy change—ie the entire prison population at that point in time—would be able potentially to sidestep the new policy. As Lord Templeman concluded in *Findlay*:[24]

> the most that a convicted prisoner can legitimately expect is that his case will be examined individually in the light of whatever policy the Secretary of State sees fit to adopt provided always that the adopted policy is a lawful exercise of the discretion conferred upon him by the statute. Any other view would entail the conclusion that the unfettered discretion conferred by the statute upon the minister can in some cases be restricted so as to hamper, or even to prevent, changes of policy.

If adoption of a policy in and of itself were held to ground enforceable expectations, this could discourage the setting of policies at all, given adoption of a policy could potentially tie the administration's hands in the future so that they would be prevented from changing tack given the changed demands of the public interest. This is problematic because policies are a good thing. They facilitate consistent decision-making, yet allow sufficient flexibility to tailor exercises of power to particular facts.[25]

If an authority were to be bound by its former policies, this would be difficult to reconcile with the no fettering principle. An authority would surely abdicate its responsibility to exercise its public powers for the public good if it were bound at t_{n+1} to exercise its powers according to its prior assessment of the public good at t_n, despite its assessment of the public good having radically changed by t_{n+1}. It is difficult to see how a court could endorse a legitimate expectation arising merely on the basis of adoption of a general policy without rendering hollow Lord Woolf's words that '[t]he court's task in all these cases is not to impede executive activity'.[26]

23 *Hamble* (n 17) [28].
24 *In re Findlay* [1985] 1 AC 318, 338.
25 *Begbie* (n 8) 1132.
26 *Coughlan* (n 10) [64].

These reasons are no doubt why courts emphasise that authorities must retain 'unfettered power to change policy':[27]

- 'It is ... common ground that there is no restriction in principle upon the power of the respondent from time to time to change its policy'.[28]
- 'no individual can legitimately expect the discharge of public duties to stand still or be distorted because of that individual's peculiar positions'.[29]
- 'By declaring a policy [the Minister] does not preclude any possible need to change it'.[30]
- 'Administrative policies may change with changing circumstances, including changes in the political complexion of governments. The liberty to make such change is something that is inherent in our constitutional form of government. When a change in administrative policy takes place and is communicated in a departmental circular ... any reasonable expectations that may have been aroused ... by any previous circular are destroyed.'[31]
- 'since [an authority] cannot abdicate its general remit, not only must it remain free to change policy; its undertakings are correspondingly open to modification or abandonment'.[32]

Logically this same reasoning applies *mutandis mutatis* to general *practices*.[33] If we accept that a *formal* policy, consciously adopted by an authority, is insufficient to generate a legitimate expectation, then it is difficult to see how *informal* administrative practices, ways of doing things, or habits could be sufficient to generate enforceable legal duties on authorities to continue those practices. This is reflected in the principle that where practice is based on a policy then 'the practice cannot logically be expected to survive a policy change'.[34]

Let us turn to the cases so as to identify the confusions that have arisen. As we shall see, that change-of-policy cases do not properly implicate legitimate expectations does not mean that policy changes occur in a legal vacuum. Several other review doctrines regulate such changes.

[27] *Hamble* (n 17) [45].
[28] *Hamble* (n 17) [2].
[29] *Hamble* (n 17) [25].
[30] *R v SOSHD, ex parte Ruddock* [1987] 1 WLR 1482, 1497.
[31] *Hughes v Department of Health and Social Security* [1985] AC 776, 788.
[32] *Coughlan* (n 10) [64].
[33] cf *Rowland* (n 5) [68](1) ('A legitimate expectation may arise from "the existence of a regular practice which the claimant can reasonably expect to continue"').
[34] *Hamble* (n 17) [42].

The Cases

Ex parte Hamble Fisheries

The claimant challenged a change in the policy governing transfer and aggregation of fishing licenses, a change driven by a concern to reduce the intensity of fishing in the relevant maritime area. Whereas under the old policy the claimant had prospects of being able to fish the maritime area, having taken steps towards fulfilling the criteria under the old policy, under the new policy it was prevented from fishing at all. The defendant gave no assurances that the old policy would continue. The new policy included transitional provisions to preserve the interests of certain classes of persons, however the claimant fell outside these provisions. The claimant nonetheless claimed a 'legitimate expectation that when radical and severe measures are adopted … there will either be proper transitional provisions, or, if no such provisions are made, proper "pipeline" provisions (i.e. provisions covering transactions already in progress)'.[35]

Having quoted higher court judgments holding that expectations based on mere existence of a policy cannot survive a policy change, Sedley J nonetheless considered that legitimate expectations could potentially arise on the basis of general policy alone and that these could possibly survive a policy change.

However, examination of the Judge's reasoning demonstrates this was a case for application of traditional substantive review grounds rather than legitimate expectations. Consider how Sedley J framed the principal issue: 'The issue in this case is whether the material change in policy, albeit lawful, ought to have been qualified by an exception having the effect which the applicants now seek to achieve through these proceedings'.[36] Whether the new policy should have contained transitional provisions preserving the claimant's interests is a question that goes to the substance of the new policy, specifically the substantive fairness of the transitional arrangements. This has nothing to do with expectations formed on the basis of the prior policy, but is a bare rationality challenge to policy design. One of the core principles relied upon was: 'it is a misuse of power for [a public body] to act unfairly or unjustly towards the private citizen when there is no overriding public interest to warrant it'.[37] It is difficult to see this as a principle concerned specifically with expectations. It is far closer to a substantive review principle of fair balance in public decision-making (which, as we shall see, constituted radical departure from the *Wednesbury* test that should have been applied).

[35] *Hamble* (n 17) [13].
[36] *Hamble* (n 17) [2].
[37] *Hamble* (n 17) [46].

Reflecting this, Sedley J considered that the 'decision-maker must ... balance the case for making no ... exception against the case for generalising [an exception]'.[38] It was this balancing that the court was concerned to scrutinise, apparently objectively. Again this reveals that the legal challenge was to the balancing of interests undertaken by the primary decision-maker in settling which individuals ought to be protected by transitional provisions. Sedley J's conclusion is similarly illustrative of the substantive nature of review here:

> it was in my judgment not unfair, in the light of the government's legitimate policy imperatives and objectives, to exclude from the policy's transitional provisions enterprises in the position of the applicant ... The means adopted bore a fair proportion to the end in view.[39]

These are conclusions as to the substantive justifiability of the transitional provisions, which form a substantive aspect of the new policy. The idea of legitimate expectations does no work here.

Sedley J rightly concluded that,

> [o]nce it is accepted that nobody has a legitimate expectation that policy will not change, it is more accurate to describe the applicant's anticipation of being permitted nevertheless [to have its interests preserved] as, objectively a hope rather than an expectation.[40]

This must be correct given the inherently transitory, fluid nature of policy. However, this analysis is difficult to square with Sedley J's view that other classes of persons subject to the prior policy, specifically those whose interests were preserved by the transitional clauses, had legitimate expectations which accrued by virtue of their being subject to the prior policy: 'In public law terms, these were classes which might very well have been held to possess an expectation which the law would protect—a legitimate expectation'.[41] The answer to this riddle is that when Sedley J referred to these other classes of persons as having a 'legitimate expectation' he was misusing that term. This is an example of a lack of discipline in invocation of the concept, which in turn has bred confusion as to the nature of legitimate expectations. Sedley J's reliance on legitimate expectations was a way of expressing a conclusion that the transitional provisions would have lacked fair balance and been irrational if they had excluded the relevant classes. On the other hand Sedley J concluded the transitional provisions had struck a fair balance in excluding the claimant's class.

[38] *Hamble* (n 17) [22].
[39] *Hamble* (n 17) [59].
[40] *Hamble* (n 17) [58].
[41] *Hamble* (n 17) [57].

Ex parte Hargreaves

The subsequent Court of Appeal decision in *Hargreaves* provides a corrective to the approach in *Hamble*.[42] Prisoners challenged a new scheme governing eligibility for home leave. The old policy entitled all prisoners to apply after serving one third of their sentence. The new scheme extended this period, so that a prisoner could only apply after serving half their sentence. The claimants were prisoners negatively affected by this change. They claimed they had a legitimate expectation of being considered for home leave after serving one third of their sentence; their case was that 'if these changes were to have been made they should have been implemented in such a way as to protect their legitimate expectations'.[43] As in *Hamble* the Minister had made transitional arrangements to preserve the position of some classes of prisoners, but considered it would be inconsistent with the new policy's purpose to include wider transitional arrangements which would have preserved the claimants' position.

The Court considered that absent a clear and unambiguous representation, the case was not one of legitimate expectations. All the prisoner could expect was to have his case dealt with under whichever was the prevailing policy at the relevant time, emphasising that government must have liberty to change policy. The Court rejected Sedley J's analysis in *Hamble*, which appeared to contemplate that legitimate expectations could arise merely on the basis of general policies. The Court also rejected as 'heresy' and 'wrong in principle'[44] Sedley J's approach to reviewing transitional arrangements, which entailed the court balancing competing interests objectively for itself. 'On matters of substance *Wednesbury* provides the correct test'.[45]

This not properly being categorised as a legitimate expectations case, the Court went on to apply other review doctrines. There was no suggestion that the Minister's decisions breached the parent statute. Nor was there any argument of irrationality: the Minister had balanced relevant interests in setting the transitional arrangements and the balance struck was not perverse. Pill LJ specifically rejected the submission, which bore the hallmarks of Sedley J's open-ended approach in *Hamble*, that:

> the court can take and act upon an overall view of the fairness of the respondent's decision of substance. The court can quash the decision only if, in relation to the expectation and in all the circumstances, the decision to apply the new policy in the particular case was unreasonable in the *Wednesbury* sense.[46]

[42] *R v SOSHD; ex parte Hargreaves* [1997] 1 WLR 906.
[43] Ibid 909.
[44] Ibid 921, 925.
[45] Ibid 921.
[46] Ibid 924.

The Court found no basis for intervention on the relevant considerations ground: the Minister had considered factors specific to those in the claimant's class in deciding to change the policy and formulating transitional provisions. Nor could there be any complaint of fettering, the decision-maker having addressed themselves to concerns peculiar to the claimant's class.

Ex parte Coughlan and Beyond

If *Hargreaves* entailed a step forward in clarifying the approach to change-of-policy cases and setting the law on a principled footing, *Coughlan* reintroduced some confusion, principally because of a lack of discipline around use of the legitimate expectations label. Lord Woolf propounded a three-fold classification of legitimate expectation cases. The first category was one where: 'The court may decide that the public authority is only required to bear in mind its previous policy or other representation, giving it the weight it thinks right, but no more, before deciding whether to change course'.[47]

There are two principal problems with the first category.

First, it is confusing to categorise such cases as legitimate expectations cases. Rather, this category includes cases where there has been a mere change of policy, where mere reliance on the previous, generally applicable policy cannot give rise to a legitimate expectation (and cases where an authority has made a representation which does not amount to a legitimate expectation).[48] In other words, the first category is a category of non-legitimate expectation cases. Lord Woolf gave *Hargreaves* as an example of a case within this category. As we have seen, that was not a case where legitimate expectations were recognised. Rather, it was held that legitimate expectations could not arise merely on the basis of general policy. That this category is not in truth one of legitimate expectations is reinforced by there being no mention of legitimate expectations in Lord Woolf's category description. Rather, change-of-policy cases are best categorised as cases of reasonableness review—of the rationality of transitional arrangements or the new policy—and/or review on the relevant considerations ground—the decision-maker must consider the detriment to those who will be negatively affected by the change in deciding whether to change policy, whether to include transitional provisions, and in formulating such provisions.

[47] *Coughlan* (n 10) [57].

[48] *Begbie* (n 8) is an excellent example of a policy change case in which no legitimate expectation could be established, so that the appropriate ground of challenge was *Wednesbury* review of the transitional provisions in the new policy. As Peter Gibson LJ observed, such a challenge will only rarely succeed (at 1128).

Second, the description of the category suggests a choice: 'The court may decide' the case is one that calls for rationality review only. However, it is wrong to frame this as a choice, and framing it as such has given rise to much confusion. Either a legitimate expectation arises or it does not. If a legitimate expectation does arise the case shall fall to be considered as a legitimate expectations case (ie it shall fall into one of Lord Woolf's other two categories: cases of substantive or procedural legitimate expectation). If it does not then the court has no choice but to consider it according to other doctrines.

Later in Lord Woolf's judgment we find a similar type of confusion to that which characterised *Hamble*. He says that where an authority has changed its policy, considered the impact of the policy-change on affected individuals, and put in place exceptions and transitional arrangements, then a court ordinarily will not intervene. 'But where no accommodation is made, it is for the court to say whether the consequent frustration of the individual's expectation is so unfair as to be a misuse of the authority's power'.[49] The use of the language of 'expectation' is unfortunate. It may suggest that those subject to a general policy will have legally-recognised legitimate expectations simply by virtue of their being subject to that policy for the time being. This cannot be right as recognition of such expectations could utterly undermine an authority's ability to effectively change its policy, which Lord Woolf was adamant ought not to be the consequence of legitimate expectations doctrine. The better view of Lord Woolf's dictum is that not much weight should be placed on use of 'expectation', and nor should the term be read as meaning 'legitimate expectation'. If the authority changes policy but gives no consideration to the fact this change will bare harshly on some, then the change, or the omission of transitional clauses, may be impugned on ordinary grounds of review. Intervention does not require nor depend upon legal recognition of legitimate expectations among those subject to the prior policy. Invocation of legitimate expectations would do no work here, but it can cause significant confusion.

Happily, it seems that recent case law is returning the law to the clear position articulated in *Hargreaves*. In *Bhatt Murphy*, Laws LJ observed that outside an exceptional case an authority will not be 'bound by the law to maintain in being a policy which on reasonable grounds it has chosen to alter or abandon'; 'establishment of any policy, new or substitute, by a public body is in principle subject to *Wednesbury* review'.[50] In this judgment we also find explicit support for the view that recognising legitimate expectations solely on the basis of existence a general policy would extend the doctrine beyond acceptable limits:

[49] *Coughlan* (n 10) [82].
[50] *Bhatt Murphy* (n 1) [35], [41].

> Once set in place, *every* policy of a public authority, not subject to a stated terminal date or terminating event, may no doubt be expected to continue in effect until rational grounds for its cessation arise. A promise of its continuance, if it points to no particular date or future event to mark the end of the policy, represents little more than this ordinary expectation. And nothing is added by referring to a practice of the policy in operation over time. In this context, then, the notion of a promise or practice of present and future substantive policy risks proving too much. The doctrine of substantive legitimate expectation plainly cannot apply to every case where a public authority operates a policy over an appreciable period. That would expand the doctrine far beyond its proper limits.[51]

These views were echoed in the subsequent case of *DM*, in which the Court gave short shrift to an argument that the petitioner had a legitimate expectation to be dealt with under an older policy—'There is … no compulsitor to follow the earlier policy'—and observed: 'Policy may be changed at any time, and a change might be rendered largely ineffective if it were still necessary to apply the policy that existed at an earlier date'.[52] Any protection was limited to the doctrine of relevant considerations: 'To the extent that the decision made after the change in policy is discretionary, it may be appropriate to take into account the change in considering how the discretion should be exercised'.[53]

Summary

The best reading of the law governing policy changes is as follows.

First, in general a mere change in policy does not implicate the doctrine of legitimate expectations. All that one may expect is that one's case will be governed by the currently-prevailing policy. To hold otherwise would be to radically undermine the Government's liberty to adjust policy given the demands of the public interest. Logically the same approach should apply to changes in general practices.

Second, where a policy change prejudices one's accrued interests under a prior policy, one may seek review on other grounds. Most obviously one may challenge the rationality of the new policy, transitional provisions within the new policy, or an omission to make transitional arrangements. Other review doctrines may also apply. For example, consistently with the requirement that decision-makers not fetter their discretion, the decision-maker, in applying the new policy to individual cases, must be alive to the fact that the change may impact upon some more harshly than others; policy should not be applied with 'rigidity' or 'as a set of rules'.[54]

51 *Bhatt Murphy* (n 1) [34]–[35].
52 *DM v SOSHD* 2014 SC 635 [25]–[26].
53 Ibid [25].
54 *Hamble* (n 17) [19]; *Begbie* (n 8) 1132.

Consistent with the ill-disciplined invocation of legitimate expectations, this principle itself has been expressed in terms of legitimate expectations, ie one can legitimately expect the decision-maker will consider one's individual circumstances.[55] But the no-fettering principle is recognised as a free-standing doctrine, which does not rely on the presence of legitimate expectations for its application. Closely linked to the principle of individual consideration is the doctrine of relevant considerations; in policy-change cases there is no deviation from 'the standard requirements of any exercise of discretion: namely that the decision take into account all relevant matters'.[56] However, that a decision-maker may be lawfully required, in determining the new policy or transitional provisions, or making a decision under the new policy, to take into account that the policy-change will bear or has borne particularly harshly on the claimant or their class 'is a different point from that of legitimate expectations'.[57] Lastly, courts, in exercising remedial discretion on review, may take into account, as a factor favouring grant of relief, that individual prejudice has been suffered through a policy change. Similarly, courts may give weight to an official representation made to the claimant, but which does not generate a legitimate expectation.[58]

Deviations from Existing Policies or Practices

On occasion the courts have applied the concept of legitimate expectations where an authority has a policy or established practice of treating those in the claimant's class in a particular way—for example a policy of always consulting those subject to decision-procedures before a final decision is reached—but deviates from or fails to apply that policy or practice in the claimant's case without good reason.[59]

These are cases which the courts clearly consider warrant intervention on review. But these cases are not properly categorised as legitimate expectations cases, even if the language of legitimate expectations has been deployed at times.[60] The better view is that such cases entail application of a discrete

[55] *Findlay* (n 24) 338.
[56] *Coughlan* (n 10) [73].
[57] *R (Bloggs 61) v SOSHD* [2003] 1 WLR 2724 [74].
[58] *South Bucks DC v Flanagan* [2002] 1 WLR 2601 [26].
[59] The prime example is *Rashid v SOSHD* [2005] INLR 550. The cases of *R v SOSHD; ex parte Asif Mahmood Khan* [1984] 1 WLR 1337 and *Ruddock* (n 30) arguably provide further examples in that the main complaint was simply that the authority had not applied its existing policies. *Ruddock* is a particularly interesting case as there is no way the claimant could have known there was a policy in place or that they were subject to it, as the policy was a *secret* policy governing phone tapping, and the claimant's phone had been tapped without their knowledge.
[60] This view is shared by other commentators: eg M Elliott, 'Legitimate Expectation, Consistency and Abuse of Power: The *Rashid* Case' [2005] *Judicial Review* 281; R Clayton,

doctrine of review, which we might term a doctrine of consistency or equal treatment.[61] The principal concern in such cases is that the claimant has been dealt with arbitrarily rather than that they have had some expectation defeated. This is clear if we assume that the claimant in our scenario has no prior knowledge of the authority's practice or policy. It is difficult to see how one could legitimately expect to be treated according to a particular policy or practice if one has no knowledge of it. However, we may still expect a court to intervene in such a case, despite the claimant's imperfect knowledge, on the basis that a deviation from established policy or practice without justification smacks of arbitrariness.[62] Equality of treatment is a principle of such importance that it should not depend for its application on whether a particular claimant happens to be able to establish a legitimate expectation. Another way to put this is that all people are entitled to expect officials to act consistently, applying policies they have adopted, unless there are reasons for doing otherwise. On the other hand, to analyse such cases as legitimate expectations cases will ultimately lead courts to distort the coherence of that concept. Thus, where courts have relied on legitimate expectations in such cases, they have been forced to stretch the concept to apply where the claimant has no knowledge of the relevant policy.[63] As already discussed, the idea that someone can have a legitimate expectation of being dealt with according to a particular policy where they have no knowledge of that policy is perplexing.[64]

The concept of legitimate expectations does no extra work here; indeed, if judicial intervention were to depend on legitimate expectations in such cases this could only serve to unduly narrow protection against inconsistent decision-making. We can see this clearly if we consider statements of principle such as Sedley LJ's in *Begbie*: 'discretion must not be exercised arbitrarily

'Legitimate Expectations, Policy, and the Principle of Consistency" (2003) 62 *Cambridge Law Journal* 93. For an interesting attempt to explain consistency cases as cases of legitimate expectations, see F Ahmed and A Perry, 'The Coherence of the Doctrine of Legitimate Expectations' (2014) 73 *Cambridge Law Journal* 61.

[61] There are close similarities between this ground of judicial intervention and two other doctrines of review; indeed the similarities are so close one might argue the doctrines are the same, or ought to be amalgamated. First, inconsistency is an indicium of irrationality, and if that inconsistency cannot be explained by the defendant the court may intervene on the *Wednesbury* ground (P Daly, 'Wednesbury's Reason and Structure' [2011] *Public Law* 238, 245). Second, a decision which appears inexplicable—eg because it deviates from a consistent pattern of decisions on similar facts—will likely give rise to a duty to give reasons, and if reasons are not given this shall be sufficient basis for judicial intervention: *R v Civil Service Appeal Board; ex parte Cunningham* [1991] 4 All ER 310.

[62] *Rashid* (n 59) [25].

[63] *Rashid* (n 59) [24]ff.

[64] *Mandalia v SOSHD* [2015] UKSC 59 [29].

or inconsistently'.[65] There is no need for recourse to legitimate expectations in stating this principle. Similarly, in *Lumba* Lord Dyson stated as a general proposition, '[t]he individual has a basic public law right to have his or her case considered under whatever policy the executive sees fit to adopt provided that the adopted policy is a lawful exercise of the discretion conferred by the statute'.[66] There is again no recourse to legitimate expectations nor any need for recourse. Making this patent is Lord Dyson's endorsement of the following quote from *De Smith's Judicial Review*: 'there is an independent duty of consistent application of policies, which is based on the principle of equal implementation of laws, non-discrimination and the lack of arbitrariness'.[67] The point has now been put beyond any doubt by the recent Supreme Court decision in *Mandalia*.[68] On the other hand, consistency cases do not sit 'comfortably with the conventional concept of legitimate expectation'.[69] The tell-tale sign that such cases are not naturally analysed as implicating legitimate expectations is that judges have determined these cases on the basis that 'the degree of unfairness was such as to amount to an abuse of power requiring the intervention of the court'.[70] Appeal to such open-ended concepts of 'conspicuous unfairness'—'unfairness which … "leaps from the page"'[71]—reflects that the courts are unsure how legitimate expectations apply here.

Let us consider a variation of the scenario we started with. Instead of the complaint being that the defendant deviated from a prevailing general policy or general practice, let us assume the defendant has adopted an idiosyncratic practice in respect of a particular claimant, in repeat interactions with that claimant over a significant period, but then deviates from that practice without reason. Legitimate expectations have entered judicial analysis of such cases. However, such cases do not fit neatly within a legitimate expectations framework, they can be explained according to established grounds, and they fall within the consistency principle.

The best example is *Unilever*.[72] The Revenue disallowed Unilever's claim to set trading losses incurred during the relevant financial year against profits as the claim was not made within time. Importantly, the Revenue had

[65] *Begbie* (n 8) 1132.

[66] *R (Lumba) v SOSHD* [2012] 1 AC 245 [35].

[67] Ibid [26], quoting H Woolf et al, *De Smith's Judicial Review*, 6th edn (Sweet and Maxwell, 2007) [12-039].

[68] *Mandalia* (n 64) [29]ff ('the applicant's right to the determination of his application in accordance with policy is now generally taken to flow from a principle, no doubt related to the doctrine of legitimate expectation *but free-standing*' (emphasis added)).

[69] *Rashid* (n 59) [26], [34]; *R (A) v SOSHD* [2006] EWHC 526 (Admin) [30].

[70] *Rashid* (n 59) [26].

[71] *Rashid* (n 59) [23], [26].

[72] *R v IRC; ex parte Unilever Plc* [1996] STC 681.

a discretion to accept late claims, and there was a consistent pattern, over a significant number of years, of the Revenue allowing Unilever to lodge claims outside the time limit. The Court granted review of the Revenue's decision to exclude the claim. The Court had recourse to the concept of legitimate expectation. However, this was far from being a clear case of legitimate expectations: the Revenue did nothing positive to induce in Unilever an expectation that late claims would invariably be accepted, the Revenue had not always accepted late claims from Unilever though it had in the vast majority of their interactions, and the Revenue had no general policy or practice of accepting late claims—which all depended on individual exercises of discretion. Reflecting the difficulty in categorising this case as one of legitimate expectations, Lord Bingham considered this was an exceptional case concerning 'unique facts',[73] and only recognised legitimate expectations on this basis. Further, in reaching his decision he took into account a host of factors irrelevant to legitimate expectations, suggesting the true ground for intervention was more likely substantive unreasonableness: eg it is a basic principle of the tax system that corporations should be able to set off losses, the rule breached was only a procedural one, and the Revenue should not enjoy an 'adventitious windfall'.[74] In addition, there was the tell-tale appeal to the decision being 'so unfair as to amount to an abuse of power'.[75] More generally it was difficult to discern from Lord Bingham's judgment how the legitimate expectations doctrine had actually been applied. Lord Bingham followed the lower court judge in finding the Revenue's conduct irrational, adding that he did 'not think that in truth this raises a new point'.[76] But the matter is the other way around: legitimate expectations add nothing to other doctrines here. The Court's core concern in the case seems to have been one of arbitrariness or capriciousness: the authority dealt with Unilever in a particular way consistently, and then deviated from that individualised practice inexplicably. This concern is clearest in Simon Brown LJ's judgment. He considered the case did not fall within the legitimate expectations doctrine. He explicitly disposed of the case, which he described as 'wholly exceptional[]', on the basis that the Revenue's decision was 'so outrageously unfair that it should not be allowed to stand' and a 'plainly wrong exercise of discretion' *given a clear pattern of prior administrative conduct*.[77] He also referred to the 'demonstrable pointlessness of imposing a two year time limit on the particular facts of the case'; ie there was no good reason for deviating from consistent practice.[78]

[73] Ibid 691.
[74] Ibid.
[75] Ibid.
[76] Ibid 692.
[77] Ibid 696–97.
[78] Ibid.

Secret Policies

The twin ideas that authorities ought to publish their policies, and not operate secret policies at variance with published policies, have sometimes been associated with legitimate expectations. For example, in the important legitimate expectations case of *Begbie*, Sedley LJ said

> there are today cogent objections to the operation of undisclosed policies affecting individuals' entitlements or expectations. It is right and proper that a policy such as [the one under consideration] be published ... The necessary consequence and indeed purpose of publication is that people will, where appropriate rely upon it.[79]

There is certainly some connection between expectations, in the ordinary sense of that word, and an imperative to publish policies. One justification for requiring publication of policies might be that publication enables those subject to the policy to know what to expect when powers are exercised. However, there is no necessary connection between emergent norms of transparency and the legal concept of legitimate expectations. This is made clear in *Lumba*, where the norm that policies should ordinarily be published was enunciated as a general rule, not one dependent on legitimate expectations.[80] Thus Lord Dyson, giving the lead judgment, stated as a general proposition that

> [t]he rule of law calls for a transparent statement by the executive of the circumstances in which the broad statutory criteria will be exercised ... [w]hat must ... be published is that which a person who is affected by the operation of the policy needs to know in order to make informed and meaningful representations to the decision-maker before a decision is made.[81]

Further, it is a general rule that 'a decision-maker must follow his published policy (and not some different unpublished policy) unless there are good

[79] *Begbie* (n 8) 1132.

[80] *Lumba* (n 66). In his minority judgment in *Lumba*, Lord Phillips observed that the question of whether it was unlawful for the defendant to operate a secret policy which was different to its public policy 'overlaps with the question of the nature and effect of a legitimate expectation' (at [303]). But little light was shed on the nature of this overlap and the interrelationship between the two concepts within his Lordship's judgment. Aspects of the judgment tend to suggest that the existence of a policy gives rise to a legitimate expectation that one will be dealt with according to that policy. But, as discussed above, this is not a matter of legitimate expectations. Rather, Lord Phillip's proposition is the corollary of the consistency or non-arbitrariness principle already discussed above, ie if one is not dealt with according to the terms of an existing policy, the defendant will need to show good reasons for this deviation, otherwise the deviation will be unlawful. The concept of legitimate expectations is superfluous. Indeed Lord Dyson, in his lead judgment in *Lumba*, expressed as a general principle that an authority must follow its public policy: see text to n 82 below.

[81] *Lumba* (n 66) [34], [38].

reasons for not doing so'.[82] Neither of these legal propositions rely on legitimate expectations for their application. In a sense things are the other way around. Those subject to policies will be unable to form expectations of how public power will be exercised and/or sensibly make representations as to how power should be exercised if policies are secret.

Withdrawal of a Continuing Benefit

Preliminaries

The last layer to be chiselled away is the jurisprudence on withdrawal of a continuing benefit (and denial of future benefits). Such cases have often been analysed as legitimate expectation cases. The way in which legitimate expectations enter analysis of such cases has been inconsistent. For example, some courts have held that where an individual enjoys a discretionary benefit over a significant period of time, a legitimate expectation shall arise that the benefit will continue to be provided, if certain criteria are fulfilled. Such expectation will be protected procedurally by a duty on the defendant to consult with the claimant before any decision as to withdrawal. In other cases on analogous facts the legitimate expectation said to arise is a legitimate expectation to be consulted before withdrawal.

The more convincing analysis of such cases is that they are not legitimate expectations cases at all but cases of procedural fairness simpliciter. In other words, ordinary duties of procedural fairness, including obligations to consult and hear representations, arise where a claimant is threatened with withdrawal of an important benefit which they have enjoyed undisturbed over time. Within contemporary law legitimate expectations is not required to explain why obligations of fairness arise in such cases.

The reason why legitimate expectations have played a role in such cases is largely historical. Up until the 1970s and 1980s a duty of procedural fairness, then known as natural justice, could only possibly arise where an administrative decision affected an individual's legal rights. The label 'rights' was not used as loosely then as it is in contemporary administrative law.[83] Rights meant those Hohfeldian legal rights recognised as independently actionable outside of judicial review, such as private individual rights in contract or tort. Thus, the 'triggers' for duties of fairness to arise, and by extension those standing rules governing who could bring a claim of procedural unfairness, were relatively narrow. This was unsatisfactory because administrative decisions can affect interests or discretionary benefits

[82] *Lumba* (n 66) [26]; *Mandalia* (n 64) [29]ff.

[83] See JNE Varuhas, 'The Reformation of English Administrative Law? "Rights", Rhetoric and Reality' (2013) 72 *Cambridge Law Journal* 369.

which, while not legal rights, are nonetheless of importance to those who possess them, so that those individuals should at least be consulted before decisions are made affecting their interests or benefits. Thus, courts began to broaden the triggers for duties of fairness to arise and by implication standing rules on review. One of the principal ways progress towards these goals was achieved during the 1970s and 1980s was through recognition and invocation of the concept of legitimate expectations. The courts began to hold that despite a claimant not being able to demonstrate interference with recognised legal rights, duties of fairness could nonetheless arise where the claimant possessed a legitimate expectation. This concept of legitimate expectations was not well-defined. But it was clearly a concept with less normative weight than rights, yet one which could serve as a surrogate or proxy for legal rights so as to extend duties of fairness and widen standing.

So, for example, in the 1983 case of *Ng Yuen Shiu*, Lord Fraser considered, and ultimately approved, the proposition that 'a person is entitled to a fair hearing before a decision adversely affecting his interests is made by a public official or body, if he has "a legitimate expectation" of being accorded such a hearing'.[84] He considered a 'legitimate expectation' includes 'expectations which go beyond enforceable legal rights, provided they have some reasonable basis', and recalled cases where a prisoner was 'entitled to challenge ... a decision by a prison board of visitors, awarding him loss of remission of sentence, although he has no legal right to remission, but only a reasonable expectation of receiving it'.[85] In another prisoner case, *O'Reilly*, Lord Diplock observed the claimant had not been deprived of any private law right but they had a legitimate expectation based on knowledge of general administrative practice:

> such legitimate expectation gave to each appellant a sufficient interest to challenge the legality of the adverse disciplinary award made against him by the board ... and such grounds would include the board's failure to observe the rules of natural justice: which means no more than to act fairly towards him in carrying out their decision-making process.[86]

The only role legitimate expectations play here is as a trigger for standing and ordinary duties of fairness. Further, because little of normative significance flowed from recognition of legitimate expectations—the concept played an essentially procedural role in enabling access to review procedure, through which one's substantive claims of unfairness could be tested—the criteria for recognition of such expectations were not tightly regulated.

[84] *Attorney-General of Hong Kong v Ng Yuen Shiu* [1983] 2 AC 629, 636.
[85] Ibid.
[86] *O'Reilly v Mackman* [1983] 2 AC 237, 275.

In *O'Reilly* a legitimate expectation arose simply because the claimant knew of general administrative practices.

Thus, legitimate expectations, as the concept emerged through the 1970s and 1980s, played an important role in the development of judicial review. But the concept is no longer required to perform the role it once played. Standing has been broadened out, as have the triggers for ordinary duties of fairness to arise. As such, legitimate expectations are no longer required to serve as a surrogate for legal rights, so as to ensure the proper reach of procedural fairness in benefit-withdrawal cases. We shall see this clearly if we consider the key cases.

The Cases

In *CCSU* the claimants challenged the Minister's decision, pursuant to an Order in Council, to vary the terms of employment of staff at Government Communications Headquarters, specifically to prohibit their membership of national trade unions. The principal challenge concerned the Government's failure to consult on the change; there was a well-established practice of consultation with trade unions and staff on such matters.

The challenge failed because interests in national security ultimately trumped procedural fairness. However, legitimate expectations formed a core plank of their Lordships' reasoning. All found that legitimate expectations arose, except possibly Lord Scarman who engaged in a more open-ended inquiry into whether the Court should intervene 'to correct excess or abuse of power'.[87] However, the nature of the legitimate expectation was expressed in different ways. Lord Fraser described the expectation as one 'that the minister would consult' before withdrawing union membership.[88] In contrast, Lord Diplock recognised 'a legitimate expectation that [staff] would continue to enjoy the benefits of [union] membership'; for Lord Diplock this expectation would be protected procedurally via a duty to consult staff on the reasons for the proposed withdrawal before any final decision.[89] Either way this is clearly a case where the doctrine of legitimate expectations is relied upon to protect against withdrawal of a continuing benefit, where there is no legal right to those benefits, ie the benefits of union membership.

In this case we see clearly the important role of legitimate expectations in expanding the scope of procedural fairness and standing. Lord Diplock observed that where a decision does not alter legal rights but only affects legitimate expectations, '"procedural propriety" will normally provide the

[87] *CCSU* (n 12) 404.
[88] *CCSU* (n 12) 401.
[89] *CCSU* (n 12) 412–13.

only ground on which the decision is open to review',[90] while Lord Roskill observed, 'the principle [of legitimate expectations] is closely connected with "a right to be heard"'.[91] As to standing, Lord Roskill explained that 'part of the recent evolution of our administrative law' is that 'an aggrieved party [may] evoke judicial review if he can show that he had a "reasonable expectation"'.[92] Lord Diplock, in a canonical statement on the law of standing, said: '[t]o qualify as a subject of judicial review' a decision must either alter the claimant's 'legal rights or obligations ... in private law' or alternatively deprive 'him of some benefit or advantage' which amounted to a legitimate expectation.[93] He suggested two categories of legitimate expectation case: (i) where the claimant enjoyed some ongoing benefit which he had a legitimate expectation that he would continue to enjoy until the decision-maker communicated to him some reason for withdrawal and allowed opportunity for comment (the *CCSU* category of case); (ii) where the decision-maker had made an assurance that the benefit would not be withdrawn without opportunity for comment (the paradigm case: see below).[94] As Sedley J observed subsequently, Lord Diplock was here relying on legitimate expectations in enumerating 'pathways to judicial review'.[95]

Thus, *CCSU* shows very clearly the important role of legitimate expectations in the evolution of judicial review through the 1970s and 1980s. Without the conceptual tool of legitimate expectations, the claimants in *CCSU* may not have had standing, while the Minister may not have been under a duty of fairness, as legal rights—the traditional trigger for obligations of fairness to arise—were absent.

However, legitimate expectations are no longer required to perform this role. Today it is clearly established that deprivation of some important, continuing benefit, such as housing or welfare, despite not entailing deprivation of a legal right, could give rise to obligations of fairness regardless of whether the claimant could be said to have an expectation, legitimate or otherwise, that the benefit would continue or that they be consulted. In an authoritative statement of principle, Lord Mustill said:

> (5) Fairness will very often require that a person who may be adversely affected by the decision will have an opportunity to make representations on his own behalf either before the decision is taken with a view to producing a favourable result; or after it is taken, with a view to procuring its modification; or both. (6) Since the person affected usually cannot make worthwhile representations without

[90] *CCSU* (n 12) 411.
[91] *CCSU* (n 12) 415.
[92] *CCSU* (n 12) 415.
[93] *CCSU* (n 12) 408.
[94] *CCSU* (n 12) 408–09.
[95] *Hamble* (n 17) [44].

> knowing what factors may weigh against his interests fairness will very often require that he is informed of the gist of the case which he has to answer.[96]

There is no need for appeal to legitimate expectations to complete or make out these propositions: it is simply an ordinary requirement of fairness that where an adverse decision is proposed, the affected person should generally be consulted before the decision is made.

Turning to standing, while iconic, Lord Diplock's statement of the law of standing in *CCSU* plays hardly any role in the modern law. Today standing is more or less presumed if one can show a prima facie case of administrative unlawfulness. Whether one is directly affected by the challenged administrative action is generally beside the point; standing will only generally be refused if the claim is vexatious or prompted by ill-motive.

We see strong similarities with the reasoning in *CCSU* in later decisions. *Baker* is the best example.[97] A local council sought to close a care home. The key legal question was whether the council had an obligation to consult residents. Dillon LJ concluded that 'whether on the closure of a home or for any other reason, a resident is to be transferred from one home to another, she must be consulted over the home to which she is to be transferred'.[98] This is procedural fairness simpliciter in action: if an authority is to take some decision which radically affects my life, as a vulnerable person dependent on state support, then the authority should consult me as a matter of basic fairness. Legitimate expectations do no extra work here; we would expect the law to impose a consultation duty regardless of any prior practice or promise of consultation.

Similarly to the Law Lords' analysis in *CCSU*, legitimate expectations entered Dillon LJ's analysis as an issue of standing, or trigger for public law obligations. This is made clear by Dillon LJ's reliance on an Australian decision, *Haoucher*.[99] In that case, Deane J treated rights and legitimate expectations as equivalents for the purpose of determining whether duties of fairness arose; he speaks of 'a right in the strict sense or a legitimate expectation' and observes that '[t]he notion of "legitimate expectation" … gives rise to a prima facie entitlement to procedural fairness or natural justice'.[100] But, as we have seen, we no longer need to rely on legitimate expectations in such cases. Indeed, as Deane J recorded, hitching fairness to legitimate expectations may unnecessarily narrow the scope of procedural fairness:

> the vagueness of the phrase 'legitimate expectation', which enables it to be used as a convenient label for a broad category of circumstances which will give rise

[96] *R v SOSHD; ex parte Doody* [1994] 1 AC 531, 560.
[97] *Baker* (n 4).
[98] *Baker* (n 4) 86.
[99] *Haoucher v Minister of State for Immigration and Ethnic Affairs* (1990) 93 ALR 51, 52–53, discussed in *Baker* (n 4) at 85–86.
[100] *Haoucher* ibid.

> to a prima facie obligation to accord procedural fairness, may convey an impression of comprehensiveness with the result that the absence of an identified legitimate expectation is wrongly seen as a legal mandate for disregarding procedural fairness in any case where no legal right in the strict sense is involved.[101]

This point effectively leads Deane J to the conclusion argued for here: a duty of fairness should arise where context demands it, and there is a 'strong presumption' that such duty will arise where an authority has power to negatively affect someone's interests. The rationale for such duties is 'ordinary notions of what is fair and just'.[102] This is the true basis upon which the obligation to consult arises in cases such as *Baker*; legitimate expectations is an unnecessary complication.

Simon Brown LJ, in his separate judgment in *Baker*, seemed to recognise the very argument made here, ie fairness simpliciter governs withdrawal cases. Although this did not lead him to take the logical next step, and acknowledge that such cases are not properly conceptualised as legitimate expectation cases. This is probably because he was bound by *CCSU*. He said that in cases of deprivation of existing benefits

> the concept of legitimate expectation ... seems to me no more than a recognition and embodiment of the unsurprising principle that the demands of fairness are likely to be somewhat higher when an authority contemplates depriving someone of an existing benefit or advantage when the claimant is a bare applicant for a future benefit.[103]

As he acknowledged earlier in his judgment, if all that legitimate expectations entail here is that some continuing benefit cannot be removed without consultation then 'there would be no point in introducing the concept ... in the first place; one would simply look at the decision in question and ask whether the administrator acted fairly'.[104]

Surprisingly, this line of jurisprudence lives on, albeit the number of successful claims of this type is 'vanishingly small',[105] and there have been moves to marginalize this category of legitimate expectations. For example courts have held that before a legitimate expectation may arise the impact on the claimant must be 'pressing and focussed', that a case with these characteristics will be 'exceptional' and that this category of legitimate expectation is of 'narrow and specific compass'.[106] It seems legitimate expectations

[101] Ibid.
[102] Ibid.
[103] *Baker* (n 4) 91.
[104] *Baker* (n 4) 90.
[105] *Application by Charles Boyle for Judicial Review* [2016] NIQB 2 [18].
[106] *Bhatt Murphy* (n 1) [58]–[59]. In this case Laws LJ describes withdrawal-of-benefit cases as the 'secondary case of procedural legitimate expectation' (at [37]–[39], [47]–[49]), directly following *CCSU* and *Baker*.

jurisprudence is gradually catching up with developments in procedural fairness and standing, which have rendered legitimate expectations otiose in withdrawal-of-benefit cases. It is to be hoped that this process is soon completed, and that the courts formally recognize that legitimate expectations have no role in withdrawal-of-benefit cases. Not only do legitimate expectations add nothing, but analysis of such cases in terms of legitimate expectations may be counterproductive in narrowing the ambit of standing and procedural fairness. Further, extension of the doctrine to such cases contributes to the doctrine's sprawling nature, which makes it impossible for the field to settle and develop coherently.

Liberating a Doctrine: The Paradigm Case

The previous section showed how the doctrine of legitimate expectations has been stretched to cover a wide range of cases, and that many of these categories of case are not properly or best analysed as legitimate expectations cases. The lack of discipline around invocation of legitimate expectations is a principal reason, if not *the* principal reason for the unsatisfactory state of the field and why courts have struggled to articulate a concrete set of rules and principles to govern the field, often falling back on abstract notions of conspicuous unfairness or abuse of power. By chiselling away at the foregoing categories we are now in a position to identify the paradigm case; that category of case in which legitimate expectations meets a distinctive set of concerns not met by other doctrines, and performs a role meaningfully distinct from more established doctrines. Once identified, the task of theorising the doctrine and fashioning a concrete set of legal principles to govern legitimate expectation cases can be sensibly undertaken. In turn formulation of general legal tests would hold out the prospect that the field could be saved from its current state of incoherence.

The paradigm case, that category of case that remains once all extraneous categories have been chipped away, is the case where an authority makes an express promise, assurance or undertaking to an individual or group of individuals that the authority will act or omit to act in some way, this act or omission having a bearing on the individual or group's interests. The courts have themselves come to recognise this in more recent case law: 'The paradigm case arises where a public authority has provided an unequivocal assurance'.[107] In *Rahman* Stanley Burnton LJ, with whom the other members of the Court agreed, put the position even more strongly: 'the concept of legitimate expectation is normally otiose in cases where there has been no representation, by words or conduct, by the public authority

[107] *Bhatt Murphy* (n 1) [29].

in question to the claimant seeking to rely on it'.[108] Courts clearly view promise cases as those in which there is the strongest normative imperative for recognition of legally-enforceable expectations: 'the principle of good administration prima facie requires adherence by public authorities to their promises'.[109] In *Loreto Grammar School's Application* the Northern Irish Court of Appeal held that the doctrine of legitimate expectations should be 'narrowly construed' so as to protect against undue fettering of administrative discretion—the courts should 'lean against the finding of a fettering of discretion'—while acknowledging that the one type of case where a concern for administrative autonomy may have to give way is where there has been a clear, unequivocal representation to an individual: 'In such a situation the balance must be struck differently'.[110] In these cases the legitimate expectation is of the authority doing what was promised.

It is the presence of a promise, a positive inducement to rely and place trust in officials, which sets such cases apart from those considered above,[111] may justify recognition of a distinct doctrine, and grounds a duty on the authority to act in a particular way.[112] The concern in such cases is not that the defendant affords an individual procedural fairness. As we saw in the context of withdrawal-of-benefit cases, an authority is under a free-standing duty to make decisions according to fair process regardless of the presence of any subjective expectations of fair process. Where an authority's promise gives rise to a legitimate expectation, the relevant expectation is not one that the authority will follow a procedure consonant with ordinary requirements of fairness. Rather, the expectation is one that the authority will adopt the promised procedure; the promised procedure would most likely be one 'not otherwise required by law in protection of an interest'.[113]

Nor is the concern in promise cases that the authority act rationally in pursuing public goals: an authority will generally be acting quite rationally, given its primary duty to pursue statutory public goals, in acting contrary to promises which would frustrate the proper pursuit of those goals; such action could certainly not be considered perverse. The legal inquiry in promise-based cases does not begin and end with an inquiry into reasonableness, nor must it. If a promise gives rise to a legitimate expectation, that expectation will provide a free-standing basis for a review claim. Further,

[108] *SOSHD v Rahman* [2011] EWCA Civ 814 [42].

[109] *Begbie* (n 8) 1123–24.

[110] *Loreto Grammar School's Application* [2012] NICA 1 [45].

[111] *DM* (n 52) [18]

[112] I leave open here whether conduct other than an express promise which nonetheless induces in the claimant an assumption about the defendant's future conduct may be sufficient to ground a legitimate expectation. The issue has been a live one in the law of estoppel: E Peel, *Treitel The Law of Contract* 14th edn (Sweet and Maxwell, 2015) [3-081]; J Paterson, A Robertson and A Duke, *Principles of Contract Law* 5th edn (Thomson Reuters, 2015) [9.60].

[113] *Baker* (n 4) 89.

it seems increasingly clear that the inquiry into whether the authority was justified in frustrating a promise-based legitimate expectation is an objective question for the judiciary rather than one filtered through a *Wednesbury* lens.[114] In other words, the courts do not ask whether the balance struck by a decision-maker between promise and countervailing interest was irrational, exercising a secondary, supervisory judgment. Rather, courts ask for themselves whether the balance struck was justifiable. Of course, substantive review is currently in flux, and there appears to be emergent recognition of at least a substantive test of fair balance in some contexts.[115] This test has arisen where what are described as basic rights are in play. But the same method could be applied to test whether an authority has, in not fulfilling a promise, struck a fair balance between the claimant's expectations and pursuit of public goals. Perhaps promise cases will come to be seen as a branch of this new substantive review. However, what will continue to mark such cases out is the normative ground for intervention and the analytical starting-point of the inquiry, which is the promise. Further, the reasons promises should be protected will be different from the reasons why we protect other phenomena which may also ground a fair balance test, such as human or constitutional rights.

Nor is the concern in promise cases that the authority looks on the promise as a relevant consideration. The specific concern addressed by legitimate expectations is that the authority should follow through with its promised actions; the claimant's expectation is not one of due consideration—the expectation speaks to an outcome and the key question in the case will be whether the authority should be held to its promise, or whether the expectation is defeated by countervailing concerns. Relevant considerations is a fall-back ground in such cases. For example, if the claimant fails to convince the court that an authority's representation gave rise to a legitimate expectation, the claimant may nonetheless convince the court that the decision-maker ought to have taken the representation into account in their decision-making. In some legitimate expectations cases courts have held that one mode of protecting a legitimate expectation may be to require the decision-maker to consider the expectation. However, as is discussed below, relevant considerations here do not go to the normative basis for judicial intervention, ie the causative event which grounds the claim is *not* the authority's failure to *consider* the promise, but the failure to *fulfil* the promise. Here, relevant considerations enter the analysis as a matter relevant to remedies. Further, specifically in promise cases, the courts hold that the ordinary response to failure to fulfil an expectation is that the authority will be held

[114] *Paponette* (n 3); *R (Patel) v GMC* [2013] 1 WLR 2801.
[115] eg *Pham v SOSHD* [2015] 1 WLR 1591.

to its promise;[116] the relevant consideration mode of protection is generally one reserved for cases in which the normative basis for the expectation is far weaker than an express promise, ie a non-paradigm case.

Nor is the concern in promise cases that the defendant treat the defendant consistently, applying its general policies or practices to the claimant's case. Rather, the concern is that the claimant should be treated in the manner the defendant promised they would treat them, whether consonant with policies or practices or not. Generally the reason a promise-based claim is brought is that the authority wishes to treat the claimant in the same way as everyone else, but the claimant objects. The claimant is typically making a claim for *exceptionalism* based on an individuated promise. Thus, in *Coughlan* all others in the claimant's class had no legal claim against being transferred away from their care homes, but the claimant did because she had been made a promise of a home for life. Similarly, in *Bibi*, the claimants were seeking to jump to the top of the secure accommodation housing list on the basis of a promise made to them; but for that promise the claimants would have had no prospect of jumping the queue. In this way promise cases are typically the polar opposite of consistency cases. This reinforces that it is utterly incoherent to include consistency and promise cases under one umbrella doctrine.

Nor is the concern in promise cases with ensuring policies are published. In promise cases the claimant is not particularly concerned with the authority's policies, let alone whether they are published, nor does any legal issue depend on this. The principal issue is whether the authority ought to be held to its promise.

Thus, the concern in promise cases is that an authority should stand by its word, and this concern is *distinct* from those concerns underpinning other grounds of review. It is the failure to stand by its promise, which would reasonably induce individuals to rely on and place their faith in officials and founds an expectation that the promised conduct will be undertaken, which affords the normative and legal ground for judicial intervention so as to prevent the authority from reneging on its commitment.[117] Why an authority should be held to its promises, particularly absent contractual relations, and why this concern warrants recognition of a doctrine distinct from estoppel is a difficult and contentious question for another day. My principal concern

[116] *Bhatt Murphy* (n 1) [50].

[117] It is unlikely that the rationale is to protect an expectation only insofar as it engenders detrimental reliance given—as we shall see—it is not clear detrimental reliance is a prerequisite, and damages are not available to remedy detriments. I note this point in passing in the light of a significant debate within the literature on the law of estoppel over whether protecting against detrimental reliance is the basis of such claims: A Robertson, 'The Reliance Basis of Proprietary Estoppel Remedies' [2008] *Conveyancer* 295; 'Three Models of Promissory Estoppel' (2013) 7 *Journal of Equity* 226.

here has been to identify the distinctive contribution legitimate expectations can make within judicial review; in Simon Brown J's words, what 'actual assistance can be derived from' it.[118]

Above, we saw that recognition of legitimate expectations can give rise to serious public interest concerns, particularly in change-of-policy cases. Recognising legitimate expectations in policy-change cases could make intolerable inroads into the 'general principle that a public authority cannot be estopped from exercising a statutory discretion or performing a public duty'.[119] If courts recognise legitimate expectations merely on the basis of general policy it would be nearly impossible for an authority to perform their first duty of taking that action required to fulfil statutory goals; an authority which wished to change policy to better serve public goals would face serious impediments as all subject to the prior policy could resist application of the new policy. Furthermore, it is not clear there are good reasons for recognising legitimate expectations; all should reasonably expect, given the inherently transitory nature of policies, that policies only govern affairs for the time being. The argument is even stronger in the case of informal practices or ways of doing things. As Laws LJ observes, a change in practice or policy is unobjectionable because it entails no abuse of power; it is an ordinary, necessary aspect of public administration.[120] Therefore, something more is required to warrant legal intervention on the basis of legitimate expectations, given concerns to ensure authorities retain liberty to set policy in the public interest.

Promise cases do not run into these problems or at least do not implicate them to the same degree. First, there is a good reason for differential treatment, and departure from the general principle that authorities should not be estopped from pursuing public goals: the authority has positively induced the claimant, through an explicit promise, to believe that they will be treated in a particular way in the future. As Laws LJ observed in *Bhatt*:[121]

> Authority shows that where a substantive expectation is to run the promise or practice which is its genesis is not merely a reflection of the ordinary fact ... that a policy with no terminal date or terminating event will continue in effect until rational grounds for its cessation exist. Rather it must constitute a specific undertaking, directed at a particular individual or group, by which the relevant policy's continuance is assured. Lord Templeman in *Preston*[122] referred (866–867) to 'conduct ... equivalent to a breach of contract or breach of representations'.

118 *Baker* (n 4) 88.
119 *R (Reprotech (Pebsham) Ltd) v East Sussex CC* [2003] 1 WLR 348 [35].
120 *Bhatt Murphy* (n 1) [49].
121 *Bhatt Murphy* (n 1) [43].
122 *R v IRC; ex parte Preston* [1985] AC 835.

Second, only promisees may claim differential treatment. Of course concerns over ossification may arise if the class of promisees is large, particularly if the promise is one guaranteeing substantive outcomes. However, in such case the promise is unlikely to generate legitimate expectations.

Third, following on from the previous point, not just any promise will do; the promise must be one giving rise to a legitimate expectation. Certain requirements must be met for a promise to generate a legitimate expectation, and these are likely to be more stringent where the promise pertains to outcome rather than procedure. Criteria may include that the promise is clear, unambiguous and unqualified; there must be a degree of formality to the promise; the promise might have to be addressed to the claimant's circumstances; and the representation may need to be such that it would induce a reasonable person to rely. It is readily apparent that the normative imperative for holding an authority to a promise with these characteristics is far stronger than holding it to some practice which may not even have been the product of a conscious decision. 'A promise is, precisely, a presentation about future conduct, making it relatively straightforward to decide whether the promisor should be held to it' whereas '[w]here expectation is based upon practice, the issue is more elusive'.[123]

Legal Tests

This chapter's main aim has been to cut through an unruly jurisprudence, eliminating categories of cases not properly analysed as legitimate expectations cases, and identify the paradigm or core case, in which a separate doctrine of legitimate expectations can perform a role meaningfully distinct from other review doctrines. The doctrine has been pinned down. However, we do not have a final product. Important outstanding questions remain. But identification of the paradigm case brings into focus the questions we should be asking, and holds out the prospect that we will be able to forge a worked-out, coherent law of legitimate expectations. There is simply no prospect of such tests emerging while so many disparate and meaningfully distinct categories of case are lumped together under one umbrella doctrine; rather this has had the opposite effect of pushing courts towards open-ended concepts such as abuse of power. The courts have come to recognise the problems with such an approach. In *Bibi* Schiemann LJ said, 'without refinement, the question whether the reneging on a promise would be so unfair as to amount to an abuse of power is an uncertain guide';[124]

[123] *Hamble* (n 17) [42].
[124] *Bibi* (n 7) [34].

> [t]he case law is replete with words such as 'legitimate' and 'fair', 'abuse of power' and 'inconsistent with good administration'. When reading the judgements care needs to be taken to distinguish analytical tools from conclusions which encapsulate value judgments but do not give any indication of the route to those conclusions.[125]

It is these analytical tools which we need to forge to bring order to the field. Schiemann LJ also voiced scepticism of attempts to pin down a set of general legal tests to govern the field on the basis that this could impede legal development.[126] With respect, it is the failure to discipline decision-making through concrete rules and principles that has plunged the field into confusion, and pushed courts towards the open-ended concepts Schiemann LJ was so critical of.

I cannot here propose fully worked-out tests to govern the paradigm case. However, I offer several observations as to the general features such a test would have, and flag up some of the important outstanding questions which need to be resolved.

During the 1990s there was some prospect of emergence of a set of worked-out criteria; in particular these criteria can be traced through the cases of *MFK*, *RAM*, *Unilever* and *Hargreaves*.[127] Many of these criteria still sit at the core of promise cases though the clear structure and rules enunciated in earlier case law have been muddied over time, while different courts have given different views on which criteria should be prerequisites for legitimate expectations to arise. Indeed, it is worth noting that it is only within promise cases that anything approaching a worked-out, coherent and general legal test has emerged. This is probably because such cases revolve around the giving of a promise, and that promise provides a clear analytical starting point, by reference to which a set of legal tests can be forged, while the presence of the promise clearly differentiates such cases, so that it is easy for courts to identify when relevant tests apply.

In *RAM*, Stuart-Smith LJ set out the following criteria that had to be fulfilled in a paradigm case of legitimate expectations, noting similarities with estoppel.[128] If the claimant proves the first four criteria, then there shall be a legitimate expectation, and the defendant shall have to justify frustration of that expectation.

1. Was the representation clear and unambiguous?
2. Was the representation made directly to the claimant or if not, was the claimant within the class of persons who were entitled to rely, or was it reasonable for the claimant to rely on the representation?

[125] *Bibi* (n 7) [18].
[126] *Bibi* (n 7) [25].
[127] *R v IRC; ex parte MFK Underwriting Agents Ltd* [1990] 1 WLR 1545; *RAM* (n 6); *Unilever* (n 72); *Hargreaves* (n 42).
[128] *RAM* (n 6) 236–37.

3. Did the claimant rely?
4. Did the claimant suffer detriment in consequence of reliance?
5. Can the defendant show that overriding public interests entitled it to depart from its promise?
6. Ought the court to exercise its remedial discretion in favour of the claimant?[129]

There are important debates to be had about each step of this inquiry, some of which are closer to being resolved in the jurisprudence than others; in particular the precise role of reliance and detriment is yet to be conclusively resolved (though it is increasingly clear that neither is a prerequisite, albeit the presence of detrimental reliance will be a factor strongly favouring recognition of an enforceable expectation),[130] while it remains uncertain whether the inquiry in step five should invariably take the form of a structured proportionality analysis. Other established criteria are not included in the six-point test; for example, the claimant must, in their interactions with the relevant authority, place their cards face up, it is now relatively clear that the claimant must have knowledge of the promise,[131] while the courts have generally set their face against giving legal force to unlawful promises. The questions that arise can only be conclusively resolved by reference to the underlying reasons why authorities should be held to their promises.[132] But the basic structure enunciated by Stuart-Smith LJ seems a good starting point, and is suggestive of the sort of structured test that could bring order, certainty, consistency, predictability and coherence to the field, for the benefit of individuals and administrators alike.

The obvious criticism of a structured test is that it may overly constrain judges' ability to intervene in cases where it seems intervention is warranted. There are several responses. First, judges must apply law; review ought not to collapse into an intuitive enterprise, which it explicitly has done in the field of legitimate expectations.[133] Second, we have seen the results of not disciplining decision-making through adoption of general legal tests. Those results are wholly unattractive. Third, while the six-point test provides an invariable structure, there is flexibility at different stages of the analysis,

[129] This element was not included in Stuart-Smith LJ's five-point list, which addressed the substantive law of legitimate expectations, but in disposing of the claim remedial discretion was the final aspect of his reasoning, and was identified by the Judge as a core issue for determination in the case. See also, eg, *Bibi* (n 7) [40]ff; *Reprotech* (n 119) [34]; *Nadarajah* (n 14) [57].

[130] M Elliott and JNE Varuhas, *Administrative Law* 5th edn (Oxford, 2016) [6.1.3].

[131] Elliott and Varuhas (n 130) [6.1.3].

[132] For discussion of possible justifications see, eg, P Reynolds, 'Legitimate Expectations and the Protection of Trust in Officials' [2011] *Public Law* 330; CF Forsyth, 'Legitimate Expectations Revisited' (29 May 2011) ALBA Summer Conference 2011 (www.adminlaw.org.uk/library/publications.php); S Schønberg, *Legitimate Expectations in Administrative Law* (Oxford University Press, 2000).

[133] *R v IRC; ex parte Matrix-Securities Ltd* [1994] 1 WLR 334, 358 ('the single issue in this case is one of impression—namely whether it is an abuse of power').

for example in determining whether public interests justify frustration of the promise, and in application of remedial discretion (see below). Fourth, where courts have felt compelled to stretch legitimate expectations, it has often been the case that alternative grounds of intervention were open. Consider *Unilever*. The Court rejected explicitly counsel's submission that the Court should stick to applying the structured tests from *MFK* and *RAM* so as to keep legitimate expectations within 'controllable limits' and promote certainty.[134] It preferred to stretch legitimate expectations to embrace a wider idea of abuse of power, whereas application of the *RAM* criteria told against intervention. But tellingly, as we saw above, judicial intervention could easily have been justified on rationality or consistency grounds. Indeed, a recurring theme of analysis of non-legitimate expectation cases was that legitimate expectations commonly added nothing to or were confused with existing grounds.

Process, Substance and Modes of Protection

Two further issues require comment. First, a significant feature of contemporary legitimate expectations jurisprudence is the drawing of a categorical distinction between procedural and substantive expectations. In promise cases, this plays out as a distinction between cases in which an authority promises to follow a particular procedure in reaching a decision, for example promising a consultation, and cases where an authority promises an outcome, for example promising a company's taxes will be calculated according to a given formula. The process-outcome distinction may be hard to draw in practice. But putting these difficulties to one side, there may be good reasons for drawing the distinction. In particular, enforcement of substantive expectations may prevent the authority from reaching that decision which it considers best serves the common good, whereas enforcement of procedural expectations only dictates the procedure to be followed in reaching an outcome. Recognition of substantive expectations may therefore place significant fetters on an authority's ability to carry out its first duty, exercising its public powers in a way that best serves public goals, especially where held by a large class. There may therefore be good reasons why, for example, it should be more difficult to establish substantive legitimate expectations, so further criteria are added to those in steps (1)–(4) of the *RAM* test. These may include requirements that the representation was made to a small group and/or addressed to the promisee's circumstances.[135]

[134] *Unilever* (n 72) 694–695.

[135] *Coughlan* (n 10) [59], [71]; *Bhatt Murphy* (n 1) [46]. Further, where a case has these features it will be more difficult for the authority to justify frustrating the expectation: *Nadarajah* (n 14) [69].

However, at times too much has been made of this distinction. In particular, some courts have seemingly suggested that the judicial approach or method of analysis should fundamentally vary as between the two types of case. In *Coughlan*, Lord Woolf distinguished three categories of legitimate expectation case. Above we saw the first category was not in fact a category of legitimate expectation case. The two other categories were procedural and substantive legitimate expectations. He distinguished the court's role in each category. In procedural cases the court's role was 'the conventional one of determining whether the decision was procedurally fair'.[136] Whereas in substantive expectations cases 'the court has when necessary to determine whether there is a sufficient overriding interest to justify a departure from what has previously been promised'.[137] This is an odd distinction as surely procedural expectations may also be defeated by countervailing considerations. Lord Woolf seemed to acknowledge as much when he said a procedural expectation would be enforced 'unless there is an overriding reason to resile from it'.[138] Thus, the court's general approach is the same in each case: the court must decide whether legitimate expectations exist, and then consider whether there are good reasons for frustrating those expectations. There may be important differences between the two categories, as already discussed, but the court's basic role is not one of them. Any suggestion of a difference of approach has now been expunged by Laws LJ's judgment in *Bhatt*. In terms of whether an expectation has been generated,

> If [the authority] has distinctly promised to consult those affected or potentially affected, then ordinarily it must consult (the paradigm case of procedural legitimate expectation). If it has distinctly promised to preserve existing policy for a specific person or group who would be substantially affected by the change, then ordinarily it must keep its promise (substantive expectation).[139]

Laws LJ clarifies that the issue of frustration of expectations arises and is to be approached in the same way across procedural and substantive cases:

> In the paradigm case [of procedural expectation] the court will not allow the decision-maker to effect the proposed change without notice or consultation, *unless the want of notice or consultation is justified by the force of an overriding legal duty owed by the decision-maker, or other countervailing public interest* (emphasis added).[140]

Similarly, in *Nadarajah*, in arguing that proportionality should govern the inquiry into frustration of the promise, Laws LJ said, '[t]his approach makes

[136] *Coughlan* (n 10) [58].
[137] *Coughlan* (n 10) [58].
[138] *Coughlan* (n 10) [57].
[139] *Bhatt Murphy* (n 1) [50].
[140] *Bhatt Murphy* (n 1) [30].

no distinction between procedural and substantive expectations. Nor should it'.[141] Explicitly doubting the *Coughlan* categories, he said:

> Of course there will be cases where the public body ... justifiably concludes that its statutory duty ... requires it to override an expectation of substantive benefit which it has itself generated. So also there will be cases where a procedural benefit may justifiably be overridden. The difference between the two is not a difference of principle.[142]

The second outstanding issue relates to the idea of 'modes of protection'. Courts and commentators sometimes suggest that after a court establishes an expectation, and finds the expectation is not defeated by countervailing concerns, a further question should be posed: 'what the court should do'.[143] In other words, that a promise gives rise to an expectation, which trumps countervailing concerns, does not mean necessarily that a court should enforce the promise, ie the court will not necessarily require the authority to actually do what was promised. I do not doubt the case law provides some support for this proposition. But the question is how it enters the analysis.

It seems some commentators and courts consider the question of whether the expectation should be enforced, or protected through some second-best means, to be an aspect of substantive law. I think this view follows from the unruly state of the jurisprudence. The idea of modes of protection has been used to try to explain cases which are not properly legitimate expectation cases. The idea emerges principally from the withdrawal-of-benefit cases considered above. In those cases the legitimate expectation is often characterised as a legitimate expectation of retaining a benefit into the future. This expectation is substantive. But in these cases it is protected through recognition of procedural duties to consult before withdrawal. So if one wished to explain these cases as legitimate expectations cases one would need to say that courts have adopted a procedural mode of protecting a substantive expectation. However, one only need reach for such explanations if one considers these cases to be legitimate expectation cases. I do not. As such I would not add such a stage of analysis to any legal test governing legitimate expectations.

Another way to think about modes of protection is as a control device which allows the courts to relieve authorities of having to fully implement legitimate expectations. Such a control device is necessary if courts are not disciplined in their approach to recognising legitimate expectations; for example if courts readily find legitimate expectations across the disparate

[141] *Nadarajah* (n 14) [68]–[69].
[142] *Nadarajah* (n 14) [69].
[143] *Bibi* (n 7) [19].

types of cases considered above. But if the doctrine is a narrow one then there shall be far less need for control devices. Furthermore, it is worth reiterating that compared to other categories of case, such as where legitimate expectations have been recognised on the flimsy basis of general policy or practice, in the paradigm case the normative imperative for full enforcement of expectations is far stronger because the authority has positively and personally assured the claimant that it will act in a particular way into the future. It is thus unsurprising that courts have indicated that there shall be far less scope to refuse enforcement of an expectation generated by promise.[144]

Does it follow from this that I consider every legitimate expectation generated by promise, and which trumps countervailing interests, should be enforced to the letter? No. The explanation for my answer lies in an axiomatic aspect of review: remedies are discretionary (see *RAM* step 6).[145] Recognition of the role of remedial discretion in expectations cases also shows that a 'mode of protection' inquiry would be otiose. The concerns that might justify such a step in the analysis are met at the remedies stage: it is typically the remedies stage where courts undertake pragmatic assessment of what action is now feasible given the facts as they stand. An observed problem with introducing this type of discretionary, pragmatic analysis into adjudication of substantive obligations, rather than reserving it for a separate remedial inquiry, is that it can swallow up the entire analysis; instead of following the type of structured inquiry encapsulated in the *RAM* test, judicial analysis may collapse into an unstructured inquiry into what is feasible.

It is clear that remedial discretion applies in expectation cases.[146] Indeed courts have placed great weight on the nature of remedial discretion on review, specifically that it implicates consideration of public and third-party interests, as that feature of legitimate expectations which marks it out as distinct from estoppel.[147] So, for example, a court might refuse to mandate fulfilment of the expectation if, given effluxion of time, actual performance is now impossible. If fulfilment of the promise would be exceptionally burdensome, the court could require the executive to consider alternative ways

[144] eg *Bhatt Murphy* (n 1) [50] (where a legitimate expectation is generated by promise then 'ordinarily [the authority] must keep its promise').

[145] In some cases the 'mode of protection' inquiry has explicitly been conceptualised as an inquiry into relief: eg *Rowland* (n 5) [132]ff.

[146] See n 129 above. *Preston* (n 122) 866.

[147] *Reprotech* (n 119) [34]; *Flanagan* (n 58) [16]. But it is questionable whether the nature of the remedial discretion on review is a sound basis for distinguishing legitimate expectations from the law of estoppel given remedial discretion in the law of estoppel is similarly broad and flexible (eg *Commonwealth v Verwayen* (1990) 170 CLR 394, 441–443) and it is increasingly clear that wider public and third party interests may be taken into account in deciding upon equitable remedies (eg *Coventry v Lawrence* [2014] 1 AC 822).

in which the expectation may be 'satisfied',[148] such as provision of compensation, or some other next-best benefit—or refuse relief because such steps have already been taken.[149]

CONCLUSION

This chapter has sought to chip away the excess, those cases often considered to be legitimate expectations cases but which are not best analysed as such, in order to liberate the doctrine and help save the field from 'the many semantic confusions that have bedevilled this area of our law'.[150] This chapter has completed the heavy hammer and chisel work, revealing the basic form of the core case of legitimate expectations; that is, cases in which the basis of the claim is a promise made by an authority. Now much more delicate work must be undertaken to finesse the finer details of the legal tests that ought to govern such cases. But identification of the basic form provides the foundation for this important work to be completed.

[148] *Rowland* (n 5) [162].
[149] eg *Bibi* (n 7) [56]; *Coughlan* (n 10) [82]; *Rowland* (n 5) [135].
[150] *Baker* (n 4) 89.

3

Legitimate Expectations and the Separation of Powers in English and Welsh Administrative Law

ROBERT THOMAS

THIS CHAPTER EXAMINES whether the courts have exceeded the proper limits of judicial review when applying the principle of legitimate expectations in English and Welsh administrative law. This principle has generated much discussion.[1] A central and perennial concern is that, when enforcing legitimate expectations, the courts have engaged in merits review. That is, they have imposed their own policy preferences upon expert administrators or democratically accountable politicians by re-making administrative decisions or telling government agencies which decisions they ought to make. In other words, judicial protection of legitimate expectations infringes the separation of powers.

To investigate whether this is so, this chapter undertakes a detailed analysis of those cases in which the English courts have protected legitimate expectations. The approach adopted is neither normative nor doctrinal. Instead, the focus is upon the outcomes and consequences of those judicial decisions that have safeguarded legitimate expectations. There has been much discussion of the principle, but only a handful of such challenges have ever succeeded. It is argued that the courts have not come anywhere near the limits of judicial review, let alone strayed beyond them. In each case, judicial intervention was necessary to protect the claimants against the adverse consequences of governmental errors and failures. If anything, the courts have adopted a highly cautious approach.

[1] See, eg, CF Forsyth, 'The Provenance and Protection of Legitimate Expectations' (1988) 47 *Cambridge Law Journal* 239; I Steele, 'Substantive Legitimate Expectations: Striking the Right Balance?' (2005) 121 *Law Quarterly Review* 300; R Moules, *Actions Against Public Officials: Legitimate Expectations, Misstatements and Misconduct* (Sweet & Maxwell, 2009).

The chapter is structured as follows. The first section outlines the principle of legitimate expectations. The second considers the meaning of the separation of powers doctrine. The third section outlines the approach and method used. The fourth section considers the number of legitimate expectation challenges. The fifth section undertakes a detailed analysis of successful legitimate expectation cases.

LEGITIMATE EXPECTATIONS

The principle of legitimate expectations is part of the duty to act fairly.[2] If a public body has raised expectations that it will in future undertake a certain course of action, then it should ordinarily fulfil those expectations unless there is otherwise good reason. The principle has a number of overlapping rationales: abuse of power; fairness; preserving trust and confidence in government; and the need for public bodies to deal straightforwardly and consistently with the public. To some degree, all of these rationales merge, but they are relative not absolute. The legitimacy of an individual's expectation depends upon the court's assessment of the force of an expectation in the face of any competing public interest. In all legitimate expectation cases, three practical questions arise:

(i) What has the public body, whether by practice or by promise, committed itself to?
(ii) Has the body acted or proposed to act unlawfully in relation to its commitment?
(iii) What should the court do?

It is common to distinguish between procedural and substantive expectations. Procedural expectations are not generally seen as problematic. A public body has generated an expectation that it will follow a certain procedure before taking a decision. This may involve a hearing or consulting with those affected. The court can require the public body to adopt the procedure, even though there would otherwise be no obligation to hold a hearing or to consult. Procedural expectations therefore represent an expansion upon the general principles of procedural fairness, but for good reason: it was the public body's own behaviour that induced the expectation.

Procedural expectations usually impose a slight, though not negligible, burden. Holding a hearing or consulting may add a small financial cost and some delay to the decision-making process. Having undertaken the procedure, the public body is able to make its decision, which can, of course, be unfavourable. The requirement to fulfil such procedural expectations has

[2] See *R (Niazi) v Secretary of State for the Home Department* [2008] EWCA Civ 755 [50]–[51] (Laws LJ).

value. It enhances dignitarian values and trust in government.[3] Further, the body may become more circumspect before raising similar expectations in the future. However, such judicial intervention in practice exerts little adverse impact upon government.

By contrast, substantive legitimate expectations are potentially more problematic. In this situation, a public body has generated an expectation that it will take a particular substantive decision. Alternatively, the expectation is that the public body will apply a previously announced policy to the claimant's circumstances and thereby exempt the claimant from the application of a new policy which the body now considers to be appropriate.[4] Substantive expectations are normally created through either an explicit representation or the publication of a policy. In the typical situation, the claimant will have relied in good faith upon that representation or policy to her detriment. The public body then seeks to act contrary to the expectations engendered. This may be because the public body's conception of the public interest has changed or there has been a change of policy, in resources, or in the underlying administrative scheme. As the courts have recognised, 'a decision-maker must follow his published policy (and not some different unpublished policy) unless there are good reasons for not doing so'.[5] The issue whether a public body can lawfully resile from a legitimate expectation is particularly fact-sensitive and will depend upon various factors: the strength of the expectation; the subject matter to which it relates; the range of affected individuals; and the consequences of giving effect to the change.

The court's task is to assess whether there is a sufficiently compelling public interest which requires the claimant's expectations to be defeated. The situation poses a tension between administrative discretion and an individual's trust. On the one hand, there is the importance of governmental discretion to amend policy in the face of changing circumstances and the consequent administrative and democratic gains. On the other hand, there is the desirability of government acting in accordance with the expectations that arose as a result of its own behaviour, thereby making administrators responsible and allowing people to plan their lives.

In the midst of this is the role of the court. A standard doctrinal issue concerns the appropriate standard of review. Should the court adopt a light-touch *Wednesbury*-style review, or should the court itself weigh up the balance of the claimant's expectations and the public body's conception of the

[3] For judicial endorsement of the importance of dignitarian values, see *Osborne v Parole Board* [2013] AC 1115, 1149 [68] (Lord Reed).

[4] See, eg, *R v Ministry of Agriculture, Fisheries and Food; ex parte Hamble (Offshore) Fisheries Ltd* [1995] 2 All ER 714 (QB).

[5] *R (Lumba) v Secretary of State for the Home Department* [2012] 1 AC 245, 265 [26] (Lord Dyson).

public interest? Beneath such doctrinal concerns are wider underlying questions: how far should the courts go when assessing administrative action? When does the court start becoming an active participant in managing the administrative process itself—as opposed to merely reviewing the lawfulness of administrative action?

In general terms, there are two possible judicial responses. The first is to establish a bright-line rule that substantive expectations are outside the scope of judicial protection. This expands the scope of administrative freedom, but the obvious downside is that public bodies could raise and then defeat expectations irrespective of the impact upon affected individuals. A second approach is for the court to assess whether the public interest claimed does in fact require the expectations to be overridden. This requires a detailed and contextual assessment of the individual facts and circumstances of the particular issue raised. Under this approach, the focus is upon the purpose why the public body is changing its policy and whether this requires the individual's expectations to be defeated. English law has shifted from the first to the second response.[6]

From one point of view, substantive expectations are a desirable addition to the judicial tool-kit to protect individuals against unfair government action and to compel administrators to give individual consideration to people caught out by changes in administrative policy. From a different point of view, the court is inappropriately constraining the ability of public bodies to assess the changing needs of the public interest in accordance with its constitutional power as a policy-formulating executive body. The perception is that the court is no longer merely supervising public administration, but is engaging in it by telling administrators which decision to make. In other words, the courts are undertaking merits review, which is impermissible.[7]

A related concern is that the courts have not properly articulated a formal framework by which they undertake this analysis. According to Forsyth, there is so much uncertainty with the principle of legitimate expectations that there is a risk that it could 'collapse into an inchoate justification for judicial intervention'.[8] Similarly, Watson has noted that '[l]egitimate expectation in its current state as a patchwork of possible elements to consider, rather than [an] organised system of rules, is little more than a mechanism to dispense palm-tree justice'.[9] Both of these concerns could be brought

[6] A third possible approach would be for the courts to always protect substantive expectations regardless of the public body's argument for overriding them, but no-one has seriously advanced this position.

[7] See, eg, *R v Secretary of State for Transport; ex parte Richmond upon Thames LBC (No.1)* [1994] 1 WLR 74 (QB) 94 (Laws J).

[8] CF Forsyth, 'Legitimate Expectations Revisited' (2011) *Judicial Review* 429.

[9] J Watson, 'Clarity and Ambiguity: A New Approach to the Test of Legitimacy in the Law of Legitimate Expectations' (2010) 30 *Legal Studies* 633, 651.

together under the general label of what might be termed the 'separation of powers critique', that is, the principle of legitimate expectations involves the courts exceeding the proper limits of their constitutional authority by interfering with the merits of administrative decisions.

THE SEPARATION OF POWERS DOCTRINE

To investigate whether the courts have exceeded their role under the separation of powers doctrine, it is necessary to define that doctrine. However, this is a problematic endeavour.

The separation of powers is deeply embedded in the nature of modern liberal constitutionalism, but there is no agreed definition of the doctrine or agreement over its precise meaning. It manifests differently in different constitutional systems—a point well illustrated by the chapters in this book, which examine different common law jurisdictions. It can mean different things depending upon the perspective adopted. For instance, the pure doctrine of the separation of powers—institutional separation of the legislature, executive, and judiciary—fails at a descriptive level to explain Westminster-style democracies. In the UK, the doctrine of separation of powers is mostly frequently mentioned in relation to the need for the legislature and executive to refrain from interfering with the judiciary.

Nonetheless, it is generally accepted that the doctrine has a core meaning—albeit at a high level of abstraction. The separation of powers works against the concentration of power by allocating governmental power to different institutions. In order to balance governmental power with individual liberty, the powers of the state should not be concentrated in few hands. Instead, such powers should be allocated to different institutions—the legislature, executive and judiciary—which then operate as a check upon each other. The separation, rather than the concentration, of powers reduces the risk of the abuse of power. These powers principally include: legislation; execution of the law; and adjudication.

A basic problem is that discussion of the separation of powers often confuses institutions and functions. The doctrine assumes three separate institutions—the legislature, the executive, and judiciary. It also assumes three separate functions: the legislative, the executive; and the judicial. The legislature is there to enact general laws; the executive exists to administer those laws through administrative decision-making and implementation; and the judiciary is there to interpret and apply those by adjudicating upon disputes. However, it is often difficult in practice to distinguish between the exercise of these functions. Given the inherent imprecision that attaches to such labels, there can be no a priori distribution of legislative, administrative and judicial functions. In practice, formal differences often break down entirely when underlying substantive matters are considered. Courts adjudicate, but so too do public bodies when they make decisions that affect individuals. It is for Parliament to legislate, but in practice, the legislative agenda is highly influenced by the Government. Government also makes the vast body of secondary legislation. It is also implements and interprets legislation, subject to judicial correction. In formal terms, the courts continue to recognise the sovereignty of Parliament, but they also act as occasional legislators whenever they establish or modify a legal rule and when they interpret legislation. The consequence of this overlapping of functions by institutions means that any clear separation of powers is often illusory in practice. As Cane has noted, a realistic assessment of the separation of powers leads 'to the conclusion that all three branches of government effectively perform all three functions'.[10] The superficial simplicity of the functional separation of powers is 'beguiling, but horribly platitudinous'.[11]

Some scholars have rejected the separation of powers doctrine in its entirety: the doctrine is 'so remote from the facts that it is better to disregard it altogether' and a 'vehicle ... for the conveyance of fallacious ideas'.[12] More recently, Rubin has argued that the doctrine is a heuristic, a mental image or shortcut for thinking about the structure of government, but that it does not itself accurately describe the structure and operation of a contemporary administrative governmental system.[13] Government is no longer divided into the simple scheme of legislature, executive, and judiciary. There is an enormous range of administrative agencies that regulate society and formulate and implement policy. The separation of powers doctrine underemphasises the reality of the administrative state.

Despite these views, for the purposes of this chapter, it will be accepted that the separation of powers doctrine retains validity. For present purposes, the separation of powers doctrine is taken to mean that the courts should not exceed the proper limits of the judicial role by improperly imposing their own policy preferences on government or by unduly interfering with public administration. The role of the courts is one of reviewing legality rather than telling public bodies which decisions they should make. To examine whether the courts have breached the separation of powers

[10] P Cane, *Administrative Law*, 5th edn (Oxford University Press, 2011) 49.

[11] EW Thomas, *The Judicial Process: Realism, Pragmatism, Practical Reasoning and Principles* (Cambridge University Press, 2005) 77.

[12] JAG Griffith and H Street, *Principles of Administrative Law*, 5th edn (Pitman, 1973) 16; WA Robson, *Justice and Administrative Law*, 3rd edn (Stevens & Sons, 1951) 16. Robson's argument was based principally upon the difficulty of distinguishing between judicial and administrative functions: 'judges often administer, and administrators often judge' (ibid at 4). For J Willis, 'Canadian Administrative Law in Retrospect' (1974) 24 *University of Toronto Law Journal* 225, 228, the doctrine was emblematic of a 'theological' approach to administrative law, that is, an approach that focuses upon the 'never-never-land of grand constitutional principles' rather than the practical affairs of governance.

[13] EL Rubin, *Beyond Camelot: Rethinking Law and Politics for the Modern State* (Princeton University Press, 2005) Ch 2.

doctrine, decided cases will be analysed in detail. However, before proceeding further, it is necessary to explain the approach adopted here in more detail.

A REALIST APPROACH

Much of the discussion of legitimate expectations is undertaken through formal doctrinal legal analysis. This is important and there are many excellent studies. However, traditional doctrinal analysis does not and cannot exhaust the study of judicial review.[14] Legalism emphasises the importance of legal doctrine and precedent in judicial decision-making; policy consequences are irrelevant.[15] A legalist would examine cases to determine how they fit into a pre-existing structure of legal doctrine. By contrast, a realist approach looks beyond legal doctrine to a wider range of factors that influence judicial decision-making. As Holmes famously explained, '[t]he life of the law has not been logic: it has been experience'.[16] A realist approach would then focus upon the policy and non-legal factors that influence courts. It would also consider the impact and consequences of judicial intervention upon public administration.[17]

It is contended here that realism offers a better way of understanding judicial behaviour than drawing out extrapolations from legal doctrine. If we want to assess whether the courts have engaged in merits review when enforcing legitimate expectations, then we need to examine the practical consequences of decided cases. Whereas a formalist would concentrate almost entirely upon doctrine and precedent, a realist would point out that judges are not academic lawyers and do not think in the same way as academics. The risk is that formalists can exaggerate the importance of legal doctrine in judicial decision-making. Doctrinal coherence is, of course, not unimportant. But unlike academics, judges must reach decisions in real cases. Judging is a largely practical matter.

[14] Whether or not a scholar adopts a doctrinal approach is likely to be influenced as much by personal preference as well as her jurisdiction. As SA Smith, 'Taking Law Seriously' (2000) 50 *University of Toronto Law Journal* 241 has noted, in the UK and Australia, doctrinal work 'is probably still the orthodox form of legal scholarship, meaning not only that it is practised widely but that it is considered academically important. … In Canada, and even more so in the United States, doctrinal scholarship is still very much alive—primarily in the form of student and practitioner texts—but it ceased to be note-worthy academically long ago.'

[15] CF Forsyth, 'Showing the Fly the Way Out of the Flybottle: The Value of Formalism and Conceptual Reasoning in Administrative Law' (1997) 66 *Cambridge Law Journal* 325.

[16] OW Holmes, 'The Common Law' in *The Path of the Law and The Common Law* (first published 1881, Kaplan Publishing, 2009) 31.

[17] See RA Posner, *The Problematics of Moral and Legal Theory* (Harvard University Press, 1999) 238–39.

It is important to note in this regard that English judges have, in their extra-judicial discussions, increasingly come to articulate a realist perspective on their role. According to Lord Steyn, '[c]onsequentialist arguments and policy factors are the very stuff of decisions in the public law field'.[18] Furthermore, 'in common law adjudication it is an everyday occurrence for courts to consider, together with principled arguments, the balance sheet of policy advantages and disadvantages'.[19] Lord Carnwath has noted that during his years as an administrative law judge he never applied the *Wednesbury* test to determine whether a decision was irrational. Instead, he adopted a pragmatic approach: the ultimate question is always whether something has gone wrong of a nature and degree which requires the court to intervene and, if so, what form that intervention should take. If the answer is 'yes', then the judge looks for a legal hook to hang it on and if there is none suitable, then it may be necessary to adapt one.[20] Other judges have highlighted that the facts and circumstances of cases provide the all-important starting point because they are what the court has to adjudicate upon.[21] Such statements highlight the importance of viewing judicial decision-making as a form of practical reasoning in which legal doctrine is one consideration amongst others.[22]

A useful way of approaching decided cases is then not to focus solely upon doctrinal considerations, but also consider the degree of judicial intervention and its consequences. This means how far the court intervened in the governmental process when deciding a judicial review case. Arguably, the notion of intervention denotes more about judicial power and control than the standard doctrinal questions of whether a court makes a finding of illegality.[23] There can be varying degrees of intervention ranging from none at all, to procedural requirements, to more substantive judicial intervention. Further, the degree of judicial intervention is related to the likely consequences. From this perspective, to criticise the principle of legitimate expectations on the ground that it does not comprise an organised system of rules is to miss the point. All the principles of judicial review—legality, fairness, reasonableness, proportionality, and legitimate expectations—are

[18] Lord Steyn, 'Does Legal Formalism Hold Sway in England?' (1996) 49 *Current Legal Problems* 43, 51.

[19] Lord Steyn, 'Deference: A Tangled Story' (2005) *Public Law* 346, 357.

[20] Lord Carnwath, 'From Judicial Outrage to Sliding Scales—Where Next For *Wednesbury*?' (ALBA Annual Lecture, 12 November 2013) www.supremecourt.uk/docs/speech-131112-lord-carnwath.pdfaccessed 7 January 2016 at 19. Cf *R v Take-over Panel ex p Guinness Plc* [1990] 1 QB 146, 160C (Lord Donaldson MR).

[21] Thomas (n 11) 321.

[22] Ibid. RA Posner, *How Judges Think* (Harvard University Press, 2008) Ch 9. See also the assessment of the Law Lords in D Robertson, *Judicial Discretion in the House of Lords* (Oxford University Press, 1998) 401: 'The ideology is one of pragmatism, indeed the sort of pragmatism that is unable to conceive that it is an ideology.'

[23] See B Atkins, 'Interventions and Power in Judicial Hierarchies: Appellate Courts in England and the United States' (1990) 24 *Law & Society Review* 71, 73.

fuzzy around the edges and take colour from their context and how they are applied in practice by the courts. General principles do not decide specific cases. In administrative law, the determinants that influence case outcomes are likely to be: the facts and circumstances of the particular case; the social and political context of a case; and the possible consequences.

A STATISTICAL NOTE ON THE NUMBER OF LEGITIMATE EXPECTATION CHALLENGES

We now turn to consider how the courts have applied the principle of legitimate expectations, but before examining in detail successful legitimate expectations cases, it is important to look at the number of such challenges and their outcomes. This may give some purchase on the scale of the issue.

To this end, Figure 1 presents data on judicial review claims handled by the Administrative Court of England and Wales over the years 2000 to 2014. The Figure shows the number of judicial review claims granted permission, those that proceed to a substantive hearing, and the number of claims ultimately allowed.[24]

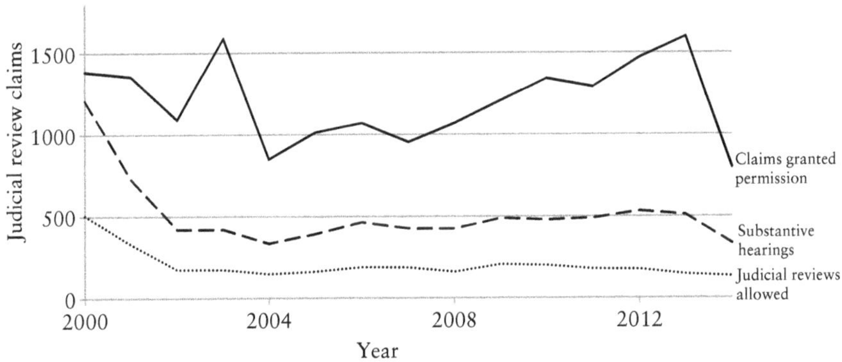

Figure 1: Judicial Review Claims in the Administrative Court of England and Wales, 2000–14

The data prompts the following points. The number of substantive judicial review hearings has rarely exceeded 500 per year since 2002. Between 2000 and 2014, the mean average of judicial review claims allowed was 204 cases per year. On average, claimants succeeded in 40 per cent of

[24] The data is drawn from the judicial review dataset produced by the Ministry of Justice, available here: www.gov.uk/government/statistics/civil-justice-statistics-quarterly-july-to-september-2015 accessed 7 January 2016. The drop in claims granted permission in 2014 coincided with the transfer of immigration judicial reviews to the Upper Tribunal (Immigration and Asylum Chamber) in 2013.

substantive hearings. Despite an increase in the number of judicial review claims lodged over this period, the number of successful challenges decreased from 504 in 2000 to 135 in 2014. Moreover, this decrease occurred during a period in which it has generally been assumed that the courts have adopted a more intensive approach to judicial review. When compared with the total volume of administrative decisions made each year, the number of judicial reviews lodged with the Administrative Court is miniscule. It is not known how many such decisions are made each year because it has never been quantified. However, it is reasonable to assume that this figure is measurable only in the millions or tens of millions of decisions per year. Whatever the precise figure may be, the proportion challenged through judicial review is very small indeed.[25] The number of judicial review claims that are granted permission, those that proceed to a substantive hearing, and are then those ultimately allowed is only a small percentage of this already miniscule figure.

It is not possible to state how many judicial review claims were made on legitimate expectation grounds. The data does not identify the grounds of challenge. Nonetheless, it is apparent from a survey of the law reports that only a small number of legitimate expectation cases have succeeded. As Wade and Forsyth note, '[a]part from *Coughlan*, successful substantive protection has been very limited'.[26]

Of course, statistics alone cannot capture the overall influence of judicial challenges and decisions. Court judgments shape the predictions and views of future litigants about what might happen to their case if it proceeds to court. Many judicial review cases granted permission are settled out of court. Judgments sometimes have wider radiating effects. But with these caveats in mind, the statistics place the application of legitimate expectations within a wider context. Though important, the principle may well have less practical importance than is sometimes assumed.

Why have there been few successful legitimate expectation cases? The following reasons may be advanced. It is relatively difficult for a claimant to succeed on legitimate expectations grounds. The principle is concerned with 'exceptional situations'.[27] Its requirements are stringent. The initial burden lies on an applicant to prove that the claimed expectation is worthy of protection. The promise or representation must be 'clear, unambiguous and

[25] Many more administrative decisions are challenged each year by way of appeal to tribunals than judicial review, but such cases can be discounted here because they are almost always appeals on the facts and merits of individual decisions rather than challenges based on principles of judicial review.

[26] HWR Wade and CF Forsyth, *Administrative Law*, 11th[t] edn (Oxford University Press, 2014) 460.

[27] *R (Association of British Civilian Detainees) v Secretary of State for Defence* [2003] QB 1397 (CA) [72] (Dyson LJ); *Niazi* (n 2) [41] (Laws LJ).

devoid of relevant qualification'.[28] Many claims fail on this ground alone.[29] When there is a clear representation, the case may fall on at least two other grounds. The public body might have introduced transitional provisions to cushion the impact of a policy change.[30] This can take the form of prior warning that change is coming or temporary preservation of the entirety or aspects of the old policy or exception from the new policy. Second, the courts are reluctant to intervene when policy changes concern the 'macro-political field'.[31] The courts often recognise that government possesses a wide discretion to formulate and re-formulate policy and to decide upon both content and frequency of change of such policy.[32]

In a 2011 survey of legitimate expectation cases, Farbey and Silverstone concluded that two factors have influenced the courts.[33] First, public policy considerations often dictate case outcomes. The courts tend to preserve the right of the executive—especially central government—to formulate, revise, and apply policy in the public interest. The courts seem to attach more importance to preserving the discretionary powers of central government than those of other public bodies, such as local authorities.[34] Some core public interests may defeat individual expectations more readily than others. For instance, prisoners have launched various legitimate expectations challenges, but few, if any, have succeeded.[35] Second, case outcomes are highly fact-sensitive and dependent on context. As Laws LJ has noted, '[w]hat is fair or unfair is of course notoriously sensitive to factual nuance'.[36] The essential challenge posed by legitimate expectations—the balance between an individual's fair treatment in the circumstances and the demands of the public interest—'is not precisely calculable, its measurement not exact'.[37] Judges retain flexibility to decide cases how they consider most

[28] *R v Inland Revenue Commissioners; ex parte MFK Underwriting Agents Ltd* [1990] 1 WLR 1545, 1569 (Bingham LJ).

[29] See, eg, *R (Bancoult) v Secretary of State for Foreign and Commonwealth Affairs (No 2)* [2009] 1 AC 453; [2009] AC 453; *Hossain & Ors v Secretary of State for the Home Department* [2015] EWCA Civ 207.

[30] See, eg, *Hamble* (n 4).

[31] *R v Secretary of State for Education and Employment; ex parte Begbie* [2000] 1 WLR 1115 (CA) 1131 (Laws LJ).

[32] *Hughes v Department of Health and Social Security* [1985] AC 776, 788 (Lord Diplock); *R (BAPIO) v Secretary of State for the Home Department* [2007] EWCA Civ 1139 [43] (Sedley LJ).

[33] J Farbey and B Silverstone, 'Promises Promises? The Scope of Legitimate Expectation in Judicial Review' (seminar paper, Doughty Street Chambers, 11 October 2011).

[34] See, eg, *Niazi* (n 2) [41] (Laws LJ): 'Public authorities typically, and central government *par excellence*, enjoy wide discretions which it is their duty to exercise in the public interest.'

[35] See, eg, *Re Findlay* [1985] AC 318 (HL); *R v Secretary of State for the Home Department; ex parte Hargreaves* [1997] 1 WLR 906 (CA).

[36] *R (Bhatt Murphy and Others) v The Independent Assessor and Others* [2008] EWCA Civ 755 [42].

[37] Ibid.

appropriate in the circumstances. In other words, they look to the likely consequences of judicial intervention. Judicial caution is prevalent. As McCloskey J has noted, '[t]he doctrine of substantive legitimate expectations is a nuanced, sophisticated one which should not be prayed in aid without careful reflection'.[38]

FIVE SUCCESSFUL LEGITIMATE EXPECTATION CASES

We now consider in detail the handful of successful legitimate expectation cases. If the courts have engaged in merits review when applying the principle of legitimate expectations, then one way of testing this hypothesis is to analyse those cases in which the courts have protected claimants' legitimate expectations. By examining successful challenges, we can assess whether the courts have engaged in merits review. The focus here therefore is not on legal doctrine, but upon the outcomes reached by the court in the context of the specific disputes and their practical consequences.[39]

A preliminary issue is that the term 'merits review' is unclear and potentially problematic. The courts should not engage in merits review, but there is no accepted definition as to what this entails.[40] The dividing line between legality and the merits is mutable and contestable. It can vary between different legal jurisdictions. It can vary within the same jurisdiction over time[41] and between different judges.[42] To some extent, the dividing line depends upon the nature of both the impugned administrative decision and the legal challenge. Nonetheless, for the purpose of this chapter, 'merits review' is taken to mean that the court has exceeded the limits of its role by imposing its own policy preferences upon public bodies by telling them which decisions they should make. We now examine five successful legitimate expectation cases.

[38] *Secretary of State for the Home Department v Iqbal (Para 322 Immigration Rules)* [2015] UKUT 434 (IAC), [11].

[39] In a similar vein, see M Shapiro, *Courts: A Comparative and Political Analysis* (Chicago University Press, 1981) 111–25.

[40] As Lord Sumption noted in *R (Lord Carlile of Berriew QC) v Secretary of State for the Home Department* [2015] AC 945 [30]: 'it has never been sufficiently clear what kind of inquiries a "merits review" embraces'.

[41] See R Rawlings, 'Modelling Judicial Review' (2008) *Current Legal Problems* 95.

[42] Consider, for instance, the different approaches as to the role of courts in assessing the legitimacy of an expectation: *Hamble* (n 4) and *Hargreaves* (n 35). Consider also the debate as to whether proportionality involves engaging in merits review: *R v Secretary of State for the Home Department; ex parte Brind* [1991] 1 AC 696 (HL); *R (Daly) v Secretary of State for the Home Department* [2001] 2 AC 532 (HL); *Kennedy v Charity Commission* [2015] 1 AC 455; *Pham v Secretary of State for the Home Department* [2015] 1 WLR 1591.

Khan

Mr Khan had settled in the UK from Pakistan and wanted to bring his nephew over. The Home Office had informed Khan that, while there was no provision in the Immigration Rules for such cases, it would exercise its extra-statutory discretion and apply certain criteria when considering his application. These criteria were whether: the child's welfare was assured; the Court was likely to grant an adoption order; and one of the intending adopters was domiciled in the UK. Khan duly collected the documentation and applied in person at the UK entry clearance post in Islamabad. However, the Home Office refused the application on the basis of a new criterion not previously disclosed to Khan, namely that the Home Office was 'not satisfied that serious and compelling family or other considerations make exclusion [of the child from the UK] undesirable'.[43] The Court of Appeal held that the Home Office had acted unfairly by frustrating Khan's legitimate expectations. It had changed its policy without notifying Khan of this and not giving him the chance to argue that only the old policy criteria should be applied in his case.[44]

So, the Court held that the Home Office should either consider Khan's case under its previously stated criteria or, if it wanted to apply the new criteria, notify Khan of this and then let him have his say. The Court explicitly disclaimed any ability to prevent the Home Office from changing its policy in its entirety. It only insisted on fair treatment for Khan given his reliance on correspondence from the Home Office. It is difficult to see how the Court could be said to have engaged in merits review. Moreover, the impact of the case seems to have been entirely limited to Khan's circumstances; it appears to have exerted no wider impact upon the handling of immigration applications.

Luton Borough Council

In 2003, the UK Government introduced the 'Building Schools for the Future' programme to rebuild or refurbish 3,500 secondary (high) schools in England. Many local authorities had applied for funding under the programme. In 2010, the Coalition Government was elected and introduced spending cuts to reduce the UK's fiscal deficit. Accordingly, the new

[43] It is difficult to even make sense of this response from the Home Office, which simply seems to mean that 'we reject your application because we don't think it should be granted'.

[44] *R v Secretary of State for the Home Department; ex parte Khan* [1984] 1 WLR 1337 (CA).

Education Secretary, Michael Gove MP, cancelled the Building Schools for the Future programme. While some building projects would proceed, most would be scrapped.[45] Luton Borough Council and five other local authorities had applied for and almost, but not quite, been awarded funding. They had already invested substantial sums as part of the application process and would be left with contractual liabilities of circa £1–3.5 million. By contrast, the Department for Education had consulted other local authorities about the way forward. According to the leader of Waltham Forest Council, Councillor Chris Robbins, his council stood to lose millions of pounds of investment. He also said that judicial review was the only option to take because Mr Gove and his officials would not 'sit down amicably and explain their decision to us'.[46]

Unsurprisingly, the Court swiftly dismissed the challenge on rationality grounds: the Court could not act as the umpire of a social and economic controversy that has been settled by due political process.[47] The Court also dismissed the challenge on substantive legitimate expectation: no clear and unambiguous promise. However, the Court did find that the Education Secretary had breached a procedural legitimate expectation by abruptly stopping the building projects without consulting the local authorities. The department had given individual consideration to certain schools in 14 other areas in the same position. The Court held that the claimant authorities should have a similar opportunity to discuss the possible ways ahead and for them to press their case.

The Court's ruling attracted some media attention at the time—perhaps because it was one of the first legal challenges against the new Government. Alternatively, the case illustrated the all too frequent high-handedness shown by a newly appointed minister in a hurry to make his name by taking a headline-grabbing decision even though this involved cutting a few corners. Whatever the reason, the case was a straightforward application of procedural legitimate expectations. The Department for Education had consulted with some local authorities, but not others. Following the judgment, the Education Secretary told Parliament that he would shortly contact the claimant local authorities, but sternly reminded them that 'no one should gain false hope' from this. In other words, all the Court required was for the Minister's civil servants to consult the six local authorities to discuss the

[45] The Government's rationale was that the programme had been inefficiently run and was beset by massive overspends and needless bureaucracy.

[46] 'High Court Battle over Building Schools for the Future' *BBC News*, 24 January 2011 www.bbc.co.uk/news/education-12265758 accessed 7 January 2016.

[47] *R (Luton Borough Council and others) v Secretary of State for Education* [2011] EWHC Admin 217. For a similar successful consultation legitimate expectation case, see *R (Greenpeace) v Secretary of State for the Environment* [2007] EWHC 311 (Admin).

options (this would require a few telephone calls or meetings) and then the Minister could still make negative decisions—hardly merits review.

Nonetheless, the case was seen within government as an instance in which the courts were encroaching too deeply into policy issues. As the former Treasury Solicitor, Sir Paul Jenkins, has noted, the case was seen within government as another illustration of the increasing clash between the courts and the Government, with the former being seen as second-guessing the democratic will of the people. In such circumstances, the ministerial response is: 'Why are the courts telling us we've got to consult again? We consulted the electorate!'[48]

The Government subsequently introduced a package of measures to reform judicial review to address such concerns.[49] The courts must now refuse a remedy if it appears to be highly likely that the outcome for the applicant would not have been substantially different if the conduct complained of had not occurred.[50] This controversial measure attracted criticism on the ground that it instructs the courts to ignore unlawful conduct by public authorities; it is in the public interest for public bodies to make lawful decisions.[51] Given the stand-off between the two Houses of Parliament over the measure, a compromise solution was found to enact the 2015 Act. The court can disregard the requirement to refuse a remedy for reasons of exceptional public interest.[52] This episode generated concerns over the willingness and ability of central government—a frequent litigant in legal proceedings—to constrain and limit the effectiveness of judicial review in order to serve its own ends. The widely-shared view is that the 2015 reforms weaken judicial review.[53]

In any event, for the Government to predicate this discussion upon the facts of the *Luton Borough Council* case is misleading. The legitimate expectation arose because the Department for Education had given individual consideration to similarly placed local authorities. In short, rather than engaging in merits review, the case demonstrates ministerial misunderstandings of the role of judicial review.

[48] M Ross, 'Interview: Sir Paul Jenkins' *Civil Service World*, 20 March 2014 www.civilserviceworld.com/interview-sir-paul-jenkins accessed 7 January 2016.

[49] Ministry of Justice, *Judicial Review: Further Proposals for Reform* (White Paper, Cm 8703, 2013); Criminal Justice and Courts Act 2015.

[50] *Senior Courts Act 1981* s 31(2A) (as inserted by the *Criminal Justice and Courts Act 2015* s 84(1)).

[51] Joint Committee on Human Rights, *The Implications for Access to Justice of the Government's Proposals to Reform Judicial Review* (2013–14, HL 174 HC 868) [43] and [45].

[52] *Senior Courts Act 1981* s 31(2B) (as inserted by the *Criminal Justice and Courts Act 2015* s 84(1)).

[53] A Mills, 'Reforms to Judicial Review in the Criminal Justice and Courts Act 2015: Promoting Efficiency or Weakening the Rule of Law?' (2015) *Public Law* 583.

Coughlan

This case has generated much discussion. If there was ever a legitimate expectation case in which a court's intervention arguably exceeded the limits of its proper jurisdiction, this would be it.

Miss Coughlan had been seriously disabled following a car accident in 1971 and for many years lived in a hospital in Exeter. In 1993 Coughlan, along with seven other comparably disabled people, were moved from hospital to a purpose-built facility, Mardon House. The North and East Devon Health Authority promised that Mardon House would be their home for life. Nonetheless, in 1997, Coughlan and the other residents were informed that Mardon House was to be sold because the NHS did not consider any of the residents to be their responsibility—thereby effectively deciding that the residents were not entitled to continuing NHS healthcare. The health authority had not identified any alternative accommodation. This was challenged before the courts. The issue was whether there was a sufficient overriding public interest to justify a departure from the home for life promise. The Court took into account the following factors: the importance of the promise to the applicant; the fact that it was limited to a few individuals; and that the consequences to the health authority of honouring the promise were likely to be financial only. The Court of Appeal concluded that Coughlan had a substantive expectation. The closure decision resulted in unfairness amounting to an abuse of power. It also infringed the right to respect for a home under Article 8 of the European Convention on Human Rights (ECHR).

Before proceeding further, it is apparent that the Court had a great deal of sympathy for Coughlan. She had lived for many years in a hospital, moved to Mardon House in 1993, been promised a home for life there, and had adjusted to this state of affairs—only to then be told five years later that she would be moved again against her will to an unspecified location. The Court accepted that Coughlan's enforced move would 'be emotionally devastating and seriously anti-therapeutic'.[54] Closing Mardon House not only breached the home for life promise, but also meant 'perhaps more importantly, the loss of her only home and of a purpose-built environment which had come to mean even more to her than a home does to most people'.[55]

Part of the background to the case was the widespread closure of care homes in England since the mid-1990s and the impact upon vulnerable people. Residents, charities, and groups campaigned against such closures. A central concern is that the upheaval for residents arising from the closure

[54] *R v North and East Devon Health Authority: ex parte Coughlan* [2001] QB 213 (CA) [92].

[55] Ibid.

of a care home and relocation elsewhere causes fear, anxiety and, in many cases, a higher mortality rate for vulnerable and/or elderly people.[56] In other words, residents' health would not only suffer as a result of such involuntary relocation, but they could die. Closing a care home having previously promised to keep it open seems like odd behaviour for a health authority—given that its purpose is to promote public health. Such concerns did not explicitly find their way into the Court's judgment, but they clearly formed an essential part of its background.

Concerns have been raised with *Coughlan*—in particular that the Court interfered in policy and administrative matters by directing the health authority not to close Mardon House. That does not seem much like judicial review, but more like merits review. More specifically, there are four concerns with *Coughlan*. First, the Court interfered with the allocation of public resources. Any such interference could represent the thin end of the wedge with the result that the Court would end up acting as a *de facto* health authority. Second, the Court lacked the required expertise to take decisions such as allocating resources. Third, other people affected by the Court's decision were unable to participate in the litigation. There were 'other residents of North and East Devon whose treatment was denied or delayed as a result of the money that had to be expended fulfilling Ms Coughlan's substantive expectation. These voices were simply not heard before the court'.[57] Fourth, Parliament clearly intended that such decisions were to be taken by the health authority and not the Court. All of these are standard grounds in favour of limited judicial intervention and this line of critique seems to be quite robust. However, for the following reasons, these concerns do not have the practical force commonly attributed to them. On the contrary, the Court's intervention was entirely appropriate.

First, the task of allocating limited resources can be difficult, but difficult decisions often go wrong and can benefit from external scrutiny. In any event, the financial savings of closing Mardon House and moving Coughlan to local authority care were modest—the Court described them as 'not dramatic'.[58] What was at issue in the case was not whether the

[56] J Wilson and A Netten, *Guidelines for the Closure of Care Homes for Older People: Prevalence and Content of Local Government Protocols* (University of Kent at Canterbury, Personal Social Services Research Unit Discussion Paper 1861/2, October 2003) www.pssru.ac.uk/pdf/dp1861_2.pdf accessed 7 January 2016. In a detailed review of the medical research, AE Smith and P Crome, 'Relocation Mosaic—A Review of 40 Years of Resettlement Literature' (2000) 10 *Reviews in Clinical Gerontology* 81 concluded that while the medical research literature is ambiguous and sometimes contradictory with numerous inherent methodological problems, individuals who are physically or mentally impaired and have no preparation in advance for relocation are at increased risk of death or a decline in functional mental health status. Whatever the finer findings of a large medical research literature, it is widely believed that there is a link between care home closures and the premature mortality of residents.

[57] Forsyth (n 8) 437.

[58] *Coughlan* (n 54) [92].

health authority would continue to provide care for Coughlan; whatever the outcome of the case, the local authority and the health authority between them were to remain responsible for Coughlan's care.[59] The only issue was whether Coughlan and the other residents would continue living in Mardon House. The financial saving would only have been in terms of the economic and logistical efficiency of no longer accommodating the eight vulnerable people in Mardon House, but in the unspecified local authority home.

In other words, the amount of savings was more likely to amount to a few hundred thousand pounds—a relatively small sum given the total NHS budget for England (£44.6 billion in 1998/99).[60] The effect, if any, upon waiting lists and operations for other patients would have been negligible. The health authority would still have remained responsible for Coughlan's care. Whereas the health authority was seeking to impose an 'emotionally devastating and seriously anti-therapeutic' decision upon a small group of vulnerable people, the consequences of the Court's judgment was to spread the limited financial costs more thinly upon the wider public.[61] A further point is that on the facts it seems very far from the case that the health authority was trying to balance its budget. Rather, it had been trying to evade its responsibility for the residents onto the local authority—passing the buck rather than providing healthcare for vulnerable people.

Second, to say that the Court lacked the required expertise to take decisions such as allocating resources is not a knock-down argument. Instead, it opens up debate over the relative expertise of the Court and the health authority. A health authority has expertise in managing its budget. At the same time, we should not overlook the behaviour of people in organisations. They often ignore the negative impact of their decisions on affected individuals. There is often a psychological bias to cherry-pick the upsides of a decision and ignore the unpalatable downsides. Decisions taken by a committee can be passed down to other people to communicate them to those concerned. By contrast, a court's attention is always directly focused upon the facts and circumstances of a claimant's case and how they are affected by administrative action. This is of no lesser importance than trawling over

[59] The other major issue in *Coughlan* was an important point of statutory interpretation concerning who bore the financial responsibility for healthcare needs over and above those which local authority social services can be expected to provide and are therefore primarily health needs. The Court of Appeal ruled that health authorities had a responsibility to provide for those needs, and to fund the necessary care. Following the judgment, every health authority was instructed to review its local criteria for providing continuing healthcare to ensure that it was not too restrictive and that it was 'Coughlan compliant'.

[60] House of Commons Library, *NHS Funding and Expenditure* (House of Commons Standard Note SN/SG/724) http://researchbriefings.files.parliament.uk/documents/SN00724/SN00724.pdf accessed 7 January 2016 table 1.

[61] *Coughlan* (n 54) [92].

financial data. Expertise is not therefore a binary choice, but it is relative, depending upon the particular perspective and behaviour of the public authority and the court.

Third, it is argued that other members of the public affected by the Court's decision were unable to have their voice heard by the Court. This argument presupposes that members of the public both can and do participate in decisions taken by health authorities. Yet, for all practical purposes, the public is rarely involved in the making of such decisions. When public bodies do consult the public, it is often for presentational reasons. In practice, only those people with the ability, resources, and time and who can shout loudest tend to participate—and even then such people mostly do so to pursue their own self-interested agendas. It is difficult to envisage many members of the public feeling disgruntled because court procedures precluded their involvement.

Fourth, Parliament conferred the responsibility to administer resources upon the health authority. However, this does not mean that the courts were to have no role at all in supervising such decision-making. No such intention can be discerned from the legislation. If Parliament had been concerned at the judgment, then it could have reversed the Court's decision, but this did not happen. A final point is that the Court did not base its decision solely upon legitimate expectations ground, but also upon the breach of her right to respect for her home under Article 8 ECHR.

In summary, *Coughlan* had little, if any, impact on public policy, the organisation of government, or the delivery of public services.[62] It was not a major judicial challenge to the exercise of the massive discretionary powers wielded by central government. It was a perfectly reasonable decision that a health authority should not close down a care home when it had previously promised eight vulnerable people that they could live there for the rest of their lives. The health authority had bungled the entire matter (going back on its promise, proposing to move the residents to alternative accommodation, but unable to say where because it had not yet decided). The adverse consequences were to fall exclusively upon a small group of vulnerable people—in other words, the clearest possible case for judicial intervention. It is difficult to see how the Court's intervention could be classified as an illegitimate breach of the separation of powers. Instead, the Court was enforcing basic fairness in public administration.

Looking at the case more broadly, any prior anxiety that government might have had that legitimate expectation would really be used as a wide-ranging ground of intervention was gently assuaged by the Court.

[62] That is, the legitimate expectation point. The statutory interpretation point concerning the responsibility of health authorities to provide healthcare over and above ordinary social care needs had a major impact on the NHS and local authorities.

Government could only have been pleased with the Court's confirmation of the narrow scope of substantive expectations as being limited to 'cases where the expectation is confined to one person or a few people, giving the promise or representation the character of a contract'.[63] *Coughlan* did not then signal the start of a judicial revolution—on the contrary. Despite the flurry of attention the case attracted, it stands out as the almost sole example of a successful substantive legitimate expectation claim. Widely discussed, *Coughlan* has been rarely applied in practice.[64]

Bibi

Newham London Borough Council had promised to provide secure accommodation to two homeless families within 18 months, but then failed to keep its promise. Before the Court, the council accepted that it had promised to provide secure accommodation. However, the council did not accept that it should be held to that promise because its statutory housing allocation scheme had changed.[65] The council subsequently devised a new allocation scheme and the two families were placed on the housing register alongside other applicants. However, the council had not taken any account of the promises made to the families. The Court of Appeal held that the council was obliged to provide secure accommodation to the families.[66] It recognised that decisions on the allocation of public housing entailed invidious choices as to the allocation of limited public resources, which were essentially political rather than judicial. However, the council had to take another look at the matter taking account of the families' circumstances. If it then decided not to provide them with secure accommodation, then reasons must be given.

[63] *Coughlan* (n 54) [59].

[64] The facts of *R (Bodimeade) v London Borough of Camden* [2001] EWHC Admin 271 were almost on all fours with *Coughlan*—closure of a care home; and promise of a home for life—but the expectation had not been take into account in the decision-making process. The Court quashed the closure decision and required the local authority to make a fresh and lawful decision taking account of its home for life promise. In *R (Patel) v General Medical Council* [2013] EWCA Civ 327, the Court of Appeal held the GMC to a substantive expectation that it stand by its previously announced policy of accepting as primary medical qualification the course that the claimant, a pharmacist, had studied at an overseas university in order to retrain as a medical practitioner. In *Paponette v Attorney-General of Trinidad and Tobago* [2010] UKPC 327, the Privy Council upheld a legitimate expectation concerning the conditions for taxi drivers who were moved to a different taxi strand. Both cases seem sensible decisions on their facts. Also, both concerned minor and low-level administrative decisions.

[65] Before *R v Brent London Borough Council; ex parte Awua* [1996] 1 AC 35 (HL), local authorities were obliged to provide permanent accommodation to homeless people. This meant that in practice the homeless leaped to the front of the queue for local authority housing. However, following *Awua*, homeless people were placed in much the same situation as anyone else likely to get a council house.

[66] *R (Bibi) v Newham London Borough Council* [2002] 1 WLR 237 (CA).

In summary, all that the court required here was that the council consider the families' expectations as a relevant consideration and then give reasons if it did not provide them with secure accommodation. The doctrine of relevant considerations is amongst the more mundane grounds of judicial. Reason-giving is a desirable norm of administration. Put together, this was an appropriate intervention by the Court.

The case also needs to be placed in its social context. For many years there has been a chronic housing shortage in England—especially in London. That city needs some 63,000 new homes built each year, but only a third of these are being built. London councils are under intense pressure and do not possess enough housing stock for all applicants.[67] In this context, giving full substantive effect to the legitimate expectations of both families could well be seen as unfair to other people on the housing register by giving them special preference. The Court was well aware of this:

> [w]here one is dealing with a promise made by an authority a major part of the problem is that it is often not adequate to look at the situation purely from the point of view of the disappointed promisee who comes to the court with a perfectly natural grievance.[68]

In other words, the court must also consider the wider public interests at stake—another factor that weakens any claim that the courts have been second-guessing administrative decision-making. That the Court considered the families' expectations to be a relevant consideration, but did not require them to be given full substantive effect because of the limited housing supply available to the local authority, demonstrates that the Court was fully aware of the need not to intrude into merits review.

Highly Skilled Migrant Programme Forum

In this case, the Court upheld a substantive legitimate expectation that some 49,000 migrants be able to settle permanently in the UK. In 2002, the Home Office had established the Highly Skilled Migrant Programme (HSMP) so that migrants with the requisite skills and experience could help the UK compete in the global economy. The programme was designed to provide an avenue to permanent settlement in the UK for the migrants and their families. Home Office guidance issued in 2002 stated that once applicants had entered under the programme that they would be allowed to stay and apply for settlement regardless of any future revisions to the programme. Some

[67] Since 2010, London local authorities have been relocating families out of the capital and into areas some distance away (sometimes hundreds of miles away) to ease the pressure on housing.

[68] *Bibi* (n 66) [35].

49,000 people entered under the scheme. In 2006, the Home Office revised the programme by tightening up the eligibility criteria. However, and crucially, by the Home Office's own subsequent admission, only a small percentage of the migrants were clearly not making the financial contribution expected of them. Nonetheless, new immigration rules were laid before Parliament by the Immigration Minister, Liam Byrne MP. These rules extended the required period of residence from four to five years and tightened the requirements which have to be met in order to qualify for an extension of leave.

The new rules applied not just to future applicants, but also to the large number of people who had already relocated to the UK. A significant number of people who had moved their homes, families and careers to the UK in the expectation that they would be eligible for permanent residence now found that they were no longer eligible because of the new rules. Many had sold businesses and houses in their home countries before coming to the UK and some faced the prospect of taking their children out of education. Instead of becoming permanently resident, as they had been led to expect, they and their families now faced deportation. In other words, the Home Office had shifted the goalposts for a significant number of people who had taken a number of important and long-term steps to establish their main home in the UK. There had been no attempt to consult them or put them on notice about the changes—let alone make special provision for such people given the investment they had already made.

The new immigration rules provoked some opposition. One of the migrants concerned, Amit Kapadia, established the HSMP Forum to campaign against the changes.[69] MPs became deluged with complaints. The opposition criticised the Government for its stupidity of having both 'broken faith' with the migrants and acted against the country's economic interests.[70] The UK Parliament's Joint Committee on Human Rights was highly critical of the retrospective nature of the changes.[71] The Home Office dismissed these concerns, repeating the time-honoured constitutional fiction that the new rules were subject to parliamentary scrutiny.[72] Given the Government's dominance of the House of Commons, such scrutiny is virtually non-existent. No changes to the Immigration Rules have been voted down in the House of Commons since the 1970s.

[69] See www.hsmpforumltd.com/index.html accessed 7 January 2016.

[70] A Browne, 'Skilled Immigrants Forced out of their Jobs by Visa Changes' *The Times*, London, 3 January 2007.

[71] Joint Committee on Human Rights, *Highly Skilled Migrants: Changes to the Immigration Rules* (2006–07, HL 173 HC 993).

[72] Home Office, *The Government Reply to the Joint Committee on Human Rights: Highly Skilled Migrants: Changes to the Immigration Rules* (Cm 7268, 2007).

The judge, Sir George Newman, recognised that there was a balance between the Home Office's ability to control immigration and the desirability of requiring government to adhere to its past statements.[73] But the judge rejected the Home Office's argument that there were macro-political reasons for the changes to the programme and that the Court was not competent to adjudicate upon the matter. Given that only a very small number of migrants had not been making the required financial contribution, this was insufficient to found a sufficient public interest to outweigh the unfairness done to those migrants who had already been admitted. The judge was not persuaded that there were significant political or economic reasons for the change of policy. Further, the Home Office had repeatedly failed to take any account of the hardship that would be imposed. The judge concluded that

> the terms of the original scheme should be honoured and that there is no good reason why those already on the scheme shall not enjoy the benefits of it as originally offered to them. Good administration and straightforward dealing with the public require it. Not to restrain the impact of the changes would, in my judgment, give rise to conspicuous unfairness and an abuse of power.[74]

The *HSMP Forum* decision could be taken as a stronger case than *Coughlan* or *Bibi* on which to test whether the courts have gone too far. The challenge concerned a decision taken personally by a minister that affected tens of thousands of people in a politically sensitive area. Yet, there are features of the case that justify the Court's intervention, the principal reason being the Home Office's over-reaction to the scale of the problem it was seeking to address. The Home Office had positively encouraged the migrants and their families to enter and set up their lives in the UK. It had reassured them that the scheme would not change. The Home Office had then changed the rules on the basis of its analysis that showed that only a small percentage of migrants were not making the required financial contribution—yet the changes affected all of them. The Home Office had repeatedly refused to consider the impact of the changes on the migrants. It had argued that the changes were not retrospective when they demonstrably were. Further, a Parliamentary Committee had been highly critical of the changes. In short, the goals posts had been shifted for no reason and in a way that would cause unnecessary hardship.

This was then a case in which the Court intervened in a large way in a sensitive policy area because of the disproportionate consequences of inadequate policymaking. It also stands out as the sole instance of a successful

[73] *R (HSMP Forum) v Secretary of State for the Home Department* [2008] EWHC Admin 664.

[74] Ibid, [61].

substantive legitimate expectation challenge against a ministerial decision. The general message of the case is that government should not make wide-ranging and retrospective changes that override people's expectations without adequate evidence to justify them, a sensible norm of administrative good behaviour. It could hardly be argued that the Court here went too far—that would merely amount to saying that the Court should have left undisturbed a manifest injustice that a government department was seeking to impose upon thousands of people for no good reason. That would be a pretty odd decision for any court to make. A final point is that this was a first-instance decision. If the Home Office had been concerned about excessive judicial activism, it could have appealed the decision or reversed it through legislation—but it did neither.

CONCLUSIONS

This chapter has assessed whether the courts have infringed the doctrine of the separation of powers when applying the principle of legitimate expectations. It has been seen that, in quantitative terms, the number of legitimate expectations cases is very small. Only a handful of legitimate expectations challenges have succeeded. Many claims fail because of the stringency of the principle's requirements or because the courts confer significant freedom upon public authorities—central government in particular—to change their policies.

From a detailed examination of five successful cases, it has been argued here that, on a detailed analysis, all of them were justifiable instances of judicial intervention to correct injustice caused by unfair administrative behaviour. All of the claimants stood to lose out in some way or other and this prompted their challenge. Further, the challengers had been unable to utilise effectively the systems of political accountability—either because their position was too weak or because those systems are all too often ineffectual. The courts were then, to some degree, re-assessing the allocation of political and social resources already made by government. Yet, the courts' intervention was fairly modest. In three of the cases, the Court imposed procedural requirements to consult (*Luton Borough Council*), to take account of the expectations (*Bibi*) or either to apply the original policy or consult (*Khan*). In only two other cases (*Coughlan* and *HSMP Forum*) did the courts enforce substantive legitimate expectations. In both cases, individuals stood to lose out because they had relied to their detriment upon statements made by government.

The cases do not provide evidence of excessive judicial intervention. On the contrary. In each case, the public body's attitude and behaviour left much to be desired. The public body had failed in some way because of its own ineptitude, or made an error because it rushed the matter or was indifferent to the expectations it had itself raised. In each case, but for the courts, the fall-out would have fallen squarely upon those people who had the misfortune to place their trust in an earlier representation. There is nothing like the type of judicial activity that could be used to launch, let alone sustain, a credible allegation that the courts have illegitimately interfered in public administration. What can be drawn from the cases is not so much excessive judicial intervention, but the failure of public bodies to show a considerate attitude. If anything, it could be argued that the courts have not gone far enough. There are likely to be many other potentially unlawful and unfair decisions that override an individual's reasonable expectations.

It is possible that the courts could apply the principle of legitimate expectations in a more expansive way so that they could dictate to public bodies the content of their decisions. However, this seems unlikely. The cases considered show that the courts recognise the need to consider the consequences of their intervention from the perspectives of the individual claimant, the public body concerned, and the wider public interest. In other words, the courts acknowledge the need to attain a balance between ensuring fairness for individuals without at the same time unduly interfering with public administration. Looking forward, the courts are likely to intervene on legitimate expectation grounds only when the facts and circumstances of the case demonstrate real hardship upon individuals created by unfair governmental action.

4

Substantive Fairness: A Case for Reconsidering the Breach between English and Australian Law

KRISTINA STERN SC AND JOANNA DAVIDSON

INTRODUCTION

THE IDEA THAT substantive fairness might have a role to play in judicial review of administrative decisions continues to receive short shrift in Australia. The gap between the two jurisdictions is illustrated by the rarity with which Australian courts now cite the line of English cases recognising a right to relief in judicial review proceedings based upon conspicuous unfairness amounting to an abuse of power.[1] The rejection of the English jurisprudence is well-entrenched in Australia, while English courts continue to recognise and apply the doctrine.

Analysis of Australian public law decisions continues, however, to demonstrate that fairness and equality remain alive and well as motivating judicial concerns or values. In particular, Australian courts increasingly recognise the existence of an 'outcome-focused' application of the concept of legal unreasonableness, in which no specific ground of jurisdictional error is identified but a remedy is justified.[2] At the same time, consideration of the

[1] The High Court has neither cited nor considered *R v North and East Devon Health Authority; ex parte Coughlan* [2001] QB 213 ('*Coughlan*') since *Re Minister for Immigration and Multicultural and Indigenous Affairs; ex parte Lam* (2003) 214 CLR 1 ('*Lam*') at [28] (Gleeson CJ), [68]–[80] (McHugh and Gummow JJ). The Full Federal Court last cited *Coughlan* in *Singh v Minister for Immigration and Citizenship* (2011) 190 FCR 552 [47], but only to note that it had not found favour in Australia. See also *Habib v Commonwealth of Australia (No 2)* (2009) 175 FCR 350 at [70] (Perram J finding that an argument was not open because 'it has been held on high authority that Australian law knows no action based on substantive legitimate expectations'); *Rush v Commissioner of Police* (2006) 150 FCR 165 at [80]–[82] (Finn J).

[2] *Minister for Immigration and Border Protection v Singh* (2014) 231 FCR 437 at [44]–[45], ('*Singh*') citing *Minister for Immigration and Citizenship v Li* (2013) 249 CLR 332 ('*Li*') [28]

English jurisprudence indicates a degree of restraint in granting substantive protection to legitimate expectations, with a relatively narrow construction given to the doctrine of substantive protection of such expectations[3] and, more broadly, concern that the categorisation of conduct as an abuse of power should not, without more, achieve remedial results.[4] As has been previously argued,[5] the apparent gap between the two jurisdictions is narrower than is generally articulated. The aim of this chapter is to compare the development of the English jurisprudence with Australian cases in which the concept of substantive fairness is either considered or apparently underpins judicial reasoning.

English and Australian courts continue[6] to exhibit differing approaches to the accommodation of concerns with equality and fairness. The Australian jurisprudence seeks to accommodate those concerns within recognised categories of reviewable error, while acknowledging that the categories of jurisdictional error are not closed.[7] Articulation of the value of fairness in the course of judicial reasoning focuses primarily on the subject-matter (or statutory context) of the case. English courts continue to seek to determine how a principle that finds its justification in fairness and equality might be acceptably defined in order to enable the principle to resolve cases, rather than simply express a conclusion.[8] While the Australian approach might be thought to maintain greater restrictions on the role of the court in a judicial review claim, the elasticity of the unreasonableness ground once divested of the constraints imposed by the *Wednesbury* test[9] may well belie that appearance.

The first section of this chapter considers the progress of the English case law concerning substantive unfairness as a head of abuse of power. The second section turns to the Australian cases, arguing that the 'outcome-focused' category of unreasonableness has considerable elasticity and scope for considerations of substantive fairness to enter into identification of the ambit of unreasonableness as a species of jurisdictional error in Australia. The chapter concludes by assessing whether there remains scope to develop a doctrine of substantive unfairness in Australian law.

(French CJ), [66] (Hayne, Kiefel and Bell JJ), [105] (Gageler J); *Minister for Immigration and Border Protection v Stretton* [2016] FCAFC 11 ('*Stretton*') [6] (Allsop CJ).

3 See eg *Re Loreto Grammar School's Application for Judicial Review* [2012] NICA 1 [46].

4 *TN (Afghanistan) v Secretary of State for the Home Department* [2015] 1 WLR 3083 [42], [71], approving *R(S) v Secretary of State for the Home Department* [2007] EWCA Civ 546, [2007] Imm AR 781 ('*R(S)*') at [39] (Carnwath LJ).

5 Kristina Stern, 'Substantive Fairness in UK and Australian law' (2007) 29 *Australian Bar Review* 266.

6 Ibid, 266–67.

7 *Kirk v Industrial Court of NSW* (2010) 239 CLR 531 ('*Kirk*') [71].

8 Stern (n 5) 267.

9 *Associated Provincial Picture Houses Ltd v Wednesbury Corporation* [1948] 1 KB 223 ('*Wednesbury*').

ENGLISH CASE LAW—THE LIMITATIONS OF ABUSE OF POWER

Fairness, in the context of this chapter, operates as a constraint upon the scope of decision-making by administrative decision-makers by reference to the private interests of those affected by the decision (the usual basis for an obligation of fairness being the interests of the object of the obligation).[10] Both procedural and substantive fairness impose this type of constraint, altering the public interest balance which a decision-maker might otherwise reach as to how to exercise administrative powers or perform administrative duties to ensure that the interests of the subject are properly met.[11] The Court of Appeal in *Coughlan* adopted this approach. Lord Woolf MR (who delivered the Court's judgment) considered that Lord Templeman's speech in *In re Preston*[12] demonstrated an insistence upon 'the adjudicative role of the court to ensure fairness to the individual'[13] and explained:

> In the ordinary case there is no space for intervention on grounds of abuse of power once a rational decision directed to a proper purpose has been reached by lawful process. The present class of case is visibly different. It involves not one but two lawful exercises of power (the promise and the policy change) by the same public authority, with consequences for individuals trapped between the two. The policy decision may well, and often does, make as many exceptions as are proper and feasible to protect individual expectations. ... If it does not, as in [R v Inland Revenue Commissioners; ex parte Unilever plc [1996] STC 681], the court is there to ensure that the power to make and alter policy has not been abused by unfairly frustrating legitimate individual expectations. In such a situation a bare rationality test would constitute the public authority judge in its own cause, for a decision to prioritise a policy change over legitimate expectations will almost always be rational from where the authority stands, even if objectively it is arbitrary or unfair.[14]

Coughlan represented an attempt to reconcile different strands of English authority on substantive unfairness.[15] It is discussed in greater detail elsewhere in this book,[16] but it should be noted that the Court's statement that fairness in the context of an abuse of power 'must for the reasons we have considered include fairness of outcome'[17] suggests the existence of more extensive reasoning on the justification for judicial intervention in cases of substantive unfairness than is easily discernible in the preceding parts of

[10] Stern (n 5) 267.
[11] See eg *R(A) v Secretary of State for the Home Department* [2006] EWHC Admin 526 [29].
[12] *R v Inland Revenue Commissioners; In re Preston* [1985] AC 835.
[13] *Coughlan* (n 1) [70].
[14] *Coughlan* (n 1) [66]
[15] Stern (5) 268–70.
[16] See chapters 3, 6, 10 and 11 of this volume.
[17] *Coughlan* (n 1) [71].

the judgment.[18] What is much clearer is the adoption of abuse of power as a unifying principle underlying the basis for intervention (including on *Wednesbury* grounds). Lord Woolf MR held that '[o]nce it is recognised that conduct which is an abuse of power is contrary to law its existence must be for the court to determine'.[19]

'Conspicuous unfairness'[20] was subsequently recognised as a head of abuse of power justifying relief. Well before *Coughlan*, Simon-Brown LJ in *Unilever* had distinguished between unfairness that was and was not 'conspicuous' by contrasting 'conduct which may be characterised as "a bit rich" but nevertheless understandable' with 'a decision so outrageously unfair that it should not be allowed to stand'.[21] In *R (Rashid) v Secretary of State for the Home Department*,[22] all members of the Court of Appeal considered that the administrative errors that had occurred led to conspicuous unfairness to the applicant, amounting to an abuse of power. The applicant in *Rashid*, an Iraqi Kurd, applied for asylum in December 2001 and had his claim refused that month. He unsuccessfully appealed to an adjudicator in 2002 and unsuccessfully applied for permission to appeal against that decision later in 2002. Throughout that time, however, the Secretary of State's policy was to allow asylum claims from Iraqi Kurds. Thus, all decisions taken in relation to the applicant, including those on appeal which flowed from submissions by a representative of the Secretary of State, were inconsistent with (and taken in ignorance of) the Secretary of State's policy. The error was applied multiple times, in that the initial decision-maker, the adjudicator, the appellate tribunal and counsel instructed by the Secretary of State were not notified of the correct policy.[23] In March 2003, the applicant's advisors became aware of the Secretary of State's policy and applied for reconsideration of the asylum claim. By that time, however, the Secretary of State's policy had changed (as a result of the invasion of Iraq) and asylum was refused—a proper application of the post-invasion policy. On judicial review, the primary judge quashed the refusal decision.

Lord Justice Pill (May LJ agreeing) accepted in *Rashid* that legitimate expectation is only 'one application' of a claim of unfairness rising to abuse

[18] The Court proceeds to note that some prior consideration of legitimate expectation did not distinguish between procedural and substantive unfairness: *Coughlan* (n 1) [73], [77].

[19] *Coughlan* (n 1) [81]. This is consistent with justification requirements imposed on government in judicial review more generally in England, including where proportionality is not involved: see eg *Secretary of State for Foreign and Commonwealth Affairs v Rahmatullah* [2013] 1 AC 614 [65]–[70] (Lord Kerr, with whom Lord Dyson MR and Lord Wilson agreed).

[20] The phrase is drawn from Simon Brown LJ's judgment in *R v Inland Revenue Commissioners; ex parte Unilever plc* [1996] STC 681, 695 ('*Unilever*') and was adopted by Lord Hoffman in *Secretary of State for the Home Department v Zeqiri* [2002] Imm AR 296 [44].

[21] *Unilever*, ibid 697.

[22] *R (Rashid) v Secretary of State for the Home Department* [2005] Imm AR 608; [2005] EWCA Civ 744 ('*Rashid*').

[23] Ibid, [32].

of power.[24] There was an abuse of power 'based on an expectation that a general policy for dealing with asylum applications will be applied and will be applied uniformly'.[25] No countervailing public interest was claimed, save for contemporaneous review, the determination of asylum claims based on a current risk of persecution. Pill LJ acknowledged this point as 'important'.[26] Other relevant factors in determining the unfairness in *Rashid* was 'conspicuous' included the persistence of the conduct and the lack of explanation for it. This factor arose in the context that many asylum applications from Iraq were being processed at the same time, so that the country 'would have been expected to be in the forefront of the [Secretary's] deliberations'. Nevertheless, Pill LJ cautioned that administrative errors would not often lead to a finding of conspicuous unfairness.[27]

Lord Justice Dyson's analysis in *Rashid* relied more extensively on the notion of legitimate expectation, categorising *Rashid* as a case of a general policy choice being departed from in the circumstances of a particular case.[28] However, his Lordship endorsed Laws LJ's proposal in *R v Secretary of State for Education and Employment; ex parte Begbie*[29] that the intensity of review applied to the identification of an abuse of power will depend on the factual (and statutory) context:

> ... the facts of the case, viewed always in their statutory context, will steer the court to a more or less intrusive quality of review. In some cases, a change of tack by a public authority, though unfair from the applicant's stance, may involve questions of general policy affecting the public at large: in such cases the judges may not be in a position to adjudicate save at most on a bare *Wednesbury* basis 'without themselves donning the garb of policy-maker, which they cannot wear.' In other cases, where, for example, there are no wide-ranging policy issues, the court may be able to apply a more intrusive form of review to the decision. The more the decision which is challenged lies in the field of pure policy, particularly in relation to issues which the court is ill-equipped to judge, the less likely it is that true abuse of power will be found.[30]

In addition to the type of policy issues involved, the extent of the temporal effect of holding a public authority to its representation or policy, as well as the number of people affected by the decision were, in Dyson LJ's view, relevant to the satisfaction of the test for whether conspicuous unfairness (here frustration of an expectation) amounts to an abuse of power.[31] The degree

[24] Ibid, [34].
[25] Ibid.
[26] Ibid, [35], citing *Adan v Secretary of State for the Home Department* [1999] 1 AC 293.
[27] Ibid, [36].
[28] Ibid, [45], adopting the categorisation in Paul Craig, *Administrative Law*, 5th edn (Sweet & Maxwell, 2003) 641.
[29] *R v Secretary of State for Education and Employment; ex parte Begbie* [2000] 1 WLR 1115, 1130 ('*Begbie*').
[30] *Rashid* (n 22) [49].
[31] *Rashid* (n 22) [50].

of unfairness was likewise relevant to whether unfairness would be characterised as abuse of power, although the only example his Lordship gave of 'extreme' unfairness likely to amount to an abuse of power was the frustration of a legitimate expectation in bad faith (whilst his Lordship did not refer to this, bad faith is, of itself, likely to provide a sound basis for seeking judicial review in England,[32] and is recognised as a jurisdictional error in Australia).[33,34] His Lordship balanced what he inferred—in the absence of an explanation as to the reasons for what had occurred—to be flagrant and prolonged incompetence, aggravated by a failure to treat the applicant in the same manner as applicants in other, procedurally linked cases, against the importance of contemporaneous review in determining asylum claims.[35] Like Pill LJ, he held that the applicant should have a grant of indefinite leave to remain in the United Kingdom.

This was not a remedy which was within the Court's power to grant, as the Supreme Court later pointed out.[36] The Supreme Court has now stated that *Rashid* should no longer be followed to the extent that it creates an exception to the principle that, on an asylum appeal, the question is one of a person's present status. This occurred without discussion of conspicuous unfairness as a head of abuse of power, in remarks directed to the specific context of asylum-seeker appeals but generally criticising the reasoning in *Rashid* as confusing the remedial effect of identification of an abuse of power. In *TN*, the Court was not addressing legitimate expectations, although it was argued throughout that the respondent had breached her statutory obligation[37] to endeavour to trace members of the unaccompanied minor applicant's family. If properly carried out, it was said that this might have produced evidence to support his account of risk of persecution. The discussion of *Rashid* arose in the context of a remedial issue, namely the power of an asylum tribunal to dispense 'corrective relief' as a sanction

[32] See eg *Board of Education v Rice* [1911] AC 179, 182; see also HWR Wade and CF Forsyth, *Administrative Law*, 11th edn (Oxford University Press, 2014) 355, suggesting that bad faith now has little independent existence as a distinct ground of invalidity.

[33] See eg *Kirk* (n 7) [71]; *Commissioner of Taxation v Futuris Corporation Ltd* (2008) 237 CLR 146 [55]–[56] (Gummow, Hayne, Heydon and Crennan JJ, referring to 'deliberate failures to administer the law according to its terms'); *SBBS v Minister for Immigration and Multicultural Affairs* (2002) 194 ALR 749 [43]–[48] (Tamberlin, Mansfield and Jacobson JJ).

[34] *Rashid* (n 22) [50].

[35] His Lordship attributed this principle to *Ravichandran v Secretary of State for the Home Department* [1996] Imm AR 97, in which the Court of Appeal held that asylum appeals should be determined by reference to the position at the time of the appellate decision rather than by reference to the factual situation at the time of the original decision against which the appeal was brought. In Australia, this approach is a hallmark of merits review in tribunals but not of judicial review; see *Shi v Migration Agents Registration Authority* (2008) 235 CLR 286, 327–28.

[36] *TN* (n 4) [42] (Lord Toulson, Lord Neuberger, Baroness Hale, Lord Wilson and Lord Hughes agreeing).

[37] Imposed by reg 6 of the Asylum Seekers (Reception Conditions) Regulations 2005 (SI 2005/7).

for the alleged breach of duty, so as to confer a right to remain on a person who had been found on the evidence before the tribunal not to be in need of protection. No such relief having been dispensed by the Upper Tribunal, the Supreme Court's remarks were by way of *obiter*. The Court endorsed Carnwath LJ's analysis of the reasoning in *Rashid* as 'not altogether convincing' notwithstanding the justice of the result in *R(S) v Secretary of State for the Home Department*.[38] The Supreme Court held that the principle of contemporaneous review in asylum-seeker appeals applied without exception, and that *Rashid* should no longer be followed.[39]

In passages endorsed by the Supreme Court in *TN*, Carnwath LJ suggested in *R(S)* that instead of treating abuse of power as an underlying, unifying theory in public law cases, in *Rashid* it was transformed into a 'special and more extreme category of illegality' containing a 'magic ingredient, able to achieve remedial results which other forms of illegality cannot match'.[40] His Lordship also expressed doubt as to the weight placed in *Rashid* on the Department's conduct, suggesting that the Court had enabled abuse of power to operate as a 'new and more potent category of judicial review, depending on the flagrancy of the administrative failing',[41] and emphasised that 'the court's proper sphere is illegality, not maladministration'.[42] Lord Justice Carnwath queried the utility of categorising unfairness as obvious or conspicuous, stating that the test should be 'whether it amounts to illegality which on reconsideration the Department has the power to correct'.[43] By contrast, Moore-Bick LJ's concurring judgment in *R(S)* endorsed the existence of a category of cases satisfying the test of 'conspicuous unfairness' without obviously falling within another ground of judicial review.[44]

In a concurring judgment in *MM (Zimbabwe) v Secretary of State for the Home Department*,[45] Hughes LJ sought to confine the scope of *Rashid* and of conspicuous unfairness as a ground of review to cases involving administrative errors amounting to illegality by the initial decision-maker (relevantly the Secretary of State), suggesting there must be 'very considerable doubt' as to whether *Rashid* could apply to judicial errors or errors by an administrative tribunal, such as had occurred in *MM*. Lord Justice Kay did not express the same level of doubt, though having noted the appellant's reliance on *Rashid*, his Honour did state that '[t]he cases in which "conspicuous unfairness" and legitimate expectation have been considered

[38] *R(S)* (n 4) [39].
[39] *TN* (n 4) [71], [72].
[40] *R(S)* (n 4) [39], [40] (Moore-Bick LJ and Lightman J agreeing).
[41] *R(S)* (n 4) [43].
[42] *R(S)* (n 4) [41].
[43] *R(S)* (n 4) [54].
[44] *R(S)* (n 4) [71].
[45] *MM (Zimbabwe) v Secretary of State for the Home Department* [2012] EWCA 135 (Lewison LJ agreeing) ('*MM*').

have generally been cases in which the Secretary of State has changed her policy on a relevant issue upon which she has some discretion'.[46]

This judicial caution as to the scope of conspicuous unfairness can also be seen in decisions of the Court of Appeal outside the context of asylum claims, but with a broader emphasis on the essential connection between abuse of power and illegality. The Court of Appeal in *Dudley Muslim Association v Dudley Metropolitan Borough Council*[47] cited Hughes LJ's judgment in *MM* for the proposition that 'abuse of power is not a freestanding ground on which a court can act in the absence of unlawful action on the part of the public authority in question'.[48] That is a broader proposition than Hughes LJ ventured in *MM*, where his Lordship's remarks were confined to conspicuous unfairness as a freestanding ground for judicial review. The Court in *Dudley Muslim Association* repeated *TN*'s endorsement of Carnwath LJ's remark in *R(S)* that the proper sphere of the court is illegality.[49] This reasoning should be regarded as *obiter*, in light of the Court's finding that it was impermissible for the appellant to rely on concepts such as abuse of power to improve its private law case against the respondent Council, and given the respondent Council's concession in relation to the abuse of power allegation that it had not acted unlawfully in its capacity as a planning authority.[50] On the other hand, the Court heard sustained argument on the abuse of power point and determined it on its legal and factual merits.[51]

The Court of Appeal's emphasis in *Dudley Muslim Association* on the need for abuse of power to amount to illegality is in a sense conventional—the Court did not express any doubt as to the proposition that 'a citizen can rely on an allegation of abuse of power to impugn a decision by a public authority even if there has been no clear representation which created a legitimate expectation'.[52] Indeed, Lewison LJ accepted that this was 'clear'.[53] The context was the Council's exercise of contractual rights contained in a transfer of title to land. The source of those rights was the contract (and thus ultimately the respondent's consent), and no unilateral exercise of public power was involved.[54] The Court of Appeal suggested that it could not usually be an abuse of power for a public authority to exercise contractual rights freely conferred, even if the result appeared to be harsh. At the same

[46] With whom Lewison LJ also agreed: ibid [19].
[47] *Dudley Muslim Association v Dudley Metropolitan Borough Council* [2015] EWCA Civ 1123 (Lewison LJ, with whom Tracy and Gloster LJJ agreed) ('*Dudley Muslim Association*').
[48] Ibid, [47].
[49] Ibid.
[50] Ibid, [21]–[30], [46], [48].
[51] Ibid, [45].
[52] Ibid, [46].
[53] Ibid, citing *Unilever* (n 20).
[54] Ibid, [50].

time, their Honours confirmed that the law will intervene to protect the citizen against abuse of unilateral statutory power.[55] Lord Justice Lewison appeared to endorse a variant of Dyson LJ's context-driven test for conspicuous unfairness in *Rashid*, quoting with approval Lord Hoffman's remarks (in a very different context) in *O'Neill v Phillips*:

> Although fairness is a notion which can be applied to all kinds of activities its content will depend upon the context in which it is being used. Conduct which is perfectly fair between competing businessmen may not be fair between members of a family. In some sports it may require, at best, observance of the rules, in others ('it's not cricket') it may be unfair in some circumstances to take advantage of them. All is said to be fair in love and war. So the context and background are very important.[56]

On the other hand, the judgments in *Dudley Muslim Association* reinforce the perceived difficulties with both conspicuous unfairness as a head of abuse of power, and abuse of power more generally, if those concepts are to serve as anything more than conclusory labels. Their Lordships repeated Laws LJ's admonition in *Begbie* that 'fairness and reasonableness are objective concepts, otherwise there would be no more than palm tree justice'.[57]

Lord Justice Laws' related concern that abuse of power 'goes no distance' in identifying unlawfulness, expressed in *R (Abdi & Nadarajah) v Secretary of State for the Home Department*,[58] led his Lordship to propose an alternative core value, good administration, as offering a better explanation for the protection of legitimate expectations, and an alternative test, namely the existence of a 'good reason' for departing from a promise or practice adopted by a public authority.[59] It is questionable whether Laws LJ's alternative formulation in *Nadarajah* is of greater assistance in identifying illegality, in an individual case, than abuse of power (or conspicuous unfairness), though his Lordship's adoption of proportionality as the test for a sufficiently 'good reason' of 'good administration' may provide some additional rigour in the analysis.[60] The Supreme Court has accepted that the principle of good administration articulated by Laws LJ in *Nadarajah*, rather than legitimate expectation, is the source of an individual's right to

[55] Ibid, [49].

[56] *O'Neill v Phillips* [1999] 1 WLR 1092, 1098.

[57] *Dudley Muslim Association* (n 47) [47], citing *Begbie* (n 29) 1130.

[58] *R (Abdi & Nadarajah) v Secretary of State for the Home Department* [2005] EWCA Civ 1363 ('*Nadarajah*') [67].

[59] Ibid, [68].

[60] The use of proportionality in this context was endorsed by the Privy Council in *Paponette v Attorney General of Trinidad and Tobago* [2012] 1 AC 1 ('*Paponette*') [38]. For an argument that proportionality (at least under present English case law) adds nothing, see Janina Boughey, 'Proportionality and Legitimate Expectations' in chapter 6 of this volume.

determination of his or her case in accordance with policy, in the interest of avoiding strain on the doctrine of legitimate expectation.[61]

Lord Justice Laws has also advocated constraints on the nature of agency conduct capable of giving rise to a protectable substantive legitimate expectation, referring in *R (Bhatt Murphy) v Independent Assessor* to 'the pressing and focussed nature of the kind of assurance required if a substantive legitimate expectation is to be upheld and enforced'.[62] His Lordship's remarks have been applied by the Supreme Court in the tax context, the Court clarifying that a statement formally published to the world by the Inland Revenue (as it then was) must also be clear, unambiguous and devoid of relevant qualification to give rise to a substantive legitimate expectation of particular tax treatment.[63] Further, to elevate a practice of the Revenue into an assurance to taxpayers from which it would be abusive to resile, and to which the agency should therefore be held by virtue of the legitimate expectation so created, 'the promise or practice...must constitute a specific undertaking, directed at a particular individual or group, by which the relevant policy's continuance is assured'.[64] These principles are consistent with a concern to constrain the substantive protection of legitimate expectations, a concern which is in turn consistent with the relative paucity of cases since *Coughlan* in which such expectations are successfully relied upon.[65]

Some recent cases considering the protection of substantive legitimate expectations, both inside and outside the tax setting, have repeated earlier statements that the degree of unfairness (or disproportionality) which must be demonstrated is very high, if judicial review remedies are to be granted,

[61] *Mandalia v Secretary of State for the Home Department* [2015] 1 WLR 4546 [29], [30] (Lord Wilson, with whom Baroness Hale, Lord Clarke, Lord Reed and Lord Hughes agreed); see also *R (Kambadzi) v Home Secretary* [2011] UKSC 23 [39] (Lord Hope); Wade and Forsyth (n 32) 318–19, arguing that the requirement that policy be consistently applied in order to avoid abuse of discretion establishes no new principle.

[62] *R (Bhatt Murphy) v Independent Assessor* [2008] EWCA Civ 755 ('*Bhatt Murphy*') [46]. See also *R v Inland Revenue Commissioners ex p MFK Underwriting Agents Limited* [1990] 1 WLR 1545, 1569 (Bingham LJ), approved by Lord Hoffmann in *R (Bancoult) v Secretary of State for Foreign and Commonwealth Affairs (No 2)* [2009] 1 AC 453 [60]; *R (on the application of Patel) v General Medical Council* [2013] 1 WLR 2801 [50] (Lloyd-Jones LJ, Lord Dyson MR and Lloyd LJ agreeing).

[63] *R (on the application of Davies and another) v Commissioners for HM Revenue and Customs* [2011] 1 WLR 2625 ('*Davies*') [29] (Lord Wilson). The dissent of Lord Mance, and the judgments in the Court of Appeal, indicated sympathy for the unsuccessful appellants and hinted strongly that HMRC had abused its power; see G Weeks, *Soft Law and Public Authorities: Remedies and Reform* (Hart Publishing, 2016) 117.

[64] *Davies* (n 63) [49], approving *Bhatt Murphy* (n 62) [43] (Laws LJ).

[65] See Wade and Forsyth (n 32) 460, stating that such protection has remained 'exceptional' and citing *R (BAPIO Action Ltd) v Home Secretary* [2008] 2 WLR 1073 as one of the few successful examples; see also *HSMP Forum UK Limited v Secretary of State for the Home Department* [2009] EWHC 711 (Admin) and *Bhatt Murphy* (n 62) [41] noting that the protection of substantive legitimate expectations amounts to an 'exceptional situation'.

drawing on Simon-Brown LJ's distinction[66] between 'mere' unfairness and 'conspicuous' unfairness.[67] That is not to say that any coherent doctrine of deference is developing in the English cases, beyond general statements about a sliding scale of intensity of review depending on the character of the decision.[68] The shifting of the burden of proof from an applicant to an authority to justify frustration of a legitimate expectation, once such an expectation has been established,[69] is hardly a deferential approach. However, the recent cases discussed above are consistent with the existence of an ongoing concern (of a type expressed early in the development of the substantive legitimate expectation jurisprudence)[70] about courts 'assum[ing] the power of the executive', and a continuing judicial insistence that the threshold for intervention into executive decision-making is set at a very high level.

THE AUSTRALIAN POSITION—UNREASONABLENESS UNBOUND?

The trajectory of the doctrine of legitimate expectation in Australia is explored in detail elsewhere in this collection.[71] Twice in the last four years, the High Court has stated that legitimate expectation, even in the context of procedural fairness, is an 'unfortunate expression which should be disregarded'[72] and that recourse to it 'is both unnecessary and unhelpful'.[73] In *WZARH*, the High Court's most recent expression of disdain for the doctrine, the position was said to be sufficiently clear as not to require elaboration:

> ... it is not necessary for this Court to engage again in discussion of the concept of 'legitimate expectation' in administrative law or to trace its progress from its

[66] In *Unilever* (n 20) 697.

[67] See eg *R (on the application of Hely-Hutchinson) v The Commissioners for Her Majesty's Revenue and Customs* [2015] EWHC 3261 (Admin) [47].

[68] See eg *United Kingdom Association of Fish Producer Organisations v Secretary of State for Environment, Food And Rural Affairs* [2013] EWHC 1959 (Admin) [92] (summarising earlier cases); see also Mark Elliott, 'From Heresy to Orthodoxy: Substantive Legitimate Expectations in English Public Law' in chapter 10 of this volume, 229–34, for a discussion on deference, which notes three distinct sites where deference may operate and describes the case law in this area as 'complex and somewhat disjointed'.

[69] *Paponette* (n 60) [36], [37], applied *R (on the application of Patel) v General Medical Council* (n 62) [58], [59] (Lloyd-Jones LJ, Lord Dyson MR and Lloyd LJ agreeing).

[70] *R (Bibi) v Newham London Borough Council* [2002] 1 WLR 237 [41].

[71] See Matthew Groves, 'Legitimate Expectations in Australia: Overtaken by Formalism and Pragmatism' in chapter 14 of this volume; see also the discussion of *Minister for Immigration and Ethnic Affairs v Teoh* (1995) 183 CLR 273 and *Lam* (n 1) in Stern (n 5) 276–80.

[72] *Plaintiff S10/2011 v Minister for Immigration and Citizenship* (2012) 246 CLR 636 [65] (Gummow, Hayne, Crennan and Bell JJ).

[73] *Minister for Immigration and Border Protection v WZARH* (2015) 90 ALJR 25 ('*WZARH*') [30] (Kiefel, Bell and Keane JJ).

controversial origins, to its tentative acceptance in Australian law, to its rejection as a touchstone of the requirement that a decision-maker accord procedural fairness to a person affected by an administrative decision.[74]

WZARH was a procedural fairness case, with no consideration given to substantive legitimate expectation. The High Court's most recent consideration of substantive expectation was in *Lam*. A few points should be recalled about the consideration of the English case law in *Lam*. Chief Justice Gleeson expressly disavowed the prospect of any public law principle of good administration (of the type advocated by Laws LJ) giving rise to any entitlement to relief under s 75(v) of the Constitution.[75] Justices McHugh and Gummow gave more detailed consideration to the English jurisprudence, rejecting abuse of power as a unifying principle on the basis that it appeared to evince a concern with 'the judicial supervision of administrative decision-making by the application of certain minimum standards now identified by the English common law'.[76] In their Honours' judgment, it would go too far to give values concerned in general terms with abuse of power an immediate normative operation in applying the Constitution.[77] The role and function of the courts pursuant to s 75 of the Constitution does not extend to the performance of legislative or executive functions, and this demarcation is manifested in the distinction between jurisdictional and non-jurisdictional error.[78] Justices McHugh and Gummow's conclusion reiterated that the concern is with the fairness of the procedure adopted, not with fairness of outcome.[79]

This analysis (and that of Hayne J)[80] does not resolve the question of whether or not conduct amounting to an abuse of power would amount to a jurisdictional error in a particular case. Analytically, an exercise of statutory power which abused that power could readily be seen to be inconsistent with and beyond the legitimate ambit of that power, to be irrational or unreasonable, or flawed on the basis of a failure to take account of the desirability of consistency as a relevant consideration (provided a basis for such an implication could be found in the statute). While it could be justified on any such ground, the emphasis upon identifying a recognised category for seeking judicial review may deflect attention from the underlying flaw, that is, that an abuse of power has occurred.

[74] Ibid, [30], see also [61] (Gageler and Gordon JJ, who stated, in less emphatic tones than the majority, that legitimate expectations were a 'distraction' on the basis of their limited relevance).
[75] *Lam* (n 1) [32].
[76] *Lam* (n 1) [73].
[77] *Lam* (n 1) [72].
[78] *Lam* (n 1) [76].
[79] *Lam* (n 1) [105], see also [148] (Callinan J).
[80] *Lam* (n 1) [119].

It is questionable whether reliance by Australian courts on the 'constraint' of jurisdictional error reveals any lesser degree of normative judgment by the Court than that involved in the characterisation of conduct as an abuse of power.[81] The extent to which the deliberately open-ended concept of jurisdictional error provides a greater constraint on judicial intervention than does the English concept of abuse of power, in a context where the High Court has recognised that functionality concerns and an assessment of the relative gravity of the error are important to the classification of an error as jurisdictional,[82] is debatable.[83] As has previously been argued, the true question is one of drawing the appropriate boundaries by which the law will constrain the executive in the exercise of power. Once that is appreciated, a question of law arises as to whether a particular boundary is consistent with the proper exercise of judicial power in the circumstances. That is something which may well be better analysed by reference to the precise subject matter (or statutory context) of the decision than categories or principles upon which relief could be based.[84]

A concern to avoid giving 'values' such as abuse of power immediate normative operation in judicial review was one of the principal reasons for McHugh and Gummow JJ's rejection of the English approach in *Lam*. It is obviously true that the conclusion that conduct amounts to an abuse of power relies upon and reveals a normative judgment. However, it is artificial to suggest that normative judgments are generally absent from the analysis of jurisdictional error in Australian law. While this is not acknowledged in analysis expressed in terms of statutory or constitutional construction (where power is exercised pursuant to s 61 of the Constitution), properly understood a conclusion that a consideration is relevant or irrelevant, that conduct is procedurally unfair or that action has been taken for an improper purpose involves a normative judgment. Similarly, the process of determining legislative intention for the purposes of statutory construction as to the intended consequences of a failure to comply with statutory conditions[85] is likely to involve normative judgments as to the desirability of a decision being treated as void in the circumstances.[86]

Nor can the Australian recourse to a judicial concern with process rather than outcome entirely explain rejection of the English case law's engagement

[81] See Stern (n 5) 279–81.

[82] *Kirk* (n 7) [64].

[83] See eg M Aronson and M Groves, *Judicial Review of Administrative Action*, 5th edn (Lawbook Co, 2013) [1.170] arguing that the recognition of jurisdictional error as a conclusory term requires a resumption of the 'search for sustaining principles behind the indicative tests for reviewable error'.

[84] Stern (n 5) 281.

[85] The exercise required by *Project Blue Sky Inc v Australian Broadcasting Authority* (1998) 194 CLR 355.

[86] See Stern (n 5) 283.

with substantive unfairness. Several of the well-recognised grounds of review, including the relevant/irrelevant considerations grounds and improper purpose, require the court to focus on matters of substance rather than process, albeit not necessarily by express consideration of the outcome of a decision. Further, any consideration of irrationality or unreasonableness will necessarily involve consideration of outcome. The constrained nature of such consideration (and its consistency with the separation of powers, a concern of McHugh and Gummow JJ in *Lam*) has traditionally been defended in Australia by recourse to the *Wednesbury* test or something very like it, including in the context of accepting illogicality or irrationality as a type of error distinct from *Wednesbury* unreasonableness.[87]

However, in *Li*, the High Court reconsidered the standard of judicial review for reasonableness, in a manner that reveals an increased openness to considerations of substantive unfairness, even while reiterating the need for judicial restraint. *Li* concerned the exercise of a statutory power, conferring a discretion on the Migration Review Tribunal, to adjourn a review from time to time. The High Court held that legal reasonableness (or an absence of unreasonableness) was essential to lawfulness. Parliament was taken to intend that statutory discretionary power of the type that was at issue would be exercised reasonably.[88] The plurality (Hayne, Kiefel and Bell JJ) held that *Wednesbury* unreasonableness is neither the starting point nor the end point for the standard of unreasonableness, which 'should not be considered as limited to what is in effect an irrational, if not bizarre, decision—which is to say one that is so unreasonable that no reasonable person could have arrived at it'.[89] Rather, by analogy with the test applied in appellate review of a judicial discretion in *House v R*,[90] in the absence of 'an evident and intelligible justification' for a decision, even where some reasons have been given, a reviewing court can infer from the facts that a discretionary decision is unreasonable or plainly unjust.[91]

The plurality in *Li* also held that statutory construction determines the legal standard of reasonableness. The legal standard to be applied 'must be the standard indicated by the true construction of the statute'.[92] That is so because, in the plurality's view, legal unreasonableness is linked to abuse of discretionary power: 'the question to which the standard of reasonableness is addressed is whether the statutory power has been abused'.[93]

[87] *Minister for Immigration and Citizenship v SZMDS* (2010) 240 CLR 611 [131] (Crennan and Bell JJ); cf *Li* (n 2) [72] (Hayne, Kiefel and Bell JJ).

[88] *Li* (n 2) [29], [29] (French CJ), [63] (Hayne, Kiefel and Bell JJ), [88] (Gageler J).

[89] *Li* (n 2) [68].

[90] *House v R* (1936) 55 CLR 499.

[91] *Li* (n 2) [75]–[76].

[92] *Li* (n 2) [67], citing HWR Wade and CF Forsyth, *Administrative Law*, 10th edn (Oxford University Press, 2009) 296.

[93] *Li* (n 2) [67].

The plurality added that more specific grounds of judicial review including misdirecting oneself as to the operation of a statute, taking into account irrelevant considerations or failing to take into account irrelevant considerations, giving disproportionate weight to a consideration and reasoning illogically or irrationally may all be 'encompassed' by unreasonableness.[94] One of the means by which unreasonableness may be identified is via proportionality analysis, conducted by reference to the scope of the power.[95]

The plurality's abandonment of the constraint imposed by *Wednesbury* was accompanied by a characteristically Australian reference to the need for judicial restraint and the avoidance of merits review, by reference to the much-cited formulation in *Attorney-General (NSW) v Quin*.[96] Their Honours stated that, within the bounds of legal reasonableness, 'there is an area within which a decision-maker has a genuinely free discretion'.[97] Thus, according to the plurality:

> Properly applied, a standard of legal reasonableness does not involve substituting a court's view as to how a discretion should be exercised for that of a decision-maker. Accepting that the standard of reasonableness is not applied in this way does not, however, explain how it is to be applied and how it is to be tested.[98]

The plurality stated that the error in the exercise of the discretion must be 'evident': as in appellate review pursuant to *House v R*, it will not be sufficient that the reviewing court would have taken a different course.[99] By contrast, Gageler J's separate judgment affirmed the 'stringency' of the *Wednesbury* test.[100]

The Court in *Li* held that the Migration Review Tribunal had fallen into jurisdictional error in refusing the appellant an adjournment. The result itself was held to bespeak error, even though it was not possible to identify what sort of error was made (two possible errors were posed by the plurality: giving too much weight to the fact that Ms Li had had some opportunity to present evidence and/or insufficient weight to her need to present further evidence; and failing to have regard to the scope and purpose of the statutory discretion).[101] The Tribunal acted beyond its jurisdiction because it did not conduct the review in the manner required by the *Migration Act* 1958 (Cth).[102] Chief Justice French held that there was an 'arbitrariness about the

[94] *Li* (n 2) [71]–[72].

[95] *Li* (n 2) [73], citing *Fares Rural Meat and Livestock Co Pty Ltd v Australian Meat and Live-stock Corporation* (1990) 96 ALR 153, 167–68 (Gummow J).

[96] *Attorney-General (NSW) v Quin* (1990) 170 CLR 1, 36–37.

[97] *Li* (n 2) [66].

[98] *Li* (n 2) [66].

[99] *Li* (n 2) [75], see also [30] (French CJ).

[100] *Li* (n 2) [105]–[113].

[101] cf *Li* (n 2) [30] (French CJ stating that 'The requirement of reasonableness is not a vehicle for challenging a decision on the basis that the decision-maker has given insufficient or excessive consideration to some matters').

[102] *Li* (n 2) [85].

decision', rendering it unreasonable in the limiting sense that his Honour had previously identified by reference to *Wednesbury*, as follows:

> Beyond unreasonableness expressive of particular error however, it is possible to say, as Lord Greene MR said, that although a decision-maker has kept within the four corners of the matters it ought to consider 'they have nevertheless come to a conclusion so unreasonable that no reasonable authority could ever have come to it.' In such a case the court may interfere. That limiting case can be derived from the framework of rationality imposed by the statute. As explained by Lord Greene MR, it reflects a limitation imputed to the legislature on the basis of which courts can say that parliament never intended to authorise that kind of decision. After all the requirements of administrative justice have been met in the process and reasoning leading to the point of decision in the exercise of a discretion, there is generally an area of decisional freedom. Within that area reasonable minds may reach different conclusions about the correct or preferable decision. However, the freedom thus left by the statute cannot be construed as attracting a legislative sanction to be arbitrary or capricious or to abandon common sense.[103]

The scope for 'outcome-focused' judicial review on unreasonableness grounds within this 'area of decisional freedom' where no other ground of judicial review may be identified, has since been the focus of two Full Federal Court decisions: *Minister for Immigration and Border Protection v Singh*[104] and *Minister for Immigration and Border Protection v Stretton*.[105] The most recent of these decisions reveals an express concern with the protection of fundamental values, including a rejection of unfairness and equality.[106] While currently confined to the unreasonableness ground, this type of reasoning reveals an increased judicial willingness to give normative operation to administrative law 'values' such as substantive fairness, albeit in the context of a multi-factorial analysis relying upon principles of statutory construction.

This approach is not entirely new, though *Li* gave it wider scope for operation. It is consistent with the focus of the Full Federal Court in procedural fairness cases, for example Allsop CJ's adoption of the proposition that 'subject to any clear contrary statutory intention, fairness is an inhering requirement of the exercise of state power'.[107] This is an application of Gleeson CJ's remark that where Parliament confers a power to destroy or defeat rights, interests or legitimate expectations, 'Parliament is taken to intend that the power be exercised fairly and in accordance with natural

103 *Li* (n 2) [28].

104 *Singh* (n 2) (Allsop CJ, Robertson and Mortimer JJ).

105 *Stretton* (n 2) (Allsop CJ agreeing with Griffiths J subject to his additional remarks; Wigney J agreeing with both Allsop CJ and Griffiths J).

106 See especially *Stretton* (n 2) [9] (Allsop CJ).

107 *SZRMQ v Minister for Immigration and Border Protection* (2013) 219 FCR 212 ('*SZRMQ*') [7]; *SZRUI v Minister for Immigration and Border Protection* [2013] FCAFC 80 [5].

justice unless it makes the contrary intention plain'.[108] In *SZRMQ v Minister for Immigration and Border Protection*, Allsop CJ described (procedural) fairness as: '*normative, evaluative, context specific and relative*'.[109] His Honour accepted in *SZRMQ* that some irregularities in a decision-making process (relevantly, errors in interpretation or translation) may render that process unfair even if no 'operative causal influence' of any irregularity on the decision could be established, because of the possibility that the irregularity may have had such effect 'through its materiality or repetition or context', upon consideration of the whole of the hearing.[110] Allsop CJ was prepared to accept that errors in interpretation or translation might affect a decision so as to render it procedurally unfair, even though a causal effect of such errors on the reasons for decision could not be demonstrated one way or the other.[111] This holistic approach reveals an emphasis upon normative values as an aid to identifying error of law, albeit in the context of the procedural fairness ground for seeking review.

The Full Court in *Singh*, like *Li*, was concerned with the exercise of the Migration Review Tribunal's discretion to grant an adjournment of a hearing. The Court, in a joint judgment, first rejected the proposition that *Li* creates a 'factual checklist' to be followed in determining whether the unreasonableness ground is made out, stating that 'legal unreasonableness is invariably fact dependent'.[112] The Court suggested that the judgments in *Li* had identified two different contexts in which the concept of unreasonableness is employed: first, as a conclusion after the recognition of another jurisdictional error (the sense in which the plurality in *Li* referred to unreasonableness 'encompassing' other grounds); and second, as an 'outcome-focused' conclusion without identification of specific jurisdictional error.[113] The second category was said to occur within what French CJ identified in the passage extracted above as the 'area of decisional freedom'.[114]

Consistent with *Li*, the Court in *Singh* noted that the indicia of unreasonableness are found in the scope, subject matter and purpose of the statutory provisions in issue. In *Singh*, as in *Li*, the Tribunal was subject to a duty to discharge its functions in a manner that was 'fair, just, economical and quick' and 'according to substantial justice and the merits of the case'.[115] The Court adopted an observation by French CJ in *Li* that the statutory source of the requirement to comply with the fairness criteria did

108 *Jarratt v Commissioner of Police for NSW* (2005) 224 CLR 44 [26].
109 *SZRMQ* (n 107) 215 [7].
110 *SZRMQ* (n 107) [10]; see also at [25].
111 *SZRMQ* (n 107) [10]. On the facts of *SZRMQ* no such unfairness could be identified, once the whole of the hearing was considered.
112 *Singh* (n 2) [42].
113 *Singh* (n 2) [44].
114 *Singh* (n 2) [44], citing also the plurality in *Li* (n 2) [66] and [105] (Gageler J).
115 *Migration Act* 1958 (Cth), ss 353(1), 420(1).

not alter its content,[116] before going on to consider other aspects of the statutory scheme relevant to the exercise of the adjournment power. In the result, *Singh* appears to fall into the second 'outcome-focused' category of unreasonableness—the Court held that there was a lack of active consideration by the Tribunal of the adjournment request, and that there was no objective or intelligible justification given for its refusal, but did not identify those failures as falling within another recognised ground of judicial review.[117]

The potential scope for values such as those that underpin a concern for substantive fairness to operate in the 'outcome-focused' category of unreasonableness identified in *Li*, including in contexts where there is no statutory duty to act fairly, was expanded by the Full Federal Court in *Stretton*. That case arose in the same statutory context (the *Migration Act*) as *Li* and *Singh*, but concerned a substantive discretion to cancel a person's visa, which is conferred on the Minister but may be delegated.[118] The primary judge found that the Minister's decision to cancel Mr Stretton's visa was unreasonable in the sense described in *Li*. The Full Court allowed the appeal, holding that the primary judge misapplied the relevant principles in coming to the opposite conclusion. In Allsop CJ's view, his Honour erred by reaching his own view of what was reasonable, and then, without more, supplanting the view of the Minister.[119] Justice Griffiths identified error in the assessment of whether the Minister's decision was capable of being seen as an exercise of the relevant power of visa cancellation.[120]

Chief Justice Allsop's concurring judgment most openly confronts the difficulties involved in identifying error in the 'outcome-focused' category of unreasonableness described in *Singh*. His Honour explained that in this category 'precise definition, beyond explanation of the operative notion and of the legal technique by which to make the assessment, becomes productive of complexity and confusion'.[121] Having reiterated that unreasonableness does not provide a vehicle for courts to substitute their own views for those of decision-makers,[122] his Honour refuted criticism that explanations for judicial review on unreasonableness grounds are 'circular and vague' by the proposition that the appropriate course is to:

> … attend[] to the terms, scope and policy of the statute and the values drawn from the statute and the common law that fall to be considered in assessing the decision.

[116] *Singh* (n 2) [49]. Along with lawfulness and rationality, fairness was said to 'lie at the heart of administrative justice' (quoting *Li* (n 2) [14] (French CJ)).

[117] The Court conducted a proportionality analysis (*Singh* (n 2) [77]) and found the exercise of powers disproportionate to 'the Tribunal's conduct of the review to that point, to what was at stake for the first respondent, and what he might reasonably have hoped to secure through a re-mark', but this analysis was *obiter*.

[118] *Migration Act* 1958 (Cth), s 501(2) (see also s 496).

[119] *Stretton* (n 2) [21].

[120] *Stretton* (n 2) [76].

[121] *Stretton* (n 2) [7].

[122] *Stretton* (n 2) [8], [12].

> The terms, scope and policy of the statute and the fundamental values that attend the proper exercise of power—a rejection of unfairness, of unreasonableness and of arbitrariness; equality; and the humanity and dignity of the individual—will inform the conclusion, necessarily to a degree evaluative, as to whether the decision bespeaks an exercise of power beyond its source.[123]

The weight and relevance of these fundamental values attached to any proper exercise of power (and any other values that are explicit or implicit in the statute) will depend on 'the statutory source of the power in question'.[124] Chief Justice Allsop expressly stated that nothing in his reasons was directed to the exercise of power under the prerogative or s 61 of the Constitution or otherwise unsupported by statute.[125]

Justice Griffiths was less prepared than Allsop CJ to discuss indicia of unreasonableness in the abstract. He nonetheless stated that the standard of unreasonableness will be informed by whether the subject matter of the power is substantive or procedural, adding that 'generally speaking, the intensity of the legal standard is likely to be higher in the case of review of the exercise of discretion which is of a procedural character'.[126] Furthermore, Griffiths J suggested that, following *Li* and *McCloy v New South Wales*,[127] proportionality analysis can be accommodated within unreasonableness[128] but also, more broadly, that the concept of proportionality 'is an aspect of judicial review of administrative action'.[129] Particular statutory indicia that the discretion to decide whether or not to cancel a person's visa under consideration were broad and included, in Griffiths J's (non-exhaustive) list: the absence of an express list of considerations to be taken into account; the reference to the 'national interest' in the objects provision of the *Migration Act*; the fact that the power is conferred on the Minister (who holds political office) and if delegated, the delegate is subject to binding instructions on the Minister; the absence of merits review if the Minister exercises the power personally and the obligation to provide reasons.[130]

Stretton is notable for its acceptance that, in the 'outcome-focused' category of unreasonableness, the concept defies textual formulation. As Wigney J put it in his concurring judgment, referring in particular to the outcome-focused category, '[a]ny addition to, or gloss on, the existing descriptions, explanations or explications of the concept is unlikely to assist'.[131] It is too early to assess the scope that recognition of such a

[123] *Stretton* (n 2) [9].
[124] *Stretton* (n 2) [11].
[125] *Stretton* (n 2) [27].
[126] *Stretton* (n 2) [71].
[127] *McCloy v New South Wales* (2015) 89 ALJR 857 [3].
[128] As pointed out in *Li*, this is not itself a new idea in light of *Fares Rural* (n 95) 167–68.
[129] *Stretton* (n 2) [21].
[130] *Stretton* (n 2) [70].
[131] *Stretton* (n 2) [91].

category of unreasonableness opens up for explicit consideration of substantive unfairness and/or abuse of power. Given the limited trajectory of substantive legitimate expectations in Australia to date, it is nevertheless significant that an opening for such consideration has appeared at all.

THE SCOPE FOR A DOCTRINE OF SUBSTANTIVE UNFAIRNESS IN AUSTRALIAN LAW

Assuming the ongoing currency in Australia of the *Lam* objections to the English case law on substantive fairness, in the absence of any indication from the High Court to the contrary, it remains the case that the underlying basis for the clearly stated Australian rejection of substantive unfairness as a ground of review may be regarded as one of form. More particularly, the objection is that it would be too significant a trespass on the roles of the executive and the legislature were judicial review openly (rather than through mechanisms such as interpretation and construction of legislative powers or duties accommodated within traditionally recognised categories of grounds for seeking judicial review) to be based on adjudication as to the substantive fairness of the outcome of the exercise of statutory power.[132] This does not undermine the validity of the objection, but may indicate that substantive unfairness as a motivating value underlying judicial decision-making on judicial review claims is not itself considered to be objectionable, provided that it can be accommodated within the formal constraints operating in such claims.

The acceptance by the Full Federal Court of an 'outcome-focused' category of unreasonableness, in which fundamental common law values such as fairness and equality have a role to play in the identification of error (again, at least in cases involving the exercise of statutory discretion), opens the way for express consideration of substantive unfairness and abuse of power in Australia, albeit always in a particular statutory setting and not as distinct grounds of judicial review. This development has the potential to go a little distance towards reconciling the Australian and English case law. In the realm of unreasonableness, it avoids the anomalies involved in the Australian rejection of the explanatory force of concepts such as abuse of power and substantive unfairness.[133] Those anomalies arise in particular given that many of the recognised grounds of judicial review require judicial consideration of the substance or merits of the manner of executive decision-making. Once that is accepted, it is not clear why unfairness rising

[132] See Stern (n 5) 285–88, setting out the various contexts in which considerations of substantive fairness have been considered as an aspect of unreasonableness and in the process of statutory construction.

[133] See Stern (n 5) 289.

to the level of abuse of power should fall outside the bounds of jurisdictional error provided that it can be, and is, kept within appropriate limits.

While the English case law involves a more open acknowledgement of the normative judgments being made than has been seen in Australia to date, the English cases considering substantive fairness place great emphasis on the importance of the factual and legal context, including the statutory context, of the relevant decision in controlling the intensity of review applied, whether or not that involves a proportionality analysis. A similar emphasis on statutory context is apparent in considering the ambit of the unreasonableness ground in the recent Australian decisions. The practical difference between the two approaches (albeit that the Australian case law is limited to the unreasonableness ground) is smaller than a reading of some of the more emphatic remarks in *Lam* might suggest.

Where substantive or conspicuous unfairness is the true impetus for granting relief in judicial review claims, judicial acknowledgement of that would have the advantage of transparency as to the administrative (and common law) values being applied, with open recognition of the normative judgment being deployed. Also, it may avoid the eliding of concepts of fairness and reasonableness which could otherwise result from accommodating substantive fairness values within the rubric of legal unreasonableness. However, it would have the disadvantage, from an Australian perspective, of departing from the certainty provided by a rule precluding relief on such a ground, and of potentially reigniting the debate as to the appropriate place for notions of substantive legitimate expectation in Australian law. Accepting that tests in this area are not susceptible to minute characterisation or, to adopt Allsop CJ's expression, 'a precise textual formulary',[134] the extent to which the advantage outweighs the disadvantage probably depends on the extent to which the threshold and criteria for granting relief on grounds of substantive unfairness can properly be delineated to enable certainty and predictability in the determination of judicial review claims. The English experience seems to indicate that that may well be an enduring difficulty and it may be that this provides an ongoing roadblock to the reconciliation of Australian and English doctrine in this area.

[134] *Stretton* (n 2) [10].

5

A Pluralist Account of Deference and Legitimate Expectations

PAUL DALY*

LEGITIMATE EXPECTATIONS, LORD Fraser of Tullybelton said in the early 1980s, is an 'apt' term 'to express the underlying principle', but 'it is somewhat lacking in precision'.[1] Decades later it was described as 'a relatively young doctrine'[2] that is 'still developing'.[3] Authors have questioned the status of the doctrine of legitimate expectations. Courts are said to have 'experienced some difficulty in producing a coherent body of law',[4] because '[i]t has never been precisely clear what jurisprudential basis has been adopted' for the development of legitimate expectations.[5] A period of 'rapid growth' has occurred 'without proper exploration as to why legitimate expectations ought to be protected'.[6] As a result, the doctrine is 'highly uncertain'[7] and 'many questions about it remain unanswered'.[8]

Such a crescendo of criticism may cause one to doubt the existence of any coherent doctrine of legitimate expectations. In my view, however, coherence can be attained. That the doctrine may not map clearly onto the various justifications offered for it from time to time is not a great surprise. The doctrine is of recent provenance and, as is the case with the common

* With thanks to Vincent-Alexandre Fournier for his research assistance.

1 *Attorney-General of Hong Kong v Ng Yuen Shiu* [1983] 2 AC 629, 636.

2 M Elliott, 'Legitimate Expectations and the Search for Principle: Reflections on *Abdi & Nadarajah*' (2006) *Judicial Review* 281, 282.

3 *R (Niazi) v Secretary of State for the Home Department* [2008] EWCA Civ 755 [3].

4 I Steele, 'Substantive Legitimate Expectations: Striking the Right Balance?' (2005) 121 *Law Quarterly Review* 300, 303.

5 CJS Knight, 'Expectations in Transition: Recent Developments in Legitimate Expectations' (2009) *Public Law* 15, 17.

6 P Reynolds, 'Legitimate Expectations and the Protection of Trust in Public Officials' (2011) *Public Law* 330, 330.

7 J Watson, 'Clarity and Ambiguity: A New Approach to the Test of Legitimacy in the Law of Legitimate Expectations' (2010) 30 *Legal Studies* 633, 633.

8 F Ahmed and A Perry, 'The Coherence of the Doctrine of Legitimate Expectations' (2014) 73 *Cambridge Law Journal* 61, 61.

law, its development has not followed inexorably from an agreed set of first principles. More generally, a doctrine that imposes constraints on officials' freedom of action has necessarily both substantive and procedural aspects and may draw on different values in different circumstances. Some underlying theory is needed to assist in answering the difficult doctrinal questions that will inevitably arise.

In the pages that follow, I will set out a pluralist account of legitimate expectations, building on the apparently diverse values found in decided cases.[9] I begin with an overview of the different values provided in the case law, some of which support judicial enforcement of legitimate expectations, and some which seem to counsel against it. I then proceed to outline how these values should be meshed together by focusing on the contentious areas of knowledge and reliance, substantive legitimate expectations and enforcement of *ultra vires* representations, explaining along the way the role that deference ought to play.

THE PLURALITY OF LEGITIMATE EXPECTATIONS

Legitimate 'expectation[s] may take many forms'.[10] A distinction is typically drawn between procedural and substantive responses to legitimate expectations.[11] An individual with the legitimate expectation of a certain procedure will benefit from procedural protection—such as notice and an opportunity to comment—before a decision can lawfully be made against her. A legitimate expectation of a substantive outcome would, if enforced, prevent an administrative decision-maker from resiling from a promise or changing a policy without good reasons for doing so. Accordingly, substantive enforcement of a legitimate expectation represents a much greater interference by the courts with the administration, for it reduces the range of options available to a front-line decision-maker, whereas a legitimate expectation of a certain procedure simply imposes a procedural barrier without reducing the range of options. But this distinction should not be over-emphasised. The line between procedure and substance is a notoriously slippery one,[12] especially so in this area because individuals will typically

[9] I refer throughout to values. One could equally refer to justifications, rationales or reasons, but as I explain, some of the values found in the case law mitigate against recognition of legitimate expectations, such that it may be misleading to refer to them as justifications, rationales or reasons. See generally P Daly, 'Administrative Law: A Values-Based Approach' in J Bell, M Elliott, P Murray and J Varuhas (eds), *Public Law Adjudication in Common Law Systems: Process and Substance* (Hart Publishing, 2016).

[10] *Council of Civil Service Unions v Minister for Civil Service* [1985] AC 374, 415 (Lord Roskill).

[11] Elliott (n 2) 285.

[12] See generally D Dyzenhaus and E Fox-Decent, 'Rethinking the Process/Substance Distinction: *Baker v Canada*' (2001) 51 *University of Toronto Law Journal* 193.

seek to use additional procedural rights to develop additional substantive arguments.[13] Moreover,

> [i]t is difficult to see why it is any less unfair to frustrate a legitimate expectation that something will or will not be done by the decision-maker than it is to frustrate a legitimate expectation that the applicant will be listened to before the decision-maker decides whether to take a particular step.[14]

Drilling further down into this distinction, Paul Craig has suggested that there are four very different ways in which a legitimate expectation might arise:

i. A general norm or policy choice, which an individual has relied on, has been replaced by a different policy choice.
ii. A general norm or policy choice has been departed from in the circumstances of a particular case.
iii. There has been an individual representation relied on by a person, which the administration seeks to resile from in the light of a shift in general policy.
iv. There has been an individualised representation that has been relied on. The administrative body then changes its mind and makes an individualised decision that is inconsistent with the original representation.[15]

One of the frustrations for the scholar who wishes to synthesise the learning on legitimate expectations is that relevant materials may be found in many different places, layered by many different concerns. Indeed, at times, the language of legitimate expectations may seem inapposite. For instance, where an individual holds a protected interest[16] accorded by an administrative decision-maker, courts will impose procedural protections should the administrative decision-maker seek to withdraw the interest; but this is part of the general administrative law requirement of fairness,[17] to which

13 See eg *Minister for Immigration and Border Protection v WZARH* [2015] HCA 40, esp [42]–[44].

14 *R v Ministry of Agriculture, Fisheries and Food; ex parte Hamble (Offshore) Fisheries Ltd* [1995] 2 All ER 714, 724 (Sedley LJ). See also G Cartier, 'A "Mullanian" Approach to the Doctrine of Legitimate Expectations: Real Questions and Promising Answers' in G Huscroft and M Taggart (eds), *Inside and Outside Canadian Administrative Law: Essays for David Mullan* (University of Toronto Press, 2006) 185.

15 P Craig, *Administrative Law*, 7th edn (Sweet and Maxwell, 2012) 679–80.

16 Interest here is shorthand for a longer list of triggers for judicial review, for example, 'the rights, privileges or interests of an individual': *Cardinal v Director of Kent Institution* [1985] 2 SCR 643 [14].

17 For example, Denning LJ employed the terminology of 'legitimate expectation' in a sense related purely to the overall fairness of the administrative process in *Schmidt v Secretary of State for Home Affairs* [1969] 2 Ch 149, 170. See similarly, *Council of Civil Service Unions* (n 10) 401 (Lord Fraser of Tullybelton). See also *Gutrani v Minister for Justice* [1993] 2 IR 427, 436 (McCarthy J); *Haoucher v Minister for Immigration and Ethnic Affairs* (1989-90) 169 CLR 648, 658–59 (Dawson J); *Re Minister for Immigration and Multicultural Affairs; ex parte Lam* (2003) 214 CLR 1, 12–13 (Gleeson CJ); *Minister for Immigration and Ethnic Affairs v Teoh* (1995) 183 CLR 273, 310–12 (McHugh J).

the idea that an individual has a legitimate expectation that the interest will not be withdrawn without due process seems not to add a great deal. Similarly, where an administrative decision-maker seeks to change a policy, constraints[18] may be imposed independently of the existence of any subjective expectation held by an individual or group.[19] In short, '[l]egitimate expectation may play different parts in different aspects of public law'.[20] Nonetheless, each of the situations Craig enumerates has an important common feature: a legally cognisable interest[21] engendered by official action at Time X which is defeated by official action at Time Y.[22] Anxious to resist the 'lure of over-classification',[23] I will concentrate on this common feature.

JUSTIFYING LEGITIMATE EXPECTATIONS: JUDICIAL PERSPECTIVES

'Perhaps unhelpfully', many different conceptual bases for legitimate expectations can be found in the case law.[24] Abuse of power figures prominently, as do the rule of law and good administration. These are often tempered, however, by reference to the democratic decision to vest power in a non-judicial body, an idea with overtones of a separation of decision-making functions. My goal in this section is both descriptive and normative, to demonstrate that the values of good administration, the rule of law, democracy and separation of powers *have* and *ought to have* a role in the development of the law of legitimate expectations.

[18] See eg *Attorney General of New South Wales v Quin* (1990) 170 CLR 1, 18 (Mason CJ).

[19] For a recent example, see *Altus Group Limited v Calgary (City)* 2015 ABCA 86, where a municipality's change of position in respect of a taxing by-law was quashed as unreasonable, a notable decision given that Canadian courts do not officially protect substantive legitimate expectations. See generally, *Canada (Attorney General) v Mavi* [2011] 2 SCR 504.

[20] *R v North and East Devon Health Authority; ex parte Coughlan* [2001] QB 213 [71].

[21] It is difficult to improve upon Lord Diplock's suggestion that the term 'legitimate expectation' simply means 'consequences to which effect will be given in public law…' *Council of Civil Service Unions* (n 10) 408. Where I use 'legitimate expectation' in this chapter, it is as shorthand for the more cumbersome 'legally cognisable interest'. The term 'legitimate expectation' is somewhat unfortunate because it suggests by reference to 'expectation' that courts must inquire into the subjective view of an individual as to the effect of official action and that it will only be 'legitimate' for them to enforce such subjective expectations in limited circumstances. See eg *Lam* (n 17), 45–47 (Callinan J); *Teoh* (n 17) 314 (McHugh J). I think this is to put the linguistic cart before the conceptual horse. Whether knowledge and reliance are prerequisites is not a matter of linguistic analysis but depends on conceptual analysis. I defer until later questions about whether knowledge and reliance are necessary to justify judicial enforcement of 'legitimate expectation'.

[22] See also Laws LJ's formulation in *R (Abdi & Nadarajah) v Secretary of State for the Home Department* [2005] EWCA Civ 1363 [68]: 'Where a public authority has issued a promise or adopted a practice which represents how it proposes to act in a given area, the law will require the promise or practice to be honoured unless there is good reason not to do so'.

[23] *Nadarajah*, ibid [49] (Laws LJ). Compare *Mount Sinai Hospital Center v Quebec (Minister of Health and Social Services)* [2001] 2 SCR 281 [27] (Binnie J): 'it is inevitable that sub-classifications must be made to differentiate the situations which warrant highly intrusive relief from those which do not'.

[24] Knight (n 5) 17.

Abuse of power is a term found in some foundational cases on legitimate expectations.[25] However, abuse of power is probably better understood as an overarching principle of judicial review of administrative action in general, a 'rationale' rather than a free-standing rule.[26] It is a 'conclusory statement'[27] that 'goes no distance to tell you, case by case, what is lawful and what is not'.[28] It may be significant that abuse of power first came to prominence during a period of rapid development in administrative law.[29] One might suggest that judges were casting around for a general term that would capture their new responsibilities: abuse of power fulfils that function admirably. But it does not provide much in the way of concrete guidance to judges charged with determining whether an individual has a legally cognisable interest that can be overridden by a subsequent administrative decision.

Good administration features regularly in the jurisprudence.[30] Christopher Forsyth suggests that the term is as vague as abuse of power.[31] Properly understood as a concern with the efficient attainment of statutory objectives, however, good administration is neither a hopelessly general term nor beyond the ken of judges. While judges are not generally well-equipped, by reason of evidentiary limitations and a relative lack of institutional competence, 'to impose upon the executive branch [their] ideas of good administration',[32] they may properly take some account of the effect of judicial review doctrine on the administrative process. For instance, it is surely reasonable for judges to suggest that participation by affected individuals prior to an administrative decision being taken is likely to increase the accuracy of outcomes.[33] And in the context of legitimate expectations, judges may reasonably take the view in the absence of empirical evidence to the contrary that holding officials to policies, published or unpublished,[34] would

[25] See eg *In re Preston* [1985] AC 835, 851 (Lord Scarman), 864 (Lord Templeman); *Coughlan* (n 20) 246–47 [71]. See also *Apotex Inc v Canada (Attorney General)* [2000] 4 FCR 264 [123] (Evans JA).

[26] *R v Department of Education and Employment; ex parte Begbie* [2000] 1 WLR 1115 [76].

[27] Reynolds (n 6) 333.

[28] *Nadarajah* (n 22) [67] (Laws LJ).

[29] See eg *Preston* (n 25).

[30] See eg *Apotex* (n 25) [123] (Evans JA); *Coughlan* (n 20) 246–47 [71]; *R (Bibi) v London Borough of Newham* [2001] EWCA Civ 607 [24]; *Nadarajah* (n 22) [68] (Laws LJ).

[31] C Forsyth, 'Legitimate Expectations Revisited' (2011) *Judicial Review* 429.

[32] *Lam* (n 17) 12 (Gleeson CJ). See similarly *R (S) v Secretary of State for the Home Department* [2007] EWCA Civ 546 [41] (Carnwath LJ).

[33] See generally *Matthews v Eldridge* 424 US 319 (1976). See also P Craig, 'Legitimate Expectations: A Conceptual Analysis' (1992) 108 *Law Quarterly Review* 79, 85: 'Giving a person a hearing of some kind can help to ensure that the desired end is attained; the procedural rights perform an instrumental role in the sense of rendering it more likely that there will be an accurate decision on the substance of the case'.

[34] See generally *Lumba (WL) v Secretary of State for the Home Department* [2012] 1 AC 245.

further the ends of effective administration.[35] It is true that reference to 'good administration' alone will not resolve all of the difficult questions that arise in administrative law cases. Nevertheless, reminding judges to focus on the efficient and effective achievement of statutory goals by administrative decision-makers can assist in resolving these questions.

Reference is often also made to unfairness operating against an individual or group of individuals. The formulation in *Attorney-General of Hong Kong v Ng Yuen Shiu*, that 'expectations may be based upon…[action] that would make it unfair *or* inconsistent with good administration…' (emphasis added), is especially telling because it came so early in the evolution of the law of legitimate expectations.[36] Good administration has not been the only driver of the judicial imagination on this subject.

In its evident concern with fairness *to* individuals—that 'holding government to a procedural undertaking that was solemnly given on its behalf to an individual is more a matter of individual justice'[37]—unfairness in this context plays a role distinct from the general common law guarantee of fair procedures. Courts intervene to provide fair outcomes rather than fair procedures alone.[38] Clear examples can be found in *ex parte Unilever plc*, where Simon Brown LJ commented that a legitimate expectation will be enforced where 'it is illogical or *immoral* or both for a public authority to act with conspicuous unfairness and in that sense abuse its power' (emphasis added);[39] in *R (Bibi) v London Borough of Newham*, where Schiemann LJ for the Court of Appeal invoked the 'moral detriment' suffered by a refugee family that sought enforcement of a legitimate expectation to secure housing;[40] and in *Webb v Ireland*, where Finlay CJ noted that it would be 'inequitable and unjust' for the State to 'repudiate' an assurance that individuals who had handed over valuable treasure would be honourably treated.[41] Similarly, in explaining the foundations of legitimate expectations, Bingham LJ invoked the inter-personal relationship created by the law of contract: 'If in private law a body would be in breach of contract in so acting or estopped from so acting [contrary to a legitimate expectation] a public authority should generally be in no better position'.[42] This is surely quite telling: when a public

[35] Though equally, '[t]o hold that…pre-election promises bound a newly elected Government could well be inimical to good government' (*Begbie* (n 26) [56] (Peter Gibson LJ)).

[36] *Ng Yuen Shiu* (n 1) 637. See also ibid 638 where good administration is said to be 'primarily' the justification for enforcing legitimate expectations.

[37] *Apotex* (n 25) [121] (Evans JA).

[38] cf *SZBEL v Minister for Immigration and Multicultural and Indigenous Affairs* (2006) 228 CLR 152, 160.

[39] *R v Inland Revenue Commissioners; ex parte Unilever plc* [1996] STC 681, 695.

[40] *Bibi* (n 30) [55].

[41] *Webb v Ireland* [1988] IR 353, 379.

[42] *R v Inland Revenue Commissioners; ex parte MFK Underwriting Agents Ltd* [1990] 1 WLR 1545, 1569–70.

body makes a representation to an individual, it finds itself in a domain where promises may be enforced.

Judicial concern for the dignity and autonomy of individuals in their dealings with administrative decision-makers evokes the rule of law, as 'a principle of institutional morality'.[43] A cautious reader would no doubt protest that the rule of law has an 'all things to all people' quality that reduces its value as a tool of analysis; indeed, it may be an 'essentially contested concept' that means different things to different judges.[44] What is true of 'abuse of power' may be equally true, if not more so, of the 'rule of law'. From the cases, however, the core sense of the rule of law as applied to legitimate expectations is relatively stable and readily comprehensible because it is underpinned by a concern for human autonomy and dignity. Even so-called 'formal' conceptions of the rule of law,[45] which emphasise that laws should be published, accessible and clear, respond to the needs of humans as autonomous agents capable of planning their lives to achieve personal goals.[46] As Raz explains, 'Observance of the rule of law is [seen as] necessary' on this approach to allow the law 'to respect human dignity'.[47] In legitimate expectations cases where the rule of law is invoked, courts are typically concerned by the effect on individuals of promises being broken or settled expectations disrupted. As Schiemann LJ put it, for the Court of Appeal in *R (Bibi) v London Borough of Newham*, 'there is value in holding authorities to promises which they have made, thus upholding responsible public administration *and allowing people to plan their lives sensibly*' (emphasis added).[48] Where individuals use official action to plan their affairs, their autonomy is very much in play, and it is impinged upon when officials go back on their word or change a policy. The human dimension of a case like *R v North and East Devon Health Authority; ex parte Coughlan*[49] cannot be overstated: promising a home for life was an important engagement by the Authority

[43] J Jowell, 'The Rule of Law' in J Jowell, D Oliver and C O'Cinneide (eds), *The Changing Constitution*, 8th edn (Oxford University Press, 2015) 13, 27.

[44] J Waldron, 'Is the Rule of Law an Essentially Contested Concept (In Florida)?' (2002) 21 *Law and Philosophy* 137; *Trial Lawyers Association of British Columbia v British Columbia (Attorney General)* [2014] 3 SCR 31 [102] (Rothstein J). At the very least it is a 'highly textured expression': *Re: Resolution to Amend the Constitution* [1981] 1 SCR 753, 805–06.

[45] P Craig, 'Formal and Substantive Concepts of the Rule of Law: An Analytical Framework' (1997) *Public Law* 467.

[46] P Craig, 'Substantive Legitimate Expectations in Domestic and Community Law' (1996) 55 *Cambridge Law Journal* 289, 304.

[47] J Raz, 'The Rule of Law and its Virtue' (1977) 93 *Law Quarterly Review* 195, 204.

[48] *Bibi* (n 30) [24]. See similarly *Glenkerrin Homes Ltd v Dun Laoghaire-Rathdown Corporation* [2007] IEHC 298 (Clarke J): 'where third parties reasonably arrange their affairs by reference to...a practice...[they] are entitled to rely upon an expectation that the practice will not be changed without reasonable notice being given'.

[49] *Coughlan* (n 20).

towards the severely disabled applicant; departing from the promise was a significant blow to her dignity and autonomy.

The cautious reader might next object that good administration and the rule of law are simply two sides of the same coin: is it not always good administration to respect the rule of law and, in particular, enforce promises made to individuals; indeed, does not holding decision-makers to their promises increase trust in government thereby enhancing good administration?[50] In many cases, no doubt, good administration and the rule of law will point to the same outcome. But not always.[51] A representation might have been mistaken, in which case, 'the court should be slow to fix the public authority permanently with the consequences of that mistake'.[52] Or giving effect to a representation made to an individual or group of individuals might have negative wider consequences:

> Seen from the point of view of administrators focusing on the problem immediately before their eyes a promise seems reasonable…[b]ut when they, or their superiors, focus on a wider background it appears that the making of the promise was unwise or that, in any event, its fulfilment seems too difficult.[53]

Good administration and the rule of law serve primarily to underpin the legitimacy of expectations, but establishing a legitimate expectation is not the end of the analysis. As courts repeatedly emphasise, invoking concerns for democracy and separation of powers, a decision can be made contrary to a legitimate expectation in appropriate circumstances: judges will offer have to defer to administrative decision-makers. Where decision-making authority has been granted by the legislature to an administrative decision-maker, it would be inappropriate for a court to step into the other body's shoes and take the decision it ought to have taken: 'to do so would be to assume the powers of the executive'.[54] On occasion, indeed, a statutory provision may shut the door to the recognition of a legitimate expectation.[55] Moreover, the administrative decision-maker cannot, by adopting a decision or policy at Time X, bind itself; it must remain free at Time Y to depart from the earlier decision or policy:[56] 'To regard a legitimate expectation as requiring the decision-maker to act in a particular way is tantamount to treating it as a

[50] See eg C Forsyth, 'The Provenance and Protection of Legitimate Expectations' (1988) 47 *Cambridge Law Journal* 238, 239; SJ Schønberg, *Legitimate Expectations in Administrative Law* (Oxford University Press, 2000) 25.

[51] Steele (n 4) 301.

[52] *Begbie* (n 26) [61].

[53] *Bibi* (n 30) [36].

[54] *Bibi* (n 30) [41]. See also *Thames Valley Electric Power Board v NZFP Pulp & Paper Limited* [1994] 2 NZLR 641, 653; *Minister for Immigration, Local Government and Ethnic Affairs v Kurtovic* (1990) 21 FCR 193, 210 (Gummow J).

[55] See eg *Mount Sinai Hospital* (n 23) 29 (Binnie J): 'The expectations must not conflict with the public authority's statutory remit'.

[56] See eg D Gwynn Morgan and G Hogan, *Administrative Law in Ireland*, 4th edn (Roundhall, 2010) 1033: 'This bar on the fettering of future executive action is part of a wider principle that statutory powers must be freely exercised'.

rule of law'.[57] Performance of an undertaking must be 'compatible with [a decision-maker's] public duty':[58]

> Public authorities typically, and central government *par excellence*, enjoy wide discretions which it is their duty to exercise in the public interest. They have to decide the content and the pace of change. Often they must balance different, indeed opposing, interests across a wide spectrum. Generally they must be the masters of procedure as well as substance; and as such are generally entitled to keep their own counsel.[59]

As Lord Templeman explained in *In re Preston*, a case in which a taxpayer complained of a change of policy by the Inland Revenue Commissioners:

> [A] taxpayer cannot complain of unfairness, merely because the commissioners decide to perform their statutory duties ... to make an assessment and enforce a liability to tax. The commissioners may decide to abstain from exercising their powers and performing their duties on grounds of unfairness, but the commissioners themselves must bear in mind that their primary duty is to collect, not to forgive, taxes. And if the commissioners decide to proceed, the court cannot in the absence of exceptional circumstances decide to be unfair that which the commissioner by taking action against the taxpayer have determined to be fair.[60]

I quote this passage from Lord Templeman's speech at length because it helpfully illustrates two related ideas. First, an administrative decision-maker must act pursuant to the mandate given to it by the legislature. A democratic choice made by a parliamentary majority ought to be respected. Second, judges should not second-guess the merits or wisdom of courses of action taken by administrative decision-makers. There is *a* (rather than *the*) separation of powers between them. The distinction is subtle but important: *the* separation of powers implies to the legal mind the Montesquian distinction between legislative, executive and judicial branches, whereas *a* separation of powers implies only some separation of functions between different bodies. The difference is between assuming that some functions are magically 'legislative', 'executive' or 'judicial' in nature and should be assigned accordingly and understanding simply that distinct parts of the governmental apparatus should exercise distinct functions, leaving the precise allocation to be worked out by an appropriate theory. The latter idea features often in the legitimate expectations cases.

[57] *Teoh* (n 17) 291 (Mason CJ and Deane J).
[58] *R v Liverpool Corporation; ex parte Liverpool Taxi Fleet Operators' Association* [1972] 2 QB 299, 308 (Lord Denning MR). See also *Laker Airways v Department of Trade* [1977] 1 QB 643, 707, where Lord Denning MR explained that:

> The underlying principle is that the Crown cannot be estopped from exercising its powers, whether given in a statute or by common law, when it is doing so in the proper exercise of its duty to act for the public good, even though this may work some injustice or unfairness to a private individual...

[59] *Niazi* (n 3) [41].
[60] *Preston* (n 25) 864.

Accordingly, respect for legislative choice and a concern to ensure that some sort of distinction can be drawn between legislative, executive and judicial power both underpins and motivates arguments for judicial deference in the enforcement of legitimate expectations.[61]

JUSTIFYING LEGITIMATE EXPECTATIONS: A PLURALIST APPROACH

These competing values might seem to give rise to difficulties. Even the rule of law and good administration might be unruly bedfellows, for a breach of a promise may sometimes be very good administration indeed, even if it undermines the dignity of the individual concerned. It may be that the judges have been lurching wildly from case to case with no guiding principle in mind, that these values are 'little more than a smokescreen for an erratic and subjective assortment of judicial ideas',[62] in which case the better approach may simply be to concentrate on the individual strands of case law in isolation, allowing judges to refine them case-by-case with the incrementalism for which the common law is famous.

This, however, is an unattractive approach. As I suggested above, there is a common thread to the legitimate expectations cases: a legally cognisable interest engendered by official action at Time X which is defeated by official action at Time Y. Moreover, jurists have spent decades searching for 'more precise principles'[63] behind this common thread. As a branch of the law, legitimate expectations is relatively new; as a result, some confusion is surely unavoidable,[64] but surely not ineradicable: 'it is all too easy to make separate compartments of the law where, in truth, different applications represent a single principle or at least interlocking principles'.[65]

Without doctrinal frameworks to guide the work of courts and commentators, the law will only become more confused. As Lord Scarman wisely put it:

> The mark of the great judge from Coke through Mansfield to our day has been the capacity and the will to search out principle, to discard the detail appropriate (perhaps) to earlier times, and to apply principle in such a way as to satisfy the needs of their own time.[66]

Those who inveigh against 'top-down' legal reasoning should not recoil in horror.[67] The law of judicial review has 'evolved',[68] which—given that this

[61] See similarly *Mount Sinai Hospital* (n 23) [47]–[51].

[62] M Groves, 'Substantive Legitimate Expectations in Australian Administrative Law' (2008) 32 *Melbourne University Law Review* 470, 487.

[63] Reynolds (n 6) 335.

[64] See *Abrahamson v Law Society of Ireland* [1996] 1 IR 403, 422 (McCracken J): 'it is only to be expected that in an evolving concept there will be contradictory judgments'.

[65] *Nadarajah* (n 22) [49] (Laws LJ).

[66] *Gillick v West Norfolk and Wisbech Health Authority* [1986] AC 112, 183.

[67] See eg *McGinty v Western Australia* (1996) 186 CLR 140, 231–32 (McHugh J).

[68] *Council of Civil Service Unions* (n 10) 414 (Lord Roskill).

is a field of human, not biological or divine, endeavour—suggests some sort of intelligent design; jurists may properly 'shape the development...'[69] of the subject. Searching out principle and discarding detail may occasionally provoke criticisms that the author is rewriting history, but so far as legitimate expectations are concerned, all the values are found in judicial decisions that overtly seek to explain the law in terms of general principles or values. In any event, interpreting cases with a view to identifying a defensible general framework for judicial decision-making is a perfectly legitimate mode of scholarly inquiry.[70]

Faced with values found in the cases that are individually appealing but which may come into conflict with one another, one response is to adopt a pluralist approach. Rather than assigning priority to any one value—or casting about for an alternative meta-value that is not easily found in the cases[71]—the scholar attempts to accommodate them all, reconciling them where necessary.[72] The utility of this approach is best appreciated in the treatment of concrete problems, where the limits of the competing values can be better understood, but some preliminary comments are in order.

First, a pluralist approach is explicitly normative. It speaks to how jurists *ought* to think about legitimate expectations. It is descriptive only to the extent that it draws its values from sources of positive law. As a result, only values that are attractive on their own terms may be accommodated: hence the time I spent above in describing the values found in the case law and mounting a defence of each of them.

Second, if values are genuinely irreconcilable, one of them must yield. Should it prove to be the case, there would be reason to doubt the attraction of a pluralist approach based on the values found in the cases. However, declarations of irreconcilability should only be a last resort. Often, what seems to be an irreconcilable difference could be resolved by further study, especially by consideration of empirical evidence, for instance as to whether enforcement of legitimate expectations really increases trust in officialdom or the efficiency of public administration. Moreover, it may be possible to resolve any conflict by revising the values which, when applied to concrete problems, may prove to have been drawn too broadly in the abstract. Where this is the case, critics should not hastily blurt out declarations of irreconcilability but carefully consider whether the conflict might disappear on closer inspection.

Third, although it would be possible in theory to formulate priority rules to address conflicts, these are unlikely to be appropriate. The rules would

[69] *Council of Civil Service Unions* (n 10) 417 (Lord Roskill).

[70] A Beever and C Rickett, 'Interpretive Legal Theory and the Academic Lawyer' (2005) 68 *Modern Law Review* 320.

[71] See eg Reynolds (n 6) 341, advocating for a meta-value of 'trust in the public authority'.

[72] What follows owes a significant debt to SR Munzer, *A Theory of Property* (Cambridge University Press, 1990).

only operate in situations where one or more values come into conflict. If all values point to the same result, there is no conflict to resolve: indeed, that common law courts have 'had little difficulty in recognising the existence of procedural legitimate expectations',[73] which vindicate rule of law and good administration concerns without impinging on decision-makers' autonomy on matters of substance, reflects the absence of any conflict in this particular area. The problem with priority rules is that they may not take account of the strength of the competing values in more difficult areas. For instance, a plausible priority rule would be majoritarian. But even in a situation where three values are ranged against one, the one value may nonetheless be extremely strong, so much so that it could override the others. As a rule of thumb, a majoritarian preference might be useful, but it would be a dangerously facile priority rule if cast in absolute terms.

PROTECTING LEGITIMATE EXPECTATIONS: PLURALISM IN ACTION

Three controversial doctrinal questions form a crucible within which the appropriate interaction of the rule of law, good administration, democracy and separation of powers can be observed. These are: first, the role of knowledge and reliance; second, substantive legitimate expectations; and third, expectations based on *ultra vires* representations. I argue that neither knowledge nor reliance should be a prerequisite to the enforcement of legitimate expectations. On substantive legitimate expectations, I take the side of the Court of Appeal in *Coughlan*, arguing in the teeth of strong criticism of that decision that there are indeed good reasons for courts to enforce substantive legitimate expectations, though I also observe that the Court of Appeal probably went too far in one important respect. As to *ultra vires* representations, I ally myself with Paul Craig and others in advocating an approach that would permit courts to enforce them in some circumstances.

Knowledge and Reliance

Does an individual need to know of and rely on the official action said to give rise to a legitimate expectation? In respect of knowledge it has been suggested, for instance, that '[a] person cannot lose an expectation that he or she does not hold'.[74] And as to reliance, Binnie J would have refused to protect substantive legitimate expectations in the absence of a need to demonstrate detriment: 'One would normally expect *more* intrusive forms

[73] Craig (n 46) 290.
[74] *Teoh* (n 17) 314 (McHugh J).

of relief to be accompanied by *more* demanding evidentiary requirements'.[75] The objection here seems to be that in the absence of knowledge and reliance there is little or no imperative for judicial intervention because the individual's dignity and autonomy interests have not been compromised by a broken promise. I suggest, however, that neither knowledge nor reliance should be required.

To begin with, good administration supports a requirement that policies and decisions should be departed from only where there is a 'reasoned justification'[76] to do so. Personal knowledge of and reliance on a policy or decision is not a prerequisite:[77]

> When a legitimate expectation arises from an agency's past practice, or non-statutory procedural guidelines, it serves to preclude procedural arbitrariness, not the actual expectation of the individual who may have been unaware of its existence.[78]

Although rule-of-law concerns about the non-performance of personalised promises to individuals are absent, good administration points to the desirability of judicial enforcement even where there has been no knowledge or reliance.

But, of course, the force of knowledge and reliance in a particular case may vary. For instance, an individual whose legitimate expectation is based on 'a policy which itself is liable to change' cannot expect the expectation 'to survive a policy change'.[79] That a policy may be changed at some point in the future is inherent in the policy's very existence:[80] it follows inexorably from the decision-maker's appointed role as the regulator of the portion of the administrative state assigned to it by the legislature that it should be able to change policy to suit changed circumstances. Knowledge of and reliance on a policy does not generate expectations as forceful as those engendered by personalised representations, for the rule of law concerns are less weighty.[81] Indeed, good administration counsels against imposing a high threshold for policy changes, for fear of 'ossify[ing] administrative policy'.[82]

[75] *Mount Sinai Hospital* (n 23) [31].

[76] *Nadarajah* (n 22) [38] (Laws LJ).

[77] See *Begbie* (n 26) [101] (Sedley LJ): 'in cases where the government has made known how it intends to exercise powers which affect the public at large it may be held to its word irrespective of whether the applicant had been relying specifically upon it'. Indeed, in the foundational case of *Ng Yuen Shiu* (n 1) 635, the individual concerned had no personal knowledge of the announcement that gave rise to his enforceable legitimate expectation of a procedural protection (although he later learned of it). See also *Heatley v Tasmanian Racing and Gaming Commission* (1977) 14 ALR 519; *Keogh v Criminal Assets Bureau* [2004] 2 IR 159; *Teoh* (n 17).

[78] *Apotex* (n 25) [122] (Evans JA). See similarly, *Haoucher* (n 17) 669–70 (Toohey J).

[79] *Hamble Fisheries* (n 14) 729 (Sedley LJ).

[80] See eg *Thamotharem v Canada (Minister of Citizenship and Immigration)* [2008] 1 FCR 385.

[81] See also Schønberg (n 50), 17: 'Reliance is only relevant in so far as it strengthens the Rule of Law justification for protection of legitimate expectations'.

[82] Craig (n 33) 90.

A better way of capturing the greater moral force of knowledge and reliance—which comes from the rule of law's concern for dignity and autonomy—is to place more exacting requirements on the decision-maker who goes back on her word than on the decision-maker who changes a generally applicable policy:

> The nature and clarity of the promise or practice and of the legitimate expectation which it engenders combine with the circumstances and reasons giving rise to the proposed change of practice as factors which have to be weighed together in order to consider whether and how far justice requires that the public authority should be held to a position consistent with the promise or practice.[83]

Once this point is appreciated, the force of Binnie J's reason for rejecting substantive legitimate expectations is greatly reduced: although the evidentiary requirements are lower, the burden on the decision-maker who wishes to change a policy will be lighter than the burden on the decision-maker who wishes to resile from a personalised representation. Less exacting requirements for policy changes protect good administration by holding administrative decision-makers to their policies until such time as these are revised, reflect the relative lack of rule-of-law imperatives for heightened protection and preserve a higher degree of decisional autonomy for the legislature's chosen regulator. Conversely, where a personalised promise places a heavier justificatory burden on a decision-maker, this is offset by the more demanding evidentiary requirements placed on the applicant and, in any event, does not fatally compromise the decision-maker's authority to resile from a promise in appropriate circumstances, as the decision to do so can, in principle, be justified.

In summary, the absence of rule-of-law concerns does not mean legitimate expectations can never be enforced without proof of knowledge and reliance, because the value of good administration may also be engaged and respect for democracy and separation of powers ensures that administrative decision-makers' freedom to change policy in appropriate circumstances is preserved.

Substantive Enforcement of Legitimate Expectations

Enforcement of procedural legitimate expectations does no violence to democracy or separation of powers by comparison to substantive enforcement of legitimate expectations. Judges generally 'feel far more comfortable telling public bodies what procedures they should follow rather than what outcomes they should procure'.[84] As Laws LJ explained in *R (Niazi) v Secretary of State for the Home Department*, in this sort of case 'the

[83] *R (Bancoult) v Secretary of State for Foreign and Commonwealth Affairs* [2009] AC 453 [182] (Lord Mance).

[84] Steele (n 4) 300. See similarly, Elliott (n 2) 288.

unfairness or abuse of power which the court will check is not merely to do with how harshly the decision bears upon any individual'.[85]

However, substantive enforcement of legitimate expectations by courts is more controversial. At times, courts and commentators have claimed that democracy and separation of powers concerns have such force as to defeat substantive legitimate expectations outright:

> A significant weakness in the analysis of … academic supporters of substantive legitimate expectations is the failure to acknowledge that the doctrine clearly narrows the freedom of the executive government and, more importantly, the effect that this may have on the relationship between the judicial and executive arms of government.[86]

As an Australian judge put it, if legitimate expectations could be given substantive force, 'the notion would become a stalking horse for excesses of judicial power', liable 'to set courts adrift on a featureless sea of pragmatism'.[87]

But this represents a drastic denial of the agency of individuals who respond to and rely on promises made by officials. It would give individualised representations designed to induce action or expectation no effect whatsoever. It would permit governments to make cynical promises. Officials could instrumentalise the citizenry, treating individuals as means rather than ends. Treating reliance by individuals on official representations as entirely irrelevant to the lawful exercise of state power does great violence to the rule of law by making it more difficult for individuals to plan their affairs: 'to break a promise is to directly interfere with the liberty of the person or persons who have relied on that promise'.[88]

In addition, permitting separation of powers and democracy to predominate would prevent courts from drawing distinctions between different types of expectation. On this approach, all engagements are equally unenforceable: the engagement made in a general policy document is treated no differently from the solemn promise with 'the character of a contract'[89] offered to a citizen. Ruling out substantive enforcement of legitimate expectations altogether would deprive jurists of the opportunity to hone judicial doctrine so as to make appropriate distinctions between different types of expectation. It discounts completely the 'greater moral force' of individualised representations relative to general policies.[90] To treat policies as 'a type of promise…distorts the nature of policies and promises'; only the latter 'creates a duty or obligation' to someone to act in some way.[91]

[85] *Niazi* (n 3) [30].
[86] Groves (n 62) 492.
[87] *Quin* (n 18) 38–39 (Brennan J).
[88] Watson (n 7) 641.
[89] *Coughlan* (n 20) [59].
[90] Steele (n 4) 302–03.
[91] Ahmed and Perry (n 8) 66.

There is a better way of harmonising the values in such a way that the decision-maker's primacy in policy matters is respected and courts respect the limits of the judicial role. Concerns for democracy and separation of powers need not necessarily exclude the possibility of substantive judicial protection of legitimate expectations. The goal of substantively protecting legitimate expectations:

> is not to impede executive activity but to *reconcile* its continuing need to initiate or respond to change with the legitimate interests or expectations of citizens or strangers who have relied, and have been justified in relying, on a current policy or an extant promise (emphasis added).[92]

Indeed, procedural protection will often not be enough. For example, 'a hearing will be of no value to the applicant if the authority in making its decision is free to ignore the legitimate expectations it has previously aroused'.[93]

Recognising substantive legitimate expectations does not place an insurmountable barrier before an administrative decision-maker who wishes to resile from a promise or change a policy; it simply imposes an additional constraint in the form of a reason for the final decision that takes adequate account of the initial promise or policy: 'It recognises the primacy of the public authority both in administration and in policy development but it insists, where these functions come into tension, upon the adjudicative role of the court to ensure fairness to the individual'.[94]

Moreover, this additional constraint can be tailored to the strength of the expectation created by official action because '[t]he facts of the case, viewed always in their statutory context, will steer the court to a more or less intrusive quality of review'.[95] Where there has been an individualised representation on which there has been detrimental reliance, the burden on a decision-maker who refuses to give effect to the representation will be greater than where an individual seeks to rely on the continuance in force of an official policy that the decision-maker wishes to adapt to new circumstances. So, in *Coughlan*, where residents of a home for severely disabled patients were promised a 'home for life' that the public authority subsequently sought to close, it was appropriate to require '[s]trong reasons … to justify resiling from [the] promise'.[96]

In at least one respect, however, the Court of Appeal in *Coughlan* went too far by asserting 'that it is for the *court* to decide in an arguable case whether such a judgment, albeit properly arrived at, strikes a proper balance

[92] *Coughlan* (n 20) [65].
[93] Forsyth (n 50) 253.
[94] *Coughlan* (n 20) [70].
[95] *Begbie* (n 26) [80] (Laws LJ).
[96] *Coughlan* (n 20) [86]. On the appropriate modes of judicial review of these determinations, see especially J Boughey's contribution to this volume, as well as that of M Elliott.

between the public and the private interest' (emphasis added);[97] it adjudged the authority at fault for having 'failed to weigh the conflicting interests *correctly*' (emphasis added).[98] But this is to substitute judicial judgment on the merits for the considered wisdom of the administrative decision-maker identified by the legislature.[99] It is not for courts to determine 'fairness of outcome' or the 'propriety' of the balancing exercise undertaken by the decision-maker.[100] Separation of powers suggests that the reviewing court has a distinct role; that of providing a check on the administration by ensuring that executive action remains within acceptable boundaries:[101] 'Further they should not go'.[102]

On a pluralist approach, some effect must be given to democratic and separation of powers principles. A legitimate expectation should not be treated as sacrosanct; rather, the relative strength of the expectation would require more or less by way of explanation from the decision-maker seeking to resile from its previous representation.[103] So, 'where the representation relied on amounts to an unambiguous promise; where there is detrimental reliance; where the promise is made to an individual or specific group; these are instances where denial of the expectation is likely to be harder to justify…'[104] Conversely, an applicant will face a 'steeper climb' in cases where a policy change adopted in the public interest has a general effect on a diffuse group of individuals.[105] In addition, courts should generally be less willing to constrain administrative decision-making in the 'macro-political' realm.[106] Common law judges, who have little or no specialised knowledge of public administration, are poorly placed to pull on the spider web of carefully balanced interests woven by an expert decision-maker as it might unravel in an unfortunate way.[107]

What ultimately should matter is whether the justification provided by the decision-maker is reasonable or rational (or, perhaps, proportionate), not whether the court would prefer to have struck the balance differently. This assessment of reasonableness or rationality (or proportionality) must be performed (and the remedial consequences determined) in light of the

[97] *Coughlan* (n 20) [52].
[98] *Coughlan* (n 20) [89]. See similarly *Niazi* (n 3) [35].
[99] P Sales and K Steyn, 'Legitimate Expectations in English Public Law: An Analysis' (2004) *Public Law* 564, 590–1; Groves (n 62) 480.
[100] *Coughlan* (n 20) [71]. See also the formulation at [82].
[101] Quite what the boundaries of acceptability might be will vary from jurisdiction to jurisdiction, from Canada's increasingly all-encompassing reasonableness approach to the grounds of review approach familiar in other Commonwealth jurisdictions.
[102] C Harlow and R Rawlings, *Law and Administration*, 3rd edn (Cambridge University Press, 2009) 232.
[103] *Bibi* (n 30) [39].
[104] *Nadarajah* (n 22) [69] (Laws LJ).
[105] *Nadarajah* (n 22) [69].
[106] *Nadarajah* (n 22) [69]. See also *Quin* (n 18) 18–19 (Mason CJ).
[107] See generally P Daly, *A Theory of Deference in Administrative Law: Basis, Application and Scope* (Cambridge University Press, 2012) Chapter 3.

general principles of judicial review operative in a particular jurisdiction. In this way, a pluralist approach allows courts to take account of rule-of-law and good-administration concerns whilst respecting the distinct role of administrative decision-makers and the mandates confided to them by legislatures.

Ultra Vires Representations

The conventional view is that *ultra vires* representations can never give rise to legitimate expectations, which can only be 'founded on a lawful representation or practice'.[108] Unlawful representations cannot create enforceable rights, interests or obligations, as the Supreme Court of Canada recently explained in respect of a local authority that had long permitted a company to operate a commercial parking lot in violation of a zoning provision: 'The authorisation by a municipal employee or elected official of a use that violates a provision of a by-law cannot create rights or oust the applicable standards set out in the by-law'.[109]

Here, the democratic principle, as expressed through statutory language, dominates. In particular, courts have concluded, administrative bodies should not be able to expand the limits of their statutory mandates by making representations that are beyond their powers:[110]

> Any doctrine of estoppel in that context would threaten to undermine the doctrine of ultra vires by enabling public authorities to extend their powers both *de facto* and *de jure* by making representations beyond power, which they would then be estopped from denying.[111]

It has even been suggested that the rule of law could be threatened by the enforcement of *ultra vires* representations: 'When the Government is unable to enforce the law because the conduct of its agents has given rise to an estoppel, the interest of the citizenry as a whole in obedience to the rule of law is undermined.'[112]

Nonetheless, there are examples of judicial concern about unfairness created by non-enforcement of *ultra vires* representations. Thus in *Stretch v West Dorset District Council*, Peter Gibson LJ had 'considerable sympathy' with the individual defeated by a local authority's ability to assert the illegality of its own stance (an 'unattractive' proposition),[113] and in *Rowland v Environment Agency*, May LJ concluded that there

[108] *Rowland v Environment Agency* [2005] Ch 1 [81] (Peter Gibson LJ).
[109] *Immeubles Jacques Robitaille inc v Québec (City)* [2014] 1 SCR 784 [25] (Wagner J).
[110] See, eg, *Re Green Dale Building Co* [1977] IR 256.
[111] *Kurtovic* (n 54) 208 (Gummow J).
[112] *Heckler v Community Health Services* 467 US 51 (1984) 60 (Stevens J).
[113] *Stretch v West Dorset District Council* [1998] 3 EGLR 62, 67.

was no legitimate expectation with 'undisguised reluctance' at the 'unjust' outcome.[114]

However, a blanket rule of non-enforcement of *ultra vires* representations clashes with the rule of law and good administration values for the protection of legitimate expectations. Great unfairness may be done to an individual who relied on an official representation whose validity he or she had no reason to doubt. Accordingly, it is doubtful that the rule of law is better protected by requiring losses caused by *ultra vires* representations to fall invariably on individuals. A more nuanced approach, which permitted enforcement in some circumstances, would do less violence to the values underpinning legitimate expectations

Good administration may also be imperilled. Requiring individuals to interrogate administrative officials at length about the scope of the latter's authority, or engaging a legal representative to do so, is not a recipe for the efficient use of scarce resources. Indeed, individuals may be dissuaded from dealing honestly—or at all—with administrative decision-makers if they cannot trust the words of officials. And even though one might want to guard against the deliberate expansion of powers accorded by the legislature, causing the loss to fall on an individual is 'misdirected':

> In the rare cases of intentional extension of power it strikes at the wrong person, the innocent representee, rather than the public officials. In the more common case of careless, or inadvertent, extension of power any deterrent effect upon the public officer will be minimal.[115]

Moreover, the democratic principle is not necessarily compromised by the enforcement of all types of *ultra vires* representations. An Irish judge has suggested that there might be some cases where there may be 'greater scope' to enforce an *ultra vires* representation which involves 'something more marginal than the essence of the [administrative] action which is impugned—for example, its scope or extent rather than its nature...'[116] One might add that the fact that an official would have made the representation in the first place surely indicates—absent proof of malice or bad faith—that the official believed the representation furthered the administrative decision-maker's statutory mandate. Indeed, in jurisdictions that use a holistic reasonableness test for invalidity rather than the 'all-or-nothing' *ultra vires* principle, a blanket rule against the enforcement of *ultra vires* representations is particularly inapt, for there is a good chance that a statutory provision will ultimately be interpreted in conformity with the stated views of the administrative decision-maker.[117]

114 *Rowland* (n 108) [100].

115 P Craig, 'Representations by Public Bodies' (1977) 93 *Law Quarterly Review* 398, 420.

116 *Ashbourne Holdings v An Bord Pleanàla* [2003] 2 IR 114, 137 (Hardiman J).

117 See eg *McLean v British Columbia (Securities Commission)* [2013] 3 SCR 895 [38] (Moldaver J).

Professor Craig has advocated a balancing test: 'Where the harm to the public would be minimal compared to that of the individual, there is good reason to consider allowing the representation to bind',[118] by focusing on 'more sensitive ways of reconciling the needs of…innocent individuals and the requirements of the public body'.[119] A pluralist approach leads to a similar conclusion. Enforcement of *ultra vires* representations should not be barred outright. Rather, in principle, courts should examine the interplay of rule of law, good administration and democratic considerations to determine whether an *ultra vires* representation should be enforced, aware that in some cases '[t]he public interest may be better served by honouring [the] undertaking than by breaking it'.[120] That is, by acknowledging 'that legality is not absolute, but rather an important *aspect of* the legal system, the consequences of which are subject to important countervailing considerations'.[121] Due to democracy and separation of powers concerns, courts should not engage in an independent balancing exercise that pays no heed to the decisional autonomy of the administrative decision-maker under review, but as in the area of substantive enforcement of legitimate expectations, should assess the rationality or reasonableness (or, perhaps, proportionality)[122] of any failure to give effect to an official representation, unencumbered by a dogmatic refusal to countenance the enforcement of *ultra vires* representations.

CONCLUSION

In response to the crescendo of criticism of the incoherence of the common law doctrine of legitimate expectations, I have outlined a pluralist approach. My starting point was to recognise that diverse values have been identified in the cases. On the one hand, good administration and the rule of law have been invoked to support judicial enforcement of legitimate expectations. On the other hand, democracy and separation of powers have been relied upon by judges fearful that enforcement of legitimate expectations will cause them to trespass in the political domain.

Each of these values is important, but evidently there is tension between them. Nevertheless, by following a pluralist approach the values can be reconciled. My analysis of three difficult doctrinal issues—knowledge and reliance, substantive legitimate expectations and *ultra vires* representations—demonstrates the utility of a pluralist approach in reconciling good administration, the rule of law, democracy and separation of powers so as to achieve coherence in the common law doctrine of legitimate expectations.

118 Craig (n 15) 711.
119 Craig (n 33) 89.
120 *Liverpool Taxi Fleet Operators' Association* (n 58) 308 (Lord Denning MR).
121 Schønberg (n 50) 104.
122 I again refer the reader to the contributions of J Boughey and M Elliott in this volume.

6

Proportionality and Legitimate Expectations

JANINA BOUGHEY

INTRODUCTION

PROPORTIONALITY SEEMS TO have become the *de rigueur* balancing test in public law,[1] even within common law jurisdictions where there was initially a great deal of mistrust of the principle.[2] The suggestion that proportionality may provide a useful standard of review and guiding principle for the legitimate expectations doctrine should, therefore, come as no great surprise.[3] It is less surprising still, when one considers that the European Court of Justice's approach to legitimate expectations frequently involves a balancing test that looks very much like proportionality, though the Court itself has been reluctant to embrace that label.[4] Laws LJ suggested that proportionality would provide much needed guidance and structure to

[1] There are several recent books dedicated to the principle, including: Grant Huscroft, Bradley W Miller and Grégoire Webber (eds), *Proportionality and the Rule of Law: Rights, Justification, Reasoning* (Cambridge University Press, 2014); Hanna Wilberg and Mark Elliott (eds), *The Scope and Intensity of Substantive Review: Traversing Taggart's Rainbow* (Hart Publishing, 2015).

[2] Proportionality is now the accepted balancing standard (or forms part of such a standard) in human rights cases in the UK, Canada and New Zealand. For a brief overview see: Harry Woolf et al, *De Smith's Judicial Review*, 7th edn (Sweet & Maxwell, 2013) 627–33, 643–56. Even Australia, which was earlier described as an 'outlier' with respect to its rejection of proportionality, has recently given tentative indications of jumping on the proportionality bandwagon: see Janina Boughey, 'The Reasonableness of Proportionality in the Australian Administrative Law Context' (2015) 43 *Federal Law Review* 59. For early scepticism see: Sophie Boyron, 'Proportionality in English Administrative Law: A Faulty Translation?' (1992) 12 *Oxford Journal of Legal Studies* 237; Lord Irvine, 'Judges and Decision-Makers: The Theory and Practice of *Wednesbury* Review [1996] *Public Law* 59, 63–65.

[3] See, eg, *R (Abdi & Nadarajah) v Secretary of State for the Home Department* [2005] EWCA Civ 1363 [69] (Laws LJ) ('*Nadarajah*'); Paul Craig, *Administrative Law*, 7th edn (Sweet & Maxwell, 2012) 692; Iain Steele, 'Substantive Legitimate Expectations: Striking the Right Balance?' (2005) 121 *Law Quarterly Review* 300, 318.

[4] Paul Craig, *EU Administrative Law*, 2nd edn (Oxford University Press, 2012) 585–87.

English law on legitimate expectations in *R (Abdi & Nadarajah) v Secretary of State for the Home Department*.[5] He proposed that a proportionality test could be applied to both common law variants of legitimate expectation: procedural and substantive. As one would expect, the suggestion has subsequently been enthusiastically welcomed by some[6] and criticised by others.[7] It also contradicts earlier authority, endorsed by the House of Lords—albeit authority which is particularly confused on the issue of what standard of review should apply to legitimate expectations.[8] The aim of this chapter is to examine the balancing tests that have been, and could be, applied in legitimate expectations cases, to assess whether proportionality would provide useful guidance to either all, or some, aspects of the legitimate expectations doctrine as it applies in common law jurisdictions.

The first section outlines the various ways in which expectations are protected under common law. Other chapters in this book cover this ground in much more detail, so only a brief discussion is required here.[9] Nevertheless, it is necessary to sketch the main applications of the principle here in order to examine the balancing tests and factors that are relevant in the different contexts in which legitimate expectations are protected. The second section considers judicial attempts to bring conceptual unity to legitimate expectations, and the arguments that have been made as to the role proportionality should play. It argues that those who have proposed that proportionality should be the balancing methodology in legitimate expectation cases did so at a time when proportionality was less developed, and may have been seen as a more flexible principle than it has become, and drew on the European experience in which proportionality is indeed more flexible than it now is in the UK. The third section then assesses the question of whether proportionality is suitable in all, or some category of, expectation cases in light of the way in which proportionality is now understood under English law. That analysis shows that while the same balancing concerns that proportionality seeks to address are also present in many legitimate expectation cases—across all categories—proportionality, as it is presently applied in UK public law, is not an appropriate balancing test in all, or even most, legitimate expectation cases under common law.

[5] *Nadarajah* (n 3) [69] (Laws LJ).

[6] See, eg, Craig (n 3) 692.

[7] See, eg, Philip Sales, 'Legitimate Expectations' [2006] *Judicial Review* 186; Mark Elliott, 'Legitimate Expectations and the Search for Principle: Reflections on *Abdi & Nadarajah*' [2006] *Judicial Review* 281.

[8] *R v North and East Devon Health Authority; ex parte Coughlan* [2001] QB 213, 241–47; *R v Secretary of State for the Home Department; ex parte Mullan* [2005] 1 AC 1, 48 [60] (Lord Steyn).

[9] Each of the chapters in Part II discuss the protection given to expectations in a different common law jurisdiction.

PROTECTING 'LEGITIMATE EXPECTATIONS' UNDER COMMON LAW

The phrase 'legitimate expectations' is frequently used as if it were a single, unified principle. This may be the case in continental legal systems and under EU law, where the role of courts in reviewing administrative action is not rooted in the idea that they are giving effect to the intentions of a sovereign parliament.[10] However, under common law systems where the principles of judicial review of administrative action developed with precisely that remit, the idea of giving legal protection to expectations derived from non-legal sources has no natural place. Within common law jurisdictions the term 'legitimate expectation' developed, and continues to be used, in a variety of contexts, and there remains considerable uncertainty and confusion about its place, value and legitimacy.[11]

Expectations and Procedural Fairness

The term was initially used by Lord Denning to extend the range of decisions to which natural justice applied to include situations in which a person had no legal right to a benefit, but had an expectation of maintaining a benefit that they had already been granted.[12] It was then expanded to cases where a person who held a benefit sought to have it renewed on expiry.[13] In these contexts the doctrine did not present too great a challenge to orthodox common law thinking about the border between judicial and administrative power. All it did was expand the types of interests deemed worthy of procedural protection. It is now generally accepted that procedural fairness applies to most decisions that adversely affect individuals, regardless of the classification given to the interest affected—legal right, interest, benefit, privilege, expectation, revocation, etc. Thus, legitimate expectation is no

[10] See Craig (n 4) Ch 18.

[11] These issues are well-traversed. See, eg, Christopher Forsyth, 'The Provenance and Protection of Legitimate Expectations' (1988) 47 *Cambridge Law Journal* 238, 239–40; Matthew Groves, 'Substantive Legitimate Expectations in Australian Administrative Law' (2008) 32 *Melbourne University Law Review* 470; Philip Sales and Karen Steyn, 'Legitimate Expectations in English Public Law: An Analysis' [2004] *Public Law* 564, 567–70; Richard Moules, *Actions Against Public Officials: Legitimate Expectations, Misstatements and Misconduct* (Sweet & Maxwell, 2009) 53.

[12] *Schmidt v Secretary of State for Home Affairs* [1969] 2 Ch 149, 171 (Lord Denning); *Salemi v MacKellar (No 2)* (1977) 137 CLR 396, 404 (Barwick CJ); *Attorney General of Hong Kong v Ng Yuen Shiu* [1983] 2 AC 629, 636. See also the detailed analysis of the difficulties with, and utility of the doctrine in: Pamela Tate, 'The Coherence of "Legitimate Expectations" and the Foundations of Natural Justice' (1988) 14 *Monash Law Review* 15.

[13] *FAI Insurances v Winneke* (1982) 151 CLR 342, 348 (Gibbs CJ), 361 (Mason J); *Council of Civil Service Unions v Minister for the Civil Service* [1985] AC 374, 408–09 (Lord Diplock); *Kioa v West* (1985) 159 CLR 550, 583 (Mason J).

longer needed to play a role in expanding the range of decisions to which fairness attaches under common law.[14]

The concept soon came to be applied for a different purpose within the context of procedural fairness: to determine the content of fairness. For instance, in the Australian case of *Haoucher v Minister for Immigration and Ethnic Affairs*, there was no question that the applicant, who was the subject of a deportation order, was entitled to procedural fairness.[15] Instead, the question was whether he had received it in a context in which the Minister departed from a published policy of following the Administrative Appeals Tribunal's advice absent exceptional circumstances. According to the majority of the High Court, the policy gave Haoucher a legitimate expectation of being given a further hearing if the Minister was considering departing from the Tribunal's recommendation, and the absence of such a hearing meant that the decision was unlawful. There was no balancing involved, and no questioning of whether the Minister had a good reason for departing from the policy. Once those in the majority determined that Haoucher was entitled to be heard by the Minister and had not been, that was the end of the matter.[16]

There are actually at least two distinct ways in which legitimate expectations can affect the content of procedural fairness, though the arguments made with respect to the two frequently overlap. The first is where a policy or promise has induced an expectation that a government official will exercise their discretion in a particular way. This has been found, in many cases, to give rise to a right to be heard on the specific issue of the policy or promise that induced the expectation, before an adverse decision is made. *Haoucher*'s case is one example. Another is the famous (or perhaps infamous) Australian case of *Minister for Immigration and Ethnic Affairs v Teoh*.[17] A more recent example is found in *R (Bibi) v Newham London Borough Council* in which the Court of Appeal held that the Council was ordered to consider a family's application for 'suitable housing on the basis that they have a legitimate expectation that they will be provided by the

[14] See Woolf et al (n 2) 385–91; *Attorney-General (NSW) v Quin* (1990) 170 CLR 1, 40 (Brennan J); Mark Aronson, 'Private Bodies, Public Power and Soft Law in the High Court' (2007) 35 *Federal Law Review* 1, 5–6; Mark Aronson and Matthew Groves, *Judicial Review of Administrative Action*, 5th edn (Lawbook Co, 2013) 418–19; Grant Huscroft, 'From Natural Justice to Fairness: Thresholds, Content, and the Role of Judicial Review' in Colleen Flood and Lorne Sossin (eds), *Administrative Law in Context*, 2nd edn (Emond Montgomery, 2012) 153–54. Though note the contrasting view of Sir Anthony Mason, who argues that legitimate expectations may still usefully add to the scope of procedural fairness, citing *Winneke* (n 13) as an example: 'Procedural Fairness: Its Development and Continuing Role of Legitimate Expectation' (2005) 12 *Australian Journal of Administrative Law* 103, 106.

[15] *Haoucher v Minister for Immigration and Ethnic Affairs* (1990) 169 CLR 648 ('*Haoucher*'). The Court discussed these two distinct usages of the doctrine at: 658–59 (Dawson J), 672 (Gaudron J).

[16] Ibid, 654–55 (Deane J); 670–71 (Toohey J), 684–85 (McHugh J).

[17] *Minister for Immigration and Ethnic Affairs v Teoh* (1995) 183 CLR 273 ('*Teoh*').

authority with suitable accommodation on a secure tenancy'.[18] In all of these cases the expectation of the applicant was substantive: that the tribunal's recommendation be followed; that Australia act in accordance with its international obligations; and that the family be given a permanent home. However, the protection courts gave to the expectations was procedural in each case. This approach essentially treats a legitimate expectation as a mandatory relevant consideration, though it is one which has been created by events completely external to the empowering statute. Thus, it could not fit within the traditional understanding of the considerations grounds.

The second way in which legitimate expectations may affect the content of fairness is when the expectation itself is one of the processes to be followed. A good example of legitimate expectations being used in this way is found in *Attorney-General of Hong Kong v Ng Yuen Shiu*.[19] The Government of Hong Kong implemented a new policy of deporting all illegal entrants, but promised that those Chinese nationals who had entered via Macau would be interviewed and each case 'treated on its merits' before a deportation decision was made. The applicant, who fell within that class, was interviewed by an immigration official before a removal order was made. He contended that the interview was inadequate and had not met his expectation, induced by the Government's announcement, of being allowed to provide arguments as to why he should not be deported. The Privy Council accepted, without deciding, that illegal migrants may not generally be entitled to procedural fairness prior to a deportation decision being made.[20] However, the promise made to the Chinese nationals was held to give rise to a duty to follow the promised procedure and do so fairly.[21] The Court explained that its justification for holding the Government to its word in this situation

> is primarily that, when a public authority has promised to follow a certain procedure, it is in the interest of good administration that it should act fairly and should implement its promise, so long as implementation does not interfere with its statutory duty.[22]

Again, there was no question of a need to balance the impact of departing from the policy on the applicant, against the public interest. The only reason for departure that the Court envisaged was where the promise would 'interfere with its statutory duty'. It is hard to imagine a situation in which the application of the hearing rule would conflict with the statutory duty of a decision-maker, absent express statutory provisions barring certain matters from being considered or imposing strict time limits. Indeed, public authorities seem rarely, if ever, to argue that there is some overriding public interest

[18] *R (Bibi) v Newham London Borough Council* [2002] 1 WLR 237, 252 ('*Bibi*').
[19] *Ng Yuen Shiu* (n 12).
[20] *Ng Yuen Shiu* (n 12) 636.
[21] *Ng Yuen Shiu* (n 12) 638.
[22] *Ng Yuen Shiu* (n 12) 638.

that necessitates the defeat of a person's expectation as to process. Perhaps this is simply because taking an expectation into account and allowing a person to comment on why their expectation should not be defeated is not a terribly onerous requirement, so it is unlikely that there will be a compelling reason for a public authority not to fulfil the requirement. There seem to be few arguments that a public authority could present as to why they could not have considered a policy, promise or practice in exercising their discretion: the only obvious ones relate to the need for timely and efficient decision-making. Nevertheless, by giving protection to expectations through the procedural fairness doctrine, if any such arguments were raised, a court would likely simply weigh them into its ordinary assessment of what is fair in all of the circumstances.[23]

These variants of the legitimate expectation doctrine—involving the doctrine informing the content of fairness—are the only ways in which expectations are protected in Australia and Canada, to the extent that the doctrine remains relevant at all in those jurisdictions.[24] The highest courts in both countries have renounced the idea of giving substantive protection to expectations, on the basis that doing so involves judicial incursion into exercises of executive power.[25] It should be noted, however, that the Supreme Court of Canada has found other ways of protecting expectations induced by government promises in extreme cases, without resort to the legitimate expectations concept.[26] The highest courts in New Zealand and South Africa have neither expressly rejected nor accepted the notion of substantively protecting expectations.[27]

[23] It is not common to describe this assessment as involving 'balancing', though it clearly does in many circumstances: see John Griffiths, 'Procedural Fairness' in PD Finn (ed), *Essays on Law and Government, Volume 2: The Citizen and the State in the Courts* (LBC Information Services, 1996) 188, 198–200. The Federal Court of Australia made this clear in the recent case of *WZARH v Minister for Immigration and Border Protection* (2014) 230 FCR 130, which is discussed in the third section of this chapter.

[24] See *Baker v Canada (Minister for Citizenship and Immigration)* [1999] 2 SCR 817, 839–40 [26]. (L'Heureux-Dubé J for Gonthier, McLachlin, Bastarache and Binnie JJ); *Canada (Attorney General) v Mavi* [2011] 2 SCR 504, 534–36 [68]–[72]; *Quin* (n 14), 16–18, 23 (Mason CJ), 38–41 (Brennan J), 58–60 (Dawson J); *Re Minister for Immigration and Multicultural and Indigenous Affairs; ex parte Lam* (2003) 214 CLR 1, 24–25 [76] (McHugh and Gummow JJ); *Minister for Immigration and Border Protection v WZARH* (2015) 256 CLR 326, 335–36 [28]–[32] (Kiefel, Bell and Keane JJ), 343 [61] (Gageler and Gordon JJ).

[25] See *Mount Sinai Hospital Centre v Quebec (Minister of Health and Social Services)* [2001] 2 SCR 281, 317 [62]–[63] (Binnie J for McLachlin CJ); *Lam* (n 24)24–5 [76] (McHugh and Gummow JJ).

[26] See, eg, *Mount Sinai Hospital Centre v Quebec* (n 25) 336–37 [105] (Bastarache J for L'Heureux-Dubé, Gonthier, Iacobucci and Major JJ) (a majority of the Supreme Court found that the Minister was not able to renege on his promise to alter a Hospital's permit if it relocated to Montreal once the Hospital had in fact relocated, because his discretion had been exhausted: he was *functus officio*).

[27] See *Air New Zealand Ltd v Wellington International Airport Ltd* [2009] NZAR 138, 150–51 [52]–[62]; *Duncan v Minister of Environmental Affairs and Tourism* 2010 (6) SA 374 (SCA) [13]–[14]. See also chapters 9 and 8 by Philip Joseph and Cora Hoexter in this volume respectively.

Substantively Protecting Expectations

The UK is, thus far, alone amongst English-speaking common law jurisdictions in having afforded substantive protection to expectations induced by government policies, promises or practices. The Court of Appeal famously gave substantive protection to an expectation in *R v North and East Devon Health Authority; ex parte Coughlan*,[28] after several decades of debate as to whether courts should hold public authorities to their promises, either via estoppel, or some other method.[29] However, discussions about the appropriate standard of review to apply in cases where courts were contemplating holding public authorities to the substance of their promises or policies began well before *Coughlan*. There were several cases during the 1980s and 90s involving questions about whether there were any non-statutory limits on the Government's discretion to change its policies, and if so, what test should apply.

In two cases involving changes to prison leave policies, *In re Findlay*[30] and *R v Home Secretary; ex parte Hargreaves*,[31] the House of Lords and Court of Appeal respectively suggested that the *Wednesbury* standard should be applied to assess whether the change in policy was lawful.[32] In the latter, prisoners were given a notice from prison authorities setting out the leave policy and at the same time asked to sign a compact which linked good behaviour with eligibility under the leave policy. The policy was later changed. The Court held that the notice and compact did not give rise to a legitimate expectation, and that a prisoner's only expectation was that their case would be examined on its merits in light of whatever policy applied at that time.[33] This meant that the case could be accommodated within the framework of procedural expectations, and the only question for the Court was whether the process had been fair in the circumstances. However, the Court also considered, as a separate question, whether the new policy was

[28] *R v North and East Devon Health Authority; ex parte Coughlan* [2001] 3 QB 213, ('*Coughlan*').

[29] Lord Denning attempted to introduce principles that would enable individuals to hold government to its word into English law in 1949, via a version of estoppel: *Robertson v Minister of Pensions* [1949] 1 KB 227. The House of Lords overturned that position two years later in *Howell v Falmouth Boat Construction Co* [1951] AC 837 and decades of debate proceeded. UK courts had then begun contemplating the possibility of substantively enforcing government promises in the late-1980s: *R v Secretary of State for the Home Department; ex parte Ruddock* [1987] 1 WLR 1482, 1497; *R v IRC; ex parte MFK Underwriting Agencies Ltd* [1990] 1 WLR 1545, 1566. For an account see: Greg Weeks, 'Holding Government to its Word: Expectation, Estoppels and Substantive Unfairness in Administrative Law' in Matthew Groves (ed), *Modern Administrative Law in Australia: Concepts and Context* (Cambridge University Press, 2014) 224, 230–38.

[30] *In re Findlay* [1985] AC 318 ('*Findlay*').

[31] *R v Home Secretary; ex parte Hargreaves* [1997] 1 WLR 906 ('*Hargreaves*').

[32] *Findlay* (n 30) 334 (Lord Scarman, with whom the other justices agreed); *Hargreaves* (n 31), 921 (Hirst LJ, with whom the other justices agreed).

[33] *Hargreaves* (n 31) 918–19 (Hirst LJ), 925 (Pill LJ).

lawful, applying the *Wednesbury* standard and stating that '[o]n matters of substance (as contrasted with procedure) *Wednesbury* provides the correct test'.[34]

A quite different approach to a change in policy was taken by Sedley J in *R v Ministry of Agriculture, Fisheries and Food; ex parte Hamble (Offshore) Fisheries Ltd*.[35] Drawing extensively on decisions of the European Court, Sedley J held that in changing its policies, government will misuse its power if it acts 'unfairly or unjustly towards a private citizen when there is no overriding public interest to warrant it'.[36] He stated that a court's assessment of fairness and justice in this context must involve the balancing of the 'expectations induced by government and of policy considerations which militate against their fulfilment', and said that this balancing went beyond the courts' usual rationality test.[37] In doing so, Sedley J also referred to earlier judgments of Lord Denning which had attempted to introduce estoppel into public law.[38]

In *Hargreaves*, Hirst LJ labelled Sedley J's approach as heretical.[39] Yet, only four years later, it was accepted in *Coughlan*—albeit in an arguably different context in which a specific promise was broken, rather than policy simply being changed.[40] The judgment in *Coughlan* is well-known and traversed in detail elsewhere in this collection.[41] Only a few points about the case need be made here. The first is that the decision does not sit within the procedural fairness concept as traditionally understood, to protect the integrity of the decision-making process. Extensive public consultations preceded the decision to close Mardon House, and Miss Coughlan had made submissions on the proposal.[42] Although the Court found some flaws in the consultation process, it was not found to contain any legal error.[43] The Court in *Coughlan* made an attempt to explain the substantive protection it gave to Miss Coughlan's expectation in terms of fairness, stating that fairness

[34] *Hargreaves* (n 31) 921 (Hirst LJ).

[35] *R v Ministry of Agriculture, Fisheries and Food; ex parte Hamble (Offshore) Fisheries Ltd* [1995] 1 CMLR 533 ('*Hamble Fisheries*').

[36] Ibid 552 [46].

[37] Ibid 552 [47].

[38] Ibid 552 [46], citing *HTV Ltd v Price Commission* [1976] ICR 170. See further above n 29.

[39] *Hargreaves* (n 31) 921.

[40] The contexts of *Hargreaves* and *Coughlan* are only arguably different. The Health Authority's decision in *Coughlan*, to close Mardon House, was also prompted by a change in policy, though the decision itself affected a small number of people, and had the added element of a specific promise having been made to those people. However, given that in *Hargreaves* the prisoners were asked to sign the undertaking on the understanding that the first policy would be applied to them, it is not obvious why the two cases warranted the different approaches taken by the Court of Appeal.

[41] See, especially chapter 10 in this volume.

[42] *Coughlan* (n 28) 227–28 [15]–[16].

[43] *Coughlan* (n 28) 260 [117].

'must ... include fairness of outcome'.[44] However, the Court also appeared to draw a (rather murky) distinction between the unfairness it identified in this case, which it described as unfairness resulting in an 'abuse of power', and the principle of procedural fairness.[45] It is tolerably clear, therefore, that the Court saw the rationale for protecting substantive expectations as different from the rationale for protecting expectations as to the content of procedural fairness. This is evidenced by its rather unhelpful admission that '[l]egitimate expectation may play different parts in different aspects of public law'.[46]

Secondly, where a government policy or practice has induced a legitimate expectation of a substantive benefit, as was found to be the case in *Coughlan*, the Court of Appeal said that courts will 'have the task of weighing the requirements of fairness against any overriding interest relied upon for the change of policy'.[47] It is through this balancing process that courts are to determine whether defeat of the expectation would amount to an abuse of power. Like Sedley J had in *Hamble Fisheries*, the Court made it clear that this balancing test was quite different from the rationality or *Wednesbury* unreasonableness test which is usually applied to the substance of administrative decisions. On this, Lord Woolf (who delivered the Court's judgment) said:

> ... the court is there to ensure that the power to make and alter policy has not been abused by unfairly frustrating legitimate individual expectations. In such a sitation a bare rationality test would constitute the public authority judge in its own cause, for a decision to prioritise policy change over legitimate expectations will almost always be rational from where the authority stands, even if objectively it is arbitrary or unfair.[48]

The Court undertook such a balancing process in *Coughlan*, and concluded that the defeat of Miss Coughlan's expectation of having a home for life was not outweighed by any policy objectives on the part of the Health Authority. Two main factors led to this finding. The first was the importance and strength of the promise to Mardon House residents, which the Court described as equivalent to a contract.[49] The second was that in making its decision, the Health Authority had considered only the services provided to Miss Coughlan at Mardon House and not the fact that Mardon House was also her home.[50] The Health Authority had not made arrangements to

[44] *Coughlan* (n 28) 246 [71].
[45] *Coughlan* (n 28) 244–48 [66]–[73].
[46] *Coughlan* (n 28) 247 [71].
[47] *Coughlan* (n 28) 242 [57].
[48] *Coughlan* (n 28) 244–45 [66].
[49] *Coughlan* (n 28) 253 [86]. By contrast, when his Honour was a Justice of the Federal Court of Australia, Gummow J expressed the view that even an actual contract should not be capable of fettering the exercise of a statutory discretion: *Minister for Immigration and Ethnic Affairs v Kurtovic* (1990) 21 FCR 193, 220–21.
[50] *Coughlan* (n 28) 253 [88].

provide the Mardon House residents with new homes (perhaps not wanting to pre-empt the decision). Thus, it had not, and could not have, properly considered the effect of the decision on Miss Coughlan.[51] Although there were compelling reasons—both in terms of cost and also in terms of the effective delivery of services and care—for closing Mardon House, the Court held that because the Authority had 'failed to weigh the conflicting interests *correctly*' (emphasis added), its decision was an abuse of power.[52]

The way in which the Court approached its balancing exercise in *Coughlan* was undeniably intrusive. The Court, in effect, re-decided the balance that should be given to Miss Coughlan's legitimate expectation, on one hand, and the policy on the other. On this, the Court said that, while courts should not 'accept the policy change without demur', they should 'pay the closest attention to the assessment made by the public body itself'.[53] Although this statement suggests that some deference is appropriate, the Court's decision itself reflected very little deference to the policy concerns of the Health Authority. This review of the balance the Health Authority struck looks very much like the way UK courts now approach proportionality review under the *Human Rights Act 1998* (UK) c 42 ('*HRA*'), which was not in force at the time of the Health Authority's decision.[54] Perhaps, then, the application of a proportionality-like test in *Coughlan* runs counter to the widespread assumption that it is human rights law that has been driving developments in UK public law in recent years.

Despite looking very similar to proportionality review, however, the Court did not actually use the term 'proportionality' in its balancing assessment, perhaps because it wanted to avoid introducing two controversial European principles into English law simultaneously. Instead, it used the term 'abuse of power', which Craig points out is a conclusory label rather than a useful standard directing courts as to the balancing test that should be applied in relevant cases.[55]

ATTEMPTS TO DEVELOP A UNIFIED DOCTRINE OF 'LEGITIMATE EXPECTATIONS'

From Three Tests to One?

In *Coughlan*, the Court acknowledged that the standard it was applying was more intrusive than that which had applied in earlier cases. It justified

51 *Coughlan* (n 28) 254 [89].
52 *Coughlan* (n 28) 254 [89].
53 *Coughlan* (n 28) 254 [89].
54 The proportionality test that has developed under the *HRA* is discussed in detail below.
55 Craig (n 3) 691. A similar point was made by Laws LJ in *Nadarajah* (n 3) [67]. See below at n 73 and associated text.

the need to apply a more intrusive standard in this case, and other cases involving a possible 'abuse of power', on the basis that a lower standard would result in the authority being 'a judge in its own cause', and so it would be very hard for an aggrieved person to succeed in challenging the new policy.[56] However, the Court also recognised that such an intrusive standard would not be warranted in all substantive legitimate expectation cases. It set out three separate categories of expectation case, each of which would attract a different balancing test.

The Court proposed no change to the test in procedural expectation cases, which would continue to be reviewed according to the ordinary rules of procedural fairness.[57] As explained above, in such cases, there is usually no public interest to balance against the procedural expectation, and courts simply decide for themselves whether the process was fair in all the circumstances. Craig has thus described the standard of review as 'full review',[58] which in Canada would be termed 'correctness'.

In substantive expectation cases, *Coughlan* proposed a bifurcated approach to the standard of review. The more intrusive balancing test applied in that case, would only apply in 'abuse of power' cases, which were defined as situations in which a lawful promise had induced an expectation of a substantive benefit, 'where the expecation is confined to one person or a few people, giving the promise or representation the character of a contract'.[59] In these cases, the central question for the courts is whether defeating the expectation would amount to an 'abuse of power'. Although *Coughlan* made it clear by its application of this 'abuse of power' test, that it was more intrusive than the *Wednesbury* standard, no further clarity was offered as to what the 'abuse of power' standard might entail.

In the third category of legitimate expectation cases, *Wednesbury* would be the appropriate test. In these cases, the Court said, a public authority 'is only required to bear in mind its previous policy or representation, giving it the weight he thinks right', citing *Hargreaves* and *Findlay* as examples. It seems from *Coughlan* that this standard applies to policies and promises made to larger groups of people than in *Coughlan*, and where the expectation is somehow less 'contract-like' than in *Coughlan*.

There is some possibility that the Supreme Court's more recent decision in *R (Moseley) v London Borough of Haringey* may have overtaken any potential role for review on a *Wednesbury* standard in this last category of cases.[60] In *Moseley*, the Court indicated that procedural fairness requires public authorities to consult persons with a legitimate expectation of being

[56] *Coughlan* (n 28) 245 [66].
[57] *Coughlan* (n 28) 242 [57].
[58] Craig (n 3) 689.
[59] *Coughlan* (n 28) 242 [59].
[60] *R (Moseley) v London Borough of Haringey* [2014] 1 WLR 3947.

consulted (as, it said, was the case in *Coughlan*) before adopting or changing general policies or rules that will affect them.[61] Indeed, the majority of judges in *Moseley* suggested that procedural fairness may require consultation even absent a legitimate expectation of consultation.[62] If this is now the case, then it is hard to imagine the very strict *Wednesbury* standard having much useful work to do in the judicial review of the lawfulness of a change in policy.

In *Coughlan*, Lord Woolf acknowledged that it would be difficult to distinguish between the three legitimate expectation categories, and said that it was frequently difficult to separate procedural and substantive expectations.[63] However, what seems even less clear than the procedural/substantive distinction is the basis for distinguishing between those cases in which the *Wednesbury* standard is appropriate, and those in which the much more intrusive *Coughlan* test is required. This point was made separately by both Laws and Sedley LJJ in a decision handed down the month after *Coughlan: Department of Education and Employment; ex parte Begbie.*[64] In *Begbie*, Laws LJ stated that the 'abuse of power' concept in fact 'informs all three categories of legitimate expectation cases'.[65] He suggested that, rather than seeing the *Wednesbury* and *Coughlan* standards as a dichotomy, courts should instead view them, as well as fairness, as a 'sliding scale', explaining that

> Fairness and reasonableness (and their contraries) are objective concepts; otherwise there would be no public law, or if there were it would be palm tree justice. But each is a spectrum, not a single point, and they shade into one another.[66]

Laws LJ added that the *Coughlan* categories 'are not hermetically sealed. The facts of the case, viewed always in their statutory context, will steer the court to a more or less intrusive quality of review'.[67]

Perhaps recognising the extent to which this approach leaves courts with unwieldy discretion as to the extent to which they should scrutinise any given decision, Laws LJ added that a guiding principle was the extent to which a decision lay in the 'macro-political field': 'The more the decision challenged lies in what may inelegantly be called the macro-political field, the less intrusive will be the court's supervision'.[68]

[61] Ibid 3956–58 [23]–[28] (Lord Wilson JSC with whom Lord Kerr of Tonaghmore JSC agreed), 3961 [35] (Lord Reed JSC) (with whom Baroness Hale of Richmond DPSC and Lord Clarke of Stone-Cum-Ebony JSC agreed: 3963 [44]).

[62] Ibid 3956–57 [23] (Lord Wilson JSC with whom Lord Kerr JSC agreed). Lord Reed JSC disagreed on this point: 3961 [34]. Baroness Hale DPSC and Lord Clarke JSC saw little distinction between the two judgments and agreed with both: 3963 [44]).

[63] *Coughlan* (n 28) 242 [58]–[59].

[64] *Department of Education and Employment; ex parte Begbie* [2000] 1 WLR 1115, 1130 (Laws LJ), 1133 (Sedley LJ) ('*Begbie*').

[65] Ibid 1129.

[66] Ibid 1130.

[67] Ibid.

[68] Ibid 1131.

It is not clear that this 'macro-political' description adds much clarity to the *Coughlan* analysis.

In *Bibi* the Court of Appeal sought to bring further unity to legitimate expectations. The Court said that the same three questions arise in all legitimate expectation cases—whether procedural or substantive. Those questions are: (1) whether the public authority has committed itself to a particular course of action, or whether the claimed expectation is 'legitimate'; (2) whether the authority has unlawfully broken its commitment or frustrated the expectation; and (3) what the court should do—whether it should require procedural or substantive protection be afforded to the expectation.[69] It is the second question—of whether breach of an expectation is unlawful—that incorporates any balancing of public interests against the expectation. In *Bibi*, the Court noted the dichotomous approach to the applicable standards espoused in *Coughlan*, as well as the sliding scale approach of *Begbie*, but did not expressly state the standard that should apply in that case, nor any general thoughts on the issue.[70] However, the practical approach adopted in the case is revealing. The Court's analysis of the question of whether the Council had unlawfully departed from its promise to provide a family with permanent housing was heavily tied to the specific context in which that decision was made. The Court considered the competing factors that the Council was required to consider in making decisions about public housing, and concluded that in these circumstances the Council was required to consider the expectations of the family, but not to give them any specific weight.[71] Although the Court did not expressly say so, its approach suggests an acceptance of Laws LJ's proposal in *Begbie*, that the test for unlawfulness in expectation cases should be on a sliding scale, with intensity dependent on the context.[72]

Laws LJ's suggestion in *Nadarajah*, must be read in light of these preceding cases. The case involved a policy relating to the processing of asylum claims, which the Secretary of State had applied consistently, but incorrectly. On being told that he had misinterpreted his own policy, the Secretary of State amended it. The question for the Court was whether a person who sought asylum when the first policy was in place had a legitimate expectation that the policy would be correctly applied. Laws LJ found that the facts revealed no abuse of power on the part of the Secretary of State, which was sufficient to dispose of the appeal. He added, however, that the term 'abuse of power' 'reveals no principle' and reveals nothing about 'what is lawful

[69] *Bibi* (n 18) 244 [18].
[70] *Bibi* (n 18) 244 [23], 247–48 [33]–[39].
[71] *Bibi* (n 18) 249–51 [49]–[52], [57]–[59].
[72] Steele (n 3) 314–18.

and what is not'.[73] In its place, he then offered the suggestion that the central principle underpinning legitimate expectations cases is that:

> Where a public authority has issued a promise or adopted a practice which represents how it proposes to act in a given area, the law will require the promise or practice to be honoured unless there is a good reason not to do so.[74]

This, said Laws LJ, was a principle which reflected the core values courts sought to promote by protecting legitimate expectations: fairness and good administration.[75] Laws LJ then, for the first time, took the bold step of labelling the balancing test applied in *Coughlan* as 'proportionality'.[76] He suggested that proportionality was the appropriate test to protect the principle and values which he said lay at the centre of legitimate expectations:

> Accordingly a public body's promise or practice as to future conduct may only be denied, and thus the standard I have expressed may only be departed from, in circumstances where to do so is the public body's legal duty, or is otherwise, to use a now familiar vocabulary, a proportionate response (of which the court is the judge, or the last judge) having regard to a legitimate aim pursued by the public body in the public interest.[77]

Laws LJ added, 'This approach makes no distinction between procedural and substantive expectations. Nor should it. The dichotomy between procedure and substance has nothing to say about the duty of good administration.'[78]

What is Proportionality?

It is important to note that all of these decisions in which various judges advocated a balancing test that goes beyond the *Wednesbury* standard in some or all legitimate expectation cases, which Laws LJ labelled proportionality, occurred at a time before proportionality was a relatively established and well-settled test in UK public law. Accordingly, it is not entirely clear from the judgments what was envisaged. There are conflicting suggestions in the above cases. The judges all seem to view proportionality as involving an objective, and thus more intrusive, standard compared with *Wednesbury*. For instance in *Coughlan*, the Court's objection to the rationality standard was that it would allow a public authority to be a 'judge in its own cause'.[79] Similarly, Laws LJ in *Nadarajah* confirmed that 'the court is the judge, or the last judge' of whether a public interest justifies a public

[73] *Nadarajah* (n 3) [67].
[74] *Nadarajah* (n 3) [68].
[75] *Nadarajah* (n 3).
[76] *Nadarajah* (n 3) [67].
[77] *Nadarajah* (n 3) [68].
[78] *Nadarajah* (n 3) [69].
[79] *Coughlan* (n 28) 244–45 [66].

body departing from a promise.[80] Furthermore, in *Coughlan* itself, as noted above, the balancing test that was actually applied by the Court was both objective and intrusive, involving the Court reweighing competing factors and paying little or no regard to the Authority's justifications.

However, there are also suggestions that the test is seen as a flexible and variable standard. For instance, in *Nadarajah*, Laws LJ repeated his comments from *Begbie* that where a case involves 'macro-political' policy issues, an individual will face a 'steeper climb' in demonstrating that their expectation warrants protection than where the expectation derives from a contract-like promise made to them alone, or as a member of a small group.[81] In *Hamble Fisheries*, Sedley J reasoned that:

> The balance must in the first instance be for the policy-maker to strike; but if the outcome is challenged by way of judicial review, I do not consider that the court's criterion is the bare rationality of the policy-maker's conclusion. While policy is for the policy-maker alone, the fairness of his or her decision not to accommodate reasonable expectations which the policy will thwart remains the court's concern.[82]

The contextual approach taken in *Bibi* is also indicative of the Court's view that the single lawfulness standard it proposed was a very flexible one.

References to the European position in several of the judgments further suggest that the intended 'proportionality' test was fairly flexible and somewhat deferential, although this may not have been deliberate.[83] The European Court of Justice has long applied a test of 'significant imbalance' in legitimate expectation cases, which many have noted looks very similar to its proportionality test.[84] As noted above, it is also probably accurate to describe the Court's approach to balancing in *Coughlan* as a 'proportionality' test, as that test now applies under UK human rights law. However, that does not mean that the two proportionality tests are one and the same.

In European courts, as in Germany, the concept of legitimate expectation was used to afford substantive protection to the expectations of individuals resulting from government statements and acts from the outset.[85] It has also long been acknowledged that, in exceptional cases, expectations are capable

[80] *Nadarajah* (n 3) [68].
[81] *Nadarajah* (n 3) [69].
[82] *Hamble Fisheries* (n 35) 552 [47].
[83] See *Hamble Fisheries* (n 35) 547–49 [33]–[39]; *Nadarajah* (n 3) [68]; *Coughlan* (n 28) 243 [63].
[84] Craig (n 4) 585; Søren Schønberg, *Legitimate Expectations in Administrative Law* (Oxford University Press, 2000) 149–50.
[85] See generally Robert Thomas, *Legitimate Expectations and Proportionality in Administrative Law* (Hart Publishing, 2000) 41–46; Georg Nolte, 'General Principles of German Administrative Law—A Comparison in Historical Perspective' (1994) 57 *Modern Law Review* 191, 195; Schønberg (n 84) 58–60, 71–79, 117–28; Lord Mackenzie Stuart, 'Legitimate Expectations and Estoppel in Community Law and English Administrative Law' (1983) 10 *Legal Issues of Economic Integration* 53.

of being used to challenge regulations.[86] The wide scope of the principle and its ability to constrain governments when applied in this way is balanced by the relatively high threshold requirements that the European Court has applied to the questions of when an expectation will be 'legitimate' as well as by the ability of the administration to argue that the expectation is overridden by a public interest.[87] In his study comparing European and English case law in 2000, Thomas concluded that, as a result of these limits on the European doctrine, 'relatively few arguments based on legitimate expectations have succeeded'.[88]

A good example of the approach is found in *Dieckmann & Hansen GmbH v Commission*.[89] The applicant was a German company which had imported caviar for 130 years, predominantly from Kazakhstan. After an inspection visit to Kazakhstan, Commission experts found that Kazakh authorities were unable to meet Commission standards in relation to fishery products (albeit not having specifically inspected caviar production and processing) and the Commission decided to remove Kazakhstan from the list of countries from which fishery products could be imported into the EU. Three weeks prior to that decision being made, the applicant had entered into a contract with suppliers to import 9500kg of caviar from Kazakhstan. The applicant argued, among other things, that the decision had defeated its legitimate expectation to be able to import caviar from Kazakhstan, given that Kazakhstan remained on the list of countries from which fishery products could be imported at the date at which they had entered into the contract.[90]

The Commission argued that even if the applicant did have an expectation which had been breached, the public interest in protecting the health of consumers overrode it.[91] The company responded that the expert evidence contained no suggestion that caviar posed a risk to public health, and so the Commission ought to have obtained more evidence before making its decision. The Court acknowledged that the Commission had no evidence that caviar posed a risk, and had the Commission been less hasty, it may have been shown that there was no public health risk in the importation of that product. Nevertheless, the Court found:

> in view of the structural nature of the deficiencies found in Kazakhstan by the Community experts, even in the event that the results of an inspection of the caviar establishments had proved positive, the Commission was *entitled to adopt, within the bounds of its broad discretion*, a decision to ban importation of caviar,

[86] See, eg, Case 120/86 *Mulder v Minister van Laudbouw en Visserij* [1988] ECR 2321.
[87] See Craig (n 4) 567–78.
[88] Thomas (n 85) 46.
[89] Case T-155/99 *Dieckmann & Hansen GmbH v Commission* [2001] ECR II-3143.
[90] Ibid 3158–59 [33].
[91] Ibid 3161 [39].

> such as the contested decision, pending general improvement in the applicable legislation and the conditions of veterinary and export supervision and inspection in that country (emphasis added).[92]

This statement points to several important aspects of the European Court's approach to legitimate expectations and balancing. The first is the importance of interpretation. The Court's starting point was to examine the scope of the Commission's discretion, to determine whether changing a policy based on public health concerns was within its authority.[93] Finding that it was, and that the Commission was granted a very broad discretion, the Court then asked not whether the Commission's balancing of factors within its discretion was correct, but instead whether it was 'entitled' to balance competing factors in the way in which it did. This is more akin to a rationality assessment of the Commission's justifications, than review of whether the outcome was objectively disproportionate. In essence it gives the public authority a level of deference in balancing competing factors—in this case a legitimate expectation versus a public interest—provided that the justifications for the balance are clear and rational.

This approach to proportionality has, on occasion, also been adopted in other contexts in EU law. For instance in *Spain v Council*,[94] the Court had occasion to discuss the application of proportionality as a stand-alone ground of review in Community law. It said that in reviewing actions for proportionality, at least in areas where the Community legislature enjoys a high degree of discretion such as agricultural policy, a measure will only be unlawful if it 'is manifestly inappropriate in terms of the objective which the competent institution is seeking to pursue'.[95] Therefore, the role of courts is to ascertain 'not whether the measure adopted by the legislature was the only one or the best one possible but whether it was manifestly inappropriate'.[96] Incidentally, this is also the way in which Canadian courts now approach proportionality review of administrative decisions which limit *Charter* rights.[97] Rather than deciding for themselves whether the balance a public authority has struck between competing rights and public interests is proportionate, Canadian courts ask whether the authority has adequately justified its position, and whether the justification is reasonable.[98]

[92] Ibid 3174–75 [81]

[93] Ibid 3172 [77].

[94] *Spain v Council* [2006] ECR I-7285 (Case-310/04). The case also involved a legitimate expectation argument, but proportionality was argued and discussed separately, and not as an aspect of deciding the legitimate expectation question.

[95] Ibid 7346 [98].

[96] Ibid 7346 [99].

[97] The *Canadian Charter of Rights and Freedoms* comprises Part I of the *Constitution Act 1982*, which is itself Sch B of the *Canada Act 1982* c 11 (UK).

[98] *Doré v Barreau du Québec* [2012] 1 SCR 395. I have argued elsewhere that this is also the best interpretation of the High Court of Australia's approach in *Minister for Immigration and Citizenship v Li* (2013) 249 CLR 332: Boughey (n 2).

By contrast, in the UK, the courts have clarified their approach to proportionality since *Nadarajah*, and it is clear that proportionality is viewed as a wholly objective test, with limited scope for courts to defer to the opinion of a public authority on where the balance between rights and public interests lie. In *R (SB) v Governors of Denbigh High School*, the House of Lords rejected an approach to proportionality which focussed on the rationality of a public authority's reasoning process on the basis that it was inadequate to protect rights.[99] Lord Bingham made it clear that proportionality is a legal question for the courts, not one for decision-makers, stating 'proportionality must be judged objectively, by the court'.[100] His Lordship commented that if a decision-maker 'has conscientiously paid attention to all human rights considerations, no doubt a challenger's task will be the harder. But what matters in any case is the practical outcome, not the quality of the decision-making process that led to it'.[101]

In subsequent cases, the UK Supreme Court has stated that there is room within the concept of proportionality for some 'weight' to be accorded to the original decision-maker's views, at least in cases involving national security or foreign relations.[102] However, this does not change the central point made in *Denbigh*, that it is ultimately for the courts to determine whether limits the executive has placed on protected rights are proportionate, not one that can be finally determined by decision-makers.[103] This requires the courts to re-weigh the competing factors and reach its own assessment, which explains why UK judges, lawyers and commentators generally view proportionality as simply a more intense standard of review, compared with the traditional rationality and reasonableness standards.

These different approaches to proportionality review may well be explained by the fact that in the UK proportionality only currently applies in cases involving the *Human Rights Act 1998* (UK) c 42, whilst in Europe proportionality is not so restricted and applies generally as a ground of review. Indeed, in cases involving rights, the European Court of Justice frequently applies a more objective version of proportionality review than it does in other cases, albeit not consistently so.[104] Similarly, the European

[99] *R (SB) v Governors of Denbigh High School* [2006] 2 WLR 719, 731 [30] (Lord Bingham) ('*Denbigh*').

[100] Ibid.

[101] Ibid 731 [31] (Lord Bingham).

[102] See eg *Bank Mellat v Her Majesty's Treasury (No 2)* [2014] AC 700, 771 [21] (Lord Sumption JSC), 804–05 [125]–[129] (Lord Reed JSC); *R (Carlile) v Secretary of State for the Home Department* [2015] AC 945, 964–65 [19]–[22] (Lord Sumption JSC).

[103] This position aligns with the approach that UK courts take generally in review of executive action—whether or not the *HRA* and proportionality are involved: see, eg, *Secretary of State for Foreign and Commonwealth Affairs v Rahmatullah* [2013] 1 AC 614, 642–44 [65]–[70] (Lord Kerr of Tonaghmore JSC, with whom Lord Dyson MR and Lord Wilson JSC agreed).

[104] Craig (n 4), Ch 19.

Court of Human Rights often applies a proportionality test that appears more similar to the UK's objective standard. Although again, this is not consistently true, as ECHR jurisprudence also emphasises the need for a 'margin of appreciation', which allows deference by the Court to national authorities on matters that the latter are better placed to decide.[105]

Whatever the explanation, however, it is clear that proportionality does not always mean the same thing in the EU as it does in the UK context. In the former, it is more flexible and variable than in the latter. Nor does 'proportionality' necessarily mean now what it meant over a decade ago when Laws LJ and others advocated it take the place as the sole standard of review, or guiding principle in all legitimate expectation cases. Nevertheless, the question that must now be answered is whether proportionality, as understood in the UK context, is an appropriate standard in all or some category of legitimate expectation cases?

CAN PROPORTIONALITY SERVE AS A GUIDING PRINCIPLE FOR LEGITIMATE EXPECTATIONS?

Reactions to the suggestion that proportionality become the balancing test in all categories of legitimate expectations have been mixed. There is a general recognition that the 'doctrine' of legitimate expectation (insofar as it may be so described) is in dire need of a 'more principled footing'.[106] Paul Craig stated that Laws LJ's analysis and proposed proportionality test has 'beneficially clarified this area of law', though goes on to make the seemingly contradictory statement that proportionality 'will only be relevant if the applicant established a substantive legitimate expectation'.[107] Thus, Craig seems only to endorse a proportionality test in substantive expectation cases. In addition, it is not clear whether Craig endorses the application of a proportionality test *as it currently applies* in UK law. He describes proportionality as a 'structured analysis which facilitates review, and forces the agency to give a reasoned justification for its course of action'.[108] As discussed above, while this may be an accurate description of proportionality review as it applies much of the time in Europe and Canada, it does not accurately describe the UK approach to proportionality, in which courts care little about the subjective justifications and reasoning of public authorities.

[105] See Mark W Janis, Richard S Kay and Anthony W Bradley, *European Human Rights Law: Text and Materials*, 3rd edn (Oxford University Press, 2008) 242–52; Dragoljub Popolvić, *European Human Rights Law—A Manual: An Introduction to the Strasbourg Court and its Jurisprudence* (Eleven International Publishing, 2013) 49–52.

[106] Elliott (n 7) 288. See also similar comments by Craig (n 3) 692; *R (Bancoult) v Foreign Secretary (No 2)* [2009] 1 AC 533 [181] (Lord Mance).

[107] Craig (n 3) 692.

[108] Craig (n 3) 692–93.

Sales was more willing to accept a proportionality-style test in procedural expectation cases than in substantive expectation cases.[109] He argued that the two categories must remain distinct due to the very different consequences for governments of a court holding that the process of a decision was unfair versus a finding that the decision itself was unlawful.[110] The breach of a procedural expectation should demand a 'high standard of justification' from government, 'perhaps expressed in a proportionality rubric'.[111] However, Sales argued that a similarly high standard, involving the same balancing of factors, will not be appropriate in all, or even most, cases in which the Government has decided, within the lawful limits of its discretion, to defeat a substantive expectation.[112] Elliott has expanded on Sales' analysis of substantive expectation cases, and argued that while proportionality may be appropriate in some substantive expectation cases, the category is too varied, and cases within it too disparate, to settle on a single balancing principle.[113]

The House of Lords and Supreme Court have provided little guidance, not having had the occasion to rule on the matter. In the few instances in which Laws LJ's proposal has been considered in *obiter*, judges have been tentative in their support. Lord Phillips expressed obiter, qualified support for the approach,[114] and Lord Mance accepted the underlying principle that the purpose of protecting legitimate expectations is to safeguard good government, but said he preferred to:

> reserve for another case my opinion as to whether it is helpful or appropriate to rationalise the situations in which a departure from a prior decision is justified in terms of proportionality, with its overtones of another area of public law.[115]

Proportionality and Procedural Expectations

In a context in which proportionality is applied and viewed as an intrusive standard of review—nearer to merits review than to the deferential *Wednesbury* standard—Sales' argument that proportionality is better suited to procedural than substantive expectation cases is logical and compelling. Where a court finds that a public authority is bound, as a result of some undertaking, to follow a particular process, there is far less intrusion into the discretion of the authority than in a case where a court holds the authority to

[109] Sales (n 7) 190.
[110] Sales (n 7) 188–90.
[111] Sales (n 7) 190.
[112] Sales (n 7) 190–91.
[113] Elliott (n 7).
[114] *Lumba (WL) v Secretary of State for the Home Department* [2012] 1 AC 245, 344–45 [311]–[312].
[115] *Bancoult (No 2)* (n 106) [182].

its representations as to how it will exercise its discretion. Thus, the high level of judicial scrutiny involved in proportionality review, and the high standard to which it holds public authorities, is appropriate. Holding government to its procedural undertakings improves the integrity of administrative processes but does not involve courts overstepping the judicial role. As outlined above, in procedural expectation cases courts currently apply a 'fairness' standard, which is the court's own assessment of whether the process was fair in all of the circumstances. Replacing fairness with proportionality, or adding proportionality to the overarching test, is unproblematic from a constitutional standpoint.

It is, therefore, possible, under the common law framework of judicial review of administrative action, to replace fairness with proportionality as the balancing test in procedural expectation cases. Once a court finds that an aggrieved person had a legitimate expectation of being consulted before an adverse decision was made, or had an expectation of a decision being made via a particular process, then it could ask whether there is any overriding public interest that demands the expectation be defeated and itself balance the expectation against the public interest. As discussed above, in most cases public authorities do not argue that a public interest demanded the defeat of a person's procedural expectations. Therefore the assessment of whether procedural fairness has been denied usually does not involve any sort of balancing by courts. But the fact that public interests may very rarely justify defeat of a legitimate expectation as to procedure does not necessarily mean that they cannot, or should not.

To take a recent example, in *WZARH v Minister for Immigration and Border Protection*,[116] the Federal Court of Australia found that an asylum seeker had been denied procedural fairness in a review of his refugee status assessment because the decision-maker had failed to follow the process that the appellant legitimately expected would be followed. The appellant's initial application for refugee status was denied, and he sought merits review of that decision. He was interviewed by an Independent Merits Reviewer, with whom he then corresponded. That reviewer later became unavailable and a second reviewer completed the review process, and made a decision adverse to the appellant. The relevant legislation expressly provided that if, for any reason, a reviewer became unavailable to complete a review, the tribunal could be reconstituted.[117]

The appellant successfully argued that he had an expectation that the reviewer who made the decision about his case would first hear from him, and that defeat of that expectation resulted in him being denied procedural

[116] *WZARH* (n 23).

[117] *Migration Act 1958* (Cth) s 422 (since repealed). An equivalent provision now applies under *Administrative Appeals Tribunal Act 1975* (Cth) s 19D.

fairness.[118] In reaching this conclusion, the Court noted that no explanation had been given by the Minister as to why the first reviewer was unavailable, or as to why the second reviewer could not conduct a second interview.[119] The Court also distinguished the case from others in which a decision-maker had become unavailable, and the new decision-maker had taken steps to redress the detriment, which had been found not to breach the rules of procedural fairness.[120] This suggests that had an explanation been given as to why the reviewer was unavailable to complete the process, and had the Government made efforts to reduce any resulting unfairness, the Court would have considered these factors, and weighed them against the expectations of the appellant in assessing whether procedural fairness had been denied. Whether the test applied in such an assessment is termed 'fairness' or 'proportionality' would seem to make no great difference to its essential nature, in a context where both involve the court weighing competing interests for itself to decide whether the process was unfair to the appellant.

On appeal, the High Court of Australia suggested that the Federal Court may have overstated the role of legitimate expectations, but agreed with the result and found no error in its reasoning.[121] The High Court's reasoning focussed on what fairness required in the circumstances, finding that the change in procedure and the second reviewer's failure to conduct an oral hearing might have deprived the asylum seeker of a favourable outcome and was therefore unfair.[122] However, the High Court's approach to balancing was the same as that of the Federal Court. The Court suggested that had reasons been given for the second reviewer not conducing a further hearing, their approach would have been to examine the strength of that justification. Gageler and Gordon JJ noted that such reasons may include 'logistical considerations'.[123] Kiefel, Bell and Keane JJ stated that:

> It is difficult to identify any reasonable basis on which the Second Reviewer could fairly have refused the respondent an opportunity to be heard on the question of how the review process should proceed once that process was altered by the withdrawal of the First Reviewer.[124]

This case shows that, in procedural expectation cases, the ordinary judicial assessment of whether a process was fair in all the circumstances will

[118] *WZARH* (n 23) 137 [17] (Flick and Gleeson JJ).
[119] *WZARH* (n 23) 138 [20].
[120] *WZARH* (n 23) 139–40 [22].
[121] *Minister for Immigration and Border Protection v WZARH* (n 24) 335–36 [31]–[32], 340 [47]–[48] (Kiefel, Bell and Keane JJ). Gageler and Gordon JJ went a little further in criticising the reasoning of the majority of the Federal Court: at 343 [61].
[122] *Minister for Immigration and Border Protection v WZARH* (n 24) 339 [43]–[45] (Kiefel, Bell and Keane JJ), 343–44 [63]–[65] (Gageler and Gordon JJ).
[123] *Minister for Immigration and Border Protection v WZARH* (n 24) 345 [68].
[124] *Minister for Immigration and Border Protection v WZARH* (n 24) 340 [46].

incorporate the balancing of an individual's procedural expectations against any countervailing considerations raised by a public authority.

While it may be possible to use proportionality as a balancing test in procedural expectation cases, proportionality does not actually seem to add much to a fairness analysis. Indeed, adding proportionality to the assessment of fairness may have the effect of detracting from the clarity of the existing test. While the concept of procedural fairness is by no means clear or settled, it is arguably far more so than the newer and more contentious concept of proportionality in common law systems. Furthermore, replacing fairness with proportionality might have the effect of reducing the level of judicial oversight in some cases. Although proportionality is generally applied in a way which contains little deference to the executive's views as to the balance between competing interests, in some cases there is scope for a 'margin of judgment', or a 'margin of discretion'. No such margin is found in procedural fairness review, because fairness and justice are concepts that courts have traditionally regarded themselves as best-placed to assess. So, in any case in which courts are prepared to defer to the Government's assessment of how important a particular public interest or objective are, proportionality will produce a reduced level of judicial oversight than fairness does. Therefore, while it may be possible for proportionality to replace fairness in procedural expectation cases, doing so would neither bolster the protection given to expectations nor have a clarifying effect on the law.

Substantive Expectations and Proportionality

Applying a proportionality test in substantive expectation cases is clearly possible, as evidenced by the use of a very similar analysis in *Coughlan*. In many respects proportionality seems a more obvious fit with substantive expectation cases than procedural expectation cases. While public authorities often do not advance arguments as to public interests that warrant defeat of an expectation in procedural expectation cases, as the above discussion of case law demonstrates, they usually do in substantive expectation cases. In *Coughlan*, as in *Hargreaves, Findlay* and *Hamble Fisheries*, each of the aggrieved individuals had a clear and definable interest in the Government pursuing the promised course of action, and on the other side there were evident public interest reasons as to why the authority wished to depart from its promise or previous policy. In substantive expectation cases, there are most often two opposing interests—private and public—which are capable of being weighed and balanced, just as there are in those rights cases to which proportionality already applies.

In addition, while in the case of procedural expectations where the test and standard for fairness is both clearer and more established than proportionality, the same is not true in the case of substantive expectations. As the above discussion of UK case law on substantive expectations demonstrates, there is no consensus as to the methodology through which the balancing of overriding public interests and legitimate expectations ought to proceed. Introducing proportionality as that methodology would, as Laws LJ said, make this area of law more unified and more principled.

However, in the UK, Canada and New Zealand, proportionality is currently accepted as the appropriate standard only in cases involving an alleged breach of (or unlawful limit on) protected rights. In non-rights cases some version of reasonableness is applied.[125] In most common law jurisdictions, and most importantly in those which accept the concept of substantive expectations, or might do so in future, reasonableness is viewed as a less intrusive standard of review than proportionality. If courts apply a proportionality test in substantive expectation cases, they are, therefore, treating expectations as equivalent under law to a protected human right. Just as decision-makers may now only limit protected rights if the reviewing court agrees that the public interest outweighs the importance of the protected right, they could only renege on a promise if a court agreed that the public interest outweighed the adverse impact on a person who has a legitimate expectation as a result of the promise. Thus expectations, created by public authorities, would form as much of a binding limit on the exercise of administrative discretion as those rights which the legislature has chosen to enshrine in law. In effect, public authorities could create new rights via the making of policies or promises.

A possible justification for offering the same level of protection to legitimate expectations as to rights is found in Laws LJ's suggestion that the rationale for protecting expectations (both procedural and substantive) is the 'requirement of good administration'.[126] This is not the first time this explanation has been given for the legitimate expectations doctrine.[127] It is possible then, that Laws LJ intended to elevate the principle of 'good administration' to the status of a right in the UK, rather than the interests individuals have in the protection of their expectations in specific cases. There is, of course, a right to good administration enshrined in EU Law, which applies to UK Government but cannot be used by European Courts as a basis for invalidating its actions.[128] The difficulty with this explanation, however, is that it does not reflect the way balancing is actually done in substantive legitimate expectation cases. In *Coughlan*, the Court weighed the detriment

[125] Woolf et al (n 2) 627–33, 643–56.

[126] *Nadarajah* (n 3) [68].

[127] See, eg, *Ng Yuen Shiu* (n 12) 637. By contrast, in the High Court of Australia, Gleeson CJ dismissed 'good administration' as an adequate legal basis for any principle of judicial review: *Lam* (n 24) 11–12 [32].

[128] *Charter of Fundamental Rights of the European Union* [2000] OJ C346/01, Art 41; *Protocol on the Application of the Charter of Fundamental Rights of the European Union to Poland and to the United Kingdom* [2007] OJ C306/07, Art 1(1).

that Miss Coughlan would suffer and her interests in staying in Mardon House against the Authority's reasons for wishing to defeat her expectation, not her right to a trustworthy, honest or 'good' administration.

Finally, as Elliott has argued, even if the intrusive proportionality test was appropriate in *Coughlan*, this does not mean that it will be the appropriate balancing test in all substantive expectation cases.[129] Evidence of this is found in the fact that in so many other cases, including most of those discussed in this chapter, courts have applied a more deferential standard than in *Coughlan*, arguing that the balancing of competing expectations and public interests is for the repository of discretionary power and not the courts.[130] This was also a point that seems to have been acknowledged, either expressly or implicitly, in most of the cases proposing that proportionality be used in some or all legitimate expectation cases.[131] As discussed, in making those proposals, the judges seem to have endorsed proportionality with the assumption that it was a more flexible standard than it has subsequently become. They seem to have assumed it was a standard that was capable of applying with varying degrees of intensity so as to encompass review methodologies and outcomes as diverse as those in *Hargraves*, *Bibi* and *Coughlan*. The European and Canadian approaches to proportionality review are probably sufficiently flexible and diverse to do this effectively. However, as proportionality is currently applied in the UK, it is too blunt an instrument to perform the balancing task in all substantive expectation cases.

CONCLUSION

This chapter has explored the background to, and reasons for, Laws LJ's proposal that proportionality would be an appropriate balancing test and guiding principle in legitimate expectation cases. His Honour was rightly concerned about the coherence of the 'doctrine' of legitimate expectations, and seems to have elected proportionality as a guiding principle in part because of the fact that it was, at the time, viewed as a relatively flexible concept capable of accommodating the range of circumstances in which legitimate expectations are protected under common law. In addition, European experience of legitimate expectations and proportionality demonstrates that the two are capable of working together to balance the value of good and trustworthy administration against the pragmatic need for agencies to have

[129] Elliott (n 7) 286.

[130] See, eg, *Ibrahim v Redbridge London Borough Council* [2002] EWHC 2756 (Admin); *R (Ooi) v Secretary of State for the Home Department* [2007] EWHC 3221 (Admin); *Hannover Company Services Ltd v Commissioners for her Majesty's Revenue and Customs* [2010] UKFTT 256.

[131] See above nn 81–83 and associated text.

sufficient discretion to respond to changing circumstances. Since Laws LJ proposed that proportionality be used to balance legitimate expectations, however, the UK approach to proportionality has developed in a different, and far more rigid, direction, than its European counterpart. This chapter has argued that as a result, in its current form, proportionality is largely unsuited to perform a balancing function in most common law legitimate expectation cases. It adds nothing to, and may detract from, the existing fairness approach to procedural expectations, and is not sufficiently flexible to apply across the spectrum of substantive expectation cases. Applying proportionality to legitimate expectations, in its current, intrusive form, would result in public authorities potentially creating new 'rights' each time they made a promise or a policy. There seems to be no good reason for why this should be the case, and many for why it should not.

7

What Can We Legitimately Expect from the State?

GREG WEEKS*

THE TITLE OF this chapter asks a very broad question. There are of course many things we can and do expect of the state. Several of the later chapters in this book show that in countries with written constitutions, like Australia, South Africa and Canada, expectations may be framed by specific areas of constitutional legislative competence. Regardless of such a legal framework, we might expect many things in general from the state, such as attending to the demands of national security, providing services that are not necessarily provided by the free market (such as public transport, universal schooling, universal access to hospital facilities and so forth) and managing the economy. These *general* expectations are essentially of government fulfilling its normal role; they are not the concerns of this chapter. Rather, it will discuss *specific* expectations that we have of the state.[1]

There is no universal legal response where an individual to whom a promise has been made is then deprived of the fulfilment of that promise. This is in part because there have been a number of causes of action which turn on failure to adhere to a promise.[2] In some circumstances, such behaviour may cause a promissory estoppel to be formed. It may be negligent, whether the promise is provided as information or advice,[3] or amount to

* My thanks are due to Matthew Groves for his advice and assistance.

[1] cf *Council of the Shire of Sutherland v Heyman* (1985) 157 CLR 424, 462 (Mason J).

[2] The once-popular cause of action for breach of promise to marry was abolished in Australia by statute 40 years ago; see G Weeks, 'Holding Government to its Word: Legitimate Expectations and Estoppels in Administrative Law' in M Groves (ed), *Modern Administrative Law in Australia: Concepts and Context* (Cambridge University Press, 2014) 224, 225. There are other doctrines which deal with conveying inaccurate information, such as contractual misrepresentation and claims under statutory provisions like *The Australian Consumer Law* §18 (Sch 2 to the *Competition and Consumer Act 2010* (Cth)) which almost universally affect commercial dealings or conduct 'in trade or commerce'.

[3] *L Shaddock & Associates Pty Ltd v Parramatta City Council* (1981) 150 CLR 225; *Hedley Byrne & Co Ltd v Heller & Partners Ltd* [1964] AC 465.

deceit.[4] These actions offer different remedies to those which are possible when a legitimate expectation is raised in judicial review proceedings. The torts of deceit and negligence sound exclusively in damages.[5] Estoppels are remedied by meeting the equity which they have created, which will usually be achieved by making good the reasonable expectation of the plaintiff,[6] although enforcement of an expectation is not the only available remedy when an estoppel is raised.[7] Equitable compensation may instead be payable in some circumstances.[8]

It is implicit to the scope of this chapter that what one may expect of the state differs from what it is reasonable to expect of a private actor. This contention is perhaps recognised most notably by the more limited remedies available when one's expectations are disappointed by a public authority. Conversely, this difference is also clear from an understanding of the nature of promises and the fact that the effect of a promise is necessarily connected to the depth of belief that it provokes in its recipient. Public authorities are not necessarily believed more readily than private parties in every circumstance; for example, we might place greater faith in an expectation created by a long-term commercial advisor than in one created by the receptionist in a government agency. However, public authorities have an almost unique capacity to cause people to comply with their instructions, even if they do not think they are legally required to do so, or they believe that to do so is not in their interests.[9] In the same way, public authorities have a greater capacity than individuals to create expectations in which it is reasonable for those individuals to put their faith. The paradoxical result which follows is that, while we are more likely to put our faith in the representations of public authorities, we are less likely to obtain legal remedies against them.

Given the special position of public authorities that create expectations in other parties, it is understandable that some jurisdictions have developed a specific, public law doctrine which allows for the substantive enforcement of legitimate expectations. England, for example, has set aside the

[4] Although the tort of deceit has a very limited modern application; see RP Balkin and JLR Davis, *Law of Torts*, 5th edn (LexisNexis Butterworths, 2013) 680–92.

[5] Paul Finn noted that 'the tort of deceit came to prominence' for its capacity to provide compensation after the 'jurisdiction to enforce representations [was] colonised by the law of contract': PD Finn, 'Equity as Tort?' in K Barker, R Grantham and W Swain (eds), *The Law of Misstatements: 50 Years on from Hedley Byrne v Heller* (Hart Publishing, 2015) 135, 143.

[6] See J Hudson, 'The True Purpose of Estoppel by Representation' (2015) 32 *Journal of Contract Law* 275, 289.

[7] This is especially apt where there are other reasons preventing such a remedy. For example, Australian courts will not enforce an estoppel where that would cause the defendant to act contrary to law. This has particular relevance to public bodies, which also cannot be estopped such that they are fettered from exercising the full range of a statutory discretion; see G Weeks, *Soft Law and Public Authorities: Remedies and Reform* (Hart Publishing, 2016) 194–96.

[8] See G Weeks, 'Estoppel and Public Authorities: Examining the Case for an Equitable Remedy' (2010) 4 *Journal of Equity* 247.

[9] See eg Weeks (n 7) 224.

private law estoppel reasoning which for so long informed the debate about holding public authorities to their promises[10] and has absorbed its 'moral values' into a public law doctrine.[11] Elsewhere, the objections which existed to estopping public authorities have not been surmounted by seeking to conduct a broadly identical public law process.[12]

In addition to considering the kinds of expectations that we might reasonably have of the state, this chapter also addresses how such expectations might be created, and when and how they might be enforced. After all, this is the central point, not only of this chapter, but for the majority of people who assert that their legitimate expectation has been breached: one only asks about expectations created by the state because one wishes to bind the state to fulfill those expectations.

HOW ARE EXPECTATIONS FORMED?

Creating an expectation can be done with varying degrees of directness. One might divide the ways of creating an expectation usefully into three categories: promises, policies and practices.[13] A promise suggests that a fairly direct form of communication has been employed and has caused an expectation to be created of something relatively specific.[14] A policy, by contrast, is less direct. Rather than being directed specifically to a person or small group who then rely upon it, a policy tends to be published for the information of people more generally and need not be brought specifically to the attention of any one of them.[15] A policy speaks to what a public authority plans to do at a given time[16] rather than how its course of action

[10] See eg *Laker Airways v Department of Trade* [1977] QB 643; *R v Inland Revenue Commissioners; ex parte Preston* [1985] AC 835.

[11] *R v East Sussex County Council; ex parte Reprotech (Pebsham) Ltd* [2003] 1 WLR 348, 358 (Lord Hoffmann).

[12] The Canadian Supreme Court rejected the English approach to substantive enforcement of legitimate expectations, but achieved a similar result through another public law doctrine: *Mount Sinai Hospital Centre v Quebec (Minister of Health and Social Services)* [2001] 2 SCR 281. The Australian High Court has been even more dismissive of the legitimate expectations doctrine than it was of public law estoppel and applies neither.

[13] See F Ahmed and A Perry, 'The Coherence of the Doctrine of Legitimate Expectations' (2014) 73 *Cambridge Law Journal* 61, 64–66.

[14] eg *R v North and East Devon Health Authority; ex parte Coughlan* [2001] 3 QB 213; *Mount Sinai Hospital* (n 12). *Re Minister for Immigration and Multicultural Affairs; ex parte Lam* (2003) 214 CLR 1 also falls within this category, although there the failure to adhere to the promise had no legal consequence because Mr Lam suffered no practical disadvantage.

[15] eg *Attorney-General (NSW) v Quin* (1990) 170 CLR 1; *Nikac v Minister for Immigration, Local Government and Ethnic Affairs* (1988) 20 FCR 65; *Ng Siu Tung v Director of Immigration* (2002) 5 HKCFAR 1.

[16] This leads to the question of whether a government can change its policy without being bound to an earlier policy statement. The general response in Australia is that it can: *Quin* (n 15). The English cases, by contrast, are attended by greater uncertainty: see Ahmed and Perry (n 13) 82–84.

will affect an individual (as a promise does). A practice is less certain than either a promise or a policy. It does not comprise an active expression of intention but essentially amounts to a person concluding that a course of action adhered to in the past will continue to be adhered to in the future.[17] Even when a practice is established, it may not assist a person to establish the breach of procedural fairness obligations.[18] In any case, it is important to recognise that the 'nature of the decision will, therefore, always be relevant to the question whether the frustration of [a legitimate] expectation is an abuse of power'[19] or otherwise provides a basis for judicial intervention.

For all that public authorities have a degree of power that individuals do not, on the basis that their representations and promises are more likely to result in compliance, it remains necessary to consider what it is reasonable to expect of public authorities in any given situation. The question is not *whether* an individual can rely on that policy but *to what degree* s/he can rely on that policy. For example, imagine that the government has a policy which it has published.[20] To what group of people was the policy applicable? If a small group, or a single individual, it is more likely that a court will bind the government to its policy in some way.[21] How was the policy communicated? Policies published in writing tend to be more reliable than, say, a Ministerial speech.[22] On the other hand, politicians cannot consider themselves bound to adhere to the terms of manifesto policies once in office,[23] although policies adopted in office have been considered in

[17] eg *FAI Insurances Ltd v Winneke* (1982) 151 CLR 342; *Attorney-General (Hong Kong) v Ng Yuen Shiu* [1983] 2 AC 629; *Geelong Community for Good Life Inc v Environment Protection Authority* (2008) 20 VR 338; cf *Duncan v Minister of Environmental Affairs and Tourism* 2010 (6) SA 374 (SCA).

[18] See *Russell-Taylor v State of South Australia* [2011] SASC 238 [204]–[205].

[19] *R (on the application of Rashid) v Secretary of State for the Home Department* [2005] EWCA Civ 744 [50] (Dyson LJ).

[20] In England, the Supreme Court held by majority that the Home Secretary had a public law duty to publish her policy and that detention of the claimants under an unpublished, blanket policy was unlawful: *R (Lumba) v Secretary of State for the Home Department* [2012] 1 AC 245, 264, 268–69 (Lord Dyson); 301 (Lord Hope); 307 (Lord Walker); 311 (Lady Hale); 315–16 (Lord Collins); 322–23 (Lord Kerr). However, even an unpublished policy may give rise to a legitimate expectation: *Rashid* (n 19) [25] (Pill LJ). By contrast, Australian law encourages, but does not require, that policies and other forms of soft law be published: Weeks (n 7) 87. The High Court appears simply to have set aside the issue raised in *Lumba* for the appropriate case; see *Plaintiff S10/2011 v Minister for Immigration and Citizenship* (2012) 246 CLR 636, 665 (fn 94).

[21] That is to say procedurally if not in substance.

[22] See *Unilan Holdings Pty Ltd v Kerin* [1993] FCA 19. Most speeches are probably better characterised as undertakings or promises.

[23] *Bromley London Borough Council (LBC) v Greater London Council* [1983] 1 AC 768, 829 (Lord Diplock). Some have considered that there are 'particularly sound reasons' for an approach that allows politicians to rethink their commitments after reaching office: R Moules, *Actions against Public Officials: Legitimate Expectations, Misstatements and Misconduct* (Sweet & Maxwell, 2009) 64. With respect, such reasoning is more compelling where a government wishes to *abandon* its earlier promises than where only the intervention of a court prevents it from keeping them: *Bromley LBC* (n 23) 815 (Lord Wilberforce); 829–30 (Lord

England to form a possible basis for a legitimate expectation.[24] Written policies can also be subject to the same vagaries usually attendant only on statutory construction if challenged in court.[25] What was the subject of the policy? It should be obvious that policies in some areas of executive discretion, such as the appointment of judicial officers,[26] will seldom, if ever, be understood as binding the government.

An expectation generated by a public authority will generally be of greater significance than one *either* generated held subjectively by the claimant *or* of which s/he has only constructive knowledge.[27] Representations and conduct can form the basis of procedural fairness obligations, a proposition for which there is 'a considerable pedigree'.[28] The Full Court in *SZSSJ* concluded that:[29]

> a departure by an official from a representation about future procedure will be unfair in at least two circumstances:
>
> (a) where, but for the statement, the claimant for judicial review would have taken a different course, that is to say, situations of actual reliance by the claimant; or
> (a) where if the procedure had been adhered to a different result might have been obtained.

This summary is consistent with the High Court's previous analysis in *Lam*,[30] and also with earlier cases argued on different bases.[31] However, it is not reliant on legitimate expectation reasoning.[32] As Brennan J stated in *Quin*:[33]

> [W]hen a court is deciding what must be done in order to accord procedural fairness in a particular case, it has regard to precisely the same circumstances as those

Diplock). The view expressed by Schiemann LJ, that the consequences of election promises 'should be political and not legal', ought properly to extend to both circumstances: *R (on the application of Begbie) v Department of Education & Employment* [2000] 1 WLR 1115, 1126.

24 *Begbie* (n 23) 1134 (Sedley LJ).

25 See eg *R (Davies) v The Commissioners for Her Majesty's Revenue and Customs* [2011] 1 WLR 2625.

26 See *Quin* (n 15) 17 (Mason CJ). *Quin* can also be explained as an instance where policy was binding (perhaps only to a loose extent) but, because of the subject matter in question, could also be varied at any time and without notice or specific consultation.

27 See *Minister for Immigration and Ethnic Affairs v Teoh* (1995) 183 CLR 273 and n 50 below.

28 *SZSSJ v Minister for Immigration and Border Protection* [2015] FCAFC 125 [90]. Rares, Perram and Griffiths JJ referred specifically to *Shiu* (n 17) and *Haoucher v Minister for Immigration and Ethnic Affairs* (1990) 169 CLR 648.

29 *SZSSJ* (n 28)[94].

30 *Lam* (n 14).

31 See eg *Minister for Immigration and Ethnic Affairs v Kurtovic* (1990) 21 FCR 193.

32 The Full Court in fact decided the case on the basis that the Department's representations that there would be a fair process created a common law duty of procedural fairness: *SZSSJ* (n 28) [96]; cf T Brennan, 'Can Representations by a Decision-Maker be the Source of a Duty to Accord Procedural Fairness: A New Life For Legitimate Expectations?' (2015) 82 *AIAL Forum* 69, 72–73.

33 *Quin* (n 15) 40.

> to which the court might refer in considering whether the applicant entertains a legitimate expectation, but the enquiry whether the applicant entertains a legitimate expectation is superfluous. Again, if an express promise be given or a regular practice be adopted by a public authority, and the promise or practice is the source of a legitimate expectation, the repository is bound to have regard to the promise or practice in exercising the power, and it is unnecessary to enquire whether those factors give rise to a legitimate expectation. But the court must stop short of compelling fulfilment of the promise or practice unless the statute so requires or the statute permits the repository of the power to bind itself as to the manner of the future exercise of the power. It follows that the notion of legitimate expectation is not the key which unlocks the treasury of natural justice and it ought not unlock the gate which shuts the court out of review on the merits.

Promises and practices[34] expressed or adopted by public authorities are sufficient of themselves to create procedural fairness obligations. I would add that the same is true of policies which constitute a sufficiently 'pressing and focused ... kind of assurance'.[35] Brennan J made the point quoted above to emphasise the fact that legitimate expectations were irrelevant to the process of reasoning which led to this conclusion. However, if legitimate expectation reasoning is now forbidden in the context of determining procedural obligations,[36] the conclusions above regarding the importance of promises, practices and policies are not affected. It will be interesting to see whether the Australian decline of legitimate expectations will simply result in courts applying similar reasoning within the established rubric for determining the application and content of the rules of procedural fairness. Certainly, the High Court has itself proved adept at working around forbidden labels and proceeding as it had before.[37]

WHEN IS AN EXPECTATION 'LEGITIMATE'?

'Legitimate expectation' was a contentious label long before debate arose about whether legitimate expectations could be enforced substantively. Although the type of expectation in question had been protected in

[34] Schiemann LJ assumed that legitimate expectations could be formed by a public authority committing itself 'by practice or by promise' only: *R (Bibi) v Newham London Borough Council* [2002] 1 WLR 237, 244. However, policies were relevant to the availability of relief (at 240).

[35] *R (on the application of Bhatt Murphy (a firm)) v The Independent Assessor* [2008] EWCA Civ 755 [46] (Laws LJ). See R Moules, *Actions Against Public Officials: Legitimate Expectations, Misstatements and Misconduct*, (Sweet & Maxwell, 2009) 59–60.

[36] See below at nn 94–95.

[37] See eg the Court's response to a legislative ban on applying the *Wednesbury* ground in *Minister for Immigration & Multicultural Affairs; ex parte Applicant S20/2002* (2003) 198 ALR 59.

European law for some time,[38] Lord Denning coined the phrase 'legitimate expectation' in *Schmidt v Secretary of State for Home Affairs*[39] and is the figure with whom it is most associated.[40] His Lordship's purpose was to extend the obligation to provide a hearing to those who did not meet the existing threshold for procedural fairness of having a right or interest which would be adversely affected by the conduct of a public authority.[41] It soon attracted criticism on the basis that it had produced a memorable label but gave little guidance as to how it applied to procedural fairness.[42]

The growth of the coverage of procedural fairness by the time that *Kioa v West* was decided should have made the issue moot[43] were it not for the fact that the scope of legitimate expectations had also 'grown luxuriantly'.[44] By contrast with *Schmidt*, which concerned an applicant's legitimate expectation of receiving a hearing prior to the cancellation of the remaining period of a valid visa, *Kioa* concerned an appellant with no legal right to remain in Australia and held that he and his family were nonetheless owed procedural fairness before the decision to deport them was taken. The approach of Brennan J, whose view in *Kioa* and other cases was that the purpose of judicial review is to enforce the limits of public power through judicial construction of statutory purpose,[45] ultimately became dominant in the High Court with regard to matters of procedural fairness.[46] His Honour favoured the expansion of procedural fairness, since the power of the state had expanded 'beyond meaningful analogy to "legal rights or interests"'.[47]

Brennan J pointed out the lack of utility for that task that he observed in a doctrine which focused on 'the state of the applicant's mind' rather than on the manner in which his or her interests had been affected.[48] This was amply

[38] G Quinot, 'Substantive Legitimate Expectations in South African and European Administrative Law' (2004) 5 *German Law Journal* 65, 68; see *Case 54/65: Compagnie des Forges de Châtillon, Commentry et Neuves-Maisons v High Authority of the ECSC* [1966] ECR 185. Its use has been traced back as early as the 1950s in Germany; see R Perlingeiro, *Protection of Legitimate Expectations in Brazilian Administrative Law: 80-year-old Widow of a Pensioner* (SSRN eLibrary, 2015) 8 (available at http://ssrn.com/abstract=2627341).

[39] *Schmidt v Secretary of State for Home Affairs* [1969] 2 Ch 149, 170–71. Widgery LJ, who concurred with the Master of the Rolls, referred to 'the withdrawal of a right which the applicant *legitimately expected* to hold' (at 173, emphasis added) but his Lordship was discussing the difference between the decisions to grant a licence and to renew a licence respectively. See *FAI Insurances* (n 17).

[40] See C Forsyth, 'The Provenance and Protection of Legitimate Expectations' (1988) 47 *Cambridge Law Journal* 238.

[41] The threshold cases were *Cooper v Wandsworth Board of Works* (1863) 14 CBNS 180 and *Ridge v Baldwin* [1964] AC 40 respectively.

[42] See eg *Salemi v Mackellar (No 2)* (1977) 137 CLR 396, 404 (Barwick CJ).

[43] M Aronson, 'Private Bodies, Public Power and Soft Law in the High Court' (2007) 35 *Federal Law Review* 1, 5. See also *Shiu* (n 17).

[44] *Kioa v West* (1985) 159 CLR 550, 617 (Brennan J).

[45] Weeks (n 7) 91–94 (NB the cases cited at fn 193).

[46] Aronson (n 43) 2.

[47] Aronson (n 43) 6.

[48] *Kioa v West* (n 44) 621–22.

illustrated by the fact that, while the infant daughter of Mr and Mrs Kioa had standing in her own right to oppose her parents' deportation, she cannot have *expected* anything. McHugh J took a similar position in dissent in *Teoh*,[49] disagreeing with the earlier statement of Toohey J that '[l]egitimate expectation does not depend upon the knowledge and state of mind of the individual concerned'.[50] In *Teoh*, Toohey J reiterated his preference for legitimate expectations to be determined objectively,[51] and it is implicit that the rest of the majority did so too, since the evidence indicated that Mr Teoh had no subjective knowledge of the treaty upon which his legitimate expectation was based.

If the concept of 'expectation' has attracted criticism for being a 'fiction',[52] so too has the issue of when such an expectation will be 'legitimate'. Perhaps this infelicitous nomenclature is to blame for the view, now utterly orthodox in Australia, that to raise legitimate expectations is unhelpful and confusing. Aronson has pointed out that cases often used the term to signify 'something that the subject had not entertained in fact' but that s/he might have assumed or taken for granted.[53] Such an interpretation might have done more to extend the capacity to seek procedural fairness beyond the protection of rights and interests alone. However, the fact that, in contrast to other mechanisms for dealing with public authorities' broken promises, legitimate expectation does not 'do what it says on the tin' may not be determinative since, as Kirby J noted in agreeing that the term is a fiction, 'in this area of legal discourse, fictions abound'.[54] These words are employed other than in their normal English usage.[55]

Ultimately, the phrase 'legitimate expectation' garnered greater attention than the doctrine for which it stood. In *Lam*, Hayne J observed that it 'poses more questions than it answers', such as '[w]hat is meant by "legitimate"?'.[56] His Honour had earlier seemed to express relief in stating that it was:

> not necessary to consider … [issues] such as what is meant by 'abuse of power' and 'unfair' in a context where, by hypothesis, the relevant statute gives power

[49] *Teoh* (n 27) 313–14. There is support for this view in Brazil, where a judge placed reliance on German procedure to state that a claimant's legitimate expectation should be protected based on 'the confidence they have shown in the public powers, subject to demonstrating that [there] are serious reasons to believe in the stability of the administrative act' relied upon: Perlingeiro (n 38) 7.

[50] *Haoucher* (n 28) 670. Toohey J had not contradicted Brennan J's statement that it is the terms of the relevant statute which are relevant rather than 'the state of mind of an individual': *Kioa v West* (n 44)618.

[51] *Teoh* (n 27) 301.

[52] *Teoh* (n 27) 314 (McHugh J).

[53] He submitted that these might better be called 'reasonable assumptions' than legitimate expectations: Aronson (n 43) 5.

[54] *Applicant NAFF of 2002 v Minister for Immigration and Multicultural and Indigenous Affairs* (2004) 221 CLR 1, 22–23.

[55] Ahmed and Perry (n 13) 64. This is a common feature of the language employed in administrative law; see Weeks (n 2) 224, 228.

[56] *Lam* (n 14) 38.

> to make the decision which is impugned, and could any relief of the kinds enumerated in s 75(v) be granted? I mention this use of the phrase legitimate expectation in connection with substantive rather than procedural benefits only to emphasise the dangers of using the phrase without *careful articulation of the content of the principle which is said to be engaged in the particular case* (emphasis added).[57]

The two points are essentially the same and go to the dangers of advocating doctrine encapsulated in ill-defined language. Previously, Brennan J had remarked to similar effect in *Kioa* that 'legitimate expectation' is a term of 'uncertain connotation' and therefore apt to mislead as a 'criterion for determining the application or content' of procedural fairness.[58] The Privy Council in *Ng Yuen Shiu* commented with understatement that the phrase is 'somewhat lacking in precision'.[59]

'Legitimate' has long been read in this context as in fact meaning 'reasonable'[60] and not merely enforceable. This makes sense, since *Ridge v Baldwin* was decided on the basis that the plaintiff was owed procedural fairness before his employment was terminated even though his interest in his job fell short of being an enforceable right.[61] The difficulty with adding legitimate expectations to the position reached in *Ridge v Baldwin* may simply be that inquiries into the legitimacy of a claimant's expectations (which s/he may not even have held subjectively) went beyond the standard legal fictions which 'abound' in administrative law and reached the realms of misdirection.[62] Furthermore, part of the 'legitimacy' or 'reasonableness' in holding an expectation is to accept that an expectation cannot be legitimate in the required sense if it is not also relevant. Lord Sumption noted for the Privy Council that: 'Any expectation based on statute is by its nature defeasible. What Parliament gives, Parliament may take away provided that it does so consistently with the Constitution.'[63]

[57] *Lam* (n 14) 37.

[58] *Kioa v West* (n 44) 617.

[59] *Shiu* (n 17) 636.

[60] *Shiu* (n 17) 636 (Lord Fraser of Tullybelton); *Kioa v West* (n 44) 563 (Gibbs CJ); cf *Salemi v Mackellar* (n 42) 404 (Barwick CJ).

[61] *Ridge v Baldwin* (n 41) 66 (Lord Reid). In fact, the appellant did not want to save his job but his pension: ibid 68.

[62] The English preference for describing the doctrine whereby courts substantively enforce legitimate expectations as 'substantive unfairness' is perhaps understandable on the basis that it clearly focuses on fairness as an external 'constraint on the public interest' rather than becoming embroiled in what the claimant expected and whether s/he was reasonable to do so: K Stern, 'Substantive Fairness in UK and Australian Law' (2007) 29 *Australian Bar Review* 266, 267.

[63] *Ferguson, Maritime Life (Caribbean) Ltd v The Attorney General of Trinidad and Tobago (Trinidad and Tobago)* [2016] UKPC 2 [36]. His Lordship also noted that the 'Constitution [of Trinidad and Tobago] does not protect legitimate expectations as such, and there must be some doubt whether, and if so when, breach of a legitimate expectation can ever, in itself, be the basis of a constitutional challenge to the validity of an otherwise regular law": ibid. The same doubts apply in any other country with a written constitution.

By contrast with Australia, the English doctrine building on legitimate expectations has developed constantly: from the recognition of estoppel in public law, to the development of a substantive remedy in public law cases, to the relocation of equitable doctrine within the newly developed public law arrangements.[64] This constant surge onwards was initially accomplished regardless of any excessive concern about the syntax of its component terms, such as 'legitimate expectations' but extending to 'abuse of power'. This latter phrase was the fulcrum on which *Coughlan* turned the capacity of a court to remedy unfairness, specifically where a public authority failed to adhere to a legitimate expectation.[65] Lord Woolf MR noted in *Coughlan* that this area of law had been considered by the House of Lords in both *Preston*[66] and *ex parte Unilever plc*[67] but that there had remained a difference between the vocabulary of 'abuse of power' and the language of 'legitimate expectation', which his Lordship sought to correct.[68]

Abuse of power has been criticised on the basis that it is inherently imprecise, which is to say that 'power' is a concept that is usually defined with precision but whether it has been 'abused' is an issue on which the reasonable administrative mind might differ from the reasonable judicial mind. The orthodox judicial approach in Australia is that an exercise of statutory power which is otherwise *intra vires* can only be challenged on the narrow application of the *Wednesbury* ground.[69] The English approach is considerably broader but, as Laws LJ noted in his much-quoted consideration of the topic in *Nadarajah*, abuse of power does little to supply a principled basis for the substantive enforcement of legitimate expectations, nor does it assist in differentiating on a case-by-case basis what behaviour will fall foul of the standard.[70]

Faced with a dispute which turned on the content of the phrase 'abuse of [a public authority's] position or powers' in *Sisangia*, Lewison LJ looked at a range of judicial commentary on the related term 'abuse of power'.[71] His Lordship held that the authorities yielded no 'definition of … universal application'[72] but that the 'fact that "abuse of position or power" cannot be given a hard-edged definition does not mean that the concept itself is meaningless', since its 'ingredients' have been explained in a number of

[64] See respectively, *Preston* (n 10); *Coughlan* (n 14); and *R v East Sussex County Council* (n 11).

[65] *Coughlan* (n 14) 242; 243–54.

[66] *Preston* (n 10).

[67] *R v Inland Revenue Commissioners; ex parte Unilever plc* [1996] STC 681.

[68] *Coughlan* (n 14) 243.

[69] *Associated Provincial Picture Houses Ltd v Wednesbury Corporation* [1948] 1 KB 223.

[70] *R (Abdi and Nadarajah) v Secretary of State for the Home Department* [2005] EWCA Civ 1363 [67].

[71] *R (Sisangia) v Director of Legal Aid Casework* [2016] EWCA Civ 24 [14]–[22].

[72] Ibid, [14].

cases.[73] The Court of Appeal took the view that, although uncertain, sufficient meaning can be attached to the term 'abuse of power' to allow it to be usefully employed. To the extent that this is inconsistent with the approach of Laws LJ in *Nadarajah*, the difference might be explained by the greater number of cases which have sought to explain 'abuse of power'. However, given that the sources relied upon in *Sisangia* mostly preceded *Nadarajah*, it is perhaps more likely that the true answer is that an increasing number of common law and statutory actions[74] now oblige courts to discern meaning from 'abuse of power'. Lewison LJ made the point that any difficulty attendant on such a task does not allow a court to avoid it.

Labelling has in fact become more contentious rather than less in English law pertaining to substantive remedies against public authorities. The Supreme Court in *Keyu* deferred the constitutionally 'profound' decision on whether to replace the traditional '*Wednesbury* rationality' standard with 'more structured and principled' proportionality challenges.[75] In *Youssef*, the Court again deferred the issue, with a comment that threw doubt on the adequacy of the existing 'vocabulary' of substantive judicial review:

> It is to be hoped that an opportunity can be found in the near future for an authoritative review in this court of the judicial and academic learning on the issue, including relevant comparative material from other common law jurisdictions. Such a review might aim for rather more structured guidance for the lower courts than such *imprecise concepts* as 'anxious scrutiny' and 'sliding scales' (emphasis added).[76]

The contentiousness of labelling, and its precision, in this area may be part and parcel of the increased frequency with which the Supreme Court has elected to comment on the future of substantive judicial review in recent years without determining the issue.[77] It may also be a result of the doubt that academic authors have thrown on the content of 'traditional' grounds

[73] Ibid, [17]. See eg *R v Hillingdon London Borough Council; ex parte Puhlhofer* [1986] AC 484, 518 (Lord Brightman); *Begbie* (n 23) 1129 (Laws LJ); *Three Rivers District Council v Governor and Company of the Bank of England (No 3)* [2003] 2 AC 1, 235 (Lord Millett); *R v Lord President of the Privy Council; ex parte Page* [1993] AC 682, 693 (Lord Griffiths), 704 (Lord Browne-Wilkinson); *Lumba* (n 20).

[74] As in *Sisangia* (n 71) [3]–[4].

[75] *Keyu v Secretary of State for Foreign and Commonwealth Affairs* [2015] 3 WLR 1665, 1700–01 (Lord Neuberger).

[76] *Youssef v Secretary of State for Foreign and Commonwealth Affairs* [2016] UKSC 3 [55] (Lord Carnwath).

[77] Mark Elliott has noted Supreme Court *dicta* on this issue in *Kennedy v The Charity Commission* [2015] AC 455; *Pham v Secretary of State for the Home Department* [2015] 1 WLR 1591; *Keyu* (n 75); and *Youssef* (n 76); see M Elliott, '*Youssef*: Another Supreme Court Decision, another Set of *obiter dicta* on Substantive Judicial Review' (28 January 2016) *Public Law for Everyone*, available at: http://publiclawforeveryone.com/2016/01/28/youssef-another-supreme-court-decision-another-set-of-obiter-dicta-on-substantive-judicial-review/.

of review, such as reasonableness.[78] The attempt of Laws LJ to place substantive judicial review challenges on a 'principled' basis in *Nadarajah* demonstrates the difficulty of the task ahead of the Supreme Court. While there is no reason to believe that the Australian High Court would shirk such a task, its 'profundity' is another reason why the Court might focus on the adequacy of the existing grounds of challenge rather than attempting to create a new, 'principled' system from the ground up. Principles, like values,[79] are seductive[80] but usually turn out to be extremely hard to isolate and define. Elliott takes a more optimistic view but has nonetheless commented that '[q]uestions about substantive judicial review … often appear to be as intractable as they are beguiling'.[81]

Seemingly, since very shortly after *Coughlan*'s revolutionary elevation of the importance of legitimate expectations in English law, the Australian High Court has been at pains to state its disapproval of the public law legitimate expectations doctrine. In *Lam*, this came in the form of a frontal assault on *Coughlan*, a case upon which neither party had relied in argument.[82] That attack was conducted with such vehemence that it has never seriously been questioned since. However, *Lam* also saw the High Court withdraw from *Teoh*,[83] which had been decided by the High Court only eight years before *Lam* and had somewhat similar facts. As with *Coughlan*, neither party in *Lam* sought either to rely upon or attack *Teoh*.[84] Much of the Court's discussion of *Teoh* reflected its preference for McHugh J's dissent in that case but did not expressly overturn the majority's reasoning.[85] *Teoh*'s status has been a matter of conjecture in the years since *Lam* was decided,[86] although Taggart was certain that the High Court in *Lam* had 'done about as much as judges can by way of *obiter dicta* in a case where the point was not argued to overrule *Teoh*'.[87] There is no doubt that he is right in as much as *Lam* read down the findings in *Teoh* until their application was extremely narrow.

[78] More 'nuanced' views are said to bring that standard closer to proportionality: Elliott, ibid.

[79] M Groves and G Weeks, 'Substantive (Procedural) Review in Australia' in H Wilberg and M Elliott (eds), *The Scope and Intensity of Substantive Review: Traversing Taggart's Rainbow* (Hart Publishing, 2015) 133, 151.

[80] It is axiomatic amongst practising litigators that principles are always expensive.

[81] M Elliott, 'From Bifurcation to Calibration: Twin-Track Deference and the Culture of Justification' in Wilberg and Elliott (n 77) 61, 61.

[82] *Lam* (n 14) 22–27 (McHugh and Gummow JJ).

[83] *Teoh* (n 27). In practice, *Lam* could not overrule *Teoh* because to overrule such a recent case would have required that possibility to be put directly before a full bench of seven judges, rather than indirectly before the bench of five which sat in *Lam*.

[84] *Lam* (n 14) 28 (McHugh and Gummow JJ). See also the transcripts in *Lam* [2001] HCATrans 144 and [2002] HCATrans 248.

[85] *Lam* (n 14) 27–34 (McHugh and Gummow JJ), 37–39 (Hayne J), 45–48 (Callinan J).

[86] See eg M Groves, 'Treaties and Legitimate Expectations: The Rise and Fall of *Teoh* in Australia' (2010) 15 *Judicial Review* 323.

[87] M Taggart, '"Australian Exceptionalism" in Judicial Review' (2008) 36 *Federal Law Review* 1, 17.

What has occurred since *Lam* is that the High Court has changed its focus from substantive enforcement of legitimate expectations to the procedural consequences of legitimate expectations. In *S10*, the defendants made a submission based on the standard formula that procedural fairness applies where there exists 'some identifiable right, interest, privilege or legitimate expectation' which is affected. In the circumstances of the case, this submission might easily have been dismissed on the basis that the Minister could not have been compelled to exercise his statutory powers. However, the majority took the opportunity to inveigh against the *language* of legitimate expectations more sternly than *Lam* had done:[88]

> the phrase 'legitimate expectation' when used in the field of public law either adds nothing or poses more questions than it answers and thus is an unfortunate expression which should be disregarded. The phrase, as Brennan J explained in *South Australia v O'Shea*,[89] 'tends to direct attention on the merits of the particular decision rather than on the character of the interests which any exercise of the power is apt to affect.

Brennan J had never been persuaded that the concept of legitimate expectations added anything to the process of determining to whom procedural fairness was owed,[90] a position he was not alone in holding.[91] In any case, for many years before *S10*,[92] the application of procedural fairness had already been sufficiently broad that the importance of the formula applied by the defendants in *S10* should have been minimal.[93] It is interesting not only that the majority elected to engage again with legitimate expectations in a case where it was not necessary to do so, but that the attack was driven entirely by the distracting nature of the term rather than its content. It is a curious aspect of the different paths that have been taken in England and Australia with regard to legitimate expectations that the highest courts in each country remain, after many years, so driven by the difficulties presented by the labels of legitimate expectations and its attendant doctrines.

The High Court's comment about the language of legitimate expectation in *obiter dicta* in *S10* seemed to have done little more than to encourage further consideration of the procedural significance of legitimate expectations by the time *WZARH* was heard three years later.[94] In that matter, the Full Court of the Federal Court had previously decided that a breach of

[88] *Plaintiff S10/2011* (n 20) 658 (Gummow, Hayne, Crennan and Bell JJ).
[89] *South Australia v O'Shea* (1987) 163 CLR 378, 411.
[90] *Kioa v West* (n 44) 617–22.
[91] See Weeks (n 2) 224, 227–28.
[92] Possibly as long ago as *Kioa v West* (n 44), but at least since *Annetts v McCann* (1990) 170 CLR 596.
[93] cf AF Mason, 'Procedural Fairness: its Development and Continuing Role of Legitimate Expectation' (2005) 12 *Australian Journal of Administrative Law* 103, 106.
[94] *Minister for Immigration and Border Protection v WZARH* (2015) 90 ALJR 25.

procedural fairness resulted when an adverse review of an asylum-seeker's refugee status was commenced by one reviewer (who had interviewed the asylum-seeker) and completed by another (who made a strong adverse determination as to the asylum-seeker's credibility). The asylum-seeker's case was strong on this point and, in the Full Court, it succeeded in relatively short order.[95] The judgment of Flick and Gleeson JJ (with whom Nicholas J agreed) was in all substantive respects unimpeachable but for the fact that its reasoning on procedural fairness adopted the *language* of legitimate expectations.[96] It was ultimately adhered to in its other aspects by the High Court, a majority of which noted that the attention paid by Flick and Gleeson JJ to the failure of the second reviewer to alert the asylum-seeker to the change in the administrative process 'was a sufficient basis for their Honours' decision, which might have been more readily apparent had their Honours not been disposed to deploy the concept of legitimate expectation in their analysis of the issue'.[97]

The case therefore may not have seemed likely to receive special leave for appeal to the High Court, particularly given that counsel for the respondent asylum-seeker explicitly disclaimed the reasoning in the Full Federal Court which was founded in legitimate expectation.[98] However, it appeared that the High Court wished to reiterate forcefully some of the points it had made in *S10*. Kiefel, Bell and Keane JJ briefly recounted the history of the High Court's consideration of legitimate expectation reasoning, stating pointedly that the 'position has been made sufficiently clear that it is not necessary for this Court to engage again in discussion of the concept of "legitimate expectation"'.[99] Their Honours concluded that:

> Recourse to the notion of legitimate expectation is both unnecessary and unhelpful. Indeed, reference to the concept of legitimate expectation may well distract from the real question; namely, what is required in order to ensure that the decision is made fairly in the circumstances having regard to the legal framework within which the decision is to be made.[100]

Gageler and Gordon JJ reached the same conclusions about the appeal but put their comments about legitimate expectations in slightly different terms. Their Honours noted that the concept was a confusing tool with which to determine the content of procedural fairness and that:

> By focusing on the opportunity expected, or legitimately to have been expected, the concept can distract from the true inquiry into the opportunity that a reasonable

[95] Both judgments were delivered in a mere 57 paragraphs: *WZARH v Minister for Immigration and Border Protection* (2014) 230 FCR 130.
[96] Ibid 137–42.
[97] *WZARH* (n 94) 32 (Kiefel, Bell and Keane JJ).
[98] *Minister for Immigration and Border Protection v WZARH* [2015] HCATrans 092.
[99] *WZARH* (n 94) 32.
[100] *WZARH* (n 94).

administrator ought fairly to have given. The former is relevant only in so far as it bears on the latter.[101]

Ultimately, the distinction between legitimate expectation being an 'unnecessary and unhelpful' concept or simply confusing and of marginal relevance is less important that the overall message of *WZARH*. That was that the High Court had meant every word of its criticism of the concept in *S10*, that legitimate expectations will not only be refused substantive enforcement in Australia but can no longer be employed to determine the content of procedural fairness, and that even otherwise flawless judgments will have erred by thinking in terms of legitimate expectations. The Australian High Court was pellucidly clear on these points in *WZARH*, as it had indeed been previously in *S10*. The argument can no longer be sustained that, while *Lam* had indicated the High Court's disapproval of legitimate expectation reasoning, it had not reversed cases which had applied such reasoning but 'simply pivot[ed] … away from a doctrinal reliance upon legitimate expectation towards an examination of the fairness of the process'.[102] It would take unusually courageous[103] counsel to raise an argument based upon legitimate expectations before the High Court, or any other Australian court, again. It seems inescapable, unless a most unexpected change of approach occurs, that legitimate expectations are dead in Australian courts and will bear little further academic analysis in the Australian context. At the very least, the language of legitimate expectations will not now reappear.

WHAT FOLLOWS FROM A DISAPPOINTED EXPECTATION?

The issue of an expectation's 'legitimacy' is not only about its formation; it is essentially one that goes to whether anything follows from the state failing or refusing to do what is expected of it. Gleeson CJ distinguished the 'mer[e] departure from a representation' from unfairness consequent on any departure.[104] Defeating an expectation created by a public authority in another party is not legally significant without more. It therefore becomes important to determine what 'more' must be demonstrated in order to obtain a judicial remedy based upon the disappointment of an expectation. For the purposes of this chapter, it is not important to discuss the varying approaches to whether or not a judicial review court can or should provide substantive relief.[105]

[101] *WZARH* (n 94) 36. Their Honours cited *Lam* (n 14) 12–13 (Gleeson CJ).

[102] *SZSSJ* (n 28) [92].

[103] In the sense popularised by Sir Humphrey Appleby: A Jay and J Lynn, *The Complete 'Yes, Minister': The Diaries of a Cabinet Minister* (HarperCollins, 1988) 141–42.

[104] *Lam* (n 14) 12.

[105] Particularly since the approaches in both England and Australia are now all but fixed; see respectively *Coughlan* (n 14); *Lam* (n 14).

The first point to note is that the rights consequent on establishing a legitimate expectation are always conditional. On a procedural level, this requirement goes to whether the creation of a legitimate expectation has in practice resulted in unfairness to the applicant. As Gleeson CJ explained in *Lam*, fairness is not an 'abstract concept' but 'is essentially practical', and 'the concern of the law is to avoid practical injustice'.[106] Where a public authority seeks to resile from a legitimate expectation, whether or not substantive enforcement of the legitimate expectation is sought, the interest of the individual concerned will always be subject to the public interest. However, the onus is on the public authority to prove that there is an 'overriding public interest' which demands such action.[107]

In England prior to *Coughlan*, whether the public interest outweighed a legitimate expectation was determined on the undemanding *Wednesbury* standard.[108] The *Coughlan* Court of Appeal limited *Wednesbury*'s application to circumstances where 'the public authority is only required to bear in mind its previous policy or other representation, giving it the weight it thinks right, but no more, before deciding whether to change course'.[109] It differentiated cases in which a 'promise or practice induces a legitimate expectation of, for example, being consulted before a particular decision is taken' in which it was considered 'uncontentious that the court itself will require the *opportunity for consultation* to be given unless there is an overriding reason to resile from it' (original emphasis).[110] The Court of Appeal stipulated that the court itself and not the decision-maker would determine whether the reason for refusing a hearing was adequate, a process that would be informed by the requirements of fairness. The Court of Appeal also held that, before a public authority could disappoint a legitimate expectation of a substantive benefit, it would fall to the court to 'decide whether to frustrate the expectation is so unfair that to take a new and different course will amount to an abuse of power' by 'weighing the requirements of fairness against any overriding interest relied upon for the change of policy'.[111] The rise of proportionality reasoning in England has only reinforced the role of courts as directing their attention 'to the relative weight accorded to interests and considerations' in a given case.[112]

[106] *Lam* (n 14) 14.

[107] *R v Secretary of State for the Home Department; ex parte Asif Mahmood Khan* [1984] 1 WLR 1337, 1344 (Parker LJ); *Coughlan* (n 14) 238 (Lord Woolf).

[108] Moules (n 35) 81.

[109] *Coughlan* (n 14) 241.

[110] Ibid, 242. The Supreme Court in *Moseley* later approved key parts of what *Coughlan* said about consultation, but made clear that a duty of consultation, while related to the doctrine of legitimate expectations, was also distinct from it: *R (Moseley) v London Borough of Haringey* [2014] 1 WLR 3947, 3956–57 (Lord Wilson), 3961 (Lord Reed).

[111] *Coughlan* (n 14) 242.

[112] *R (Daly) v Secretary of State for the Home Department* [2001] 2 AC 532, 547 (Lord Steyn).

It follows that what one might legitimately expect from the state is heavily influenced by the remedial approach taken by the courts. An English claimant's expectations might take into account the fact that it falls to the court to assess what remedy should be granted based on concepts such as 'fairness' and 'abuse of power' which are either appropriately flexible or worryingly nebulous, according to one's outlook.[113] An Australian claimant, by contrast, who appealed to notions of fairness in judicial review proceedings, could only expect to be told that s/he was inviting the court to dabble in the merits of the case and apply a standard suitable to tribunal hearings. A strict *ultra vires* approach to judicial review, such as is orthodox in Australia,[114] holds that a court can inquire whether a decision-maker has operated in excess of his or her jurisdiction but cannot exercise the statutory or executive power held by that decision-maker in his or her stead. Within this restriction falls any invitation for the court to weigh fairness to an individual against the interests of the public generally.

Additionally, there is a line of thought that says that, even if courts were constitutionally able to conduct such an exercise, they ought not because they lack the expertise to reach the right solution reliably.[115] This is familiar from where review is sought of polycentric decision-making,[116] a difficult process even before specialist tribunals.[117] Much has been made of the fact that the Court of Appeal in *Coughlan* gave greater weight to the disappointed expectation of a disabled (and faultless) woman than it did to the appellant health authority's plans to develop better health care options for a wider range of people.[118] The Court of Appeal in *Bibi* was frank about this limitation, particularly where the legitimate expectations of the claimant may be at variance with the legitimate expectations of people not represented before the court.[119] Ultimately, the paths that courts in different countries have elected to take on this issue do not appear to have been driven by the concerns which are apparent with courts taking a role of balancing issues of fairness.

[113] Schiemann LJ perhaps trod the middle ground when he remarked that 'without refinement, the question whether the reneging on a promise would be so unfair as to amount to an abuse of power is an uncertain guide': *Bibi* (n 34) 247.

[114] See the seminal modern statement in *Quin* (n 15) 35–36 (Brennan J).

[115] Weeks (n 7) 164–65.

[116] Most famously in LL Fuller, 'The Forms and Limits of Adjudication' (1978) 92 *Harvard Law Review* 353.

[117] A Edgar, 'Participation and Responsiveness in Merits Review of Polycentric Decisions: A Comparison of Development Assessment Appeals' (2010) 27 *Environmental and Planning Law Journal* 36.

[118] See M Groves and G Weeks, 'The Legitimacy of Expectations About Fairness: Can Process and Substance be Untangled?' in J Bell et al (eds), *Public Law Adjudication in Common Law Systems: Process and Substance* (Hart Publishing, 2016) 165, 171.

[119] *Bibi* (n 34) 247–48 (Schiemann LJ).

CONCLUSION

There is a difference between the administration we want and what we are able to compel. Should the courts hold the answers to every issue where a public authority has created an expectation in another party? To put the question another way, must we rely on judicial enforcement to protect our expectations, or is there sometimes a preferable option? The discussion above has touched on the possibilities that certain remedial options may be better suited to the executive than the judiciary, either by dint of the former's greater expertise in certain matters or because the issue for consideration is, of its nature, political. It is worth noting, however, that the differences between the various countries which engage with the concept of legitimate expectations can in the main be explained by different judicial arrangements in each. It is likelier that each has (or is working towards) a solution which suits it, and not that any country has taken an approach which is simply wrong.

What we can legitimately expect from the state depends on multiple variables. How was the expectation engendered? Is the expectation reasonable to hold? Is the expectation of a hearing or a more substantive outcome? One of the issues that seems common across several jurisdictions is whether or not the outcome is 'fair'—although determining that issue is beset with difficulties. There is no single answer to the question posed by the chapter. However, one possibility is that that question cannot be answered without also asking: what can we legitimately expect from our courts?

8

The Unruly Horse and the Gordian Knot: Legitimate Expectations in South Africa

CORA HOEXTER*

INTRODUCTION

SOUTH AFRICA IS something of a hybrid in the common law world. Owing to our colonial past, South African administrative law was formed essentially along English lines. However, our law lost much of its common law character in the momentous year of 1994, when constitutional democracy was introduced and section 24 of the transitional or interim Constitution[1] brought in rights to just administrative action for the first time.

Today, South African administrative law is founded on a similar set of rights contained in section 33 of the 'final' or 1996 Constitution.[2] The section 33 rights have since been expressed in more detail in the *Promotion of Administrative Justice Act 3 of 2000* (PAJA), effectively giving South African administrative law a statutory basis. However, a large body of common law principles continues to exist alongside the legislative framework, and (to the extent that it is compatible with the Constitution) it informs the courts' interpretation of the section 33 rights and of the PAJA. The influence of English administrative law remains fairly strong, and the courts sometimes take note of developments in other common law jurisdictions as well.

The doctrine of legitimate expectations is a prime example of English influence. The doctrine was a latecomer to pre-democratic South African law, no

* This work is based on research supported in part by the National Research Foundation of South Africa (Grant No 96285). Any opinion, finding and conclusion or recommendation expressed in the material is that of the author, and the Foundation does not accept any liability in this regard.

1 *Constitution of the Republic of South Africa, Act 200 of 1993* (hereafter 'interim Constitution').

2 *Constitution of the Republic of South Africa, 1996* (hereafter simply 'the Constitution' unless the context requires clarification).

doubt reflecting the rather moribund state of procedural fairness generally in those days. However, in the late 1980s, during the last days of apartheid, the whole area of 'natural justice' was reinvigorated by means of some bold and creative judicial lawmaking—including the adoption of the legitimate expectation doctrine in the case of *Administrator, Transvaal v Traub*.[3]

In that case Corbett CJ observed that as a concept new to our law, legitimate expectations could become an 'unruly horse' that might require curbing from time to time.[4] But the horse proved tractable enough, and the Chief Justice could hardly have foreseen just how useful it would be. The concept of legitimate expectations had a great impact on South African law at the time and, as I hope to show in what follows, it remains a vigorous and exciting part of our administrative law.

In the second part of this chapter, I explain the significance and scope of legitimate expectations in South African law, both before and since 1994. I then discuss the requirements for establishing such an expectation. The case law in this regard suggests that the courts are (again) becoming more flexible about the ways in which a legitimate expectation may be established.

In the third part, I speculate about the substantive enforcement of legitimate expectations, something most public lawyers probably regard as an inevitable development in this country. Some degree of substantive enforcement has in fact taken place in a sporadic and more or less inadvertent fashion in the case law. But although the superior courts[5] have amply acknowledged the possibility of substantive enforcement, they have not yet practised it officially.

Finally, I draw attention to an intriguing Constitutional Court judgment, *KZN Joint Liaison Committee*,[6] in which an official promise was in fact enforced without reliance on legitimate expectations—yet in a manner strongly reminiscent of the English jurisprudence on substantive enforcement.

LEGITIMATE EXPECTATIONS: THEIR SIGNIFICANCE AND SCOPE

Traub and its Impact on the Common Law

For much of the pre-democratic era, the South African law relating to procedural fairness was characterised by twin tendencies that I have described

[3] *Administrator, Transvaal v Traub* [1989] ZASCA 90; 1989 (4) SA 731 (A).

[4] Ibid, 761F–G.

[5] Apart from a few specialist courts, the superior courts consist of divisions of the High Court (formerly the Supreme Court of South Africa). Above the High Court is an intermediate court of appeal, rather confusingly styled the Supreme Court of Appeal. It is the successor to the Appellate Division, the highest court of the pre-1994 era. At the apex of the system is the only new court created for the post-1994 era, the Constitutional Court.

[6] *KwaZulu-Natal Joint Liaison Committee v MEC for Education, KwaZulu-Natal* [2013] ZACC 10; 2013 (4) SA 262 (CC), hereafter simply *KZN Joint Liaison Committee*.

elsewhere as those of parsimony and conceptualism.[7] The courts were fearful of somehow devaluing the *audi alteram partem* principle by applying it 'outside its proper limits',[8] and they relied on the classification of functions to supply those limits. Entitlement to a fair hearing was thus restricted to *judicial* and *quasi-judicial* matters. In substance, these labels denoted cases involving an adverse effect on 'existing rights' in the strict sense of forfeiture or deprivation. But the labels themselves also did some work: action of a legislative nature, for example, could not attract the benefits of fairness even when it obviously deprived people of existing rights.[9]

As for 'purely administrative' cases, those generally involved mere applicants: people who had no right to whatever they happened to be applying for, and who had at best an interest in the application. They were not entitled to procedural fairness at all. The victims of preliminary and investigative action were fobbed off too, but on a slightly different basis: that such action did not *in itself* affect rights adversely.[10] In case after case the courts proved adept at finding technical reasons for denying most complainants the benefits of procedural fairness, and no doubt congratulated themselves on thus maintaining its value.

Against this unpromising background, it is easy to appreciate how invigorating the effects were of *Administrator, Transvaal v Traub*,[11] in which the Appellate Division approved the doctrine of legitimate expectations. The doctrine was by no means unheard of in South Africa at that stage—it had already found its way into a number of judgments,[12] but had not yet been employed by the highest court.

The case concerned six doctors who had applied for posts as Senior House Officers (SHOs) at Baragwanath Hospital, a public hospital serving the country's biggest black township, Soweto. Two of the six doctors had already held SHO posts at the hospital and were seeking reappointment, while the other four were new applicants. All six had been recommended for SHO posts by the heads of department concerned, and in the past such recommendation had led to appointment 'as a matter of course', and to

[7] Cora Hoexter, 'The Principle of Legality in South African Administrative Law' (2004) 4 *Macquarie Law Journal* 165.

[8] *Laubscher v Native Commissioner, Piet Retief* 1958 (1) SA 546 (A), 549C.

[9] *Pretoria City Council v Modimola* 1966 (3) SA 250 (A); *E Snell and Co Ltd v Minister of Agricultural Economics* 1986 (3) SA 532 (D); cf *Cooper v Wandsworth Board of Works* (1863) 14 CBNS 180.

[10] *Cassem v Oos-Kaapse Komitee van die Groepsgebiederaad* 1959 (3) SA 651 (A); *South African Defence and Aid Fund v Minister of Justice* 1967 (1) SA 263 (A).

[11] *Administrator, Transvaal v Traub* (n 3).

[12] *Everett v Minister of the Interior* 1981 (2) SA 453 (C) (expulsion of an alien); *Langeni v Minister of Health and Welfare* 1988 (4) SA 93 (W); *Mokoena v Administrator, Transvaal* 1988 (4) SA 912 (W) and *Mokopanele v Administrator, Transvaal* 1989 (1) SA 434 (O) (all relating to the dismissal of employees); *Lunt v University of Cape Town* 1989 (2) SA 438 (C) (refusal to readmit student).

reappointment 'invariably'.[13] However, the Director of Hospital Services decided not to appoint the applicants for a reason that became common cause: each of the six had put their names to a letter published in the *South African Medical Journal* which criticised in strong terms the appalling overcrowding and other deplorable conditions at the hospital, and pointed out the 'callous disregard' of the provincial administration to this 'affront to human dignity'.[14]

The essential question was whether the doctors had been entitled to a hearing before the adverse decision was made. The Court below held that in view of the prejudicial effects of the decision on the applicants, they ought to have been heard.[15] The governing legislation, Goldstone J reasoned, obliged the Director to judge the suitability of the applicants, and '[a] decision that a professional person is unsuitable for a post is potentially of the utmost importance and will, if it remains, be a permanent blot on his good name'.[16] He added that the claim to a hearing thus arose from a statutory duty, and 'not from a legitimate expectation'[17]—for Goldstone J was ahead of his time, and had already employed the English-law doctrine in his own judgments.[18]

On appeal the result was confirmed, but on a new and different basis. Writing for a unanimous court, Corbett CJ reasoned that since the doctors had no right to be appointed to the posts they had applied for, the adverse decision could not be said to have affected their existing rights prejudicially.[19] That was not the end of the matter, however, for the Court then turned to the concept of legitimate expectations. Corbett CJ first surveyed the English jurisprudence on the topic, and quoted from speeches in the *CCSU* case including these most seminal words of Lord Fraser:

> Legitimate, or reasonable, expectation may arise either from an express promise given on behalf of a public authority or from the existence of a regular practice which the claimant can reasonably expect to continue.[20]

The Chief Justice then referred to a number of South African cases inspired by English law, in which the courts had extended procedural fairness to complainants whose existing rights had not been prejudicially affected.[21]

[13] *Administrator, Transvaal v Traub* (n 3) 752E–H.

[14] *Administrator, Transvaal v Traub* (n 3) 746B–G, where an extract from the letter is quoted.

[15] The case was reported as *Traube v Administrator, Transvaal* 1989 (1) SA 397 (W).

[16] Ibid, 400I.

[17] Ibid, 402C.

[18] *Langeni v Minister of Health and Welfare* (n 12) and *Mokoena v Administrator, Transvaal* (n 12).

[19] *Administrator, Transvaal v Traub* (n 3) 754D–G.

[20] *Council of Civil Service Unions (CCSU) v Minister for the Civil Service* [1985] AC 374, 401B–C, quoted in *Administrator, Transvaal v Traub* (n 3) 756I.

[21] *Administrator, Transvaal v Traub* (n 3) 759D–E: see the cases listed in n 12 above.

While the Appellate Division had itself previously rejected an argument based on legitimate expectations,[22] there had been no basis for it in that instance and Corbett CJ did not see the earlier judgment as 'closing the door'.[23] He concluded:

> There are many cases ... where an adherence to the formula of 'liberty, property and existing rights' would fail to provide a legal remedy, when the facts cry out for one; and would result in a decision which appeared to have been arrived at by a procedure which was clearly unfair being immune from review. The law should in such cases be made to reach out and come to the aid of a person prejudicially affected.[24]

In this instance, the Court found, the prejudicial effects of the decision taken in conjunction with the past practice gave the applicants a legitimate expectation that approval of the posts would follow as a matter of course, and/or that they would be heard before the Director decided to depart from the practice.[25]

Not content with this reform, Corbett CJ went on to criticise the use of labels such as 'quasi-judicial' and 'purely administrative', which he said added nothing to the essential question whether rights had been prejudicially affected, and which in any event had little to say to the problem before him.[26] A couple of years later the classification of functions was all but jettisoned by the Appellate Division.[27]

After *Traub*, legitimate expectations achieved instant success and were relied on in a range of cases in the last years of the apartheid era. This was usually when rights had not been affected adversely, but sometimes even when they had been:[28] a measure of the popularity of the doctrine with both litigants and courts. Past practices featured in some cases,[29] but there was also a definite tendency in the early jurisprudence not to insist on the

[22] In *Castel NO v Metal & Allied Workers' Union* 1987 (4) SA 795 (A), 810E–811A.

[23] *Administrator, Transvaal v Traub* (n 3) 760D–E.

[24] *Administrator, Transvaal v Traub* (n 3) 761D–F.

[25] *Administrator, Transvaal v Traub* (n 3) 761H–762D.

[26] *Administrator, Transvaal v Traub* (n 3) 762F–763J, and without reference to *Ridge v Baldwin* 1964 AC 40, although that case was cited in argument.

[27] See *South African Roads Board v Johannesburg City Council* [1991] ZASCA 63; 1991 (4) SA 1 (A), 10J. In *Traub*, Corbett CJ was not entirely correct in supposing that labels such as 'quasi-judicial' added nothing to the inquiry, for as I have pointed out above, at the time 'legislative' action failed to attract natural justice even if it *did* affect rights prejudicially. That state of affairs was boldly ameliorated in *Roads Board* itself.

[28] See further Cora Hoexter, *1991 Supplement to Baxter's Administrative Law* (Juta & Co Ltd, 1992) 75–78.

[29] Examples are *Minister of Local Government and Land Tenure v Inkosinathi Property Developers (Pty) Ltd* 1992 (2) SA 234 (TkA) (regular practice of not refusing applications for a permit); *Union of Teachers' Associations of South Africa v Minister of Education and Culture, House of Representatives* 1993 (2) SA 828 (C) (longstanding practice of consulting school principals about appointing substitute teachers).

presence of either of the triggers expounded in the *CCSU* case.[30] In such instances the courts relied simply on broad ideas of fairness, and indeed the link between legitimate expectations and the more general 'duty to act fairly' had been noted in *Traub*.[31]

Legitimate Expectations in the Constitution and the PAJA

South Africa's transition to democracy was governed by a deliberately temporary compact, the interim Constitution, which was intended to serve while a more permanent constitution was drawn up by the Constitutional Assembly. An indication of the importance attached to legitimate expectations is that they were expressly referred to in section 24, the administrative justice clause of the interim Constitution. Section 24*(b)* conferred on 'every person' a right to procedurally fair administrative action 'where any of his or her rights *or legitimate expectations* is affected or threatened' (emphasis added).

In due course, section 24 of the interim Constitution was replaced by section 33 of the 'final' or 1996 Constitution, which consists of three subsections. Section 33(1) is broad and uncalibrated, and simply confers on 'everyone' a right to administrative action 'that is lawful, reasonable and procedurally fair'. By contrast, section 33(2) makes the entitlement to reasons contingent on a decision's adverse effect on *rights*. The third subsection mandates national legislation to give effect to the rights in subsections (1) and (2). There is thus no express mention of legitimate expectations: the sweeping language of section 33(1) evidently militated against it. The omission presents no problem, however, for it is well understood that common law principles and doctrines such as this have been absorbed by the Constitution and that they form part of the 'one system of law' that is ultimately governed by the Constitution.[32]

The PAJA, the legislation envisaged in section 33(3), does refer explicitly to legitimate expectations. Section 3(1) states that '[a]dministrative action which materially and adversely affects the rights *or legitimate expectations* of any person must be procedurally fair' (emphasis added). Oddly enough, however, the presence of the italicised words is thought to be the result of a drafting error. In its proposed version of the PAJA, the South African

[30] Notably, in *Minister of Justice, Transkei v Gemi* 1994 (3) SA 28 (TkA), the Court denied their status as prerequisites. See also eg *Khan t/a Khan's Motor Transport v Chairman, Pietermaritzburg Local Road Transportation Board* 1990 (3) SA 234 (N); *Mokgoro v Acting Rector, Setlogelo Technikon* 1994 (4) SA 104 (B).

[31] *Administrator, Transvaal v Traub* (n 3) 755D–E, with reference to Robert E Riggs, 'Legitimate Expectation and Procedural Fairness in English Law' (1988) 36 *American Journal of Comparative Law* 395.

[32] *Pharmaceutical Manufacturers' Association of SA: In re ex parte President of the Republic of South Africa* [2000] ZACC 11; 2000 (2) SA 674 (CC), [33] and [44].

Law Reform Commission had defined 'administrative action' as action affecting not only rights but also legitimate expectations and interests, and had included these concepts in the clause governing procedural fairness as well. The legislature, on the other hand, evidently intended to reinstate the 'deprivation' approach of the pre-*Traub* common law, and the various references to legitimate expectations and interests were deliberately rooted out of the PAJA shortly before it was enacted—excepting the reference in section 3(1).

The unfortunate result of this oversight was a conflict with section 1 of the PAJA, which defines 'administrative action' in terms of its adverse effect on *rights* only, with no mention of legitimate expectations or interests. Since the Act applies only to administrative action, the effect is that section 3(1) requires procedural fairness in respect of action to which the PAJA does not apply. Realising perhaps that the legislature was highly unlikely to fix (or even acknowledge) this mistake, in 2008 the Constitutional Court went ahead and resolved the tension in the case of *Walele v City of Cape Town*.[33] It did so simply by ruling that in the context of section 3 of the PAJA, administrative action has a broader meaning than usual.[34]

The Case Law of the Constitutional Era

Just over two decades of constitutional democracy have yielded a lively but not entirely consistent jurisprudence on the topic of legitimate expectations.[35] In what follows, I draw attention to two related questions that have been addressed in the case law: what makes an expectation legitimate, and whether a legitimate expectation may be based on something other than a promise or a regular practice (a category generally taken to include policies).

The Ingredients of Legitimacy

One line of cases has underscored the need for an expectation that is legitimate in an objective sense. The requirements of legitimacy were summarised in the *Phillips* case in 2002 as (i) a reasonable expectation (ii) induced by the decision-maker and based on (iii) a clear, unambiguous

[33] *Walele v City of Cape Town* [2008] ZACC 11; 2008 (6) SA 129 (CC).

[34] Ibid, [37]. In her minority judgment, O'Regan ADCJ arrived at a similar result (at [126]) by reasoning that the more general provision of the statute, section 1, had to be read as impliedly supplemented by the more specific provision, section 3(1).

[35] See further Daniel Malan Pretorius, 'Ten Years After *Traub*: The Doctrine of Legitimate Expectations in South African Administrative Law' (2000) 117 *South African Law Journal* 520 and 'Letting the Unruly Horse Gallop in the Field of Private Law: The Doctrine of Legitimate Expectation in "Purely Contractual" Cases' (2001) 118 *South African Law Journal* 503.

representation which was (iv) competent and lawful for the decision-maker to make.[36] This list was soon approved by the Supreme Court of Appeal,[37] and all four requirements have found illustration in the jurisprudence of the constitutional era.

The first has been especially prominent in practice, and the courts have often pointed out the difference between a reasonable expectation and wishful thinking. In *Szymanski*, for example, it was held not to be reasonable for the applicant to expect that the pass mark for a special veterinary exam would be 40 per cent rather than the usual 50 per cent,[38] and in *Duncan* it was not reasonable for the applicant to suppose that he would be awarded a long-term fishing licence 'whatever the circumstances'.[39]

Requirements (ii) and (iv) are also uncontroversial in the cases. Claims have generally failed where the expectation was induced by someone other than the decision-maker,[40] where a promise was *ultra vires*[41] and where the expectation consisted of doing something unlawful.[42] There is no indication that this position is likely to change.

Regarding (iii), the requirement of a 'clear and unambiguous representation', the jurisprudence illustrates a range of promises and assurances, practices and policies that evidently qualified, as well as cases in which no promise, practice or other representation could be established.[43] As has been the experience in other jurisdictions, promises have generally operated as the strongest type of representation and policies as the weakest.

Claude Neon,[44] one of the earliest cases of the post-1994 era, related to a promise of being informed of the date on which bids for a municipal street lighting contract would be due. The promise was not kept and the tender was awarded to a third party, but the Court's vindication of the right to procedural fairness led it to set aside the award.

Both a regular practice and a promise featured in another prominent case, *Premier, Mpumalanga*,[45] which concerned transport and other bursaries for

[36] *National Director of Public Prosecutions v Phillips* 2002 (4) SA 60 (W) [28], largely inspired by The Rt Hon Lord Woolf and Jeffrey Jowell QC, *de Smith, Woolf & Jowell Judicial Review of Administrative Action*, 5th edn (Sweet & Maxwell, 1995).

[37] *South African Veterinary Council v Szymanski* [2003] ZASCA 11; 2003 (4) SA 42 (SCA) [19]–[20].

[38] Ibid, [20]–[21].

[39] *Duncan v Minister of Environmental Affairs and Tourism (MEAT)* 2009 ZASCA 168; 2010 (6) SA 374 (SCA) [17].

[40] *Meyer v Iscor Pension Fund* 2002 ZASCA 148; 2003 (2) SA 715 (SCA) [28].

[41] *Khani v Premier, Vrystaat* 1999 (2) SA 863 (O), 869H–I.

[42] *Gibbs v Minister of Justice and Constitutional Development* [2009] ZASCA 73; 2009 (4) SA 109 (SCA) [26].

[43] A famous example involving the current President of South Africa is *National Director of Public Prosecutions v Zuma* [2009] ZASCA 1; 2009 (2) SA 277 (SCA).

[44] *Claude Neon Ltd v Germiston City Council* 1995 (3) SA 710 (W).

[45] *Premier, Mpumalanga v Executive Committee, Association of State-aided Schools, Eastern Transvaal* [1998] ZACC 20; 1999 (2) SA 91 (CC).

needy school children at state-aided schools. In spite of an official assurance in 1994 that the bursary scheme would continue at least until the end of 1995, it was terminated in August 1995 with retroactive effect from July of that year. An association of schools successfully established the existence of a legitimate expectation that the bursaries would continue to be provided, subject to reasonable notice being given of their termination, and the Constitutional Court held that the administrator had acted unfairly by terminating the scheme with retroactive effect.

Legitimate expectations have also been argued on the basis of a policy (or former policy), though not always with success. The cases relating to a change in parole policy have gone both ways;[46] and in a recent case, a High Court rejected a claim 'based on quotations from policy' which departed from established practice, did not emanate from the decision-maker and did not contain any 'categorical assurance'.[47]

Cases Adopting a More Contextual and Flexible Approach

Not all the cases have insisted on the *Phillips* requirements. In particular, the courts have not been consistent in requiring a 'representation' in the form of a promise or practice. Other possibilities were hinted at in *Premier, Mpumalanga*, where O'Regan J said:

> Corbett CJ … recognised that a legitimate expectation might arise in *at least* two circumstances: first, where a person enjoys an expectation of a privilege or benefit of which it would not be fair to deprive him or her without a fair hearing; and, secondly, in circumstances where the previous conduct of an official has given rise to an expectation that a particular procedure will be followed before a decision is made (emphasis added).[48]

Apart from the indication that this is not a closed list, it is interesting that only the second of these two scenarios is explicitly linked to 'previous conduct' (a category including but presumably not confined to promises and practices).

I shall refer again to this statement below. Meanwhile, one can discern two other strands in the jurisprudence that deviate from the traditional requirements of a promise or a practice. The first strand echoes some of the pre-1994 case law by associating legitimate expectations with broader

[46] Compare the conservative approach of the Court in *Winckler v Minister of Correctional Services* 2001 (2) SA 747 (C) with the more liberal High Court decisions in *Combrink v Minister of Correctional Services* 2001 (3) SA 338 (D) and *Mohammed v Minister of Correctional Services* 2003 (6) SA 169 (SE).

[47] *Comair Ltd v Minister of Public Enterprises* [2015] ZAGPPHC 361; 2016 (1) SA 1 (GP) [52].

[48] *Premier, Mpumalanga* (n 45) [35].

ideas of fairness, as was done in the *SARFU* case.[49] Here the Constitutional Court reiterated and applied the traditional requirements of a promise or practice as laid down by Lord Fraser and endorsed by Corbett CJ.[50] Having done so, however, the Court went on to link legitimate expectations with the 'duty to act fairly', another common law idea that the South African courts had toyed with in a few pre-1994 cases. In 1984, Baxter had summed up this duty as 'the duty to observe the principles of natural justice expressed in more fundamental terms', and had hailed it as a way of escaping the 'wilderness of conceptual confusion' engendered by the classification of functions.[51] But the idea was soon overtaken by constitutional events and nothing much came of it.[52]

In *SARFU*, however, the Court underscored the link. It said: 'To ask the question whether there is a legitimate expectation to be heard in any particular case is, in effect, to ask *whether the duty to act fairly requires a hearing* in that case' (emphasis added).[53] The Court also identified the quality of legitimacy with '*whether the duty to act fairly would require a hearing* in those circumstances' and 'whether, in the context of that case, *procedural fairness* ... requires a hearing' (emphasis added).[54] De Ville, for one, saw this as strong support for a looser, 'context-dependent' understanding of legitimate expectations.[55] Indeed, he argued that Corbett CJ never intended to restrict legitimate expectations to promises and practices, and that there is no warrant for doing so in the context of procedural protection.[56]

In a second strand of jurisprudence, the Supreme Court of Appeal has been known to find a legitimate expectation without identifying a promise or practice giving rise to it, and has seemed to say (without express reliance on the duty to act fairly) that an expectation may arise out of the prejudicial effects of a decision alone. The prime example of this, *Nortje*, concerned the transfer of convicts to the maximum security section of a prison, a decision having prejudicial effects in the form of reduced privileges.[57] (The facts might have attracted procedural fairness in any event, as they do in English law.)[58]

[49] *President of the Republic of South Africa (RSA) v South African Rugby Football Union (SARFU)* [1999] ZACC 11; 2000 (1) SA 1 (CC).

[50] Ibid, [212]–[215].

[51] Lawrence Baxter, *Administrative Law* (Juta & Co Ltd, 1984) 595–96.

[52] See further Cora Hoexter, *Administrative Law in South Africa*, 2nd edn (Juta & Co Ltd, 2012) 394.

[53] *President of the RSA v SARFU* (n 49) [216].

[54] *President of the RSA v SARFU* (n 49) [216].

[55] JR de Ville, *Judicial Review of Administrative Action in South Africa*, rev edn (LexisNexis Butterworths, 2005) 231.

[56] Ibid, 229ff.

[57] *Nortje v Minister van Korrektiewe Dienste* [2000] ZASCA 20; 2001 (3) SA 412 (SCA) [14]. According to Brand JA (using the translation in the headnote), 'the *audi* rule is applicable where the administrative decision can prejudice a person to such an extent that, in accordance with that person's legitimate expectation, the decision ought not to be taken unless he is heard'.

[58] *R (Bourgass) v Secretary of State for Justice* [2015] UKSC 54; [2015] 3 WLR 457.

Another noteworthy case is *Bullock*, which arose out of the decision of the Premier of a province to register a servitude over part of the foreshore of a dam, to the detriment of a yacht club whose lease was consequently not renewed.[59] In finding that the yacht club had a legitimate expectation of being heard on the renewal, the Court relied on the length of its tenancy, the fact that negotiations for a new lease were well underway and various improvements the club had made to the property. Even though it was not clear whether these changes had been made with the approval of the lessor, the nature and scale of the improvements alone, the Court reasoned, 'went a long way to establishing' the legitimate expectation.[60] Oddly, no reliance seemed to be placed on the successive renewal of the lease. That, commentators pointed out, would have amounted to a regular practice and would have been a more orthodox foundation for a legitimate expectation.[61]

In her minority judgment in the *Walele* case, O'Regan ADCJ referred to both *Nortje* and *Bullock* in observing that '[f]rom time to time our courts have taken the view that a legitimate expectation may also arise simply because the administrative action in question constitutes a dramatic impairment of interests less than rights'.[62] She speculated that '[i]t may well be that the concept ... is not limited to the narrow requirement of a promise or a practice as set out in Lord Fraser's reasoning', particularly given the broad terms of section 33(1) of the Constitution.[63] By contrast, the majority of the Constitutional Court in *Walele* appeared to insist on the orthodox triggers of an express promise or a regular practice, which were stated not once but twice in the judgment of Jafta AJ.[64]

More recently, in *Rivonia Primary School*,[65] a majority of the Constitutional Court again signalled support for a more flexible approach to legitimate expectations and reverted to the duty to act fairly. In this case, the principal of a public school[66] had refused admission to an applicant for Grade 1 for the following year on the basis that the school had already filled all the places available for the grade. Two or three weeks into the new school year, an internal appeal against this decision came belatedly to the attention of the head of the provincial department of education (HOD).

59 *Bullock NO v Provincial Government, North West Province* [2004] ZASCA 21; 2004 (5) SA 262 (SCA).

60 Ibid, [22].

61 Wandisile wakwa-Mandlana and Clive Plasket, 'Administrative Law' (2004) *Annual Survey of South African Law* 74, 91–92.

62 *Walele v City of Cape Town* (n 33) [133], footnoting both *Nortje* (n 57) and *Bullock* (n 59).

63 *Walele v City of Cape Town* (n 33) [133].

64 *Walele v City of Cape Town* (n 33) [35] and [42].

65 *MEC for Education, Gauteng Province v Governing Body, Rivonia Primary School* [2013] ZACC 34; 2013 (6) SA 582 (CC).

66 The Schools Act 84 of 1996 distinguishes between 'public' schools, which are run and funded by the state, and 'independent' schools, which are essentially private but subsidised by the state.

Soon after this, the HOD overturned the principal's decision and instructed the school to admit the child (or 'learner' in terms of the Act) forthwith. The principal's failure to co-operate with this instruction led to disciplinary action being taken against her, and the school sought a court order affirming its sovereignty in matters of admission. That relief was denied in the High Court but granted by the Supreme Court of Appeal.

On further appeal by the department, the Constitutional Court held that the HOD had indeed been empowered to override the principal even at that late stage. However, a majority of the Court went on to hold that such action had to be taken reasonably and fairly, and that the HOD's failure to hear the school before issuing the instruction had been procedurally unfair in the circumstances. Discussions between the department and the school had culminated in a meeting towards the end of the previous year at which the principal's decision had apparently been accepted by the department. Given the timing of the HOD's instruction (four weeks into the school year) and that it represented an about-turn, Mhlantla AJ concluded for the majority that the HOD ought first to have given the school a further opportunity to make representations.[67] 'In other words', she added by way of a footnote, 'the school's legitimate expectation of a hearing was materially and adversely affected when the Gauteng HOD made his decision without allowing such a hearing'.[68]

The Court did not analyse the ingredients of this legitimate expectation in any detail. The diagnosis was, however, presaged by another footnote earlier in the judgment, in which Mhlantla AJ referred to the doctrine and quoted the 'duty to act fairly' passage from the *SARFU* case as well as the dictum of O'Regan J in *Premier, Mpumlanga*.[69] Mhlantla AJ went on to say:

> As will follow from my analysis … below, I am of the view that the Gauteng HOD had a *duty to act fairly*. In the least, the school had a legitimate expectation that it would be heard by the Gauteng HOD prior to a decision being made regarding the placement of the learner (emphasis added).[70]

That is a helpful signpost, but the quotation from *Premier, Mpumalanga* adds ambiguity. Did Mhlantla AJ quote it to underscore the point that legitimate expectations may indeed arise in circumstances *other* than those enumerated by O'Regan J; or did she mean that the situation in the case before her actually *fitted* one or other of the two circumstances mentioned by O'Regan J? Or perhaps she meant a bit of both? Although the department

[67] *MEC for Education v Rivonia Primary School* (n 65) [67]–[68].

[68] *MEC for Education v Rivonia Primary School* (n 65) [68] fn 64. The minority held that procedural unfairness had not been pleaded or established in evidence, and that the Constitutional Court ought to have confined itself to issues that had been properly pleaded and proved.

[69] *MEC for Education v Rivonia Primary School* (n 65) [60] fn 56, referring to *President of the RSA v SARFU* (n 49) [216] and *Premier, Mpumalanga* (n 45) [35].

[70] *MEC for Education v Rivonia Primary School* (n 65) [60] fn 56.

did not seem to have promised anything or established a regular practice, its previous conduct had given the school the impression that the matter had been resolved, and as a result the school expected that the decision of its principal would be upheld. In those circumstances, the duty to act fairly would surely require it to be warned of the HOD's impending *volte-face* and to be given an opportunity to respond.

It seems fair to conclude that, *Walele* notwithstanding, the highest Court is again adopting a more contextual approach and becoming less literal about promises and practices. But greater clarity is required, and the increasingly awkward gulf between the 'strict' and the 'flexible' case law must somehow be bridged. What is needed now is a new sort of *Traub*: an authoritative judgment that will survey the jurisprudence, acknowledge the variety of ways in which a legitimate expectation may arise and the forms it may take, and find a way of reconciling or accommodating the differences described above.

If that is one of the big issues relating to legitimate expectations in South African law today, the other is whether and to what extent the courts will prove willing to protect them in a substantive and not merely procedural manner.

THE GORDIAN KNOT: SUBSTANTIVE PROTECTION

Background

In *Traub*, Corbett CJ acknowledged that expectations may range from the procedural to the substantive, and he suggested that substance and procedure might sometimes be intertwined: the applicant might expect a favourable decision 'or at least that before an adverse decision is taken he will be given a fair hearing'.[71] However, there was no suggestion that the *protection* offered by the doctrine could go beyond procedural fairness.

Ten years later, in *Premier, Mpumalanga*,[72] things had progressed to the extent that the possibility of substantive enforcement was acknowledged. Writing for a unanimous Constitutional Court, O'Regan J stated that a legitimate expectation would entitle a person to procedural fairness, and found it unnecessary for the court to decide 'in what circumstances, if any, a legitimate expectation will confer a right to substantive relief beyond that ordinarily contemplated by a duty to act fairly'.[73] Ironically, however, the order in that case itself entailed a measure of substantive enforcement, for the Constitutional Court upheld the order of the court *a quo* requiring the

[71] *Administrator, Transvaal v Traub* (n 3) 758F.
[72] *Premier, Mpumalanga* (n 45).
[73] *Premier, Mpumalanga* (n 45) [36].

bursaries to be paid out until the end of 1995. Not long after this, in *Bel Porto*, one member of the Constitutional Court expressed enthusiastic support for substantive enforcement in a minority judgment,[74] but the majority remained unconvinced. Twenty years after *Traub*, O'Regan J summed up the situation by saying that the South African courts had 'expressly refrained from deciding whether a legitimate expectation may give rise to a substantive benefit'.[75]

This may not sound like much progress. On the other hand, opinion has moved well beyond the flat denial issued by a High Court judge in 2001, when he stated that substantive protection was 'not permissible' in our law.[76] There is in fact no constitutional reason why that should be so, and most public lawyers in this country probably regard the development as inevitable now. For one thing, there is a growing number of cases in which expectations seem actually to have been enforced in a substantive manner, particularly in the area of employment, even if this has not officially or consciously been achieved by means of the legitimate expectation doctrine. For instance, on the basis of a practice the applicants in one case were held entitled to be sent a letter from the department outlining their conditions of employment;[77] in another, applicants were actually awarded the promotions they had been promised.[78] And at least one South African Court has explicitly purported to enforce a substantive legitimate expectation as such (again linking it to the duty to act fairly).[79]

Secondly, there has been some influential writing on the subject of substantive enforcement and how it might be managed in South African law. Quinot has written thoughtfully on the subject and has canvassed various options open to the South African courts.[80] He divides these into a 'direct protection' model, including the formula used in *Coughlan*[81] and variations on it that rely on a proportionality test; and a second model involving review for rationality, including the *Wednesbury*[82] approach and the less

[74] *Bel Porto School Governing Body v Premier, Western Cape* [2002] ZACC 2 [88]–[89]; 2002 (3) SA 265 (CC) [212]–[213] (Madala J).

[75] *Residents of Joe Slovo Community, Western Cape v Thubelisha Homes* [2009] ZACC 16; 2010 (3) SA 454 (CC) [306].

[76] *Durban Add-Ventures Ltd v Premier, KwaZulu-Natal (No 2)* 2001 (1) SA 389 (N), 408E–F.

[77] *Ampofo v MEC for Education, Arts, Culture, Sports and Recreation, Northern Province* 2002 (2) SA 215 (T).

[78] *Coetzer v Minister of Safety and Security* 2003 (3) SA 368 (LC). This and other cases are discussed by Geo Quinot, 'The Developing Doctrine of Substantive Legitimate Expectations in South African Administrative Law' (2004) 19 *SA Public Law* 543, 548ff.

[79] *Quinella Trading (Pty) Ltd v Minister of Rural Development* 2010 (4) SA 308 (LCC) [23]–[24] (enforcement of contractual obligation to sign documents and transfer land).

[80] Quinot (n 78).

[81] *R v North and East Devon Health Authority; ex parte Coughlan* [2001] 3 QB 213.

[82] Referring to the deferential test that emerged from *Associated Provincial Picture Houses Ltd v Wednesbury Corporation* [1948] 1 KB 223.

deferential 'modified *Wednesbury*' alternative. Quinot looks at the advantages and disadvantages of both models from a South African point of view and rightly suggests that a central question for our courts will be the precise standard to be applied when balancing the expectation against countervailing considerations. No real obstacles would be presented by the PAJA, as he sees it, for that statute 'leave[s] room for the development of a doctrine of substantive protection of legitimate expectations without requiring major constitutional interventions'.[83]

In an earlier piece, Campbell argued in favour of the modified *Wednesbury* approach to substantive enforcement which, he suggested, would fit particularly well with existing South African law (including the PAJA).[84] In his proposal, a legitimate expectation would in essence be treated as a relevant consideration, and the offending administrative action would be reviewable on grounds of rationality; but the administrator would also be expected actively to justify the denial of the expectation by pointing to an imperative public interest. In the absence of such justification, Campbell envisaged the use of the South African courts' well-established power of substitution: a device actually used during the litigation in *Traub*.[85] In this regard it may be worth adding that, while section 8 of the PAJA is stricter than the common law and reserves the power of substitution for 'exceptional' cases, that threshold does not seem to be as high in practice as it might sound.[86]

Thirdly, the courts have not merely left the way open for substantive enforcement of legitimate expectations, but have actually predicted this development. In his judgment for the Supreme Court of Appeal in *Duncan*, Brand JA summed up the current position in some detail and speculated that the time, and an appropriate case, would eventually come 'for our courts to cut the Gordian knot'.[87] While that case has not yet arisen, it is

[83] Quinot (n 78) 570.

[84] John Campbell, 'Legitimate Expectations: The Potential and Limits of Substantive Protection in South Africa' (2003) 12 *South African Law Journal* 292; and see further John Campbell, 'Legitimate Expectations: Developments at Home and Abroad' (2004) 121 *South African Law Journal* 538.

[85] See Campbell, 'Potential and Limits' (n 84) 315. Before the Appellate Division handed down its judgment in *Traub*, the administrator actually gave Dr Traub a hearing and again decided not to approve her appointment. In *Traube v Administrator, Transvaal* 1989 (2) SA 396 (A), Dr Traub successfully challenged the reasonableness and procedural fairness of this decision, and Goldstone J used his common law power of substitution to order that she be appointed to the post—an outcome that he justified as a foregone conclusion.

[86] This is suggested especially by *Gauteng Gambling Board v Silverstar Development Ltd* [2005] ZASCA 19; 2005 (4) SA 67 (SCA), where the Court raised eyebrows by effectively awarding a coveted provincial casino licence to the respondent. More recently, in restating the principles governing substitution in *Trencon Construction (Pty) Ltd v Industrial Corporation of South Africa* [2015] ZACC 22; 2015 (5) SA 245 (CC), the Constitutional Court seems to have made fairness, rather than exceptional circumstances, the overriding consideration.

[87] *Duncan v MEAT* (n 39) [14]. See further, on the use of a legitimate expectations methodology in socio-economic rights cases, Marius Pieterse, 'Procedural Relief, Constitutional Citizenship and Socio-economic Rights as Legitimate Expectations' (2012) 28 *South African Journal on Human Rights* 359.

interesting to consider a case that might have effected this knot-cutting if it had been argued differently: *KZN Joint Liaison Committee*.[88]

KZN Joint Liaison Committee

Facts and Reasoning

Towards the end of 2009 the applicant, an association of independent schools[89] in the province of KwaZulu-Natal, sought to enforce a promise of subsidy made the previous year by the provincial department of education. The department had sent out a notice in September 2008 with a table showing the 'approximate' levels of subsidy such schools could expect to receive in four tranches during 2009. The first tranche of subsidy was due in April 2009 but was not in fact paid. A month later, in May 2009, the department sent a second notice warning the schools to expect a 30 per cent reduction in their subsidy allocation as a result of a budgetary cut. When the first two tranches were eventually paid in July 2009, they proved to be about 30 per cent lower than the first notice had led the schools to expect.

The applicant sought to make good the shortfall. It instituted motion proceedings in a High Court and framed its claim in contract. It was unsuccessful, however, as it failed to make out a case in its papers as is required in application proceedings. The High Court held that a promise of 'approximate' funding, even if seriously made, was too uncertain to give rise to enforceable contractual obligations.[90] The applicant appealed to the Constitutional Court, where its contractual arguments again failed. In his majority judgment, Cameron J accepted that the promise had been made seriously, but found no intention to enter into an enforceable contract, or indeed any agreement between the parties in this instance.[91]

The Centre for Child Law at the University of Pretoria, admitted as *amicus curiae* in the Constitutional Court, had a different basis for arguing that the promise ought to be enforced.[92] The *amicus* drew attention to the constitutional and legislative context within which the promise had been made,

[88] *KZN Joint Liaison Committee* (n 6).

[89] See n 66 above.

[90] *KwaZulu-Natal Joint Liaison Committee v Member of the Executive Council, Department of Education, KwaZulu-Natal* (KZP) unreported case no 9594/2010 of 26 September 2011.

[91] *KZN Joint Liaison Committee* (n 6) [35]–[37]. This instance was thus distinguishable from cases in which the courts had enforced an agreement based on an offer of subsidy or tax benefits advertised in a circular, such as *Minister of Home Affairs v American Ninja IV Partnership* 1993 (1) SA 257 (A).

[92] *KZN Joint Liaison Committee* (n 6), summarised at [25]–[28] in the judgment of Cameron J. For more detail, see 'Written Submissions on Behalf of the *Amicus Curiae*', accessed from www.constitutionalcourt.org.za on 2 June 2014.

and pointed out that a reduction in subsidy would threaten the right to basic education contained in section 29 of the Bill of Rights. It went on to argue that the applicant had a legitimate expectation of receiving the amounts actually indicated in the table contained in the first notice, and urged the Court to enforce this expectation in a substantive manner by ordering the department to pay what was promised.

According to the *amicus*, the expectation was based both on the promise and a practice; for while the promise was qualified by the word 'approximate', the past practice of the department had been to pay out subsidies exactly as promised. Notably, the applicant's papers had not only canvassed the promise thoroughly but also contained evidence of this practice. So, the *amicus* argued, though the label 'legitimate expectation' had not actually been used by the applicant, all the established requirements of a legitimate expectation were present and a legitimate expectation had effectively been made out in its papers. Moreover, upholding it would not take the respondents by surprise, for they had evidently perceived the makings of a legitimate expectation too and had addressed the possibility in their own papers.[93]

The argument did not succeed, mainly because the Court felt it did not have sufficient evidence and information before it to make a decision based on this ground. The record of the budget allocation and the department's decision-making—a record 'highly pertinent' to a claim in administrative law—was not before the Court.[94] Without that record, Cameron J held, it was not possible to consider the claim as a breach of administrative justice, particularly given the department's defence that it was unable to pay the subsidy as promised because its budget had been reduced.[95] Cameron J also pointed out that an applicant who seeks enforcement on an administrative law basis is supposed to bring review proceedings under the PAJA and in accordance with the statute's procedural requirements.[96]

The appeal might easily have been dismissed without more. Indeed, according to the dissenting judges it ought to have been dismissed, for the case pleaded had failed.[97] After the oral hearing, however, the Court threw the applicant a lifeline by asking the parties for additional written argument on the effect of the delegated legislation regulating the payment of subsidies. This effectively allowed for further public law arguments to be made[98] or, on a more cynical view, for the Court 'to pick the applicant up and make

[93] See 'Written Submissions' (n 92).
[94] *KZN Joint Liaison Committee* (n 6) [32].
[95] *KZN Joint Liaison Committee* (n 6) [32].
[96] *KZN Joint Liaison Committee* (n 6) [31].
[97] *KZN Joint Liaison Committee* (n 6) [147]–[149] in the dissenting judgment of Nkabinde J and [158] in the dissenting judgment of Zondo J, in which Mogoeng CJ and Jafta J concurred. Mogoeng CJ and Jafta J (Zondo J concurring) also contributed a further dissenting judgment refusing leave to appeal on the basis of lack of evidence as to the existence of a debt or its amount.
[98] For details see *KZN Joint Liaison Committee* (n 6) [59] and footnotes.

it stand upon a different case'.[99] It emerged that the applicable regulations envisaged payment of subsidy to independent schools 'retroactively each quarter'.[100] Further, item 195 of the Amended National Norms and Standards for School Funding of 2006 actually set deadlines for the subsidy payments. It stipulated that the subsidy for the first term had to be paid no later than 1 April in each school year, and that subsequent payments were to be made no later than six weeks after the beginning of term. On the basis of additional arguments made by the applicant and *amicus*, a majority of the Court accepted that the entitlement to receive the subsidy 'solidified' from an expectation into an accrued right once the deadline for payment had passed.[101] In the absence of an overriding public interest, there could be no lawful reduction after that point, for reasons relating to reliance, accountability and rationality.[102] In the result, by virtue of this 'sound principle of our constitutional law',[103] the applicant was entitled to payment of the 'approximate' amounts that had fallen due by 1 April.[104]

This is a remarkable judgment for a number of reasons. One is its 'anti-formalism' on both procedural and substantive fronts: for the Court was willing to rescue the applicant from ill-conceived pleadings and to overcome impediments such as the word 'approximate'.[105] Another noteworthy feature, and a more important one for present purposes, is the relationship between the constitutional principle that the majority relied on and the doctrine of legitimate expectations, on which it expressly declined to rely. The Court deliberately distinguished the two concepts, pointing out that its constitutional principle concerned the passing of a due date for payment rather than conduct that was merely expected.[106] The Court also speculated that if the case had been argued differently, the applicant might have established a legitimate expectation of receiving payment of the final three tranches of subsidy.[107]

Points of Connection with Legitimate Expectations

Notwithstanding the Court's disavowal, it is difficult to ignore certain points of connection between the principle underpinning the majority judgment

[99] *KZN Joint Liaison Committee* (n 6) [158] in the judgment of Zondo J.

[100] Regulation 4(3) of the KZN Regulations, Provincial Notice 287, *Provincial Gazette* 5387 of 28 October 1999.

[101] *KZN Joint Liaison Committee* (n 6) [60].

[102] *KZN Joint Liaison Committee* (n 6) [63]–[66].

[103] *KZN Joint Liaison Committee* (n 6) [52] (Cameron J).

[104] Cameron J indicated that the department would have to engage with the schools in this regard, adding that the schools could apply to court for relief if they regarded the payment as inadequately approximate: see *KZN Joint Liaison Committee* (n 6) [75].

[105] See further on these points Cora Hoexter, 'The Enforcement of an Official Promise: Form, Substance and the Constitutional Court' (2015) 132 *South African Law Journal* 207.

[106] *KZN Joint Liaison Committee* (n 6) [52].

[107] *KZN Joint Liaison Committee* (n 6) [69].

and the doctrine of legitimate expectations, and difficult not to hear echoes of the English jurisprudence on substantive enforcement. I have previously canvassed these similarities in a piece in the *South African Law Journal*,[108] but they bear repeating here.

The first and most obvious point of connection is the *Premier, Mpumalanga*[109] case, which was the main source of the constitutional principle elaborated in *KZN Joint Liaison Committee*. As already noted, the earlier case not only upheld a legitimate expectation but also resulted in a certain amount of substantive enforcement. A related point of connection is the concept of an 'overriding public interest' employed in *KZN Joint Liaison Committee*. Again, the immediate inspiration was *Premier, Mpumalanga*, where O'Regan J imported the concept from the jurisprudence of the European Court of Justice.[110] But the concept has also featured prominently in the English case law relating to substantive enforcement of legitimate expectations.[111] In the leading case, *Coughlan*,[112] Lord Woolf MR identified a category of cases involving a substantive legitimate expectation where the Court would be required to balance the requirements of fairness against any 'overriding interest' relied on by the public authority, and ultimately decide whether to disappoint the expectation would be so unfair as to amount to an abuse of power. He also observed that cases falling into this category were likely to involve expectations having 'the character of a contract'[113]—which might fairly describe *KZN Joint Liaison Committee*, notwithstanding the ultimate failure of the contractual argument.

Another interesting connection is that at least two of the three rationales referred to in *KZN Joint Liaison Committee* resonate with the English jurisprudence. In English law, reliance is associated most firmly with estoppel and is not generally a requirement for establishing a legitimate expectation,[114] but the authorities agree that reliance will always add weight to such an expectation,[115] and it may operate as a requirement in some

[108] Hoexter (n 105) 226–27.

[109] *Premier, Mpumalanga* (n 45).

[110] *Premier, Mpumalanga* (n 45) [41], with reference to *J Mulder v Minister van Landbouw en Visserij* [1998] ECR 2321 and *Karl Spagl v Hauptzollamt Rosenheim* [1990] ECR 4539, as well as Jürgen Schwarze, *European Administrative Law* (Sweet & Maxwell, 1992).

[111] See eg *R v Secretary of State for the Home Department; ex parte Khan* [1985] 1 All ER 40 (CA); *R v Ministry of Agriculture, Fisheries and Food; ex parte Hamble (Offshore) Fisheries Ltd* [1995] 2 All ER (QB).

[112] *Coughlan* (n 81) [57].

[113] *Coughlan* (n 81) [59].

[114] On the uncoupling of estoppel and legitimate expectations, see eg *Hamble Fisheries* (n 111) 731*g*–*j*; *R (Reprotech (Pebsham) Ltd) v East Sussex County Council* [2003] 1 WLR 308 (HL) [35].

[115] The Rt Hon Lord Woolf, Professor Jeffrey Jowell QC, Professor Andrew Le Sueur, Catherine Donelly and Ivan Hare, *De Smith's Judicial Review*, 7th edn (Sweet & Maxwell, 2013) 12–059. Notably, in *Coughlan* itself Lord Woolf seemed to place considerable weight on the applicant's reliance on the promise made to her: *Coughlan* (n 81) [86]–[93].

instances.[116] Rationality, in turn, is the standard of scrutiny that is generally used in relation to policy-laden decisions that disappoint or defeat a legitimate expectation.[117] The third rationale used in *KZN Joint Liaison Committee*, accountability, is not prominent in the English cases but may well underlie the notions of unfairness and abuse of power that are so often referred to by the English courts.[118]

Differences

These intriguing similarities should not blind us to differences between the constitutional principle used in *KZN Joint Liaison Committee* and the legitimate expectation doctrine. For one thing, their animating philosophies are quite different. The constitutional principle is informed by the idea of an 'accrued right'.[119] Here there is a definite connection with the doctrine of estoppel, where reliance is said to 'crystallise the right in the representee'.[120] Legitimate expectations, on the other hand, are not about rights but were invented to make things easier for applicants who *lack* rights.

Another important difference is that, as far as we know, the constitutional principle protects only promises of payment, and possibly only publicly promulgated promises,[121] whereas legitimate expectations may be substantively enforced (in English law) even when founded on the flimsier bases of practices and policies. The relief available is also potentially more extensive, addressing what was reasonably expected and not merely what has already fallen due.[122] As the Court itself speculated, the applicant in *KZN Joint Liaison Committee* might have been entitled to payment of the entire year's worth of subsidy, and not simply the first tranche, if it had based its case on a legitimate expectation.[123]

Of course, the two ideas also have different origins. The legitimate expectation doctrine developed in the context of the *audi alteram partem* principle in administrative law and, as we have seen, is in that context expressly embodied in the PAJA, the statute that gives effect to the administra-

[116] Forsyth suggests that a taxpayer 'must rely on a representation from the Revenue before his protection will be protected': see Wade and Forsyth, *Administrative Law*, 10th edn (Oxford University Press, 2009) by Christopher Forsyth, 452.

[117] *R v Secretary of State for Education and Employment; ex parte Begbie* [2001] 1 WLR 1115 [66]–[68].

[118] Either singly or in combination, as in *Coughlan* (n 81) [78]: 'so unfair as to amount to an abuse of power'.

[119] *KZN Joint Liaison Committee* (n 6) [60].

[120] John Cartwright, 'Protecting Legitimate Expectations and Estoppel in English Law' (2006) 10 *Electronic Journal of Comparative Law* 1, 7.

[121] Cameron J refers to a 'publicly promulgated promise to pay' in a key paragraph of *KZN Joint Liaison Committee* (n 6) [48]. Elsewhere in his judgment, however, it is merely a 'promise'.

[122] *KZN Joint Liaison Committee* (n 6) [69].

[123] *KZN Joint Liaison Committee* (n 6) [69].

tive justice rights. As a procedural doctrine, it is thus very much part of 'regular' South African administrative law. The constitutional principle is not. It seems to be associated with higher and more abstract ideas, and has to do with substantive rather than procedural fairness.

In fact, two of its underlying rationales, rationality and accountability, are strongly associated with a constitutional 'principle of legality' that the Constitutional Court has identified as an aspect of the rule of law.[124] The rule of law, in turn, is one of several founding values listed in South Africa's Constitution.[125] The principle of legality was supposed to provide a mere safety net[126] for exercises of public power that do not amount to administrative action as defined, and initially it was held to impose only the most basic standards of legality on those wielding public power.[127] But these soon mushroomed to include a minimum requirement of rationality between means and ends,[128] and that minimum has itself expanded into something considerably more onerous in more than one instance.[129] Rationality has also given rise to further requirements of good administration: it has been held to imply the need for procedural fairness[130] and the giving of reasons[131] in appropriate cases. Because of these features, the principle has sometimes been called the principle of 'legality and rationality',[132] and has been said to include accountability.[133]

Now, it is true that the kind of rationality Cameron J had in mind was not rationality between means and ends: rather, he was concerned with the impossibility of the schools tailoring their behaviour 'to a promise made in relation to a period that has already passed'.[134] Still, to the extent that the two constitutional principles are connected by rationales of rationality and accountability, it may be that the Court in *KZN Liaison Committee* has

[124] *Fedsure Life Assurance Ltd v Greater Johannesburg Transitional Metropolitan Council* [1998] ZACC 17; 1999 (1) SA 374 (CC) [56]–[58].

[125] Section 1*(c)* of the Constitution.

[126] *Minister of Health v New Clicks South Africa (Pty) Ltd* [2005] ZACC 14; 2006 (2) SA 311 (CC) [97].

[127] *Fedsure* (n 124) [56]–[59]; *President of the RSA v SARFU* (n 49) [148].

[128] *Pharmaceutical Manufacturers' Association* (n 32) [85].

[129] See Cora Hoexter, 'A Rainbow of One Colour? Judicial Review on Substantive Grounds in South African Law' in Hanna Wilberg and Mark Elliott (eds), *The Scope and Intensity of Substantive Review: Traversing Taggart's Rainbow* (Hart Publishing, 2015) 163, 178–79.

[130] *Albutt v Centre for the Study of Violence and Reconciliation* [2010] ZACC 4; 2010 (3) SA 293 (CC) [68] and [70]–[72]; *Minister of Home Affairs v Scalabrini Centre* [2013] ZASCA 134; 2013 (6) SA 421 (SCA) [68]–[72]; *Minister of Home Affairs v Somali Association of Southern Africa* [2015] ZASCA 35; 2015 (3) SA 545 (SCA) [14]–[17].

[131] *Judicial Service Commission v Cape Bar Council* [2012] ZASCA 115; 2013 (1) SA 170 (SCA) [21]–[23] and [43]–[45].

[132] Most notably in *Masetlha v President of the Republic of South Africa* [2007] ZACC 20; 2008 (1) SA 566 (CC) [78].

[133] *Wessels v Minister for Justice and Constitutional Development* [2009] ZAGPPHC 81; 2010 (1) SA 128 (GNP), 141I–J.

[134] *KZN Joint Liaison Committee* (n 6) [65].

inadvertently added to the meaning of the burgeoning principle of legality—and thus made it even more attractive to litigants. This principle is already overtaking the PAJA as the preferred avenue to judicial review. In terms of detailed grounds of review, the PAJA is still somewhat ahead; but the principle of legality is catching up fast. (No doubt the principle of legality will soon be held to encompass legitimate expectations too, if it does not do so already.) Furthermore, it has the great advantages of generality and flexibility, whereas the PAJA is more tightly constrained by its elaborate definition of administrative action, a strict duty to exhaust internal remedies and a rigid time limit within which review applications have to be brought.[135]

Bypassing the Gordian Knot?

It would seem that, because the constitutional principle discovered by Cameron J is so limited in its scope and in the relief it offers, the majority judgment in *KZN Joint Liaison Committee* has not substantially reduced the need for South African courts to explore the substantive enforcement of legitimate expectations in future, and thus to cut the Gordian knot. This conclusion is supported by Murcott, who argues that while the underlying bases of the constitutional principle bear a striking resemblance to those of the doctrine of substantive legitimate expectations developed under English law, it 'cannot be described as the doctrine by another name'.[136] Rather, its effect is to leave the way open for the development of a doctrine of substantive enforcement, 'except in a small category of cases where the *KZN JLC* mechanism will apply'.[137]

Murcott is not wrong on the law as it stands. However, as she is aware,[138] the gap between the two devices is considerably narrower in the minority judgment of Froneman J. Unlike the majority, Froneman J was prepared to enforce the promise for the entire year—*essentially on the same logic as that used by the majority judgment.* As Froneman J saw it, the implications of that logic were wider than the majority seemed to realise.[139] As to reliance, he reasoned that the schools had budgeted for the entire year on the strength of the first notice, and not merely for the first term.[140] The accountability of the respondents was 'an ongoing and fundamental responsibility under the

[135] See further Hoexter (n 105) 218–24.

[136] Melanie Murcott, 'A Future for the Doctrine of Substantive Legitimate Expectation? The Implications of *KwaZulu-Natal Joint Liaison Committee v MEC for Education, KwaZulu-Natal*' (2015) 18 *Potchefstroom Electronic Law Journal* 3133, 3154.

[137] Ibid.

[138] This emerges from an earlier version of her piece: Melanie Murcott, 'A Future for Substantive Legitimate Expectations?' (Unpublished paper presented at a conference of the Society of Law Teachers of Southern Africa, University of the Witwatersrand, Johannesburg on 13–16 January 2014) 9.

[139] *KZN Joint Liaison Committee* (n 6) [90].

[140] *KZN Joint Liaison Committee* (n 6) [87].

Constitution', and similarly did not stop at the end of the first term.[141] And as to rationality (using the concept in the usual means/ends sense), he could see no rational link between reducing the subsidy to independent schools and advancing the right to basic education. Indeed, on the respondents' own version, it would have been considerably more costly to accommodate the learners in public schools than to pay the subsidy as promised.[142]

The judgment of Froneman J demonstrates that the reasoning of the majority could fairly easily be pushed so as to achieve the sort of relief that substantive protection of legitimate expectations would offer, at least in relation to promises. And the leap from promises to other sorts of official representations (or simply 'previous conduct', as *Premier, Mpumalanga* had it) does not seem very great—particularly if one considers the increasing flexibility demonstrated by the Constitutional Court and the Supreme Court of Appeal to representations *within* the doctrine of legitimate expectations itself. With the aid of the guiding stars of reliance, accountability and rationality, it does not seem inconceivable that the constitutional principle discovered by Cameron J could be used substantively to protect reliance on a broader range of representations in future, thus possibly bypassing the doctrine of legitimate expectations—and procedural fairness—altogether. More worryingly, such a development would also bypass the PAJA; but that is something South Africans have already become accustomed to.

CONCLUSION

As shown in this chapter, in the late 1980s the doctrine of legitimate expectations brought welcome relief from the strict 'deprivation' approach of South African law to the entitlement to procedural fairness. Legitimate expectations did not turn into an unruly horse but rapidly became an important and vibrant area of the law, and remained so after the introduction of constitutional democracy in 1994. Legitimate expectations received an explicit mention in the interim Constitution and they also feature in the PAJA, albeit by mistake.

Two big questions about the doctrine are currently being explored in the case law. The first relates to the ingredients of legitimacy and the extent to which the traditional requirements of a promise or a practice still apply. The second is not so much whether, but when and how the courts will extend

[141] *KZN Joint Liaison Committee* (n 6) [88].

[142] *KZN Joint Liaison Committee* (n 6) [89]. Froneman J did not stop there: at [101]–[107], he went on to hold that the promise was also enforceable on the ordinary principles of South African contract law, as argued all along by the applicant; for our law of contract enforces promises seriously made and does not insist on consideration. Importantly, too, the department had not argued anything to the contrary, such as impossibility of performance or fettering of discretion.

the doctrine from merely procedural to substantive protection of legitimate expectations. This chapter has investigated both questions and has also drawn attention to a curiosity: a case that almost introduced substantive protection into South African law. While the Constitutional Court chose to enforce an official promise by other means in that instance, the device it employed resonates strangely with the legitimate expectation doctrine and with the English jurisprudence on substantive enforcement; and as demonstrated by a minority judgment, the same device could conceivably be pushed further to achieve similarly substantive results.

9

Law of Legitimate Expectation in New Zealand

PHILIP A JOSEPH

INTRODUCTION

FORTY-FIVE YEARS AGO, Lord Denning MR coined the concept 'legitimate expectation' to escape the constraints on judicial review then prevalent. In *Schmidt v Secretary of State for Home Affairs*,[1] he used the concept almost casually, without elaborating upon it. Then, in *R v Liverpool Corporation; ex parte Liverpool Taxi Fleet Operators' Association*,[2] he transformed his concept into a coherent administrative law principle, breaking the doctrinal shackle that only enforceable (justiciable) rights might warrant protection in judicial review. A decision-maker's representation that a fair procedure would be followed created a legitimate expectation that embraced more than enforceable legal rights. This development broadened the range of protectable interests and provided a much-needed fillip for judicial review.[3] Legitimate expectation was a liberating concept at a time of enervating judicial deference and doctrinal formalism.

This chapter explains the breakthrough that Lord Denning made and catalogues the primary elements of the doctrine in New Zealand. These elements broadly replicate those applying throughout the common law jurisdictions; although the similarities between the jurisdictions may vary given the nuanced way that national courts apply the doctrine. Even where

[1] *Schmidt v Secretary of State for Home Affairs* [1969] 2 Ch 149 (CA).

[2] *R v Liverpool Corporation; ex parte Liverpool Taxi Fleet Operators' Association* [1972] 2 QB 299, 304 (CA).

[3] *Attorney-General (Hong Kong) v Ng Yuen Shiu* [1983] 2 AC 629, 636 (PC); *O'Reilly v Mackman* [1982] 3 WLR 1096, 1100 (HL); *Fowler & Roderique v Attorney-General* [1987] 2 NZLR 56, 74 (CA); *New Zealand Association for Migration and Investments Inc v Attorney-General* [2006] NZAR 45 [142] (HC); *Comptroller of Customs v Terminals (NZ) Ltd* [2014] 2 NZLR 137 [123] (CA).

there is broad agreement over the elements, national courts still encounter difficulties in applying them. The law in New Zealand, the courts concede, is 'contentious',[4] prone to 'very considerable difficulties',[5] 'not well settled'[6] and 'far from straightforward'.[7] Uncertainties arise over two important questions: first, whether a legitimate expectation might be as to a substantive outcome as distinct from a fair procedure (and, if so, what remedy might issue where it has been defeated), and second, whether an applicant must establish knowledge of and detrimental reliance on a decision-maker's representation or promise. The courts equivocate over those questions, leaving it uncertain as to what elements claimants must establish.

The principles of legitimate expectation may be contested but its rationale is refreshingly uncomplicated. The administrative law principles of fairness and good public administration anchor the doctrine and inform its primary elements.[8] Honouring legitimate expectations is 'fair play in action',[9] 'fairness writ large',[10] and 'in the interests of proper public administration'.[11] Breach of a legitimate expectation is sometimes labelled an 'abuse of power'[12] or 'conspicuous unfairness',[13] merging into or overlapping substantive unfairness as a ground of challenge.[14] Decision-makers who promise, by word or deed, that a fair procedure will be followed ought to be held to their promise. Honouring legitimate expectations promotes observance of the constitutional principle of the rule of law, which encourages regularity, predictability and certainty in public decision-making.[15]

[4] *Coromandel Peninsula Watchdog Inc v Hauraki District Council* [1997] 1 NZLR 557, 568 (HC).

[5] *Northern Roller Milling Co Ltd v Commerce Commission* [1994] 2 NZLR 747, 750 (HC).

[6] *New Zealand Association for Migration and Investments* (n 3) [137]. See also *Te Heu Heu v Attorney-General* [1999] 1 NZLR 98, 125 (HC).

[7] *New Zealand Association for Migration and Investments* (n 3) [137].

[8] *Terminals (NZ) Ltd (n 3)* [121]. See also *Ng Yuen Shiu* (n 3) 637–38; *Diagnostic Medlab Ltd v Auckland District Health Board* [2007] 2 NZLR 832 [239] (HC).

[9] *Furnell v Whangarei High School Board* [1973] 2 NZLR 705, 718 (PC). See also *Fowler & Roderique* (n 3) 78; *Bennett v Superintendent, Rimutaka Prison* [2001] 3 NZLR 803 [63] (HC).

[10] *Furnell v Whangarei High School Board* [1973] 2 NZLR 705, 718 (PC).

[11] *Te Runanga O Ngati Awa v Attorney-General* 28 March 2008, Miller J, HC Wellington CIV-2006-485-001025 at [9]. See also *Ng Yuen Shiu* (n 3) 637–38; *Diagnostic Medlab* (n 8) [239].

[12] *Brierley Investments Ltd v Bouzaid* [1993] 3 NZLR 655, 670 (CA); *Staunton Investments Ltd v Chief Executive of the Ministry of Fisheries* [2004] NZAR 68 [29] (HC); *New Zealand Association for Migration and Investments* (n 3) [141].

[13] *R v Inland Revenue Commissioners; ex parte Unilever* (1999) 68 TC 205 (CA), quoted in *R (Zeqiri) v Secretary of State for the Home Department* [2002] UKHL 3, [2002] Imm AR 296 [44].

[14] *Northern Roller Milling* (n 5) 750 (HC); *White v New Zealand Stock Exchange* [2000] NZAR 297 [56] (CA).

[15] H Woolf, J Jowell, A Le Sueur, C Donnelly and I Hare, *De Smith's Judicial Review*, 7th edn (Sweet & Maxwell, 2013) 662.

DOCTRINAL BREAKTHROUGH

In *Schmidt v Secretary of State for Home Affairs*,[16] Lord Denning MR coined the expression 'legitimate expectation' in the context of procedural fairness, as a basis for challenge in judicial review. Until then, the law had laboured under the restriction that judicial review was confined to 'questions affecting *the rights of subjects*' (emphasis added).[17] This became a formulaic restraint on the scope of review and seriously hampered the courts' supervisory role. Private interests not legally recognised within the Hohfeldian matrix lacked protection at law. That remained the position until *Schmidt*, when Lord Denning finally broke the doctrinal stranglehold.[18]

In *Schmidt,* Lord Denning did not pause to explain the rationale of legitimate expectation. However, he did so three years later in *R v Liverpool Corporation; ex parte Liverpool Taxi Fleet Operators' Association*.[19] In this case, the council increased the number of taxi proprietor licences contrary to a council resolution not to do so. Lord Denning used the adjective 'settled' rather than 'legitimate' to describe the expectation but the adjectives meant the same thing.[20] He explained:

> So long as the performance of the undertaking is compatible with their public duty, they must honour it ... At any rate they ought not to depart from it except after the most serious consideration and hearing what the other party has to say: and then only if they are satisfied that the overriding public interest requires it. The public interest may be better served by honouring their undertaking than breaking it.

In the early decisions that applied *Schmidt*, legitimate expectation was not a carefully crafted legal concept. In some cases, it was not possible to separate a legitimate expectation from a justiciable legal interest. In *Schmidt*, Lord Denning ran the two together. The revocation of a current residence permit, he said, would have given the student 'an opportunity of making representations: for he would have a legitimate expectation of being allowed to stay for the permitted time'.[21] But under that scenario the law of legitimate expectation would be superfluous. A current permit with time to run would confer a *justiciable* legal right to remain, which the courts might enforce or protect against revocation.

Lord Denning's concept was initially exploratory and under-developed but it served a valuable purpose in relaxing the rigidity of the law. Later courts embraced the concept to review decisions where applicants otherwise

[16] *Schmidt* (n 1).

[17] *The King v Electricity Commissioners* [1924] 1 KB 171, 204–05 (Atkin LJ). See also *Cooper v Wandsworth Board of Works* (1863) 14 CBNS 180.

[18] *Schmidt* (n 1) 170.

[19] *Liverpool Taxi Fleet Operators' Association* (n 2).

[20] *Liverpool Taxi Fleet Operators' Association* (n 2) 304 in response to a submission from counsel.

[21] *Schmidt* (n 1) 171.

lacked a protectable legal interest. In a leading decision, the Privy Council quashed a deportation order where the immigration authorities had reneged on a promise that illegal immigrants who approached the authorities would be given a fair opportunity to present their case.[22] The promise gave rise to a legitimate expectation that the applicant's case would be fairly considered on its merits.

The law of legitimate expectation evolved alongside broader developments in scope-of-review doctrine. Today, judicial review extends beyond the protection of private rights in the Hohfeldian sense (legal rights balanced by correlative legal duties). It may lie to review the grant or refusal of a licence (a privilege, not a right),[23] or an inquiry whose functions are investigatory only,[24] or an interlocutory decision which precedes a final determination affecting rights.[25] In New Zealand, the *Judicature Amendment Act 1972* codifies the position at common law for the review of the exercise of statutory powers. The term 'statutory power of decision' means a power to inquire into or make a decision affecting '(a) [t]he rights, powers, privileges, immunities, duties, or liabilities of any person', or '(b) [t]he eligibility of any person to receive, or to continue to receive, a benefit or a licence, whether he is legally entitled to it or not'.[26]

LEGITIMATE EXPECTATION TEMPLATE

The New Zealand Court of Appeal has adopted a template for applying the doctrine of legitimate expectation,[27] but this chapter does not organise discussion around it.[28] The template requires applicants to establish three things:

(i) a commitment by way of a promise or settled practice or policy to act in a certain way;

[22] *Ng Yuen Shiu* (n 3).

[23] *Liverpool Taxi Fleet Operators' Association* (n 2) (taxi licences); *R v Barnsley Metropolitan Borough Council; ex parte Hook* [1976] 1 WLR 1052 (CA) (street trader's licence).

[24] *Re Erebus Royal Commission* [1983] NZLR 662 (PC); *Bradley v Attorney-General* [1988] 2 NZLR 454 (HC).

[25] *Fay, Richwhite & Co Ltd v Davison* [1995] 1 NZLR 517, 524 (CA); *Peters v Davison* [1999] 2 NZLR 164, 183 (CA); *Zaoui v Attorney-General* [2004] 2 NZLR 339, 360–61 (HC); *Zaoui v Attorney-General (No 2)* [2005] 1 NZLR 690, 720 (CA).

[26] *Judicature Amendment Act 1972*, s 3.

[27] *Terminals (NZ) Ltd* (n 3) [125]–[127]; *Green v Racing Integrity Unit Ltd* [2014] NZAR 623 [13] (CA).

[28] Contrast the following High Court decisions which treated the template as authoritative: *Singh v Chief Executive of the Ministry of Business, Innovation and Employment* [2013] NZHC 3273 [32]; *Pub Charity v Department of Internal Affairs* [2014] NZHC 1096 [48]; *Edmonds v New Zealand Parole Board* [2015] NZHC 386 [38].

(ii) legitimate or reasonable reliance on the promise or commitment; and
(iii) the appropriate remedy (if any) that should be granted.

The template has the virtue of clarity but its utility is limited. Not all matters of relevance to the doctrine can be subsumed within the three limbs. The template naturally addresses the establishing of legitimate expectations, the reasonable basis standard, the requirements of knowledge and detrimental reliance, and the difficulties associated with remedies. But it does not address other matters: for example, the closely aligned duty to consult, intensity of scrutiny, the relevance (or otherwise) of estoppel and the utility of the doctrine. There is also a problem with the template. There is no agreement over the second limb, which categorically proposes that detrimental reliance is an essential element of the doctrine. Most courts acknowledge that detrimental reliance is a relevant consideration where it can be established but not all courts consider it to be an essential element.[29] A claim might conceivably succeed in the absence of proof of knowledge or reliance.

CREATING LEGITIMATE EXPECTATION

Rationale

The requirements of fairness and good public administration hold decision-makers to their word. Legitimate expectation promotes consistency of treatment and equality before the law. On numerous occasions, the New Zealand courts have followed *Attorney-General of Hong Kong v Ng Yuen Shiu*.[30] There, the Privy Council explained:

> [W]hen a public authority has promised to follow a certain procedure, it is in the interest of good administration that it should act fairly and should implement its promise, so long as [it] does not interfere with its statutory duty.[31]

A legitimate expectation of being treated in a certain way is enforceable in the absence of any other legal basis on which to claim the treatment.[32] The expectation arises by reason of the decision-maker's conduct: by representation or promise, promulgated policies or guidelines, or settled past

[29] See under the heading, 'Detrimental Reliance' below.
[30] *Ng Yuen Shiu* (n 3). See *New Zealand Maori Council v Attorney-General* [1994] 1 NZLR 513, 525 (PC); *Awan v Minister of Immigration* [2000] NZAR 655, [23] (HC); *Vea v Minister of Immigration* [2002] NZAR 171, 180 (HC); *Te Heu Heu* (n 6) 126; *New Zealand Association for Migration and Investments* (n 3) [139]; *Terminals (NZ) Ltd* (n 3) [121]; *Green* (n 27) [14]–[15].
[31] *Ng Yuen Shiu* (n 3) 638.
[32] *New Zealand Association for Migration and Investments* (n 3) [142]; *Terminals (NZ) Ltd* (n 3) [123].

practice. A claim will succeed where a decision-maker breaches a reasonable expectation of a fair procedure.

Commitment Founded on Word or Deed

The notion of *commitment* lies at the heart of legitimate expectation. There must be 'a commitment by the public authority, whether made by promise, policy or settled practice, to act in a certain way'.[33] A promise need not be explicit but can arise by implication from past practice or policy.[34] Where reliance is placed on a practice or policy, its existence and content must amount to a commitment,[35] or an undertaking,[36] and it must be settled 'in the sense that it is regular and well-established'.[37] A regular practice is one where it is reasonable for the affected party to expect it to continue.[38] In some statutory contexts, a regular practice of itself may be unlikely to support a legitimate expectation. In *Brierley Investments Ltd v Bouzaid*,[39] the Commissioner of Inland Revenue had a statutory obligation to assess and collect taxes and his action in acting on successive annual returns could not establish a legitimate expectation. The Commissioner could not fetter the exercise of his statutory audit functions, which might require him to reopen past assessments or depart from past practices.

The effect of a decision on a particular party can give rise to a legitimate expectation of discrete application. A duty may lie on a decision-maker to consult a party, or take into account his or her interests, where the party is uniquely or specially affected.[40] Fixed-term occupational licence holders typically fall into this category. Where a licence-holder has a reasonable and legitimate expectation that the licence will be renewed, 'the Court will normally intervene to protect that expectation by judicial review'.[41]

[33] *Pub Charity* (n 28) [48], citing *Terminals (NZ) Ltd* (n 3) [125]. See also *R (Bibi) v Newham London Borough Council* [2002] 1 WLR 237, 244 (CA); *New Zealand Association for Migration and Investments* (n 3)[146].

[34] *Nichols v Health and Disability Commissioner* [1997] NZAR 351, 369–70 (HC); *Vea* (n 30) 181–82; *New Zealand Association for Migration and Investments* (n 3) [142]; *Terminals (NZ) Ltd* (n 3) [123]; *Green* (n 27) [14].

[35] *Terminals (NZ) Ltd* (n 3) [125]; *Green* (n 27) [14].

[36] *Ng Yuen Shiu* (n 3) 637, 638.

[37] *Green* (n 27) [14], citing *Council of Civil Service Unions v Minister for the Civil Service* [1985] AC 374, 401 (HL) ('regular practice … so well established'); *R (Bhatt Murphy) v The Independent Assessor* [2008] EWCA Civ 755, [29], [33], [42] and [46] ('established … pressing and focussed'); *Terminals (NZ) Ltd* (n 3) [125].

[38] *Air New Zealand Ltd v Nelson Airport Ltd* 27 November 2008, Miller J, HC Nelson CIV-2007-442-584 at [51]; *Terminals (NZ) Ltd* (n 3) [123]–[124].

[39] *Brierley Investments* (n 12) 670.

[40] *Fowler & Roderique* (n 3) 74; *Gallagher v Attorney-General* 28 July 1988, Ellis J, HC Wellington CP 402/88 at 21.

[41] *Fowler & Roderique* (n 3) 74. See also *Webster v Auckland Harbour Board* [1983] NZLR 646, 650 (CA); *Diagnostic Medlab* (n 8) [235].

A licence-holder will be entitled to be heard and given fair consideration before a decision is made to terminate the licence, or to renew it on less favourable terms.[42]

For a claim to succeed, there must be a 'holding out'. A representation must have been made with the intention that it be communicated or disseminated. In *Westpac Banking Corporation v Commissioner of Inland Revenue*,[43] an internal administrative memorandum which was not intended for dissemination, and was not externally communicated, could not found a legitimate expectation. The representation must be to the plaintiff personally or to a class of persons of whom the plaintiff is a member.[44] In *McLean v Commissioner of Inland Revenue*,[45] the plaintiff and other taxpayers were involved in a scheme that was the subject of a tax assessment and the Commissioner offered to settle shortfall penalties with the other taxpayers on more favourable terms than offered to the plaintiff. The plaintiff's legitimate expectation claim failed as his position differed from the other taxpayers', which placed him outside the class to whom the offer was made. The other taxpayers were parties to live litigation against the Commissioner and were able to pay the outstanding core tax.

The doctrine of legitimate expectation might raise issues of agency because an expectation might be raised by word or deed of someone having actual or ostensible authority to act for or on behalf of the decision-maker.[46] In *Back Country Helicopters v Minister of Conservation*,[47] helicopter operators held concessions to operate trophy hunting ventures on conservation land. The concessions officer recommended renewing the concessions on 10-year terms but the Minister granted the concessions on two-year terms. The applicants relied on the concessions officer's report but the officer had no actual or apparent authority to bind the decision-maker. 'It must have been apparent', observed the Court, 'that [the officer], at a level below that of decision-maker, could not make any binding decision or give any binding assurance on matters such as term'.[48]

Evidentiary Foundation

Legitimate expectations must have a sound evidentiary foundation. Legitimate expectation claims will be defeated through failure to establish an

[42] *Webster* (n 41) 650.

[43] *Westpac Banking Corporation v Commissioner of Inland Revenue* 26 October 2007, Harrison J, HC Auckland CIV-2004-404-6444 at [144].

[44] *E v Attorney-General* [2000] NZAR 354 [22] (HC).

[45] *McLean v Commissioner of Inland Revenue* (2005) 22 NZTC 19, 231 [39]–[42].

[46] *Air New Zealand Ltd v Nelson Airport Ltd* (n 38) [51] *Zhao v New Zealand Law Society* [2012] NZAR 894, [95] (HC).

[47] *Back Country Helicopters v Minister of Conservation* [2013] NZAR 1474 (HC).

[48] Ibid, [186].

unequivocal representation, or a clear past practice or announced policy, to act in a particular way. A practice sometimes followed will not discharge the evidential burden.[49] The evidence must satisfy 'the high threshold required to establish an unambiguous and settled commitment'.[50] A reasonable expectation requires more than a mere possibility.[51]

Whether or not the evidentiary foundation is established is a question of fact, having regard to all the surrounding circumstances.[52] The onus on the claimant is not a light one; happenstance will not discharge it. The courts distinguish between 'representations' (things uttered) and 'understandings' (things thought).[53] The former may establish a legitimate expectation claim but not the latter. A claimant must entertain more than a hope or unsubstantiated belief that something will happen:[54] 'The fact that we expect something to happen, or consider it should happen, does not in itself give us the right to have it happen.'[55] In *Te Heu Heu v Attorney-General*,[56] the evidence did not support the plaintiff's contention of a commitment to consult 'on a continuing and invariable basis'. The local authority engaged with local Maori, kept them advised and considered their views, but its openness of process and willingness to talk did not establish a legitimate expectation. The Court explained:[57] 'The question is whether the Council by its words, actions or assurances, were offering something and failed to deliver. What the plaintiffs wanted never developed beyond a hope or expectation on their part.'

Where a legitimate expectation is based on things uttered, the representation must be 'sufficiently focused',[58] and 'clear, unambiguous and unqualified'.[59] In *R (Bancoult) v Secretary of State for Foreign and Commonwealth Affairs (No 2)*,[60] the plaintiffs failed to establish that an assurance given by the Foreign Secretary gave rise to a legitimate expectation. In 1965, the

[49] *Supreme Sikh Council of New Zealand v Minister of Immigration* [2012] NZHC 1754 [39].

[50] *Green* (n 27) [31].

[51] *Wire Supplies Ltd v Commissioner of Inland Revenue* [2007] 3 NZLR 458 [151].

[52] *New Zealand Association for Migration and Investments* (n 3) [146].

[53] *New Zealand Federation of Commercial Fishing (Inc) v Minister of Fisheries* 24 April 1997, McGechan J, HC Wellington CP 237/95 at 134.

[54] *White* (n 14) 314; *Talleys Fisheries Ltd v Cullen* 31 January 2002, Ronald Young J, HC Wellington CP287/00 at 48; *Council of Social Services in Christchurch/Outautahi Inc v Christchurch City Council* [2009] 2 NZLR 123 [109] (HC); *Okahu Haulage Inc v Auckland City Council* [2010] NZAR 82, [28] (HC); *Terminals (NZ) Ltd* (n 3) [124].

[55] *New Zealand Federation of Commercial Fishing (Inc) v Minister of Fisheries* (n 53) 136.

[56] *Te Heu Heu* (n 6) 127.

[57] *Te Heu Heu* (n 6) 127.

[58] *New Zealand Federation of Commercial Fishing (Inc) v Minister of Fisheries* (n 53) 136.

[59] *Talleys Fisheries Ltd* (n 54) 48. See also *Terminals (NZ) Ltd* (n 3) [125]; *Green* (n 27) [13]–[15]; *Attorney-General v Ririnui* [2015] NZCA 160 [102].

[60] *R (Bancoult) v Secretary of State for Foreign and Commonwealth Affairs (No 2)* [2009] 1 AC 453 (HL).

British Government constituted the Chagos Archipelago a separate colony and forced the removal of the inhabitants in order to establish a military base. In 2000, following a successful challenge in the courts, the Foreign Secretary announced that the Chagossians would be allowed to return to their homeland but this announcement was not able to establish a legitimate expectation.[61] The Foreign Secretary's policy of resettlement was equivocal, not a firm promise. The Government had commissioned a feasibility study and a policy of permanent resettlement was contingent on the outcome of the study.[62] Promises, practices or policies which are ambiguous will not support an actionable claim. A claimant must establish that reliance was reasonable and it is not reasonable to rely upon one's preferred interpretation of an ambiguity.[63]

A Misnomer?

Might the expression 'legitimate expectation' be a misnomer? Need a claimant personally hold any expectation? Affected parties might not reasonably be expected to have knowledge of the decision-making and the practice or policy followed. In a refugee case, the House of Lords ruefully quipped that 'Kosavar refugees cannot be expected to check the small print'.[64] Basic fairness would support dispensing with the need for an actual expectation where it would be unreasonable to expect claimants to have the requisite knowledge. In *Lalli v Attorney-General*,[65] the plaintiff lacked knowledge of the guidelines applied and the Court applied an objective test based on the notional expectation of the objective bystander. What would that person, vested with full knowledge of the facts, legitimately expect as a matter of natural justice?

The bias in favour of actual knowledge and detrimental reliance arises by analogy to the private law of promissory estoppel. However, it is questionable whether the analogy is a valid or helpful one. The principles of fairness, certainty and good public administration are the driving imperatives of public law duties, not individualised responses that typically trigger private law principles. The law ought to encourage public officials to honour their undertakings and respect legal certainty.[66] In *Lalli*, the Court thought that a decision-maker which publicises a course of practice might properly be held

[61] Compare *Secretary of State for Foreign and Commonwealth Affairs v R (Bancoult)* [2008] QB 365 (CA) (reversed on appeal).

[62] *Bancoult (No 2)* (n 60) [61], [115], [134].

[63] *New Zealand Association for Migration and Investments* (n 3) [143], [146]; *Terminals (NZ) Ltd* (n 3) [124].

[64] *Zeqiri* (n 13) [44].

[65] *Lalli* (n 46) [26]–[27].

[66] PP Craig, *Administrative Law*, 7th edn (Sweet & Maxwell, 2012) 680–81.

to account, even in the absence of knowledge or detrimental reliance.[67] This approach has added force where representations are made to the public at large.[68] Inquiries as to individualised responses are moot where decision-makers publicly commit to particular policies or practices.

Dispensing with the need to establish knowledge and detrimental reliance (where the claimant personally entertains no expectation) raises issues of taxonomy. The language of natural justice seems more fitting than legitimate expectation to articulate the requirements of fairness in the circumstances of the case. To speak of legitimate expectation seems awkward where a duty of fairness arises by operation of law, rather than from one's personal circumstance.

DEFEATING LEGITIMATE EXPECTATION

Policy Changes

The law of legitimate expectation is built upon two countervailing public interests. On the one hand, governments and public authorities ought to be held to their promises in the interests of good public administration. But, on the other hand, they must optimise their decision-making where circumstances require reassessment and policy change.[69] Where these two public interests clash, the latter must prevail: 'the adoption of new policy to meet changing circumstances may be viewed as the duty of any government in furthering the public interest'.[70] The courts accept that the liberty to make policy changes is simply 'inherent' in Westminster parliamentary government.[71]

The courts' approach to policy changes is 'very much fact dependent'.[72] Their supervision will be less intrusive in what Laws LJ termed 'the macro-political field',[73] where high level policy choices are made in the public interest.[74] In *R v Secretary of State for Education and Employment; ex parte Begbie*,[75] Laws LJ explained:

> [I]n that field, true abuse of power is less likely to be found, since within it changes of policy, fuelled by broad conceptions of the public interest, may more readily be

[67] *Lalli* (n 46) [28].
[68] *E v Attorney-General* (n 44) [22]; *R v Department for Education and Employment; ex parte Begbie* [2000] 1 WLR 1115, 1133 (CA).
[69] *New Zealand Association for Migration and Investments* (n 3) [140]; *Lalli* (n 46) [20].
[70] *New Zealand Association for Migration and Investments* (n 3) [140].
[71] *Hughes v Department of Health and Social Services* [1985] AC 776, 788 (HL).
[72] *New Zealand Association for Migration and Investments* (n 3) [157].
[73] *Begbie* (n 68) 1131.
[74] *Talleys Fisheries Ltd* (n 54) 48.
[75] *Begbie* (n 68) 1131.

accepted as taking precedence over the interests of groups which enjoyed expectations generated by an earlier policy.

Ministers who make representations will seldom be held to fetter their decision-making freedom when exercising their statutory powers.[76] The Crown must remain unconstrained and flexible 'in matters which concern the welfare of the State',[77] and what is appropriate executive action 'must necessarily be determined by the needs of the community when the question arises'.[78] Governments are bound to revisit existing policies and adopt new ones in response to changing circumstances.[79] The courts readily countenance policy choices where ministers publicly resolve that a new policy is in the public interest.[80] Just as the Crown cannot be estopped from legitimately exercising the State's power—even should this cause harm to private individuals[81]—the courts will not entertain a legitimate expectation challenge if the minister acts in accordance with law, fairly and reasonably.[82] A plaintiff must establish that there was no good reason to depart from a policy, or that the reasoning justifying the departure was capricious or perverse.[83]

A kindred principle applies to public decision-makers generally. Public bodies established by statute may not renounce part of their statutory birthright.[84] A legitimate expectation must be compatible with a decision-maker's statutory functions and not fetter or constrain them: 'A public authority cannot bind itself not to exercise a power or to exercise it in a particular way if the statute requires it to retain a free and unhindered discretion to exercise it … according to its judgment.'[85] Clear statutory words override any countervailing expectation.[86] However, the courts are naturally circumspect where it is claimed that a statute prevents a decision-maker from making binding commitments. They give due weight to the public interest in holding

[76] *Staunton Investments* (n 12) [29]. See also *Vilceanu v Attorney-General* 11 May 2011, Faire J, HC Auckland CIV-2010-404-4358 [25].

[77] *Rederiaktiebolaget Amphitrite v R* [1921] 3 KB 500, 503 (DC). See also *Brierley Investments* (n 12) 661.

[78] *Rederiaktiebolaget Amphitrite* (n 77) 503 (DC).

[79] *New Zealand Association for Migration and Investments* (n 3) [140].

[80] *New Zealand Association for Migration and Investments* (n 3) [157]. See also *Bancoult (No 2)* (n 60) [63] (Lord Hoffmann).

[81] *Lumber Specialities Ltd v Hodgson* [2000] 2 NZLR 347 [138] (HC).

[82] *New Zealand Association for Migration and Investments* (n 3) [158]. See also *R v Secretary of State for Health; ex parte US Tobacco International Ltd* [1992] QB 353, 368–69 (CA).

[83] *Staunton Investments* (n 12) [29].

[84] *Ayr Harbour Trustees v Oswald* (1883) 8 App Cas 623; *Birkdale District Electric Supply Co Ltd v Southport Corporation* [1926] AC 355 (HL); *The Power Co Ltd v Gore District Council* [1997] 1 NZLR 537, 548 (CA); *Te Runanga-a-iwi o Ngati Kahu v Carrington Farms Ltd* (2011) 16 ELRNZ 664 [110] (HC).

[85] *Brierley Investments* (n 12) 661. See also *Commissioner of Inland Revenue v New Zealand Wool Board* (1999) 19 NZTC 15, 476 [62] (CA).

[86] *Te Tai Tokerau Mapo Trust v Chief Executive of Ministry of Health* 5 August 2011, Woodhouse J, HC Whangarei CIV-2010-488-307 [145].

decision-makers to their word, and will excuse a departure only where the statute clearly requires it.

General Principles

Miscellany

A public duty defeats a legitimate expectation.[87] The general principle is that a decision-maker's promise, policy or past practice must not interfere with the discharge of its mandated statutory duty.[88] Nor will the courts uphold a legitimate expectation where to do so would require a decision-maker to act contrary to law (be it the general law or the decision-maker's own empowering instrument).[89] A legitimate expectation is defeated if the decision-maker gives notice that a policy or practice no longer applies,[90] or if there was a 'satisfactory reason' not to follow it.[91] The need to optimise decision-making or respond to changing circumstances justifies changing policies or past practices: 'By making a promise or following a practice, a public authority cannot "preclude any possible need to change it".'[92] When a change of policy is communicated, any reasonable expectations based on earlier policy are extinguished.[93] Moreover, expectations may come to an end naturally without any action by the decision-maker.[94] A representation may be made operative for a finite period or be discharged upon a particular occurrence.

Ameliorative Action

No one may be heard to complain if a change of policy or practice was rationally supported.[95] Nevertheless, the duty of fairness continues to apply and may require ameliorative action to mitigate any adverse consequence. A change of policy or practice should, if possible, be accompanied by notice

[87] *Staunton Investments* (n 12) [29].

[88] *Hg Yuen Shui* (n 3) 638, approved in inter alia *New Zealand Maori Council* (n 30) 525; *New Zealand Association for Migration and Investments* (n 3) [139]; *Terminals (NZ) Ltd* (n 3) [121]; *Green* (n 27) [40].

[89] *Talleys Fisheries Ltd* (n 54) 48.

[90] *Te Tai Tokerau Mapo Trust* (n 86) [145].

[91] *New Zealand Maori Council* (n 30) 525; *New Zealand Association for Migration and Investments* (n 3) [140]; *Terminals (NZ) Ltd* (n 3) [121]; *Green* (n 27) [40].

[92] *Te Tai Tokerau Mapo Trust* (n 86) [145], quoting *R v Secretary of State for the Home Department; ex parte Ruddock* [1987] 2 All ER 518, 531 (DC).

[93] *Hughes* (n 71) 788.

[94] *Unitec Institute of Technology v Attorney-General* [2006] 1 NZLR 65, [138] (HC) (reversed on appeal in *Attorney-General v Unitec Institute of Technology* [2007] 1 NZLR 750 (CA)).

[95] *R v Ministry of Agriculture, Fisheries and Food; ex parte Hamble (Offshore) Fisheries Ltd* [1995] 2 All ER 714 (DC); *New Zealand Association for Migration and Investments* (n 3) [154].

to those affected, and, where appropriate, with a transitional period 'to ensure that there is not undue unfairness to those whose expectations are not realised'.[96] When making policy changes, decision-makers should also be prepared to adopt transitional ('pipeline') provisions so as to ameliorate obvious cases of hardship or unfairness.[97] They must give proper consideration to the position of affected parties and ask what provision, if any, might be made to accommodate them. In *Lawson v Housing New Zealand*,[98] Housing New Zealand staged a rent increase over several years, did not evict tenants who refused to pay the additional rent, and made special provision for vulnerable classes of tenant. The legitimate expectation claim failed as there was no unfairness in the way the rent increase was implemented. Other transitional provisions might include exceptions from the application of a new policy or, in appropriate cases, payment of compensation by the public authority.[99]

Exceptions/Plaintiff's Actions

The making of exceptions to a new policy can be a double-edged sword: they may defeat any legitimate expectations otherwise held. '[T]he inclusion of "thought-out" exceptions in the policy itself', the High Court has held, 'might well be exhaustive of the obligation'.[100] Action taken by the plaintiff might likewise defeat a legitimate action. In *Staunton Investments Ltd v Chief Executive of the Ministry of Fisheries*,[101] fishers claimed breach of a legitimate expectation when the Ministry refused to apply the standard discount to offset payments for harvested fish not covered by the fishers' quota. The claim failed as the fishers had already claimed a deduction for fishing costs relating to by-catch: 'It was that claimed—and granted—deduction that thwarted any expectation.'[102] Their legitimate expectation would have been met had they not claimed the deduction.

Fraudulent Misconduct

A claim for a legitimate expectation will fail where the action complained of was founded on the claimant's falsehood or fraud. Fraudulent misconduct, false or misleading representations or concealment of relevant information

[96] *Lalli* (n 46) [20].
[97] *Hamble Fisheries* (n 95); *New Zealand Association for Migration and Investments* (n 3) [154], [157].
[98] *Lawson v Housing New Zealand* (1996) 3 HRNZ 285, 326 (HC).
[99] *New Zealand Association for Migration and Investments* (n 3) [157].
[100] *New Zealand Association for Migration and Investments* (n 3), quoting from *Hamble Fisheries* (n 95).
[101] *Staunton Investments* (n 12).
[102] *Staunton Investments* (n 12) [34].

will defeat a legitimate expectation.[103] A foreign national who fraudulently procured a residence permit and returning residence visa could not claim a legitimate expectation that a further entry permit would be granted.[104] Acceptance of the false visa by the immigration authorities on the pervious occasion might have raised a hope of re-entry but not a legitimate expectation.

Statutory Context

The statutory context may limit the scope for legitimate expectations, and may even preclude them.[105] Before 1995, New Zealand's income tax legislation precluded the Commissioner of Inland Revenue from being bound by any representations to taxpayers.[106] That position was relaxed in 1995 when legislative amendments introduced a binding rulings regime, which made the Commissioner's representations to taxpayers legally binding. This codified the common law of legitimate expectation but only where taxpayers made a formal request for a ruling.[107] All other representations made outside of the binding rulings regime remained legally unenforceable. '[T]he Commissioner', the Court of Appeal ruled, 'cannot estop himself from enforcing the law'.[108] Accordingly, past assessments of or unsolicited representations as to taxpayer liabilities cannot found legitimate expectations. The Commissioner must make assessments in accordance with the *Income Tax Act 2007*, which trumps any expectation based on a taxpayer's previous assessments or the Commissioner's representations.[109]

The statutory context may sanction policy development over time. In liquor licensing cases, for example, the courts accept that policy development is a constantly evolving process.[110] Legitimate expectations based on past practice or policy may be defeated as the licensing authority refines its approach to the licensing regime. In *PP and G Basra Ltd v Rangitoto College Board of Trustees*,[111] the legitimate expectation claim was based on the authority's earlier practice of granting liberal licensing hours, and then reducing them if cause were shown. Over time the authority had become

103 *Chen v Minister of Immigration* [1992] NZAR 261 (CA).

104 Ibid.

105 *Northern Roller Milling* (n 5) 750 (CA) (the particular decision-making power might exclude any legitimate expectation).

106 *Brierley Investments* (n 12) 661; *New Zealand Wool Board* (n 85) 476 [62].

107 *Westpac Banking Corporation v Commissioner of Inland Revenue* [2009] 2 NZLR 99 [56]–[57] (CA).

108 Ibid, [84].

109 *Wire Supplies* (n 51) [74].

110 *The Ole Forge Ltd v Papakura District Licensing Agency* [1996] NZAR 305 [34] (CA); *Buzz & Bear Ltd v Woodroffe* [1996] NZAR 404, 409–10 (HC); *Johnsonville Club v Wellington District Licensing Agency* [1999] NZAR 360, 364 (HC).

111 *PP and G Basra Ltd v Rangitoto College Board of Trustees* 21 December 2009, Allan J, HC Auckland CIV-2009-404-3632.

more conservative in fixing licensing hours, which defeated any expectation based on its earlier practice. 'The Authority must be entitled', the High Court held, 'to fine tune its approach in the light of its experience and the emergence of fresh perspectives'.[112]

Remedial Discretion

Sometimes, the courts have relied on the remedial discretion in judicial review rather than hold that the public interest had defeated a legitimate expectation. In *Te Runanga o Ngati Awa v Attorney-General*,[113] the High Court held that, where there are good reasons for a decision-maker to change a policy, the court may withhold relief in the exercise of discretion. The public interest supported the impugned decision and enforcing a legitimate expectation of consultation would have been disruptive. However, it is puzzling why a court should rely on a residual remedial discretion when the law of legitimate expectation provides the requisite mechanism. The court might simply have held that the public interest defeated any legitimate expectation.

Regularising Misapplied Policy

No question of defeating an expectation arises where the aberrant application of a promulgated policy is corrected, involving no change to the policy itself. In *Singh v Chief Executive of the Ministry of Business, Innovation and Employment*,[114] immigration officers had incorrectly applied immigration instructions and granted residence applications lodged by the plaintiff's fellow employees. An internal ministry memorandum regularised the decision-making, which resulted in the Ministry declining the plaintiff's application in circumstances similar to the other employees. 'Regularising an errant approach', the Court held, 'does not render future decision-making arbitrary, unfair or unlawful'.[115] The plaintiff's expectation was personally held but was neither reasonable nor legitimate, 'once all the circumstances were known'.[116] Nor will a legitimate expectation claim succeed where, on the facts, the expectation has been met. Discharging the obligation the decision-maker undertakes satisfies the expectation.[117]

[112] Ibid, [63].
[113] *Te Runanga o Ngati Awa v Attorney-General* 28 March 2008, Miller J, HC Wellington CIV-2006-485-1025 [9].
[114] *Singh* (n 28).
[115] *Singh* (n 28) [59].
[116] *Singh* (n 28) [62].
[117] *Raea v Attorney-General* (2009) 24 NZTC 23, 951 [28] (HC); *Vilceanu v Attorney-General* (n 76) [24]; *Imported Motor Vehicle Industry Association v Minister of Transport* 1 December 2011, Miller J, HC Wellington CIV-2011-485-1972 [54].

Retrospective Policies

The principle against retrospectivity applies to the making of policies. Retrospective policies, applying to events which have already been concluded, will rarely defeat legitimate expectations. One suggestion is that such policies may be adopted, provided adequate notice is given to allow those affected to adjust their position.[118] However, it is difficult to comprehend parties altering their position to accommodate policy changes that apply to past events: how might one mitigate the effect of such policies on actions already carried out? As a matter of principle, such policies ought not to defeat legitimate expectations.

REASONABLE BASIS

The adjectives 'legitimate' and 'reasonable' are synonymous and interchangeable when describing expectations.[119] A legitimate expectation must have a reasonable basis to be actionable; it must, in the circumstances, be reasonable for the affected party to rely on it.[120] The reasonableness of the expectation must be assessed objectively, having regard to the circumstances claimed to support it.[121] Where the expectation is based on a practice or policy, the claimant must reasonably expect that it will continue and the belief that it will do so must be rationally supported.[122] In addition, the expectation itself must be rationally supported. In *Green v Racing Integrity Unit Ltd*,[123] the alleged expectation was unreasonable as it asserted a practice that was not rationally based. For many years, the racing authorities did not have the technology to test for the banned substance arsenic. The authorities introduced a new testing regime that could detect arsenic and the owners of a harness racer sought judicial review after their horse tested positive. They claimed to hold a legitimate expectation that the authorities would warn industry participants before introducing a new testing regime. The High Court and Court of Appeal described the alleged expectation as 'counter-intuitive'[124] and 'odd' respectively,[125] as lacking any reasonable basis. 'It would be an odd expectation on the [owners'] part,' their Honours

118 *Hamble Fisheries* (n 95) 726, followed in *New Zealand Association for Migration and Investments* (n 3) [156].

119 *Hg Yuen Shui* (n 3) 636; *Lalli* (n 46) [29], [67].

120 *E v Attorney-General* (n 44) [22]; *Begbie* (n 68); *New Zealand Association for Migration and Investments* (n 3) [143].

121 *Te Heu Heu* (n 6) 126–27.

122 *Talleys Fisheries Ltd* (n 54) 48; *New Zealand Association for Migration and Investments* (n 3) [142]; *Te Tai Tokerau Mapo Trust* (n 86) [145].

123 *Green* (n 27).

124 *Green v Racing Integrity Unit Ltd* [2013] NZHC 1137 [73].

125 *Green* (n 27) [33].

observed, 'that HRNZ would commit to warning them of its enhanced ability to detect rules infringements'.[126]

The sufficiency of the representation or practice relied on may affect the reasonableness of the expectation. An alleged representation or practice must, in fact, be established. An express promise of a fair procedure that is clear and unambiguous will usually suffice.[127] In contrast, a single precedent, or the fact that something had happened in the past, is unlikely to establish a settled practice: 'One [precedent] does not a practice make.'[128] It is neither reasonable to rely on a single precedent nor realistic to expect that decision-makers will necessarily follow a single precedent. To give rise to a legitimate expectation, a decision-maker must make it clear that its decision lays down a general policy or approach for the future.[129] An expectation will lack a reasonable basis if it is based on a hope or unsubstantiated belief,[130] a misinterpretation of a decision-maker's representation,[131] or a representation that is ambiguous, uncertain or qualified.[132] The sufficiency of the representation or practice will depend upon the circumstances of each case. In *Controller of Customs v Terminals (NZ) Ltd*,[133] it was not reasonable to rely on a verbal clarification by Customs that excise duty would not be levied. The scale of the proposed investment and the fiscal consequences of excise duty made it reasonable to expect that any clarification would be in writing.

An expectation is likely to have a reasonable basis where a refusal to recognise it would undermine public confidence in the decision-making process.[134] Conversely, there cannot be any reasonable basis if the expectation is defeated through the actions of the claimant,[135] or as a result of the decision-maker's statutory function or duty.[136] The Commissioner of Inland Revenue, for example, must maintain the integrity of the tax base and make assessments in accordance with the tax laws.[137] Neither Commissioners' representations nor past assessments of taxpayer liabilities can found

[126] *Green* (n 27) [33].
[127] *Zhao* (n 46) [95]–[96].
[128] *Back Country Helicopters* (n 47) [185].
[129] *Talleys Fisheries Ltd* (n 54) 49.
[130] *White* (n 14) 314; *Talleys Fisheries Ltd* (n 54) 48; *Challis v Destination Marlborough Trust Board Inc* [2003] 2 NZLR 107 [102] (HC); *New Zealand Association for Migration and Investments* (n 3) [143]; *Okahu Haulage* (n 54) [28].
[131] *Lawson v Housing New Zealand* [1997] 2 NZLR 474, 490 (HC).
[132] *Talleys Fisheries Ltd* (n 54) 48; *New Zealand Association for Migration and Investments* (n 3) [146]; *Terminals (NZ) Ltd* (n 3) [125]; *Howard v Accident Compensation Commission* [2013] NZHC 188 [24] (HC).
[133] *Terminals (NZ) Ltd* (n 3).
[134] *Aoraki Water Trust v Meridian Energy Ltd* [2005] 2 NZLR 268 [41] (HC).
[135] *Staunton Investments* (n 12) [34].
[136] *Ng Yuen Shiu* (n 3) 638; *Brierley Investments* (n 12) 661; *New Zealand Wool Board* (n 85) 476 [62].
[137] *Westpac Banking Corporation* (n 107) [55]–[57].

legitimate expectations.[138] The only representations that bind the Commissioner are those made under the binding rulings regime, which was introduced to the legislation to provide certainty about how the tax laws would apply to taxpayers.[139]

DETRIMENTAL RELIANCE

It remains unresolved whether or not knowledge and detrimental reliance are necessary elements of the doctrine. Detrimental reliance necessarily implies knowledge, as an aggrieved party cannot rely on that of which the party is unaware. A party must know of the representation, policy or practice (as the case may be) in order to establish reliance. Detrimental reliance and reliance simpliciter will usually be indistinguishable as the party doing the relying will almost always suffer detriment. In *Air New Zealand Ltd v Wellington International Airport Ltd*,[140] the Court rejected counsel's argument that reliance simpliciter must be established but not detrimental reliance. The Court could not see 'daylight between the two concepts' and dismissed any difference as 'semantic'.[141]

The suggestion that detrimental reliance is a necessary element of legitimate expectation arises by analogy to the private law concept of promissory estoppel. These concepts bear similarities but their rationales differ fundamentally: legitimate expectation promotes fairness in the interests of good public administration, whereas estoppel protects private parties who rely on others' undertakings. In *R v Independent Television Commission; ex parte TSW Broadcasting Ltd*,[142] Lord Donaldson testily observed that '[t]he test in public law is fairness, not an adaptation of the law of contract or estoppel'. The New Zealand courts have echoed Lord Donaldson ('estoppel has no place in modern public law ... adding nothing but confusion'),[143] although some courts have not discarded the private law analogy entirely.[144]

138 *Wire Supplies* (n 51) [74], [76].

139 *Westpac Banking Corporation* (n 107)[55]–[57].

140 *Air New Zealand Ltd v Wellington International Airport Ltd* [2009] NZAR 138 (HC).

141 Ibid, [64].

142 In *R v Independent Television Commission; ex parte TSW Broadcasting Ltd*, *The Times*, 7 February 1992 (quoted in *R v North and East Devon Health Authority; ex parte Coughlan* [2001] QB 213 [80] (CA)). See also *Russell v Attorney-General* 11 November 2002, France J, HC Wellington CP100/02 at [84] eschewing an adaptation of the law of contract or estoppel.

143 *Challis* (n 130) [105]. See also *Terminals (NZ) Ltd* (n 3) [156] where the Court 'seriously doubted' whether there was any room for the private law concept in a public law setting.

144 See, eg, *Coromandel Peninsula Watchdog* (n 4) 569; *Khouri v Waitakere City Council* 6 August 1997, Elias J, HC Auckland CP886/91 at 66 ('In general, the principles of estoppel and agency apply to public bodies'); *Westpac Banking Corporation v Commissioner of Inland Revenue* (2008) 23 NZTC 21, 694 [105] (HC); *Lalli* (n 46) [24].

In contrast, the United Kingdom courts have grasped the nettle and categorically rejected the place of estoppel in public law.[145]

The law of legitimate expectation, while broadly analogous to estoppel, is more appropriately moulded to the working assumptions of public law.[146] It may not be realistic to expect claimants to have knowledge of the decision-making: for example, as when asylum seekers arrive in a country and apply for refugee status.[147] In *Lalli*,[148] the Court extemporised that claimants who lacked knowledge might claim a 'prescriptive expectation' based on an objective test: What would the objective bystander legitimately expect as a matter of natural justice?[149] It was what this hypothetical person (in reality *the Court*) might legitimately expect, not what the claimant in person did or did not expect. The Court believed that this was a reasonable compromise but conceded that there were possibly no New Zealand decisions that fell into this category.[150]

The question concerning detrimental reliance remains unresolved.[151] Some courts have categorically stated that evidence of reliance is required (or treated it as being required),[152] while others have categorically stated that it is not required.[153] The preferable view is that evidence of detrimental reliance is not essential but clearly relevant,[154] and in most cases will be so beneficial to the applicant's case as practically to be required.[155] Absence of detrimental reliance in a successful legitimate expectation challenge will be 'rare',[156] and 'very much the exception, rather than the rule'.[157] In *Air New Zealand*,[158] the Court explained that legitimate expectation was tethered to fairness and '[t]he issue of fairness is inextricably bound up with detrimental reliance: if Air NZ did not suffer from the alleged departure, then its claim for relief is unlikely to become airborne'. The presence of reliance

[145] *R v East Sussex County Council; ex parte Reprotech (Pebsham) Ltd* [2003] 1 WLR 348, 358 (Lord Hoffmann).

[146] Ibid, [33]–[35].

[147] *Zeqiri* (n 13) [44].

[148] *Lalli* (n 46).

[149] *Lalli* (n 46) [26]

[150] *Lalli* (n 46) [26].

[151] *New Zealand Association for Migration and Investments* (n 3) [144]. See also *Air New Zealand* (n 140) [69].

[152] *Attorney-General v Waikato Regional Airport Ltd* [2002] 3 NZLR 433 [132] (CA); *R v Mohi* [2007] NZCA 139 [9]; *Terminals (NZ) Ltd* (n 3) [125]–[127]; *Green* (n 27) [13].

[153] *Lawson* (n 131) 489; *Awan* (n 30) [38]; *E v Attorney-General* (n 44) [22]; *Begbie* (n 68) 1124, 1133; *Bibi* (n 33) 245; *Lalli* (n 46) [28]–[29].

[154] *Talleys Fisheries Ltd* (n 54) 48–49; *Bibi* (n 33) 245–46; *Aoraki Water Trust* (n 134) [41]; *New Zealand Association for Migration and Investments* (n 3) [144]; *Lalli* (n 46) [29].

[155] *Air New Zealand* (n 140) [69].

[156] *Talleys Fisheries Ltd* (n 54) 48.

[157] *Begbie* (n 68) 1124.

[158] *Air New Zealand* (n 140) [70]. See also *Begbie* (n 68) 1124.

may provide objective evidence of the reasonableness of the expectation (an expectation that is not rationally supported is unlikely to engender reliance) and may therefore also be a relevant factor in determining the legitimacy of the expectation.[159]

SUBSTANTIVE LEGITIMATE EXPECTATION

The New Zealand courts have not followed their United Kingdom counterparts and embraced substantive legitimate expectations. They have generally resisted extending the law beyond procedural expectations or, when granting relief, imposing substantive outcomes or results. They have confined the law to the procedures of law-making and held decision-makers to expectations that ensure a fair process. In *Air New Zealand*, the High Court reflected that this 'is obviously a softer position than that adopted in *Coughlan* and *Begbie* for the United Kingdom'.[160]

The England and Wales Court of Appeal decision in *R v North and East Devon Health Authority; ex parte Coughlan*[161] was a game-changer for the United Kingdom. *Coughlan* established an exception to the rule that the courts will not direct the grant of a substantive benefit. The Court upheld the applicant's expectation as to a particular outcome in view of the small number of persons affected, the importance of the promise to them and the purely financial consequences of honouring it. The reneging on the promise was an abuse of power lacking any public interest justification. One month later, in *Begbie*,[162] a differently constituted Court of Appeal endorsed *Coughlan* and the concept of substantive legitimate expectation it countenanced.

The courts distinguish the two types of expectation but the question is whether or not the distinction is appropriate and helpful. Administrative law doctrine last century was wedded to a raft of false dichotomies (jurisdictional v non-jurisdictional, judicial v administrative, mandatory v directory, statutory v prerogative, void v voidable, etc) that seriously impeded judicial review.[163] Those dichotomies misdirected the focus of the law, imbuing it with distracting formalism and technicality. Might distinguishing between procedural and substantive expectations do the same for the law of legitimate expectation? Fairness and good public administration are the driving imperatives of administrative law and breaching a promise of a substantive

[159] *Begbie* (n 68) 1124, 1133; *Bibi* (n 33) 245; *New Zealand Association for Migration and Investments* (n 3) [144]; *TAP (NZ) Pty Ltd v Origin Energy Resources NZ Ltd* 14 February 2006, Miller J, HC Wellington CIV-2005-485-1500, [49].

[160] *Air New Zealand* (n 140) [52].

[161] *Coughlan* (n 142).

[162] *Begbie* (n 68). Sedley LJ sat in both *Coughlan* and *Begbie* but the other judges on these panels were different in each case.

[163] For an examination of these dichotomies, see PA Joseph, 'False Dichotomies in Administrative Law: From There to Here' [2016] *New Zealand Law Review* 127.

outcome might be as unfair to a claimant as breaching an undertaking of a fair procedure. Substantive legitimate expectations ought, in principle, therefore, to be enforceable, subject to the nature of relief that might properly issue.

Exceptional cases do arise. Some cases call for flexibility and adroitness. Enforcing anything less than a substantive outcome might fail properly to remedy a wrong and do justice to the case. In *McGuire v Wellington Standards Committee (No 1)*,[164] disciplinary proceedings against a lawyer were resolved by the tribunal agreeing that the lawyer would plead guilty to a lesser charge and undertake supervision and mentoring as a requirement for future practice. The lawyer completed the supervision and did what was required under the agreement. When the tribunal called for submissions on the final orders it should make, the lawyer applied for a discharge without conviction and costs against the standards committee which presented the charges, arguing that he had not been treated fairly in the disciplinary process. The standards committee's riposte was to seek a censure, and the tribunal resolved that a censure was appropriate to mark the unacceptability of the lawyer's conduct.

Where did the interests of justice lie? The lawyer had fulfilled the agreement to resolve the disciplinary proceeding and to justify his future practice but he was then subjected to an additional penalty of censure. The High Court ruled that this breached his legitimate expectation and quashed the censure. The nature of the expectation was as to substantive outcome: the penalty and supervision the lawyer had agreed to in order to resolve the matter and remain in practice. Merely to have directed the tribunal to reconsider its decision, while allowing the censure to stand, would have been an underwhelming response.

The New Zealand courts have accepted in principle that legitimate expectations might be substantive in nature (a holding out of a benefit, outcome or result),[165] but they have baulked at enforcing substantive outcomes. In *Association for Migration and Investments Inc v Attorney-General*,[166] Randerson J resolved that there were three possible recourses: (a) the court might hold that the decision-maker was required to accord due weight to the legitimate expectation before deciding whether or not to defeat it; (b) the court might decide that the claimant had a legitimate expectation of being consulted before a decision was taken, 'unless there [was] an overriding reason to resile from [the consultation]' (in which event 'the Court will itself judge the adequacy of the reason advanced for the change of policy');[167] or (c) the

164 *McGuire v Wellington Standards Committee (No 1)* [2014] NZHC 3042.

165 See for example *E v Attorney-General* (n 44) [22]–[23]; *Staunton Investments* (n 12); *New Zealand Association for Migration and Investments* (n 3) [145]; *Unitec Institute of Technology* (n 94) [135]; *Lalli* (n 46) [29].

166 *New Zealand Association for Migration and Investments* (n 3) [147], following *Coughlan* (n 142) [57].

167 *New Zealand Association for Migration and Investments* (n 3).

court might consider that a promise or practice had induced a legitimate expectation of a substantive benefit, in which case 'the Court would have the task of weighing the requirements of fairness against any overriding interest relied upon for the change of policy'.[168] However, unlike in *Coughlan*, Randerson J refused to entertain enforcing a substantive outcome. That, he said, would be to usurp the mandated function of the decision-maker.[169]

The policy of the law lies against granting relief in the form of substantive outcomes.[170] Such relief is 'rarely, if ever, granted'.[171] Nevertheless, the categories of legitimate expectation 'are not closed'[172] and the courts have not bolted shut the door on substantive relief. Such relief might conceivably lie 'in a truly exceptional case',[173] as in *McGuire*,[174] for example, where the justice of the case warranted it. Such cases may arise from time to time but two considerations will usually oppose substantive relief. Enforcing substantive outcomes: (a) usurps the mandated functions of the decision-maker,[175] and (b) imposes an impermissible fetter on the exercise of administrative discretion.[176]

The problematic dynamic is that substantive legitimate expectations trigger contradictory principles. Public decision-making must promote fairness and good public administration, requiring decision-makers to honour their undertakings (whether or not as to outcome or procedure). But, equally the courts must not usurp the decision-making function or be complicit in fettering discretion. How these contradictory principles play out determines the legitimacy or otherwise of enforcing substantive expectations. Should decision-makers be held to their word in the interests of good public administration, or free to exercise discretion and flexibility according to the circumstances of the case? The relative virtues of fairness and flexibility pull in opposite directions.

[168] *New Zealand Association for Migration and Investments* (n 3).

[169] *New Zealand Association for Migration and Investments* (n 3) [159].

[170] *Air New Zealand* (n 140) [52], [61]–[62]; *GXL Regulatory Ltd v Minister of Energy* [2010] NZAR 518 [45] (CA); *Terminals (NZ) Ltd* (n 3) [155]; *Back Country Helicopters* (n 47) [184]; *Green* (n 27) [40]; *Whitehouse Tavern Trust Board v Department of Internal Affairs* [2014] NZHC 662 [64]; *Oosterveen v Ministry of Business, Innovation and Employment* [2014] NZHC 1709 [46].

[171] *Terminals (NZ) Ltd* (n 3) [155]; *Green* (n 27) [40].

[172] *Burt v Governor-General* [1992] 3 NZLR 672, 679 (CA). See also *Back Country Helicopters* (n 47) [184]; *Oosterveen* (n 170)47.

[173] *Back Country Helicopters* (n 47) [184].

[174] *McGuire* (n 164).

[175] *New Zealand Association for Migration and Investments* (n 3) [159]; *Terminals (NZ) Ltd* (n 3) [155]; *Green* (n 27) [40].

[176] *Brierley Investments* (n 12) 661; *Staunton Investments* (n 12) [29]; *Unitec Institute of Technology* (n 94) [134], [137]–[138] (CA); *Back Country Helicopters* (n 47)[188]; *Green* (n 27) [40].

DUTY OF CONSULTATION

The doctrine of legitimate expectation and the duty to consult are closely aligned: '[T]he law of legitimate expectation has created a common law foundation for a duty to consult.'[177] Legitimate expectations typically require consultations and an opportunity to be heard before a decision may be taken to depart from a settled practice, policy or representation.[178] However, not every breach of legitimate expectation triggers the duty. Fairness in the circumstances of the case might require only that the decision-maker accord due weight to the legitimate expectation before deciding to depart from it.[179] Each case must be assessed according to its own particular circumstances.

The common law fixes the minimum requirements of consultation.[180] Consultations must be 'meaningful',[181] 'genuine and not a sham',[182] 'a reality, not a charade'.[183] Consultation requires more than prior notification: '"To consult" is not merely to tell or present.'[184] Consultation is an opportunity for persuasion and reassessment, having regard to all of the factors at hand. Consultees 'must know what is proposed'[185] and have a 'reasonable opportunity of stating their views'.[186] The decision-maker must allow sufficient time for the process, listen to what consultees are saying and consider their responses.[187] Decision-makers may properly form and express provisional views, provided such views do not become fixed and immutable.[188] The decision-maker must keep 'an open mind and be ready to change and even start afresh'.[189]

[177] *Whakatane District Council v Bay of Plenty Regional Council* [2009] 3 NZLR 799 [108] (HC).

[178] *Turners & Growers Ltd v Moyle* 15 December 1988, McGechan J, HC Wellington CP 720/88 at 55, 61; *Coromandel Peninsula Watchdog* (n 4) 568; *Te Heu Heu* (n 6) 126; *New Zealand Association for Migration and Investments* (n 3) [187]; *Napier Public Health Action Group Inc v Minister of Conservation* [2007] 3 NZLR 559 [97] (HC); *Zhao v New Zealand Law Society* [2012] NZHC 2169 [95]–[96].

[179] *New Zealand Association for Migration and Investments* (n 3) [147].

[180] This paragraph draws on PA Joseph, *Constitutional and Administrative Law in New Zealand*, 4th edn (Thomson Reuters, 2014) 1067–68.

[181] *Wellington Airport Ltd v Air New Zealand Ltd* [1993] 1 NZLR 671, 675 (CA); *Te Heu Heu (n 6)* 127 (HC).

[182] *Diagnostic Medlab* (n 8) [258].

[183] *Wellington Airport* (n 181) 675.

[184] *Wellington Airport* (n 181) 675.

[185] *Port Louis Corporation v Attorney-General (Mauritius)* [1965] AC 1111, 1124 (PC).

[186] *Hamilton City v Electricity Distribution Committee* [1972] NZLR 605, 643 (SC).

[187] *Ryder v Treaty of Waitangi Fisheries Commission* 6 April 2000, Anderson and Paterson JJ, HC Auckland CP171/97 at [43]; *Diagnostic Medlab* (n 8) [258].

[188] *Bishop v Central Regional Health Authority* 11 July 19997, McGechan J, HC Palmerston North M47/97 at 23.

[189] *Diagnostic Medlab* (n 8) [258]; *Aorangi School Board of Trustees v Ministry of Education* [2010] NZAR 132 [32] (HC).

There are no universal requirements as to form.[190] The essence of the duty is good faith,[191] meaning that consultations must be genuine and meaningful:[192]

> The requirement of consultation is never to be treated perfunctorily or as a mere formality. [Consultees] must know what is proposed: they must be given a reasonably ample and sufficient opportunity to express their views or to point to problems or difficulties: they must be free to say what they think.

A duty of consultation imposes a kindred duty of disclosure. Consultees must be 'adequately informed' so as to encourage 'intelligent and useful responses'.[193] They must receive sufficient detail of what is proposed so as to know what it is that they are responding to.[194] Where a merger of two schools was proposed, the Minister had to inform the schools of the reasoning which supported the proposed merger, '[b]ecause unless [consultees] know the reasons why, [they] are hampered in engaging in the process [when] responding to those reasons'.[195]

Where there are bone fide consultations, decision-makers discharge their duty and bear no greater responsibility. The duty does not enjoin them to negotiate with a view to reaching agreement or a consensus.[196] The obligation is fairly to listen and consider, not agree. Moreover, undue reliance should not be placed on a decision-maker's commitment to act fairly and engage with interested parties. In *Te Heu Heu v Attorney-General*,[197] the local authority had shown commendable willingness to engage with local Maori in matters of mutual interest but this did not manifest a commitment to engage on all matters before the authority. The Court cautioned:[198]

> It is important that the Courts do not quickly find a willingness to talk is deemed to have given rise to a legitimate expectation when all it has done is demonstrated an openness of process and a willingness to be receptive to ideas.

[190] *Wellington Airport* (n 181) 675.

[191] *Waikato Tainui Te Kauhanganui Inc v Hamilton City Council* [2010] NZRMA 285 [49], [73]–[74] (HC).

[192] *Port Louis Corporation* (n 185) 1124.

[193] *Wellington Airport* (n 181) 675. See also *Board of Trustees of Phillipstown School v Minister of Education* [2013] NZHC 2641 [60].

[194] *McInnes v Minister of Transport* [2001] 3 NZLR 11 [11] (CA); *Friends of Turitea Reserve Society Inc v Palmerston North City Council* [2008] 2 NZLR 661 [113] (HC).

[195] *Board of Trustees of Phillipstown School* (n 193) [63].

[196] *Wellington Airport* (n 181) 676; *Health Advocates Trust v Director of Health and Disability Services Consumer Advocacy* [2008] NZCA 67 [15]; *Walsh v Pharmaceutical Management Agency* [2010] NZAR 101, [207] (HC).

[197] *Te Heu Heu* (n 6). The High Court repeated this warning in *New Zealand Association for Migration and Investments* (n 3) [189].

[198] *Te Heu Heu* (n 6) [127].

INTENSITY OF SCRUTINY

Some courts have declined to extend variable intensity review to the law of legitimate expectation.[199] They have confined this judicial method to unreasonableness challenges which focus on rationality of the outcome rather than fairness of the process. However, not all courts have adopted this approach. For some courts, the intensity of judicial scrutiny may vary, depending on the specificity of the legitimate expectation, the consequences of defeating it, and the context of the decision-making.

The more specific a promise or undertaking, the more intensive the court's scrutiny to ensure that legitimate expectations are not unfairly thwarted.[200] The court's scrutiny will also intensify where the promise is to a single individual or to a small and discrete class of individuals. In *Coughlan*, the small number of persons affected was a key consideration in the Court enforcing the outcome promised. The court's scrutiny will likewise intensify where reneging on a promise has potentially serious consequences.[201] Thus, the courts have declared a particular willingness to intervene in refugee cases, where persons may be at risk of persecution if returned to their homeland.[202] Refugee cases warranted a 'generous approach',[203] requiring 'great care',[204] as 'questions of life, personal safety and liberty are at stake'.[205] In cases inviting intensive scrutiny, a decision-maker must identify sound and logical reasons for reneging on a promise, conscientiously consider the position of those affected, and act 'lawfully, fairly, and reasonably in the administrative law sense'.[206]

The context of decision-making might also affect the intensity of judicial scrutiny. The courts have recognised the ambulatory nature of public administration in the macro-political field and urged a more tolerant application of legitimate expectation principles. They have accorded leeway in the wider public interest and exercised less intensive scrutiny of the decision-making.[207] The greater good lies in protecting decision-making flexibility and optimising government decision-making, even at the expense

199 *Gordon v Auckland City Council* 29 November 2006, Fogarty J, HC Auckland CIV-2006-404-4417 [11]; *Isak v Refugee Status Appeals Authority* [2010] NZAR 535 [21], [28]–[29] (HC).

200 *New Zealand Association for Migration and Investments* (n 3) [158].

201 *New Zealand Association for Migration and Investments* (n 3) [158].

202 *Khalon v Attorney-General* [1996] 1 NZLR 458, 463 (HC); *Butler v Attorney-General* [1999] NZAR 205, 211 (CA).

203 *Jiao v Refugee Status Appeals Authority* [2003] NZAR 647 [27] (CA).

204 *A v Chief Executive of the Department of Labour* 19 October 2005, Winkelmann J, HC Auckland CIV-2004-404-6314 [33].

205 *Khalon* (n 202) 463.

206 *New Zealand Association for Migration and Investments* (n 3) [158].

207 *Begbie* (n 68) 131. See also *New Zealand Association for Migration and Investments* (n 3) [158].

of expectations reasonably held. Governments and public decision-makers must exercise policy choices as circumstances dictate, and rational and planned policy changes will rarely be justiciable. As a matter of policy, the courts will not entertain challenges to government decision-making based on politicians' promises during election campaigns, or on unrealised policy announcements when in government. Freedom of political expression promotes a vibrant and informed democracy, and is more appropriately adjudged in the court of public opinion.

CONCLUSION

The law of legitimate expectation was one of several post-war developments that liberated administrative law from the excesses of legal formalism. It released claimants from the need to establish a justiciable interest in order to allege an unfair process. As a general proposition, decision-makers ought to be held to their word in the interests of fairness and good public administration.

The concept of legitimate expectation is relatively uncomplicated, although aspects of it still remain unsettled. The courts remain divided over whether claimants must establish knowledge of the circumstances giving rise to an expectation and a claimant's consequential reliance upon it. A consensus is emerging that these are *inessential* but *relevant* elements, with claimants seldom succeeding where they cannot show detrimental reliance. This registers a pragmatic accommodation but it is a less than satisfying one, papering over uncertainty over the core elements of the concept. The question remains: must claimants establish detrimental reliance? In principle 'no' but in practice 'yes'.

Questions also linger over substantive legitimate expectations. Some courts acknowledge these while other courts do not. In truth, little meaningful distinction can be drawn between procedural and substantive expectations as breach of either type may amount to an abuse. The more exacting question is how to respond to breach of a substantive expectation. Exceptional cases apart, the appropriate recourse will be to direct the decision-maker to consult those affected and reconsider its decision, properly taking account of its promise of a particular outcome or result. For the New Zealand courts, preserving the proper exercise of administrative discretion militates against enforcing a substantive outcome.

The final question concerns the utility of the concept. When Lord Denning first raised the idea in *Schmidt*, legitimate expectation was a liberating concept that freed up the reach of judicial review. Does the concept retain that same vitality today? Administrative law doctrines reaching a certain stage of development have a tendency towards introspection and complication of the law. They become ends in themselves, obfuscating rather than facilitating the ends of judicial review. The false dichotomies of last century, for example, became disembodied skirmishes over legal principle at the margins.[208] Has the law of legitimate expectation reached that same stage of development, where skirmishes over its core elements have become a distraction? Might, for example, legitimate expectation usefully be subsumed under the generic ground of unfairness in judicial review? In one case, the Court subsumed under 'unfairness" five pleaded causes of action: illegality, mistake of fact, breach of fiduciary duty, breach of natural justice and breach of legitimate expectation.[209] In other cases, claims of breach of legitimate expectation have only complicated the proceedings and added nothing to the other pleaded causes of action.[210] Robin Cooke's celebrated struggle for simplicity in administrative law should sound warning bells.[211]

So, has the law of legitimate expectation reached that stage where it invites overhaul and reassessment? Probably not, although one might entertain reservations about some elements of the concept. Agonising over issues of detrimental reliance and substantive expectations does little to advance the objectives of judicial review, which might be collapsed into a simple but penetrating question: has something gone wrong with the decision-making of a nature and degree that requires the intervention of the court, and, if so, how might the court put right the wrong?[212] The doctrine of legitimate expectation is at the cross roads: whether it might continue to perform a useful role or lapse into yet another end unto itself, impeding rather than facilitating the aims of judicial review.

[208] See n 163 above.

[209] *Chambers v Waitangi Tribunal* 23 February 2005, Wild J, HC Wellington CIV-2004-485-1170 [24].

[210] *East Pier Developments Ltd v Napier City Council* 26 November 1988, Wild J, HC Napier CP28/98 at 34; *Naidu v Minister of Immigration* 28 March 2000, Rodney Hansen J, HC Auckland M.1661-SW99 [133]; *Krokova v Minister of Immigration* 7 September 2010, Venning J, HC Auckland CIV-2010-404-5674 [55].

[211] Sir Robin Cooke 'The Struggle for Simplicity in Administrative Law' in M Taggart (ed), *Judicial Review of Administrative Action in the 1980s: A New Zealand Perspective* (Butterworths, 1991).

[212] *R v Panel on Take-overs and Mergers' ex parte Guinness plc* [1990] 1 QB 146, 160 (CA).

10

From Heresy to Orthodoxy: Substantive Legitimate Expectations in the United Kingdom

MARK ELLIOTT*

INTRODUCTION

ITS UNEQUIVOCAL ACKNOWLEDGMENT that there could be such a thing as a substantive legitimate expectation made Sedley J's judgment in *Hamble Fisheries* a notable milestone in the development of this aspect of English administrative law.[1] Yet only two years later, a key aspect of Sedley J's judgment was overruled by the Court of Appeal in *Hargreaves*.[2] And not merely overruled, but deprecated as nothing less than 'heresy'.[3] However, the castigation in *Hargreaves* of Sedley J's judgment in *Hamble Fisheries* notwithstanding, the doctrine of substantive legitimate expectation is now a settled feature of English administrative law's doctrinal landscape. Heresy thus appears to have become orthodoxy.[4]

This chapter charts how and why this happened by situating the emergence of the substantive legitimate expectation principle within the context of wider changes that have taken place in English public law in recent decades, arguing that the patina of doctrinal orthodoxy that substantive legitimate expectations now enjoy is warranted. The chapter will take as its starting-point the English courts' judgments in *Hamble Fisheries* and *Coughlan*,[5] which collectively marked a turning-point in this area, and will

* I am grateful to Matthew Groves, Jason Varuhas and Greg Weeks for their comments on an earlier draft of this chapter. The usual disclaimer applies.

1 *R v Ministry of Agriculture, Fisheries and Food; ex parte Hamble (Offshore) Fisheries Ltd* [1995] 2 All ER 714 (QBD).

2 *R v Secretary of State for the Home Department; ex parte Hargreaves* [1997] 1 WLR 906 (CA).

3 Ibid, 921 (Hirst LJ).

4 As Sedley LJ could not resist pointing out in *R (Bhatt Murphy) v Independent Assessor* [2008] EWCA Civ 755 [69].

5 *R v North and East Devon Health Authority; ex parte Coughlan* [2001] QB 213 (CA).

argue that while characterising those cases (and *Coughlan* in particular) as heretical may be justifiable, it does not follow that the doctrine of substantive legitimate expectation is itself necessarily vulnerable to being so characterised.

That position will be advanced by reference to two lines of argument. First, it will be shown that the doctrine of substantive legitimate expectation can be understood in terms more subtle and less uncompromising than those implied by *Coughlan*, such that the doctrine can be conceptualised in a form that is more palatable from an orthodox perspective. Second, as well as addressing the substantive legitimate expectation doctrine's compatibility with orthodoxy, orthodoxy's compatibility with the doctrine will be examined and two distinct but complementary propositions advanced. It will be argued that understandings of what orthodoxy *is* have evolved somewhat in the last 20 or so years. And it will be argued that understandings of what orthodoxy *requires*, in doctrinal terms, have also changed. These shifting perceptions of the nature and implications of orthodoxy carve out a space for the substantive legitimate expectation doctrine that is more generous than that which appeared to exist when, 20 years ago, Sedley J's analysis in *Hamble Fisheries* was dismissed as 'heresy'. The story of the evolution of the doctrine of substantive legitimate expectation thus forms part of a larger tableau upon which is recorded the recent evolution of English administrative law itself.

THE EARLY CASE LAW

Hamble Fisheries may have been the trailblazer, but the Court of Appeal's subsequent decision in *Coughlan* is widely regarded as the real landmark case. Taken together, these two cases embody the English courts' inaugural conception of the doctrine of substantive legitimate expectation. Although that doctrine has developed since those early cases were decided, engaging with them—and with the reasons for criticism of them—enables us to place in context how the doctrine subsequently developed and the way in which assessments of its orthodoxy have evolved. This facilitates consideration of the extent to which acceptance of the doctrine—following the early controversy it attracted—may reflect (on the one hand) its refashioning in a more orthodox form and (on the other hand) shifts in the prevailing conception of orthodoxy itself.

Three aspects of the judgments in *Hamble Fisheries* and *Coughlan* made them turning-points, and warrant reliance upon them as the embodiment of the English courts' initial take on the notion of substantive legitimate expectations. First, they acknowledged with particular clarity that administrative law recognised substantive legitimate expectations. Neither case amounted to the first occasion on which such judicial recognition had been accorded, but on previous occasions the extent, if any, of the practical import of such recognition had been, at best, uncertain.[6] The preparedness of the courts in *Hamble Fisheries* and *Coughlan* to invest the notion of substantive legitimate expectation with a real degree of practical bite rendered their recognition of the concept meaningful in a way and to an extent that previous cases' acknowledgment of it did not.

Second, that practical bite flowed from the courts' willingness in *Hamble Fisheries* and *Coughlan* to acknowledge that a public authority might be required to deliver to the claimant whatever it was that was legitimately expected, as distinct from merely requiring the defendant to undertake some or other procedural step before deciding whether to fulfil or frustrate the expectation. It is true that earlier judgments had canvassed this possibility,[7] but the directness with which it was confronted in *Hamble Fisheries* was particularly striking, as was the realisation of that possibility in *Coughlan*.

The third factor that justifies the singling out of *Hamble Fisheries* and *Coughlan* concerns not their recognition of the *existence* of the possibility of substantive enforcement but their implications concerning the *scope* of that possibility. Acknowledging—as, for example, Taylor J did in *Ruddock*[8]—that it is in principle open to a court to require adherence to the substance of a legitimate expectation is one thing. If, however, the circumstances in which such adherence may be judicially required are very unlikely to eventuate, then the possibility of substantive enforcement remains essentially theoretical. For instance, although *Ruddock* is noteworthy for Taylor J saying that the doctrine of legitimate expectation is not confined to imposing (or augmenting) a wholly procedural conception of the duty to act fairly,[9] he appeared to envisage that legitimate expectations would acquire substantive bite only in highly constricted conditions. In particular, Taylor J indicated that it was open to the decision-maker in *Ruddock* either to change or disapply the criteria that were said to have generated a substantive legitimate expectation, and that there was 'no doubt' that the giving of reasons for such disapplication 'would have afforded [the Secretary of State] a defence to judicial review as in the *GCHQ* case'.[10] Taylor J thus appeared to envisage the possibility of substantive enforcement crystallising into reality only in the event of a failure to supply *any* reasons for the frustration of the expectation. The national security context in which *Ruddock* was decided may account for such light-touch review, but, even allowing for that, the

[6] See, eg, *In re Findlay* [1985] AC 318 (HL); *R v Secretary of State for the Home Department; ex parte Ruddock* [1987] 1 WLR 1482 (QBD).
[7] See, eg, *Findlay* (n 6); *Ruddock* (n 6).
[8] *Ruddock* (n 6).
[9] *Ruddock* (n 6) 1497.
[10] *Ruddock* (n 6) 1497, citing *Council of Civil Service Unions v Minister for the Civil Service* [1985] AC 374 (HL) ('*GCHQ*').

case hardly portended the enforcement of substantive expectations absent *Wednesbury* unreasonableness.[11]

A similar point can be made about *Khan*, in which Parker LJ went out on something of a limb by deploying an 'overriding public interest' test for determining the lawfulness of a decision that would frustrate a substantive legitimate expectation.[12] Yet the rhetoric of 'overriding public interest', when push came to shove, dissolved into a relatively modest requirement that the individual concerned should be afforded a 'full opportunity to make representations why, in his case, [a policy conflicting with the legitimate expectation] should not be followed'.[13] As far as genuinely substantive enforcement is concerned, the very furthest that *Khan* can be said to have gone is to sanction the quashing of decisions to frustrate substantive legitimate expectations when such decisions could be considered *Wednesbury* unreasonable.[14]

In spite of the weight placed on cases such as *Ruddock* and *Khan* in *Hamble Fisheries* and *Coughlan*, only the latter cases unambiguously endorsed and adopted a substantive expectation enforcement trigger capable of transforming the possibility of such enforcement from a largely theoretical into a real one. They did so by invoking the overriding public interest concept employed by Parker LJ in *Khan* whilst transforming it in three respects. First, the existence of an overriding public interest became a precondition for lawful frustration of a substantive expectation as distinct from (as in *Khan*) a matter upon which the affected individual has a right to make representations. Second, it is, according to both *Hamble Fisheries* and *Coughlan*, for the reviewing court to determine whether the defendant decision-maker has established such an overriding public interest justification. Third, and crucially, the making of that judicial determination is not, according to *Hamble Fisheries* and *Coughlan*, informed by any notion of reasonableness; rather, the question is whether, on balance, the court is satisfied that frustration is justified by the policy gains that may thereby accrue.

Taken in combination, these three aspects of the overriding public interest criterion adopted in *Hamble Fisheries* and *Coughlan* supply a platform for a far from merely theoretical possibility of substantive enforcement of substantive expectations. In *Hamble Fisheries*, Sedley J said that although the balance to be struck between the interests of the expectation-holder and conflicting public policy concerns is 'in the first instance for the policy-maker', once the matter becomes subject to judicial review the court's role is not limited to assessing 'the bare rationality of the policy-maker's conclusion'.[15]

[11] *Associated Provincial Picture Houses Ltd v Wednesbury Corporation* [1948] 1 KB 223.

[12] *R v Secretary of State for the Home Department; ex parte Khan* [1984] 1 WLR 1337, 1347.

[13] Ibid, 1348.

[14] This point is most clearly apparent from Dunn LJ's judgment.

[15] *Hamble Fisheries* (n 1) 731.

And so, said Sedley J, while the court must 'recognise the constitutional importance of ministerial freedom to formulate and reformulate policy', it is 'equally the court's duty to protect the interests of those individuals whose expectation of different treatment has a legitimacy which in fairness outtops the policy choice which threatens to frustrate it'.[16] Similarly, in *Coughlan* the Court held that, where a legitimate expectation of a substantive benefit arises, it is for the court to decide whether frustration would amount to an 'abuse of power'.[17] This, it was said, would involve the court 'weighing the requirements of fairness against any overriding interest relied upon for the change of policy'[18] and intervening if the balance of fairness comes down in favour of the enforcement of the individual's legitimate expectation.

THE NATURE AND JUSTIFIABILITY OF SUBSTANTIVE REVIEW

Among those who criticised *Coughlan*—and so, implicitly, *Hamble Fisheries*—was Lord Irvine of Lairg, the first Lord Chancellor in the Blair Government. Echoing the generally conservative conception of the judicial function that he had previously advanced,[19] Irvine argued in a public lecture that *Coughlan* was 'contrary to the fundamental principles on which our system of administrative law is founded and incompatible with the leading authorities'.[20] Irvine's concern stemmed from what he perceived to be *Coughlan*'s failure to respect the distinction between matters of process and substance, the classical view being that judicial review is centrally about the former and not the latter. It is from this distinction that other classical distinctions that have shaped English administrative law—including those between appeal and review and between legality and merits—radiate. And while such thinking has never wholly precluded substantive review, it signifies that whereas process-oriented review is considered *prima facie* legitimate, substantive review is regarded as *prima facie* suspect.

Properly used, the term 'substantive review' refers to a form of review that exhibits one or both of two characteristics that respectively pertain to the *effect of review* and the *mode of review*. Review will be substantive in the first sense if its effect is to place a given decision, as distinct from a given way of making a decision, off limits. Many—non-substantive—grounds of review have only the latter effect. For instance, a decision-maker

[16] *Hamble Fisheries* (n 1) 731.

[17] *Coughlan* (n 5) [57].

[18] *Coughlan* (n 5) [57].

[19] Lord Irvine of Lairg, 'Judges and Decision-Makers: The Theory and Practice of *Wednesbury* Review' [1996] *Public Law* 59.

[20] Lord Irvine of Lairg, *Human Rights, Constitutional Law and the Development of the English Legal System* (Hart Publishing, 2003) 190. In the interest of transparency, I should disclose that I assisted Lord Irvine with the writing of this lecture.

who has reached a decision having ignored a mandatory relevant consideration, taken account of an irrelevant consideration or acted procedurally unfairly may subsequently be able to reach the same decision pursuant to a different, lawful decision-making process. In contrast, if review successfully takes place on substantive grounds, administrative reinstatement of the quashed decision pursuant to a different process is not possible. In this way, substantive review forecloses the possibility of the sort of potentially Pyrrhic victories that are considered emblematic of classical—that is, process-oriented—judicial review. Review on the ground of jurisdictional error of law is substantive in this sense, the existence of such an error signifying that making the decision in some other way would not remedy its inherent unlawfulness. The same is true of review on the grounds of *Wednesbury* unreasonableness and disproportionality (subject to arguments as to proceduralist conceptions of the latter[21] and to the possibility that a 'better' subsequent decision-making process might be capable of triggering a higher degree of judicial deference).[22]

Meanwhile, review is substantive in the 'mode of review' sense when it involves qualitative judicial assessment of the decision-maker's reasons for exercising (or not exercising) its discretion in a given way. Understood thus, substantive review may be considered to entail some degree of 'merits review', since the reviewing court's role extends to evaluation of the decision itself, in the sense of evaluating the reasons for the decision and determining whether those reasons are qualitatively capable of justifying the decision. Review on the ground of disproportionality is substantive in this sense, as, arguably, is review on the ground of *Wednesbury* unreasonableness.[23]

None of this is to suggest that substantive review is, or is considered to be, necessarily improper. Indeed, the fact that review lies on grounds such as jurisdictional error of law, disproportionality and *Wednesbury* unreasonableness demonstrates that review that is substantive in one or both of the two senses sketched above is an established part of the doctrinal landscape. Nevertheless, review that is substantive in either of those ways sits in tension with the process-oriented paradigm of judicial review and thus implies a need for justification on account of departure from that paradigm.

[21] For discussion of proceduralist approaches to proportionality, see D Mead, 'Outcomes aren't all: Defending Process-Based Review of Public Authority Decisions under the Human Rights Act' [2012] *Public Law* 61; A Kavanagh, 'Reasoning about Proportionality under the Human Rights Act 1998: Outcomes, Substance and Process' (2014) 130 *Law Quarterly Review* 235; C Geiringer, 'Process and Outcome in Judicial Review of Public Authority Compatibility with Human Rights: A Comparative Perspective' in H Wilberg and M Elliott (eds), *The Scope and Intensity of Substantive Review: Traversing Taggart's Rainbow* (Hart Publishing, 2015).

[22] See eg *Belfast City Council v Miss Behavin' Ltd* [2007] UKHL 19, [2007] 1 WLR 1420.

[23] See eg P Craig, 'The Nature of Reasonableness Review' (2013) 66 *Current Legal Problems* 107; *R (Keyu) v Secretary of State for Foreign and Commonwealth Affairs* [2015] UKSC 69, [2015] 3 WLR 1665 (Lady Hale).

Traditionally, two such justifications have been relied upon: *deference* and *characterisation*.

The former justification has obvious application to *Wednesbury* review. In that context, the substantive nature of the judicial endeavour is simultaneously acknowledged, marginalised and deprecated, the very exoticism of qualitative judicial evaluation of decision-makers' reasons for (in)action demanding that it be hobbled by reference to such criteria as absurdity[24] and outrageousness.[25] Thus the propriety of *Wednesbury* review, its essentially substantive nature notwithstanding, is purchased by means of the deference with which it is shot through. This explains why proportionality was generally resisted by English courts prior to the entry into force of the Human Rights Act 1998, the absence from that doctrine of hard-wired deference giving rise to a perception that its deployment would necessarily entail judicial overreach. However, as will be discussed later in the chapter, a more nuanced approach has emerged in recent years, according to which the degree of deference—and hence the intensity of review—that is warranted in a given set of circumstances is a function, at least in part, of the normative significance of the value that is engaged by the impugned decision. In this way, the extent of any perceived need to blunt substantive review through reliance upon deference reflects the striking of a balance between rule of law considerations that support judicial intervention and competing constitutional considerations that favour curial respect for the discretion that has been statutorily invested in the decision-maker. This has obvious implications, which are developed below, for the doctrine of substantive legitimate expectation, not least in the light of the fact that it institutionalises the core rule of law concept of legal certainty.

The substantive nature of jurisdictional error of law review is justified in a very different way. Here, there is no pretence as to the intensity of review, since the standard is (usually) correctness.[26] Propriety is thus instead secured by means of an exercise in characterisation, according to which jurisdictional review is understood to be concerned not with judicial control of discretionary authority that has been legislatively confided to the decision-maker, but with judicial determination of the scope of the authority that is, in the first place, so confided. On this analysis, review on jurisdictional grounds entails no judicial incursion into the legislatively conferred discretion, the effect of such review being confined to judicial exposition of that discretion's extent. It is this characterisation-based defence of jurisdic-

[24] *Associated Provincial Picture Houses Ltd v Wednesbury Corporation* [1948] 1 KB 223, 229 (CA) (Lord Greene MR).

[25] *GCHQ* (n 10) 410 (Lord Diplock).

[26] This follows from the modern view that, in general, questions of law are jurisdictional questions, such that all such questions must be answered correctly by a decision-maker if an excess of jurisdiction is to be avoided: *R v Lord President of the Privy Council; ex parte Page* [1993] AC 682 (HL).

tional error of law review that enables such review, its substantive nature notwithstanding, to be regarded as something other than merits review, judicial curation of matters jurisdictional being logically prior to—and determinative of the scope of—merits questions that remain for the decision-maker.

These propositions as to what makes jurisdictional review defensible can be illustrated by reference to the dubiousness with which the *Pergau Dam* case[27] is regarded in some quarters.[28] Although the relevant legislation authorised the Secretary of State to provide assistance for the purpose of 'promoting the development' of countries and territories outside the UK,[29] the Court held that the statute actually authorised only the promotion of 'economically sound' development projects.[30] The Secretary of State was thus denied the authority to determine whether a given project should be supported in the light of (among other things) its economic soundness, and was instead confined to choosing from amongst projects of whose economic soundness the Court was satisfied. In this way, what might have been a merits question was transformed into a jurisdictional precondition and subjected to correctness, rather than reasonableness, review. It is that act of judicial transformation that has led prominent advocates of a relatively conservative judicial role to cite *Pergau Dam* as an instance of judicial overreach.[31] Where jurisdictional review uncontroversially amounts to judicial enforcement of a statutory condition that plainly circumscribes the decision-maker's discretion, such review is generally considered defensible, its substantive nature notwithstanding. However, where, as in *Pergau Dam*, jurisdictional review appears to encroach upon, as distinct from defining the scope of, the decision-maker's discretion, the characterisation-based defence of jurisdictional review becomes less compelling because, in the first place, the characterisation of the matter as one that pertains to the scope, rather than the exercise, of the discretion itself becomes less persuasive.

SUBSTANTIVE REVIEW AND SUBSTANTIVE LEGITIMATE EXPECTATIONS

Against the background of the considerations set out above, levelling the charge of heresy against the early substantive legitimate expectation cases becomes readily comprehensible, the approach favoured by those cases being substantive in *both* of the relevant senses but justified in *neither* of the ways set out above.

[27] *R v Secretary of State for Foreign and Commonwealth Affairs; ex parte World Development Movement Ltd* [1995] 1 WLR 386 (DC) ('*Pergau Dam*').

[28] For criticism, see Irvine (n 19); J Sumption, 'Judicial and Political Decision-Making: The Uncertain Boundary', FA Mann Lecture, 2011.

[29] *Overseas Development Act 1980*, s 1(1) (repealed).

[30] *Pergau Dam* (n 27) 402.

[31] Irvine (n 19); Sumption (n 28).

First, judicial protection of substantive legitimate expectations, at least as conceived in the early case law, is substantive in the mode of review sense because it involves close evaluation—unvarnished by any recourse to reasonableness—of the reasons for the decision to frustrate the expectation. *Coughlan* ultimately boiled down to the question of whether scarcity of resources was a sufficient justification for frustrating the claimant's expectation and meeting her needs in another, cheaper manner. Yet determining whether the scarcity of resources argument amounted to an adequate justification was, *par excellence*, a value judgment, not to mention a highly polycentric question. The Court thus asserted jurisdiction qualitatively to assess the reasons for the defendant's decision by reference to a contestable set of values that informed the respective importance to be ascribed to the interests of the claimant and the interests that would have been served by the redeployment of the relevant resources.[32]

Second, the approach adopted in *Coughlan* is emphatically substantive in the effect of review sense. Indeed, whereas *Wednesbury* and proportionality merely close off unlawful options, the approach envisaged in *Hamble Fisheries* and *Coughlan* is capable of prescribing one lawful option—that the substantive expectation be fulfilled. (It is, of course, *possible* that *Wednesbury* and proportionality review may indirectly prescribe one lawful option if their effect is to close off all other options; but, outwith binary scenarios, this is not *inevitable*.) Thus in *Coughlan* an obligation to fulfil the obligation inevitably followed from the unlawfulness of frustrating it.

We can, however, go further than saying that *Coughlan* involved substantive review. Just as the distinction between process-oriented and substantive review exists other than as a bright line, so substantive review is itself a spectrum as distinct from a monolithic category. A question therefore arises about where, on the substantive review continuum, a given case lies. In *Coughlan* the effect of review was to prescribe a single lawful outcome by reference to an evaluation that came close to *de novo* judicial assessment of the competing factors. It follows that *Coughlan* lies not simply *within* the category of substantive review, but *deep* within that category.

Crucially, however, while review on the ground of substantive legitimate expectation can be—and in *Coughlan* was—substantive in *both* of the relevant senses, the way in which it occurred in *Coughlan* can be justified in *neither* of the ways in which substantive review is conventionally defended against charges of constitutional impropriety. The characterisation-based defence is clearly inapplicable, the question whether discretion can be exercised in a manner that breaches a substantive legitimate expectation being an entirely separate question from whether, in the first place, the matter falls within the decision-maker's jurisdiction. Indeed, the characterisation

[32] See further on this point P Sales and K Steyn, 'Legitimate Expectations in English Public Law: An Analysis' [2004] *Public Law* 564, 591.

approach will never be capable of operating to justify review on the ground of substantive legitimate expectation, such review being necessarily about the exercise, as distinct from the scope, of discretionary authority. The same is not true, however, of the deference-based defence of substantive review, since it is clearly possible for a reviewing court to evaluate the justifiability of a decision to frustrate a substantive legitimate expectation in a more or less deferential manner (as well as in a wholly non-deferential manner, as in *Coughlan* itself). In other words, the fact that the Court of Appeal in *Coughlan* did not seek to reconcile what it did with orthodoxy through reliance upon deference does not mean that such reconciliation is not possible in relation to substantive legitimate expectation cases generally.

The remainder of this chapter is concerned with three respects in which such reconciliation may be—and may have been—achieved. The first is concerned with ways in which review on the ground of substantive legitimate expectation may be modulated so as to render the extent of judicial 'interference' with administrative autonomy less extensive. The second matter concerns changing perceptions of orthodoxy: it will be argued that the prevailing perception has, for defensible reasons, shifted since the approach commended by Sedley J in *Hamble Fisheries* was branded as heretical. Third, however, it will be argued that this point should not be overstated, and that an important part of what has happened in English administrative law over the last 20 or so years—and which is highly pertinent to our understanding of the orthodoxy or otherwise of judicial enforcement of substantive legitimate expectations—concerns not changes to what orthodoxy is considered to *be* but rather changes to what orthodoxy is considered to *require* at a doctrinal level.

PROPORTIONALITY AND BALANCING

Given developments in English administrative law since *Coughlan* was decided, it might be thought that it was merely ahead of its time: that the approach to substantive review adopted in that case amounted to a form of proportionality review, and that this merely anticipated English courts' embrace of proportionality in cases like *Daly*.[33] However, the notion that *Coughlan* simply jumped the gun, such that what seemed radical at the time ought to be regarded from today's vantage point as mundane, provokes two connected responses.

[33] *R (Daly) v Secretary of State for the Home Department* [2001] UKHL 26, [2001] 2 AC 532.

First, it is true that the approach adopted in *Coughlan* is sometimes said to have amounted to a form of proportionality review.[34] For instance, in *Nadarajah*, Laws LJ said that the unlawfulness of the decision to frustrate the expectation in *Coughlan* flowed from the fact that 'the promise's denial could not be justified as a proportionate measure'.[35] And in *Paponette*, the Judicial Committee of the Privy Council held that it should apply the *Coughlan* balancing test[36] whilst agreeing with Laws LJ's observation in *Nadarajah* that

> [t]he principle that good administration requires public authorities to be held to their promises would be undermined if the law did not insist that any failure or refusal to comply is objectively justified as a proportionate measure in the circumstances.[37]

This implies that in *Paponette* the Privy Council drew an equivalence between proportionality review and the *Coughlan* balancing test. Indeed, Laws LJ went even further in *Nadarajah* by suggesting that proportionality might form a single juridical foundation for all instances of judicial review on the ground of legitimate expectation, irrespective of whether the expectation in question is procedural or substantive in nature.[38] It is unnecessary for present purposes to show why that view is misguided.[39] It is, however, necessary to make the prior point that it is not clear that what is going on in substantive legitimate expectation cases unambiguously reduces to proportionality review.

Take *Coughlan* itself. The balancing test adopted in it clearly has something—indeed, much—in common with the final, fair-balance stage of the proportionality test. However, this raises three issues. First, the balancing test does not equate to proportionality review proper: there are, after all, several stages within the proportionality test, of which the fair-balance test is only one.[40] Second, it has not been the practice of the English courts uniformly to deploy the fair-balance test when engaging in proportionality review: indeed, it was not until the House of Lords' decision in *Huang*, some years after *Coughlan* was decided, that the fair-balance test was authoritatively endorsed as an aspect of domestic proportionality review.[41] Third,

[34] On this point, see further Janina Boughey, 'Proportionality and Legitimate Expectations' in chapter 6 of this volume.

[35] *R (Nadarajah) v Secretary of State for the Home Department* [2005] EWCA Civ 1363 [70].

[36] *Paponette v Attorney General of Trinidad and Tobago* [2010] UKPC 32, [2012] 1 AC 1, [34].

[37] Ibid [38], citing *Nadarajah* (n 35) [68] (Laws LJ).

[38] *Nadarajah* (n 35) [69].

[39] For discussion of that matter see M Elliott, 'Legitimate Expectations and the Search for Principle: Reflections on *Abdi* and *Nadarajah*' [2006] *Judicial Review* 281.

[40] *Huang v Secretary of State for the Home Department* [2007] UKHL 11, [2007] 2 AC 167; *Bank Mellat v HM Treasury (No 2)* [2013] UKSC 39, [2014] AC 700.

[41] *Huang* (n 40).

even when English courts do apply the fair-balance test, they are generally sensitive to its particularly interventionist nature, given that it essentially reduces to a value-judgment.[42] As a result, the interventionist potential of the fair-balance test is not always fully realised thanks to its blunting through the adoption of a deferential stance.

This leads to the second of my two responses to the notion that *Coughlan* was merely ahead of its time. Even if it is accepted that *Coughlan* embraced a type of proportionality review, it was a type distinct from that which is found in more recent jurisprudence, deference being an integral component of the latter whilst wholly absent from the former. The Court in *Coughlan* thus overreached by taking it upon itself to determine a highly polycentric matter concerning the allocation of scarce financial resources whilst failing to acknowledge either its institutional incapacity (not least on account of its ignorance of the many knock-on effects that would ensue if public funds were diverted in order to uphold the claimant's expectation) or pertinent constitutional inhibitions (given that measuring the relative worth of upholding the expectation and spending money on other things required the balancing of two incommensurable variables).

This does not mean that a balancing test should never be applied in substantive legitimate expectation cases. What it does, however, suggest is that to the extent that that test is to be applied, it needs to be applied with reference to the same deference considerations that apply when proportionality review and, in particular, questions of fair balance are in play in other (such as human rights) contexts. This takes us to the heart of the problem with *Coughlan*. The difficulty is not that it was before its time. Rather, the problem is that it conceived of proportionality review—if that is indeed what it was—in a way that was insensitive to the very concerns that have subsequently informed the softening of proportionality review through recourse to a doctrine of curial deference. Against this background, it is worth considering the analysis of this point advanced by Janina Boughey in her contribution to this volume. She says that

> the judges seem to have endorsed proportionality with the assumption that it was a more flexible standard than it has subsequently become. They seem to have assumed it was a standard that was capable of applying with varying degrees of intensity so as to encompass review methodologies and outcomes as diverse as those in *Hargreaves*, *Bibi* and *Coughlan*. The European and Canadian approaches to proportionality review are probably sufficiently flexible and diverse to do this effectively. However as proportionality is currently applied in the UK, it is too blunt an instrument to perform the balancing task in all substantive expectation cases.[43]

[42] See eg *R (Miranda) v Secretary of State for the Home Department* [2014] EWHC 255 (Admin), [2014] 1 WLR 3140 [40] (Laws LJ).

[43] See Janina Boughey, 'Proportionality and Legitimate Expectations' in chapter 6 of this volume.

This implies that having hitched the substantive legitimate doctrine to (some sort of) proportionality wagon, the destination that has been reached has proven to be surprisingly demanding in standard of review terms, because proportionality locks courts into a uniformly high-intensity form of review. Yet when the practice of proportionality review in English law is considered, this analysis is hard to sustain. Indeed, the courts have been at pains to enable proportionality to function in a flexible manner by ensuring that its potential rigour is appropriately ameliorated via deference. These issues encroach upon the subject-matter of subsequent parts of this chapter, in which it is argued that the doctrinal boundaries demarcating different grounds of substantive review such as *Wednesbury* and proportionality are increasingly unimportant in English law. The point for the time being, however, is narrower. It is that the difficult question invited by substantive legitimate expectation cases is not the somewhat formalistic one concerning whether a 'proportionality' or 'balancing' or 'reasonableness' test should apply. Rather, the essential question concerns the appropriate *intensity* of review. This, in turn, requires the notion of curial deference to be taken more seriously than it was in *Coughlan* (in which it was essentially ignored) and to be considered more holistically and systematically than it has been in subsequent cases.

STANDARDS OF REVIEW AND DEFERENCE

How, then, should questions about standards of review and deference be tackled in substantive legitimate expectation cases? The starting-point must be an acknowledgment that once the existence of such an expectation is judicially acknowledged, this necessarily demands that the decision to frustrate the expectation be adequately justified. In the absence of adequate justification, the decision is unlawful and the expectation must be fulfilled. This raises two distinct questions.[44] The first question pertains to what should *count as adequate justification*. Just as all human rights cases are not equal, so not all substantive legitimate expectation cases are equal; the circumstances of the particular case may warrant the decision-maker being placed under a more or less onerous justificatory burden. The second question concerns how the court should assess whether what has been proffered by the decision-maker *amounts to adequate justification*. Even if the imposition of a heavy justificatory burden is warranted, the court may—on institutional grounds or constitutional grounds or both—be limited in terms of the nature and degree of the scrutiny that it can properly supply

[44] I set out and defend the distinction between these two matters in more detail in M Elliott, 'From Bifurcation to Calibration: Twin-Track Deference and the Culture of Justification' in Wilberg and Elliott (n 21).

when attempting to determine whether the justificatory burden has been discharged. However, while these matters are—and should be kept—distinct, substantive legitimate expectation cases that have engaged with standard of review issues have tended to conflate them.

Take Laws LJ's judgment in *Begbie*.[45] He identified a range of factors that he (rightly) considered relevant to standard of review issues in substantive legitimate expectation cases, including: the extent to which policy questions are engaged; whether interests not represented before the court might be affected by the court's decision; and the number of individuals affected by the promise in question.[46] To that list might be added whether the individual has suffered detriment by relying on the promise and the degree of clarity enjoyed by the promise. Indeed, in *Coughlan* itself, the Court of Appeal cited comparable factors—in particular, the 'contractual' flavour of a promise issued to an individual or a small group—by way of seeking to justify the intrusive standard of review it adopted.[47]

However, the difficulty with these analyses—both in *Begbie* and *Coughlan*—is they are insufficiently sensitive to the distinction, mentioned above, between the justificatory standard *to be met* and the question whether that standard *has been met*. It may well be that a promise issued in extremely clear terms to an individual who has relied upon the promise should result in the decision-maker being placed under a heavy burden by way of justifying a subsequent decision to frustrate the expectation. After all, in such circumstances the rule of law principle of legal certainty, respect for which lies at the heart of judicial enforcement of legitimate expectations,[48] is jeopardised in a particularly acute manner. The scale of the threat to the at-stake rule of law norm thus warrants commensurately jealous judicial protection. But it does not follow from the appropriateness of imposing upon the *decision-maker* an onerous justificatory burden that the *reviewing court* will inevitably be well-situated to determine whether that burden has been satisfactorily discharged.

This point was not, however, taken by Laws LJ in *Begbie* (or indeed by the Court of Appeal in *Coughlan*). Laws LJ said that the intensity of review seen in *Coughlan* was justified because—in contrast with situations in which only *Wednesbury* review would be appropriate—*Coughlan* played out 'on a much smaller stage, with far fewer players'.[49] This, said Laws LJ, made the case 'discrete and limited, having no implications for an innominate class of persons' and meant that it gave rise to 'no wide-ranging issues of general

[45] *R v Secretary of State for Education and Employment; ex parte Begbie* [2000] 1 WLR 1115 (CA).
[46] Ibid, 1130.
[47] *Coughlan* (n 5) [59].
[48] See eg C Forsyth, 'The Provenance and Protection of Legitimate Expectation' (1988) 47 *Cambridge Law Journal* 238; S Schønberg, *Legitimate Expectations in Administrative Law* (Oxford University Press, 2000) Ch 1.
[49] *Begbie* (n 45) 1131.

policy'.[50] This, however, is flatly incorrect. The highly directed nature of the promise in *Coughlan* did nothing to contain the wide ramifications—in terms of the diversion of public funds away from unspecified other purposes that may have benefitted large numbers of people—of enforcing the promise. The error committed in *Coughlan* and repeated by Laws LJ in *Begbie* flows directly from the conflation of the *normative case* for rigorous judicial scrutiny and the *institutional and constitutional capacity* of the court to supply such scrutiny. Matters such as the size of the group and the clarity of the promise may well point towards the imposition of a heavy justificatory burden, but this does not necessarily imply the appropriateness of a non-deferential approach when it comes to determining whether the burden has been discharged. It follows that while the acknowledgment of the need for deference found in post-*Coughlan* cases like *Begbie* is to be welcomed, the implementation of this approach is insufficiently nuanced.

A lack of nuance is also discernible in a separate stream of case law, the separateness of the stream itself being a manifestation of the broader phenomenon of doctrinal disjointedness. Whereas the cases considered so far presuppose that the court must play some role in determining whether frustrating a substantive legitimate expectation is justified, a distinct line of cases, including *Bibi*[51] and *Ibrahim*,[52] proceeds on the basis that no such justification is required. The removal of the justification requirement might be taken to reflect an attitude of judicial deference that was lacking in *Coughlan* (and an extreme form of deference at that). On another view, however, the difference runs deeper: a fundamental premise in *Coughlan* is that, any possibility of deference notwithstanding, whether frustration is justified is ultimately a question for the court. In contrast, cases like *Bibi* and *Ibrahim* treat that question as one that is not for the court *at all*.

In *Bibi*, the defendant local authority had promised the claimants permanent accommodation. When such accommodation was not forthcoming, the claimants sought judicial review on the ground that the promises had generated substantive legitimate expectations, and that those expectations had been breached. Since this case was decided nearly two years after *Coughlan*, the Court of Appeal might have been expected to hold that permanent accommodation had to be supplied absent an overriding public policy justification. However, such an approach was not adopted. This might reflect the fact that the Court in *Bibi* appeared to be alive—in a way that the Court in *Coughlan* was not—to the polycentric nature of the issue facing it. It noted, for instance, that suitable accommodation constituted a scarce resource, such that fulfilling a given claimant's legitimate expectation

[50] *Begbie* (n 45) 1131.
[51] *R (Bibi) v Newham London Borough Council* [2001] EWCA Civ 607, [2002] 1 WLR 237.
[52] *R (Ibrahim) v Redbridge London Borough Council* [2002] EWHC 2756 (Admin).

might involve denying permanent accommodation to someone else.[53] The Court also noted that 'giving every family enough money to provide its own housing' was not necessarily 'an escape from the problem' because this too might involve diverting scarce financial resources so as to deprive others of 'money which they expected to retain or of benefits which they expected to receive'.[54] Against this background—and bearing in mind that decisions in this area 'are informed by social and political value judgments as to priorities of expenditure'—the Court concluded that '[t]he law requires that any legitimate expectation be properly taken into account in the decision making process. It has not been in the present case and therefore the authority has acted unlawfully'.[55]

What is puzzling about *Bibi*, however, is the implication that this was *all* that the law required. It is of course conceivable that, having quashed the decision to frustrate the expectation on what reduced to the ground of failure to consider a mandatory relevant consideration, a second decision to frustrate (following proper consideration of the matter) could also have been challenged, this time on the ground that reneging on the promise was not justified by reference to the balancing test. But the implication in *Bibi* is that such a second challenge would not have got the claimants anywhere because the decision-maker would have entirely discharged its legal obligation in respect of the expectation by *considering* it. *Bibi* thus implies that there is a category of cases in which the decision-maker will never need to demonstrate that frustration is justified because consideration of the expectation is exhaustive of what is required. This conclusion is reinforced by the Court's statement that it

> will not order the authority to honour its promise where to do so would be to assume the powers of the executive. Once the court has established … an abuse [of power in the sense of a failure to consider a legitimate expectation] it may ask the decision taker to take the legitimate expectation properly into account in the decision making process.[56]

This does not imply that a reviewing court should *never* order a public body to 'honour its promise'—only that it should not do so when this would amount to the court 'assum[ing] the powers of the executive'. But it is unclear in what circumstances that line will be crossed so as to—according to the analysis adopted in *Bibi*—reduce the role of the court to insisting upon executive consideration of the legitimate expectation. It is equally unclear why *Coughlan* was implicitly considered in *Bibi* to fall on the other side of the line.

53 *Bibi* (n 51) [37].
54 *Bibi* (n 51) [38].
55 *Bibi* (n 51) [51], [64].
56 *Bibi* (n 51) [41].

The approach adopted in *Bibi* thus differs radically from the approach, evident in the cases discussed earlier in this section, based upon the balancing test. Whereas the latter test demands that breach of a substantive legitimate expectation be justified to the satisfaction of the reviewing court, cases like *Bibi* eschew any requirement of justification in favour of an essentially procedural obligation to take account of the expectation when making a decision that risks frustrating it. The effect is to render *review* essentially non-substantive, the substantive nature of the *expectation* notwithstanding. In mode of review terms, there is no qualitative engagement by the reviewing court with the reasons for the decision to frustrate. Meanwhile, examined in effect of review terms, treating the expectation as generative of nothing more than an obligation to consider it makes no substantive inroad into the scope of the discretionary power, frustration remaining an option lawfully on the table, provided only that the decision-making process duly takes account of the expectation's existence.

The picture that emerges in relation to the extent to which review in this area is substantive is thus a complex and somewhat disjointed one. Whilst *Coughlan* demonstrates that review can be deeply substantive, it is clear that this will not always be so because of the possibility of the judicial role being circumscribed by considerations of deference. There are, however, three distinct sites upon which deference—using that term loosely so as to connote the modulation of the extent to which review is substantive in one or other of the two senses—may operate. First, the justificatory burden triggered by the expectation may be more or less onerous. Second, the court might be more or less deferential in its assessment of the defendant's reasons by way of determining whether the justificatory burden has been discharged. Third, the court might forego any assessment of whether frustration is justified by characterising the expectation as nothing more than a mandatory relevant consideration. Meanwhile, these forms of deference can, as has been seen, operate so as to impact upon the extent to which review is substantive in either or both of the mode of review and effect of review senses.

This complexity is not in itself problematic: indeed, it might be welcomed on the ground that it evidences judicial willingness to acknowledge the need to tailor the standard of review to the circumstances of the case. What is problematic, however, is the fact that the present case law does little by way of acknowledging the existence of such complexity, let alone attempting to systematise practice in this area so as to produce a coherent scheme of deference.

In *Bibi*, the Court of Appeal said:

> The court has two functions—assessing the legality of actions by administrators and, if it finds unlawfulness on the administrator's part, deciding what relief it should give. It is in our judgment a mistake to isolate from the rest of administrative law cases those which turn on representations made by authorities. The same

constitutional principles apply to the exercise by the court of each of these two functions.[57]

In this insight lie the seeds of a more cohesive approach. In particular, the courts' legitimate expectation jurisprudence would benefit considerably from greater integration with the courts' general substantive review jurisprudence concerning matters such as proportionality, reasonableness and deference. Such integration would not constitute a silver bullet, but greater recognition of the relationship between the judicial tasks that fall to be performed in (for instance) legitimate expectation and qualified human rights cases would enable cases of the former type to benefit from the larger, and richer, standard of review jurisprudence that exists in respect of cases of the latter type. It is to be hoped, in turn, that this would assist with the development of a clearer and less disjointed framework by reference to which standard of review issues fall to be determined in substantive legitimate expectation cases.

THE NATURE OF ORTHODOXY AND ITS DOCTRINAL IMPLICATIONS

The foregoing analysis suggests that judicial review on the ground of substantive legitimate expectation, notwithstanding that it does or may amount to substantive review, can be reconciled with orthodoxy by means of recourse to deference, albeit that there is still some distance to travel in terms of fashioning a developed jurisprudence of curial deference in this context. Looked at in this way, the substantive legitimate expectation doctrine's journey from heterodoxy to orthodoxy is facilitated not so much by the eschewal of an old in favour of a new orthodoxy, but by means of injecting into that doctrine a degree of deference that is sufficient to answer the charge of heresy that was levelled in *Hargreaves*.[58] But this is only part of the story, not least because the development of the substantive legitimate expectation doctrine over the last 20 years or so has taken place against the background of much wider and deeper changes to the landscape of English public law. In this section, I argue that those changes imply a reassessment of both *what orthodoxy requires* and *how orthodoxy ought to be doctrinally delivered.*

For present purposes, an important element of orthodoxy as traditionally conceived in English administrative law is embodied in the notion that the *Wednesbury* doctrine marked the outer perimeter of the courts' legitimate role in respect of substantive review. As is apparent from Lord Irvine's powerful, if contestable, defence of that conception of orthodoxy, it rests on a particular understanding of—and normative take upon—the UK's

[57] *Bibi* (n 51) [40].
[58] *Hargreaves* (n 2).

constitutional architecture.[59] It implies a certain understanding of, and of the relationship between, the three fundamental constitutional principles of the British constitution—the rule of law, the separation of powers and the sovereignty of Parliament. And, in particular, it implies an understanding of those principles that places special emphasis upon parliamentary sovereignty, with the result that—from the perspective of substantive review—negative or limiting aspects of the rule of law and separation of powers doctrines are accentuated. For instance, from a rule of law perspective, substantive review may appear suspect because it risks disrupting extant legal arrangements fixed in place by the legislature. On this analysis, if Parliament has conferred discretion upon a decision-maker, then it is not for the court to wrest that discretion away from the decision-maker by means of substantively reviewing its exercise. The separation of powers doctrine may appear to point in a similar direction. If discretionary authority has been vested *by Parliament* in a given administrative agency then, on one view, it is dubious, in separation of powers terms, for a reviewing court to usurp the agency—thereby frustrating Parliament's sovereign allocative choice—by engaging in substantive review.

Of course, there are other ways in which the rule of law and separation of powers doctrines might be looked at: the former might be considered to require and justify judicial protection of particular standards, including legal certainty, whilst the latter might be considered to necessitate a degree of institutional oversight that extends to curial scrutiny of administrative action on the basis of substantive constitutional standards. However, when the rule of law and separation of powers doctrines are viewed through the lens of parliamentary sovereignty, they take on particular complexions that, in turn, have implications for the extent of substantive review's perceived legitimacy. More specifically, a parliamentary sovereignty-centric view of the other principles tends to de-emphasise such independent content as they might otherwise be acknowledged to have, whilst exaggerating those dimensions of them that demand respect for the legislature's intention including as to allocations of institutional authority.

On that sort of account of the fundamental constitutional principles, the characterisation of the early substantive legitimate expectation case law as heretical was wholly unsurprising. However, during the course of the last 20 or so years a somewhat different understanding of the three fundamental constitutional principles has emerged. It is of course the case that during that period certain judges, both curially[60] and extra-curially,[61] have been

[59] Irvine (n 19).

[60] See eg *R (Jackson) v Attorney-General* [2005] UKHL 56, [2006] 1 AC 262 [102] (Lord Steyn), [104]–[107] (Lord Hope), [159] (Lady Hale); *AXA General Insurance Ltd v HM Advocate* [2011] UKSC 46, [2012] 1 AC 868 [50] (Lord Hope); *Moohan v Lord Advocate* [2014] UKSC 67, [2015] AC 901, [35] (Lord Hodge).

[61] See eg Lord Woolf, '*Droit Public*—English Style' [1995] *Public Law* 57; Sir John Laws, 'Law and Democracy' [1995] *Public Law* 72.

prepared to question or even openly doubt the veracity of the principle of parliamentary sovereignty. However, significant though it might be in general terms, the debate about whether Parliament is sovereign—and the joining of that debate by the judiciary—is for present purposes a sideshow, the more significant phenomenon being a repositioning of thinking concerning the nature of the constitutional environment within which the sovereignty principle subsists, and hence the way in which the interaction of the three fundamental principles falls to be understood.

The Supreme Court's decision in *Evans* serves to illustrate this argument.[62] It concerned a judicial review challenge to the exercise of an administrative power vetoing an order issued by the Upper Tribunal—a superior court of record[63]—requiring disclosure under freedom of information legislation of correspondence between the Prince of Wales and UK Government Ministers. It is self-evident that executive override of courts' judgments is highly suspect in both rule of law and separation of powers terms. However, the extent of such concerns is necessarily a function of the extent to which those constitutional principles are viewed through the prism of parliamentary sovereignty. It was the use of precisely such a prism that led Lord Hughes to say that although '[t]he rule of law is of the first importance ... it is an integral part of the rule of law that courts give effect to Parliamentary intention'.[64] On this analysis, any rule of law concerns triggered by executive override of a judicial decision yielded to the more compelling rule of law demand that courts should give effect to Parliament's 'plainly shown' intention.[65]

However, Lord Hughes was in a minority in holding such a view,[66] the discrepancy between the majority and minority judgments being attributable to different understandings of how the three fundamental constitutional principles relate to each other—and, in particular, of the extent to which the rule of law and separation of powers doctrines fall to be viewed through the prism of, and so blunted by, the doctrine of parliamentary sovereignty. Thus, for Lord Neuberger, permitting the executive to override judicial decisions merely because it disagreed with them would 'cut across two constitutional principles which are also fundamental components of the rule of law'[67]—namely, that judicial decisions 'cannot be ignored by anyone', 'least of all ... the executive', and that executive action, 'subject to jealously guarded statutory exceptions', must be subject to judicial scrutiny.[68] Lord

[62] *R (Evans) v Attorney-General* [2015] UKSC 21, [2015] 2 WLR 813.
[63] *Tribunals, Courts and Enforcement Act 2007*, s 3(5).
[64] *Evans* (n 62) [154].
[65] *Evans* (n 62) [154].
[66] Lord Wilson also dissented, but based his reasoning on a more historical analysis of the legislative background as distinct from Lord Hughes's 'plainly shown' intention point.
[67] *Evans* (n 62) [51].
[68] *Evans* (n 62) [52].

Neuberger concluded that because broad override powers would 'flout … the first principle' and 'stand … the second principle on its head',[69] the legislation, properly construed, was to be taken to permit override only in extremely limited circumstances. Meanwhile, Lord Mance, giving the other majority judgment, held that the constitutionally suspect nature of the executive override power justified judicial scrutiny of its exercise going far beyond *Wednesbury* review.[70]

Of course, the context in which *Evans* was decided is some way from the context in which questions of substantive legitimate expectations fall to be confronted by the courts. Nevertheless, *Evans* is instructive insofar as it casts light upon a judicial conception of the relationship between the three fundamental constitutional principles that is at odds with the conception which animates traditional thinking as to the legitimate extent of substantive review. *Evans* highlights a contemporary judicial openness to the idea that the doctrine of parliamentary sovereignty, rather than straightforwardly being a constitutional trump, falls to be understood within the context of a constitutional order that contains and assigns considerable weight to other fundamental values. On this revised analysis, other values shape the constitutional implications of the sovereignty doctrine just as that doctrine in turn shapes the implications of those other principles. In particular, Lord Mance's judgment demonstrates that the ascription of greater weight to the other principles may carve out a constitutional space in which judicial review legitimately can—and sometimes should—transcend bare rationality review. This, of course, is pertinent to substantive legitimate expectation cases, bearing in mind that one of the key constitutional values at stake in such cases is the rule of law principle of legal certainty.

None of this is to say that the concerns that underpinned the *Wednesbury* doctrine have been entirely jettisoned: merely that they find expression today in different and more subtle ways. It is true that the constitutional space in which substantive review can legitimately operate is now conceived of in somewhat more generous terms than it was 20 or so years ago, but that space is not infinitely elastic. For instance, in defending judicial deployment of the proportionality test, Lord Neuberger said in *Keyu* that while proportionality involves 'considering the merits' in the sense that the court must 'consider the balance' struck by the decision-maker between competing interests, this does not mean that the court 'displace[s] the relevant member of the executive as the primary decision-maker'.[71] The additional, if implicit, normative premise is that such displacement *should not* occur.

To the extent, then, that English courts have exhibited a preparedness to move away from *Wednesbury* as the sole approach in substantive review

[69] *Evans* (n 62) [52].
[70] *Evans* (n 62) [123]–[130].
[71] *Keyu* (n 23) [133].

cases, this implies not straightforwardly, or only, a revised conception of what orthodoxy *is*, but a revised understanding of what orthodoxy *requires* in doctrinal terms. Inherent in the traditional view—that the line in the sand drawn by *Wednesbury* must not be breached because *Wednesbury* sets the 'right' balance between judicial scrutiny and administrative autonomy—is a proposition not only about the *content* but the *implementation* of orthodoxy. As to the latter, the traditional view implies that any doctrinal vehicle more nuanced than *Wednesbury* would cause curial overreach. Such thinking was articulated particularly forcefully by the House of Lords in *Brind*.[72] That view, however, is beginning to give way to a more subtle understanding of the way in which constitutional and institutional concerns ought to shape the doctrinal architecture of substantive judicial review.

That much is apparent from *Pham*, in which the Supreme Court confronted the question whether deeming European Union law to be applicable to the matter in issue would affect the approach to judicial review, proportionality being uncontroversially available in cases that are governed by EU law.[73] Although the Court did not speak with one voice at the level of detail, it is telling that all four of the judgments doubted the argument that demonstrating EU law's applicability would unlock the door to a form of substantive review that would otherwise be unavailable. This was so because in the light of the fundamental status that was at stake—namely, citizenship—relatively strict judicial scrutiny was anyway warranted as a matter of domestic law. For Lord Mance, such strict scrutiny was to be supplied by means of the explicit adoption of the proportionality test. In contrast, for Lords Carnwath and Sumption, whether review was described in terms of 'proportionality' or 'reasonableness' was relatively unimportant, the key issue being that administrative interference with a fundamental status served to found a commensurately searching degree of judicial scrutiny. Indeed, Lord Sumption indicated the porousness of the distinction between proportionality and rationality—and so the aridity of any debate that presupposes those concepts to be straightforwardly distinct—preferring instead to emphasise that 'the cogency of the justification required for interfering with a right will be proportionate to its perceived importance and the extent of the interference'.[74]

Pham forms a useful vantage point—roughly 20 years on—from which to re-examine early substantive legitimate expectation cases such as

[72] *R v Secretary of State for the Home Department; ex parte Brind* [1991] 1 AC 696 (HL). See in particular the speeches of Lords Ackner and Lowry.

[73] *Pham v Secretary of State for the Home Department* [2015] UKSC 19, [2015] 1 WLR 1591.

[74] Ibid, [106]. Notwithstanding Lord Sumption's reference to a 'right', it is clear that for at least some of the Justices in *Pham*, review that transcends *Wednesbury* review ought not to be limited to administrative decisions that engage rights *per se*.

Hargreaves, *Hamble Fisheries* and *Coughlan*, and from which to survey the subsequent trajectory of the jurisprudence in this area. Four points arise.

First, viewed from that vantage point, the balancing test that was endorsed in *Coughlan* looks less exotic (even if the uncompromising way in which it was applied in that case remains suspect). Irrespective of whether a 'proportionality' label is attached to it, there is increasing recognition, both judicially[75] and academically,[76] that substantive review is ultimately about questions of justification and balance. In this way, when *Coughlan* is situated within the wider arc of substantive review case law, its adoption of a balancing test and its rejection of bare *Wednesbury* review can be understood to form part of a trajectory initiated by pre-*Coughlan* decisions such as *Smith* that acknowledged the need for questions of balance—in the sense of assessing the capacity of reasons offered in support of a decision to justify its effects—to be examined in at least some circumstances,[77] and which culminates (for now) in judicial recognition, in cases like *Pham* and *Keyu*, that eschewal of the *Wednesbury* straightjacket need not lead to judicial overreach.

Second, that follows, at least in part, from the way in which *Pham* diffuses the tension between rationality- and proportionality-based approaches to substantive review that the juxtaposition of cases like *Hargreaves* and *Hamble Fisheries* implies. Viewed through the binary optic supplied by those cases—and which has tended to characterise the proportionality/reasonableness debate more generally—*Coughlan* represented a radical departure from orthodoxy by jettisoning the limits imposed by the *Wednesbury* doctrine in favour of a very different, and highly intrusive, approach. *Pham*, in contrast, acknowledges that the sharpness of the structural differences that are often considered to separate the reasonableness and proportionality tests have been inaccurately taken to postulate an equally crisp distinction between the intensity of review that they respectively supply.

Without prejudice to the argument that the way in which the balancing test operated in *Coughlan* resulted in judicial overreach, the analysis adopted in *Pham* casts doubt upon the notion that adherence to the strictures of *Wednesbury* is the best or only way of avoiding such overreach, the point being that the extent of the intrusiveness of substantive review is not necessarily or only a function of the doctrinal structure adopted. Indeed, adherence to 'reasonableness' or 'rationality' may not always even be *a* way of limiting judicial intervention, as Lord Mance's judgment in *Evans*—in which a notably demanding conception of reasonableness was adopted—attests.[78] The same is true of Lady Hale's judgment in *Keyu*, in

[75] See eg *Keyu* (n 23); *Pham* (n 73).

[76] See eg Craig (n 23); P Daly, '*Wednesbury*'s Reason and Structure' [2011] *Public Law* 238.

[77] *R v Ministry of Defence; ex parte Smith* [1996] QB 517 (CA).

[78] *Evans* (n 62).

which her analysis—and the degree of scrutiny it supplied—closely resembled proportionality review in certain respects, notwithstanding her insistence that it was the rationality doctrine that was in play.[79]

Third, *Pham* dissolves a further binary distinction that has hampered the development of substantive judicial review and which has served to obscure the relationship between that area of administrative law generally and that aspect of it which is specifically concerned with substantive legitimate expectations. The distinction in question holds that even if proportionality has a part to play in substantive judicial review, its part is limited to cases involving alleged infringements of (qualified) human rights. Such thinking, for instance, animated Michael Taggart's vision of a 'bifurcated' model of substantive review.[80] The rejection of such a sharp distinction is, however, at least implicit in *Pham*, not least because it repudiated slavish adherence to the *Wednesbury* doctrine within a factual matrix that was not centrally concerned with a 'right'. Once the distinction between cases that are and are not about rights is dismantled in this way, the apparently anomalistic nature of the approach adopted in relation to substantive legitimate expectation cases begins to fade away. The application of the proportionality test (or at least some elements of it) in a non-rights context ceases to be misaligned with a rigid distinction between rights and non-rights cases that are respectively the preserve of proportionality and *Wednesbury* review, that bright-line distinction being replaced by the contextual analysis that permeates *Pham* and which presupposes a more subtle relationship between the nature and normative importance of the impugned norm and the appropriate level of curial scrutiny. On this view, there is nothing anomalous about deploying the proportionality test (or elements of it) so as to evaluate a justification offered in support of frustration of a substantive expectation deriving from a clear and specific promise made to an individual who has relied upon it.

Fourth, if, as in *Pham*, a contextualist approach begins to supplant one premised on a rigid distinction between the respective provinces of the rationality and proportionality tests, it is imperative that a doctrinal vacuum is not permitted to develop. Such difficulties will be avoided only if the gap is filled by an adequately developed doctrine of deference. Considerable judicial work remains to be done in this area, not least in the particular context of substantive legitimate expectations. The point, however, is that that work needs to be undertaken, rather than relying upon the crude notion that anything more than bare *Wednesbury* review is heretical, either generally or outwith the human rights context specifically.

[79] *Keyu* (n 23) [305]–[313].

[80] M Taggart, 'Proportionality, Deference, *Wednesbury*' [2008] *New Zealand Law Review* 423.

CONCLUSIONS

The journey undertaken by the substantive legitimate expectation doctrine over the last 20 years is a complex one that is intertwined with, and emblematic of, the broader journey upon which English public law itself has been embarked. The phenomena identified in this chapter—concerning, on the one hand, the re-conception of the doctrine of substantive legitimate expectation in terms more subtle than those evidenced in *Coughlan* and, on the other hand, evolving understandings of the nature and doctrinal demands of orthodoxy in the field of substantive review—may seem to reflect disjointed, unconnected developments. Yet they actually form related elements of a single, broader narrative that is ultimately animated by the notion of what I will call 'convergence'.

Before explaining what I mean by this—and why it helps to place in context and make sense of the developments and arguments set out in this chapter—it is necessary to distinguish what I will call 'assimilation': a notion that might appear to be a close relative of convergence, but which is actually quite different. Those who advocate assimilation argue that the whole of the substantive review—or even the whole of the judicial review –landscape ought to be, or has been, colonised by singular, superior constructs. Prominent examples of such thinking include Thomas Poole's thesis concerning the 'righting' of English administrative law,[81] according to which the law of judicial review is coming to be or should be understood in terms of the protection of rights, and Paul Craig's contention that proportionality should serve as the sole doctrinal vehicle for substantive review.[82] Thus understood, assimilation theories are to be deprecated. Administrative law is not only, or even mainly, concerned with the protection of rights, and it is unhelpful and counterfactual to suggest otherwise.[83] Meanwhile, proportionality is not, and should not be, adopted as the sole ground of substantive review, not least because to stretch the concept so as to render it universally applicable would be to deprive it of meaningful content.[84]

Convergence, in contrast, involves not the forcing of the whole of substantive review (or judicial review) into pigeon-holes that can at best accommodate only parts of it, but rather liberating substantive review by means of the removal of the pigeon-holes themselves. On this approach, rigid distinctions are dismantled and replaced with more subtle tools for the purpose

[81] T Poole, 'The Reformation of English Administrative Law' (2009) 68 *Cambridge Law Journal* 142.

[82] P Craig, 'Proportionality, Rationality and Review' [2010] *New Zealand Law Review* 265.

[83] See eg J Varuhas, 'The Reformation of English Administrative Law? "Rights", Rhetoric and Reality' (2013) 72 *Cambridge Law Journal* 369.

[84] See eg J King, 'Proportionality: A Halfway House' [2010] *New Zealand Law Review* 327; T Hickman, 'Problems for Proportionality' [2010] *New Zealand Law Review* 303.

of calibrating the nature and intensity of substantive review. The distinction between rights and non-rights cases is, for instance, eroded, not least because the presence or absence of a right need not be determinative of the approach to substantive review that ought to apply. This opens up the possibility that some (but not all) decisions that frustrate substantive legitimate expectations might uncontroversially invite a style and intensity of review akin to that which is conventionally associated with rights cases. Equally, the rigid distinction between the proportionality and rationality tests is eroded, the nature and intensity of substantive review being a function of a set of underlying normative, constitutional and institutional considerations that are not adequately captured by a categorical doctrinal approach. The notion that a particular type of case—such as one entailing frustration of a substantive legitimate expectation—should, *simply because the case is that type of case*, attract a particular form of review, such as *Wednesbury* or proportionality, thus ceases to be meaningful.

On this approach, substantive judicial review converges not upon a single concept (such as proportionality) or lens (such as rights). Rather, it converges in the sense that an holistic understanding is adopted of what substantive review is, and in the sense that its operation is animated by a single, cohesive set of principles and considerations. In this way, the question whether the substantive legitimate expectation doctrine has evolved so as to satisfy orthodoxy or orthodoxy has evolved so as to accommodate that doctrine begins to ring somewhat hollow, not least because, on this view, orthodoxy's requirements cannot be reduced to a simplistic doctrinal prescription (such as 'substantive review test X is the right test for Y category of cases').

Yet this does not mean that anything goes. It does not, for instance, lead me to the conclusion that *Coughlan* involved no judicial overreach. But it does change the terms of the analysis. *Coughlan* involved judicial overreach not because the Court diminished the discretion of the decision-maker to zero by insisting upon fulfilment of the expectation. Nor did it involve overreach because it applied a balancing test instead of a reasonableness test. Rather, it involved overreach because the balancing test was applied in a way that was insufficiently sensitive to the polycentric and value-laden nature of the issues at stake and the limits of the Court's capacity to assess such matters.

When, today, the doctrine of substantive legitimate expectation is measured against orthodoxy, it is evident that there has been movement from both sides. The shrillness of *Coughlan* has given way to a more nuanced—if inadequately coherent—jurisprudence that has at least begun to grasp the deference nettle. At the same time, what orthodoxy is—in terms of the limits upon the judicial role generated by the interaction of fundamental constitutional principles—and what it requires—in terms of those principles' translation into doctrine—have evolved. Those changes have been subtle and represent different facets of a broader, overarching change of perspective.

Importantly, however, such changes do not imply a throwing away of the baby with the bathwater. Enduring institutional and constitutional concerns that were formative in the development of English administrative law have not gone away—but such concerns are conceived of today in somewhat less bald terms, and in a way that is beginning to receive expression through a jurisprudence that is more contextualist in nature. Understood thus, the doctrine of substantive legitimate expectation has been simultaneously a function of those broader changes and part of the engine that has produced them. In this way, the story of that doctrine's journey from heresy to orthodoxy represents, in microcosm, the story of English administrative law's own evolution over the course of the last two decades.

11

The (Fictitious) Doctrine of Substantive Legitimate Expectations in India

CHINTAN CHANDRACHUD

INTRODUCTION

OVER THE LAST two decades, the doctrine of substantive legitimate expectations seems to have become a regular feature in the Indian Supreme Court's jurisprudence. Leading commentaries on administrative law extol the Court's acceptance of the principle that legitimate expectations can be invoked as a source of both procedural and substantive claims.[1] These commentaries rely on consistent statements to this effect by the Court, beginning in the 1990s.

Writing in 1998, a three-judge bench of the Court observed:

> The Government and its departments, in administering the affairs of the country are expected to honour their statements of policy or intention and treat the citizens with full personal consideration without any iota of abuse of discretion. The policy statements cannot be disregarded unfairly or applied selectively ... It was in this context that the doctrine of 'Legitimate Expectation' was evolved which has today become a source of substantive as well as procedural lights.[2]

[1] CK Thakker, *Administrative Law*, 2nd edn (Eastern Book Company, 2012) 911; MP Jain and SN Jain, *Principles of Administrative Law* (Wadhwa, 2007) 251–52; NK Jayakumar, *Administrative Law* (PHI, 2005) 62.

[2] *National Buildings Construction Corporation v Raghunathan* AIR 1998 SC 2779 [18].

The very next year, the Court observed that 'the doctrine of legitimate expectation in the substantive sense has been accepted as part of our law'.[3] The Supreme Court made similar remarks in 2007,[4] 2008[5] and 2012.[6]

These observations suggest that the doctrine—giving rise to 'crucial and difficult'[7] questions elsewhere—forms part of constitutional orthodoxy in New Delhi. However, an entirely different picture emerges once we move beyond the rhetoric and examine the Indian Supreme Court's legitimate expectations docket more closely. This chapter will argue that the substantive legitimate expectations[8] doctrine is fictitious in India—not in the sense that these observations are imaginary, but because the doctrine is illusory; it has evolved in a way that makes it almost impossible for a claim to succeed.

Courts confront a distinct set of questions when a litigant makes a claim based on substantive legitimate expectations. Has a governmental policy, practice or promise given rise to a legitimate expectation and does the expectation deserve protection?[9] Can the expectation be dislodged based on public interest or other considerations? Finally, what standards of review should be applied in testing the considerations based on which the expectation has been dislodged?

The arguments in this chapter will unfold by: (a) establishing the Court's resistance to recognising the emergence of substantive legitimate expectations in specific instances where they have been claimed; (b) disclosing the broad set of grounds based on which courts will dislodge a legitimate expectation; and (c) analysing the deferential standards of judicial review applied to these grounds. The final section will argue that, in the existing doctrinal landscape, claims of substantive legitimate expectations are doomed

[3] *Punjab Communications v Union of India* AIR 1999 SC 1801 [37].

[4] *Jitendra Kumar v State of Haryana* (2008) 2 SCC 161 [40] ('We have no doubt that the doctrine of legitimate expectation operates both in procedural and substantive matters … ').

[5] *Official Liquidator v Dayanand* (2008) 10 SCC 1 [78] (' … the existence of a legitimate expectation may even in the absence of a right of private law, justify its recognition in public law.'); *Sethi Auto Service v Delhi Development Authority* AIR 2009 SC 904 [27] (' … the doctrine of legitimate expectation, now accepted in the subjective [sic] sense as part of our legal jurisprudence, arises when an administrative body by reason of a representation or by past practice or conduct aroused an expectation which it would be within its powers to fulfill unless some overriding public interest comes in the way.').

[6] *Monnet Ispat v Union of India* (2012) 1 SCC 1 [153] ('The doctrine of legitimate expectation can be invoked as a substantive and enforceable right.').

[7] Christopher Forsyth, 'Legitimate Expectations Revisited' (2011) 16(4) *Judicial Review* 429, 436.

[8] Substantive legitimate expectations can be protected procedurally (by giving the claimant an opportunity to present their case before the decision-making authority) or substantively (by giving the claimant a substantive right to something). This chapter focuses on the substantive protection of substantive legitimate expectations.

[9] See Greg Weeks, 'What Can We Legitimately Expect from the State?' in chapter 7 of this volume.

to fail—and those that have succeeded are either mischaracterised as substantive legitimate expectations claims, or have little to do with substantive legitimate expectations.

THE RESISTANCE TO RECOGNISING SUBSTANTIVE LEGITIMATE EXPECTATIONS

The Indian Supreme Court has held that substantive legitimate expectations arise when a representation is made to a person that a benefit of a substantive nature will be granted or—if the person is already enjoying the benefit—will be continued without significant variation.[10] This representation can manifest itself in different ways—including through an express policy, a promise made to a claimant or class of claimants, or established practice giving rise to the expectation that it will continue to be followed. The claimant bears the burden of producing evidence of the policy, practice, or promise. The doctrine of substantive legitimate expectations has been subsumed within the 'non-arbitrariness' branch of the right to equality under Article 14 of the Constitution.[11]

From amongst its earliest cases considering the doctrine, the Court has demonstrated reluctance to recognise the emergence of a substantive legitimate expectation. In the *Hindustan Development Corporation* case,[12] the question for the Court's consideration was whether three leading manufacturers of steel train carriages had entered into a price-fixing cartel and manipulated an auction. Suspecting cartelisation, the relevant ministry deviated from policy to offer a larger quantity of the tender to small manufacturers. The large manufacturers contended that they had a legitimate expectation to receive the same treatment as they did for past auctions, based on existing government policy.

Although the Court rejected the manufacturers' claims based on legitimate expectations,[13] it outlined the limits of the doctrine at some length. First, the Court conceptualised the 'mere anticipation' limit on substantive legitimate expectations, holding that neither a mere anticipation, nor 'a wish, a desire or a hope' regardless of the earnestness and sincerity of the

[10] *Punjab Communications* (n 3) [27].

[11] *Food Corporation of India v Kamdhenu Cattle* AIR 1993 SC 1601 [7]; *State of West Bengal v Niranjan Singha* (2001) 2 SCC 326, [4]. See Tarunabh Khaitan, 'Legislative Review under Article 14' in Sujit Choudhry, Madhav Khosla, Pratap Bhanu Mehta (eds), *The Oxford Handbook of the Indian Constitution* (Oxford University Press, 2016) (explaining that two doctrines have evolved to judge the constitutionality of a measure under Article 14—the classification test and the arbitrariness test).

[12] *Union of India v Hindustan Development Corporation* AIR 1994 SC 988.

[13] The manufacturers succeeded on other grounds: ibid [37].

claimant,[14] nor even a 'pious hope leading to a moral obligation',[15] could constitute an expectation. Rather, a legitimate expectation would only be founded upon 'the sanction of law or custom or an established procedure followed in regular and natural sequence'.[16]

It is worth spending a moment deconstructing these somewhat cryptic remarks. If the Court was attempting to explain that not every 'expectation', understood colloquially, constituted a legitimate expectation, then it was making an innocuous, unexceptionable statement. The task of courts around the world grappling with substantive legitimate expectation cases is to determine whether the governmental practice has, in fact, acquired the character which warrants recognition as a legitimate expectation.

It is possible, however, to read something deeper within the 'mere anticipation' rule. When the Court observed that a mere anticipation will not be recognised as a legitimate expectation, that begs the question with what the expression 'mere anticipation' is being contrasted. The answer in this case was simple enough—a law, a custom or an established procedure. Read in this way, the mere anticipation rule in *Hindustan Development Corporation* may have offered a word of caution to the unwary litigant that they would not have a legitimate expectation to every governmental benefit.

Subsequent judgments, however, have interpreted the 'mere anticipation' rule less innocuously. For instance, in *Bannari Amman Sugars*,[17] the question before the Court was whether the withdrawal of tax subsidies to sugar mills constituted a denial of substantive legitimate expectations. Citing the mere anticipation rule, the Court held that the '[l]egitimacy of an expectation can be inferred only if it is founded on the sanction of law'.[18] Mysteriously, the Court dropped the second half of the sentence ('or custom or an established procedure followed in regular and natural sequence') used in *Hindustan Development Corporation* without explanation.

Bannari Amman Sugars supplied a quite different meaning to the 'mere anticipation' rule. If the Court's perception of the universe of claims extended to only two kinds—anticipations and legal rights—then that would deprive the doctrine of substantive legitimate expectations of its utility. If a claimant needs to establish an *ex ante* legal right in order to succeed in a legitimate expectations claim, the claimant would succeed on the basis of illegality in any event. The Supreme Court made similar observations to deny a claim for legitimate expectation of employment with a government-funded research and development organisation.[19]

[14] Ibid, [29].
[15] Ibid.
[16] Ibid.
[17] *Bannari Amman Sugars v CTO* (2005) 1 SCC 625.
[18] Ibid, [14].
[19] *CSIR v Ramesh Agarwal* (2009) 3 SCC 35.

The second important observation in the *Hindustan Development Corporation* case that is worth highlighting is that the Court was careful to outline the dangers of taking the doctrine of substantive legitimate expectations too far, since doing so would risk stifling the room for maneuver in executive decision-making. Whereas procedural legitimate expectations were worth preserving, the Court was not quite as enthusiastic about substantive legitimate expectations:

> It can therefore be seen that legitimate expectation can at the most be one of the grounds which may give rise to judicial review but *the granting of relief is very much limited*. It would thus appear that *there are stronger reasons as to why the legitimate expectation should not be substantively protected* than the reasons as to why it should be protected ... If a denial of legitimate expectation in a given case amounts to denial of right guaranteed or is arbitrary, discriminatory, unfair or biased, gross abuse of power of violation of principles of natural justice, the same can be questioned on the well-known grounds attracting Article 14 but a claim based on mere legitimate expectation without anything more cannot ipso facto give a right to invoke these principles (emphasis added).[20]

These observations shed light on the Supreme Court's reluctance to accept substantive protection of legitimate expectations as an independent basis for judicial review. Of course, as I have already mentioned, as soon as we start thinking about whether substantive legitimate expectations should only be claimed in conjunction with other grounds, we must also begin to question whether such expectations play *any role at all* in the decision-making process.

The Court also cited *Attorney General for New South Wales v Quin* extensively,[21] in which the High Court of Australia rejected the doctrine of substantive legitimate expectations and enabled the Government to extinguish the source of those expectations.[22] In *Quin*, Brennan J observed that to strike down a power on the basis of substantive legitimate expectations would 'set the courts adrift on a featureless sea of pragmatism'[23] and 'unlock the gate which shuts the court out of review on the merits'.[24] These observations were almost emphatically endorsed by the Indian Supreme Court in *Hindustan Development Corporation*:

> As cautioned in [*Quin*] ... the courts should restrain themselves and restrict such [substantive legitimate expectation] claims duly to the legal limitations. It is a well-meant caution. Otherwise a resourceful litigant having vested interests in

[20] *Hindustan Development Corporation* (n 12) [36].

[21] *Attorney General for New South Wales v Quin* (1990) 170 CLR 1.

[22] Matthew Groves, 'The Evolution and Entrenchment of Natural Justice' in Matthew Groves (ed), *Modern Administrative Law in Australia: Concepts and Context* (Cambridge University Press, 2014) 208.

[23] *Quin* (n 21) 38.

[24] *Quin* (n 21) 40.

> contracts, licences etc. can successfully indulge in getting welfare activities ... thwarted to further his own interests.[25]

As it turned out, *Hindustan Development Corporation* was the first amongst a series of legitimate expectations cases to cite Brennan J's 'well-meant caution'. *Quin* is an unlikely mascot for India, a jurisdiction that scholars believe has eagerly embraced the notion of substantive legitimate expectations. How, then, do we explain what is transpiring in the Indian Supreme Court? *Hindustan Development Corporation* was decided after *Quin*, but well before the England and Wales Court of Appeal's seminal judgment clarifying the role of substantive legitimate expectations in *Coughlan*.[26] After *Coughlan*, the Indian Supreme Court cited both *Coughlan* and *Quin*—judgments that take different positions on the question of substantive legitimate expectations—in equal measure.[27]

The frequent citation of these conflicting judgments reflects a broader trend in Indian public law—the Supreme Court's adoption of the taxonomy, rather than the substance, of new doctrine. While the Court has enthusiastically appropriated the language of substantive legitimate expectations from *Coughlan* and other cases, it has been careful to approach these claims with the words of caution offered in *Quin*. A similar trend is noticeable in the move from reasonableness review to proportionality, a matter that is discussed later in the chapter.

Perhaps influenced by *Quin* and some of its early substantive legitimate expectations case law, the Supreme Court excluded the application of the doctrine for an entire category of cases—those concerning employment in public services. In *Umadevi*,[28] a five-judge bench of the Supreme Court[29] was confronted with the question of whether daily wagers, casual employees or temporary employees whose terms had been extended for prolonged periods of time, would have a substantive legitimate expectation of 'regularisation', with the attendant benefits of regular employment.

Conscious of the fact that the doctrine of substantive legitimate expectations could give rise to a new class of 'litigious employment' jurisprudence,[30]

[25] *Hindustan Development Corporation* (n 12).

[26] *R v North and East Devon Health Authority, ex parte Coughlan* [2001] QB 213.

[27] *Quin* has been cited in: *Hindustan Development Corporation* (n 12); *Raghunathan* (n 2); *Punjab Communications* (n 3); *Chanchal Goyal v State of Rajasthan* AIR 2003 SC 1713; *Shimnit Utsch India v West Bengal Transport Infrastructure Development Corporation* (2010) 6 SCC 303. *Coughlan* has been cited in: *Union of India v S B Vohra* AIR 2004 SC 1402; *Kuldeep Singh v Govt of Delhi* AIR 2006 SC 2652.

[28] *Secretary, State of Karnataka v Umadevi* AIR 2006 SC 1806.

[29] In the Indian Supreme Court, decisions by panels of a larger size bind panels of a smaller size, regardless of the number of dissenting opinions: see Chintan Chandrachud, 'The Supreme Court's Practice of Referring Cases to Larger Benches: A Need for Review' (2010) 1 *Supreme Court Cases Journal* 37.

[30] *Umadevi* (n 28) [3].

the Court not only rejected the claim but vetoed substantive legitimate expectations claims in all comparable employment contexts. In the Court's view, a person engaged as a temporary employee is well informed of the limited duration of his or her employment. Temporary employees are not appointed in accordance with formal and rigorous selection procedures. Even a promise of permanent employment would be inadequate, since it was a promise that the state is not permitted to make. The Court was also mindful of the fact that equity for a 'handful of people' may deny equity to the 'teeming millions' seeking employment based on fair procedures.[31] This judgment was subsequently followed in a case in which the Supreme Court held that temporary employees were informed that they would have no right to seek regularisation of employment.[32]

There are two ways of reading the Supreme Court's categorical rejection of the doctrine of substantive legitimate expectations in employment cases. The first would suggest that the Court conceived of employment as a special category of cases to which the general rules of substantive legitimate expectations should not apply. This reading of the case seems implausible, since most of the concerns punctuating employment cases would play out in *all* substantive legitimate expectations cases. Substantive legitimate expectation claims are usually not 'victimless': just as recognising the right of patients to remain in a care home would affect the quality of care available to other patients generally,[33] the regularisation of employment claimed in *Umadevi* would have denied those awaiting employment.

Thus, it would be tenuous to argue that substantive legitimate expectations claims made specifically in employment cases should be decisively rejected, regardless of the equities and the hardships suffered by the litigants.[34] It is more plausible to read the case as magnifying the Court's more general discomfort with the doctrine of substantive legitimate expectations. The Court's categorical rule was probably motivated by the desire to send a message to the High Courts, some of which were beginning to accept substantive legitimate expectations claims in employment contexts.[35]

The Supreme Court's case law is also peppered with other restrictions on the invocation of the doctrine of substantive legitimate expectations. Claims of substantive legitimate expectations must be specifically pleaded in the original petition, and be supported by 'clear, sound and positive'

[31] *Umadevi* (n 28) [4].

[32] *UP Gram Panchayat v Daya Rama Saroj* (2007) 2 SCC 138. There was initially some resistance to the *Umadevi* judgment (see *UP State Electricity Board v Pooran Chandra Pandey* (2007) 11 SCC 92) but this was refuted by the Supreme Court in *Dayanand* (n 5) [59].

[33] See eg *Coughlan* (n 26).

[34] For criticism of the *Umadevi* decision, see Ramapriya Gopalakrishnan, 'Labour Jurisprudence of the Supreme Court' in KV Ramaswamy (ed), *Labour, Employment and Economic Growth in India* (Cambridge University Press, 2015) 303.

[35] *Umadevi* (n 28) [3].

factual foundations.[36] In the context of entertainment tax, the Court held that 14 years would not be sufficient to constitute 'established practice' for the purposes of legitimate expectations.[37] The Court has quite candidly admitted that legitimate expectations are a 'weak' ground for judicial review and (consistently with the judgment of Brennan J in *Quin*) ordinarily entitle the claimant to only procedural protection of substantive legitimate expectations, in the form of an opportunity to be heard or reasons for a decision.[38]

THE GROUNDS FOR DISLODGING SUBSTANTIVE LEGITIMATE EXPECTATIONS

Having accepted that the doctrine of substantive legitimate expectations can be invoked in an appropriate case, the next question that arises for a court is what grounds the state is permitted to raise in order to dislodge the expectation. This question has a significant impact on the scope of the doctrine—a narrow set of grounds for dislodging legitimate expectations would lend the doctrine some normative force, whereas a broad set of grounds would dilute the doctrine, possibly even to the point of obsolescence.

Beginning with the early cases, two grounds have been asserted for defeating a substantive legitimate expectation claim: public interest and good faith. At first glance, these may come across as competing grounds. After all, for the Government to establish that a policy decision was taken in the public interest would be an entirely different proposition from simply having to establish that the decision—irrespective of its detrimental potential—was taken in good faith. The development of the case law, however, suggests that these two grounds have converged to set up a standard for dislodging substantive legitimate expectations that is remarkably easy to satisfy.

Food Corporation of India v Kamdhenu[39] involved an attempted auction of damaged food grains by the Food Corporation of India (FCI). FCI was unsatisfied with the bids it received and entered into negotiations with each of the bidders, eventually choosing to award the tender to someone other than the highest bidder. The highest bidder contended that, having offered the highest price in the auction, it had a legitimate expectation that it would be awarded the tender at that price.[40]

[36] *Bannari Amman Sugars* (n 17) [19]. See also *Raghunathan* (n 2) [31]; *National Board of Examiners v Ramamurthy* AIR 2006 SC 2484, [5]; *UP Gram Panchayat* (n 32) [24].

[37] *Srinivasa Theatre v Govt of Tamil Nadu* AIR 1992 SC 999 [22].

[38] *Ram Pravesh v State of Bihar* (2006) 8 SCC 381, [14].

[39] *Food Corporation of India* (n 11).

[40] Although the terms and conditions inviting tenders allowed FCI to reject all bids, the highest bidder argued that this provision could not be invoked at the 'whim' of the authority.

While recognising that the legitimate expectations of the highest bidder would be given 'due weight', the Court held:

> Whenever the question [of a substantive legitimate expectation] arises, it is to be determined not according to the claimant's perception but in larger public interest wherein other more important considerations may outweigh what would otherwise have been the legitimate expectation of the claimant.[41]

Public interest, in the Court's opinion, would require 'cogent reasons' for action that were sufficient to dislodge a legitimate expectation.[42] The Court held that the purpose of the tender was to secure the highest price for the food grains, while giving bidders an equal opportunity to compete. Procuring the highest price for the grains was in the public interest. Therefore, the inadequacy of the prices offered on the auction was a good ground for negotiating with the bidders, especially since *all* of the bidders were given an equal opportunity to revise their bids during negotiations. Although the Court held that the legitimate expectation would be defeated in this case, the case seemed to set up a fairly robust public interest test.[43] The Supreme Court's answer to the question of 'who decides' what is in the public interest seemed to be: the authority, but subject to intrusive review by the courts. Deciding what is in the public interest is far from straightforward. Many factors apart from price could have been taken into account, not least FCI's commercial standing and its willingness to honour contractual promises.

Subsequent Supreme Court decisions seemed to apply a less exacting public interest requirement. One of these involved a claim for the allotment of land in order to relocate two petrol stations that would have been rendered commercially unviable by proposed road works.[44] The claimant argued, on the basis of representations made by the developmental authority, that it had a legitimate expectation to the allotment of land. Rejecting the claim, the Court held that legitimate expectations would have 'no role to play' where the state action was in the public interest unless the action amounted to an abuse of power.[45] The Court was reluctant to 'usurp the discretion of the public authority' and would leave the decision-making authority with the full range of choices left to it by the legislature.[46] This offered a different answer to the question of 'who decides'—one that moved away from *Coughlan* and closer to *Quin*.

[41] *Food Corporation of India* (n 11) [8].
[42] *Food Corporation of India* (n 11) [10].
[43] The Court also mentioned in passing that a 'bona fide decision of the public authority' taken in the public interest would satisfy constitutional requirements (*Food Corporation of India* (n 11) [8]). The 'bona fide' requirement is discussed later in the section.
[44] *Sethi Auto Service* (n 5).
[45] *Sethi Auto Service* (n 5) [27].
[46] *Sethi Auto Service* (n 5) [27].

A similarly low public interest threshold was applied in a 2012 case involving a legitimate expectation to a mining lease on the basis of a memorandum of understanding signed by the Government.[47] The Court held that when a decision was grounded in public interest, it would be reluctant to interfere with it by applying the doctrine of legitimate expectations. The doctrine could not be relied upon to 'fetter changes in administrative policy' and personal benefit would have to 'give way to public interest'.[48]

In many cases, the Court has combined the public interest requirement with a 'good faith' argument for dislodging legitimate expectations. In *PTR Exports*,[49] textile exporters argued that a change in government policy resulting in a denial of existing export subsidies breached their substantive legitimate expectations. Rejecting the claim, the Court held that the executive would be left with its full range of choices when making economic policy. The executive was in a better position to understand the diverse considerations in play, and substantive legitimate expectations could not be successfully invoked unless:

> the refusal [of subsidies] is mala fide or is an abuse of power in which event it is for the applicant to plead and prove to the satisfaction of the Court that the refusal was vitiated by the above factors.[50]

The Supreme Court reiterated the good faith requirement in another case, in which parties who were ineligible to sit for an examination claimed a legitimate expectation to do so based on past practice.[51] The Court held that the legitimate expectation would fail because there could be no embargo on the Board of Examiners 'bonafidely' [sic] changing its procedures and that no allegation of bad faith was made in the petition.[52]

Many judgments have adopted the strategy of applying public interest and good faith as disjunctive requirements, with proof of either defeating a substantive legitimate expectations claim. A good example can be observed in a 2006 case,[53] in which the claimants were employees of an organisation that had been licensed to distribute electricity, whose work was being transferred to a state Electricity Board. The employees claimed a legitimate expectation to be employed by the Board, based on the recommendation of a committee appointed by the state Government.

The Court rejected the claim, for the reason that the state Government had specifically considered (and rejected) the recommendation of the committee

[47] *Monnet Ispat* (n 6).
[48] *Monnet Ispat* (n 6) [153].
[49] *PTR Exports v Union of India* AIR 1996 SC 3461.
[50] Ibid, [4].
[51] *Ramamurthy* (n 36).
[52] *Ramamurthy* (n 36) [6]–[7].
[53] *Ram Pravesh* (n 38).

and that the board had never taken on the employees of private licensees in the past. A legitimate expectation based on established practice was also not established, because the employees had no previous dealings with the Electricity Board. While discussing the circumstances in which substantive legitimate expectations can be dislodged, the Court said:

> A legitimate expectation, even when made out, does not always entitle the expectant to a relief. Public interest, change in policy, conduct of the expectant or any other valid or bona fide reason given by the decision-maker, may be sufficient to negative the 'legitimate expectation' (emphasis added).[54]

This judgment set a low-water mark for dislodging substantive legitimate expectations, not only suggesting that public interest and good faith were disjunctive requirements, but that any other 'valid reason' offered by the decision-maker would suffice.[55] Putatively, this means that decisions taken in bad faith but in the public interest, or good faith decisions that are either neutral as to the public interest or even detrimental to the public interest, would dislodge substantive legitimate expectation claims. Taken individually, public interest and good faith, as the Court has interpreted them, are easy to establish. Taken together as disjunctive grounds, state authorities would find it difficult *not to satisfy* one of them.

STANDARDS OF REVIEW

Once a state authority has put forward a ground for dislodging a substantive legitimate expectation, the next (and often decisive) question becomes what standards of review the court should apply in determining whether the authority has successfully established its claim. *Punjab Communications*[56] is the leading authority on this question. The claim stemmed from a government tender notification for a project aimed at establishing digital wireless telecommunications facilities in an identified set of villages. The original notification was abandoned in favour of a notification for setting up these facilities across the country more broadly, instead of targeting the identified set of villages. The claimant argued that it had a substantive legitimate expectation for the original tender notification to be processed.

The Supreme Court accepted the Government's public interest considerations for changing the policy, which recognised the fact that other regions were in greater need of telecommunications facilities than the set of villages originally identified. The case was decided just over two months before

[54] *Ram Pravesh* (n 38) [14].
[55] See also *Union Territory of Chandigarh v Dilbagh Singh* AIR 1993 SC 796 [12].
[56] *Punjab Communications* (n 3).

Coughlan changed the landscape of substantive legitimate expectations in the UK. The Court, therefore, cited *Hargreaves*[57] as the leading authority from the Commonwealth on the questions that arose in the case. There are two possible ways of interpreting *Hargreaves*:[58] the first places the judgment in ideological opposition to the doctrine of substantive legitimate expectations; and the second is that, while no substantive legitimate expectation was held to exist on the facts of the case, if it had, a change of policy based on public interest would have been subjected to *Wednesbury* unreasonableness review.[59]

The Indian Supreme Court adopted the second reading of the case, arguing that the doctrine of substantive legitimate expectations was well recognised, but that public interests seeking to dislodge such expectations would be tested for irrationality or perversity 'according to *Wednesbury* principles'.[60] The Court specifically considered, and rejected, the idea of applying proportionality review in such cases:

> The more important aspect [of the case], in our opinion, is whether the decision maker can sustain the change in policy by resort to *Wednesbury* principles of rationality or whether the Court can go into the question whether decision maker has properly balanced the legitimate expectation as against the need for a change? … the choice of the policy is for the decision-maker and not for the Court, the legitimate substantive expectation merely permits the Court to find out if the change in policy, which is the cause for defeating the legitimate expectation is irrational or perverse or one which no reasonable person could have made.[61]

Although a sizeable body of domestic jurisprudence on substantive legitimate expectations had already developed by then, the Court's judgment relied heavily on the England and Wales Court of Appeal's inclination towards applying *Wednesbury* unreasonableness in *Hargreaves*[62] and *Unilever*.[63] As we shall see, *Punjab Communications* was closely followed in subsequent judgments, despite contrasting developments in the UK. One might speculate about what would have happened had *Punjab Communications* been decided shortly after *Coughlan*,[64] in which the Court was critical of applying unreasonableness review in substantive legitimate expectation cases.

It is fairly well established that there are multiple forms of unreasonableness review or that such review can be undertaken with different levels

[57] *R v Secretary of State for the Home Department; ex parte Hargreaves* [1997] 1 WLR 906.
[58] Paul Craig, *Administrative Law*, 7th edn (Sweet & Maxwell, 2012) 684.
[59] *Associated Provincial Picture Houses Ltd v Wednesbury Corporation* [1948] 1 KB 223.
[60] *Punjab Communications* (n 3) [44].
[61] *Punjab Communications* (n 3) [38], [40].
[62] *Hargreaves* (n 57).
[63] *R v Inland Revenue Commissioners; ex parte Unilever* [1996] STC 681.
[64] *Coughlan* (n 26).

of intensity.[65] The Supreme Court has on some occasions applied more anxious forms of scrutiny than traditional *Wednesbury* unreasonableness.[66] In *Punjab Communications*, however, the Court signaled that a highly deferential standard of unreasonableness would apply in substantive legitimate expectation cases. It observed that interference with the decision of a state authority would only be justified if the Court is satisfied that it was 'irrational or perverse'.[67]

The *Punjab Communications* dictum has often been dutifully followed in subsequent cases. In *International Trading Co*,[68] operators of foreign fishing vessels challenged the Government's refusal to renew their licenses. The Court engaged in a detailed analysis of the standards of review applied to public interest considerations in legitimate expectation cases. Citing *Punjab Communications*, it held that a light-touch unreasonableness standard would be applied in such cases. This would be a 'difficult onus for an applicant to discharge' and meant that 'something overwhelming' was required in order for the Court to intervene.[69] This description calls to mind the quixotic kind of examples that are often associated with unreasonableness review: the teacher who is dismissed for the colour of her hair;[70] or the employee who is dismissed because his name begins with 'C'.

The Court offered two rationales for its decision to apply 'pure' *Wednesbury* unreasonableness in legitimate expectation cases. First, the executive had to be offered maximum room for maneuver in devising policy.[71] The Court was conscious that substantive legitimate expectation cases in which a stricter level of review is applied have the potential of closing off all but one of the options available to the Government.[72] Second, the Court was not institutionally competent at formulating policy, and should therefore leave the task to the executive.[73]

International Trading Co conceived of the public interest in an absolute (rather than a marginal) sense, with the Court holding that a restriction would not be unreasonable merely because it operated 'harshly' in a given

[65] Michael Taggart, 'Proportionality, Deference, *Wednesbury*' [2008] *New Zealand Law Review* 423; cf Mark Aronson, 'Should We Have a Variable Error of Law Standard?' in Hanna Wilberg and Mark Elliott (eds), *The Scope and Intensity of Substantive Review: Traversing Taggart's Rainbow* (Hart Publishing, 2015), 241.

[66] Tarunabh Khaitan, 'Beyond Reasonableness—A Rigorous Standard of Review for Article 15 Infringement' (2008) 50 *Journal of the Indian Law Institute* 177.

[67] *Punjab Communications* (n 3) [40].

[68] *Union of India v International Trading Co* AIR 2003 SC 3983.

[69] ibid [18].

[70] *Short v Poole Corporation* [1926] Ch 66, 91.

[71] On which, see Jason NE Varuhas, 'In Search of a Doctrine: Mapping the Law of Legitimate Expectations' in chapter 2 of this volume.

[72] See Mark Elliott, 'From Heresy to Orthodoxy: Substantive Legitimate Expectations in English Public Law' in chapter 10 of this volume.

[73] *International Trading Co* (n 68) [18].

case, especially when the interests of the country, or the business of the economy, were involved.[74] This method of framing the public interest test makes it almost impossible to defeat any asserted public interest. It is hard to imagine, for instance, the Court accepting the claim of a private licensee in the face of considerations of 'national security',[75] 'economic prosperity', 'social welfare' and the like.

When state authorities assert a public interest, the Supreme Court quite frequently accepts the assertion at face value without explicitly engaging in any review whatsoever, not even based on the *Wednesbury* standard.[76] For example, in one case,[77] a company claimed substantive enforcement of its legitimate expectation to add three extra floors to its building, based on representations made by the Government. Echoing the conception of a public interest as an absolute notion, the Court accepted the Government's argument that when it came to permission for the construction of buildings, public interest and convenience would trump private interests.

This was even clearer in a 2004 case in which the claimants argued that they had a legitimate expectation to land mistakenly allotted to them although reserved for certain purposes.[78] The Court held that legitimate expectations would be defeated in the face of countervailing public interests, without considering what standard of review would be applied to that interest. Citing the Latin maxim *salus populi est suprema lex* ('the welfare of the people is the highest law'), the Court held that all members of society impliedly agreed to the subordination of their individual welfare in favour of the welfare of the community. The Court's analysis raises more questions than it answers. For instance, even going by the Court's social contract theory, not every asserted public interest would be sufficiently strong to defeat a legitimate expectation. The judgment is silent on the method of determining *specifically which* asserted public interests the state can raise in order to dislodge legitimate expectations, and whether the social contract theory rests on the Government or the courts determining what the welfare of the people entails.[79]

[74] *International Trading Co* (n 68) [24]. For the difference between absolute and marginal approaches, see Aharon Barak, *Proportionality: Constitutional Rights and their Limitations* (Cambridge University Press, 2012) 350.

[75] See eg the fact that 'national security' was enough to trump a procedurally unfair exercise of prerogative power in *Council of Civil Service Unions v Minister for the Civil Service* [1985] 1 AC 374.

[76] It is a separate question, of course, whether there is any qualitative difference between cases where it does explicitly engage in *Wednesbury* review and where it doesn't. The Court's failure to explicitly engage in *Wednesbury* review in these cases may offer further evidence of how deferential the standard of review is in practice.

[77] *Howrah Municipal Corp v Ganges Rope Co* (2004) 1 SCC 663.

[78] *Hira Tikkoo v Union Territory of Chandigarh* AIR 2004 SC 3648.

[79] See also *Madras City Wine Merchants v State of Tamil Nadu* MANU/SC/0815/1994 [61] (observing that 'no question' of legitimate expectations arose where a change in policy was

While proportionality review is dominating the dockets of courts around the world,[80] it has not yet found much traction in the Indian Supreme Court's case law on substantive legitimate expectations. In fact, as I noted earlier, proportionality review was specifically rejected by the Supreme Court in *Punjab Communications*. In the UK, the decisive move towards proportionality review in legitimate expectation cases took place in *Nadarajah*,[81] in which Laws LJ held that a public body's promise or practice as to future conduct could only be departed from where to do so was: (a) the public body's legal duty or (b) a proportionate response having regard to a legitimate aim pursued by the public body in the public interest.[82] Somewhat surprisingly, the Indian Supreme Court has never cited *Nadarajah* in any context.[83] One cannot be sure about whether this is because counsel have seldom cited the case, or whether the Court has simply not been receptive to the decision when it was cited.[84]

However, there have been two cases in which the Supreme Court has foreshadowed a possible move towards proportionality review in substantive legitimate expectation cases. In one case, the Court recognised that although the traditional approach in legitimate expectations cases was to apply *Wednesbury* review, the European Court of Human Rights had prompted British courts to move towards the 'doctrine of balancing' (a popular, but somewhat misleading, synonym for proportionality review) in cases under the *Human Rights Act 1998* (UK).[85]

In the second case,[86] candidates who had been selected for the civil services (and were not eventually appointed) claimed a substantive legitimate expectation to be appointed to the service. Highlighting that the Supreme Court has applied proportionality review in other contexts, the Court held that this case was not apposite for any form of review to be applied, since the candidates had failed to establish the factual basis for legitimate expectations in the first place:

> This Court not only has noticed the development of law in this field [proportionality] but applied the same also ... The fact that in some jurisdictions, doctrine

prompted by public interest considerations); *Mahudeswaran v State of Tamil Nadu* (1996) 8 SCC 617 [12].

[80] Alec Stone Sweet and Jud Mathews, 'Proportionality Balancing and Global Constitutionalism' (2008) 47 *Columbia Journal of Transnational Law* 72, 74.

[81] *R (Nadarajah) v Secretary of State for the Home Department* [2005] EWCA Civ 1363.

[82] Ibid, [68].

[83] Based on a full-text search of Supreme Court judgments on the SCC Online database as at 12 February 2016.

[84] The arguments of the parties to cases in the Indian Supreme Court are not available online. In practice, the Court sets out the arguments of the parties in its judgment, but it is difficult to know whether the Court's description is comprehensive.

[85] *Ashoka Smokeless Coal v Union of India* (2007) 2 SCC 640 [82].

[86] *Jitendra Kumar* (n 4).

> of unreasonableness is giving way to doctrine of proportionality is beyond any dispute ... But, the development of law in this field could have been applied only if a case was made out.[87]

Proponents of the doctrine of substantive legitimate expectations might conceive of these as encouraging signs. Could it be argued, for example, that while the doctrine of substantive legitimate expectations is fictitious as it stands (in the light of deferential standards of review, the ease of dislodging an expectation, as well as other factors considered earlier), a shift towards proportionality review would infuse the doctrine with some meaning? In what follows, I will argue that we should remain cautious about drawing such inferences.

Several scholars claim that the Indian Supreme Court is already applying the test of proportionality in public law adjudication.[88] At first glance, the abundance of references to proportionality review in the Supreme Court's case law seems to confirm these claims. However, a different picture emerges on examining the Supreme Court's case law more closely, namely that even when the Supreme Court has explicitly claimed to be applying the proportionality test, it has done so only in name.[89] In other words, while the Court has quite enthusiastically embraced the taxonomy of proportionality review, it continues to apply reasonableness review under the garb of proportionality.

Although there is no universal test for proportionality review, the most commonly applied version has a four-part structure:[90] (i) does the law seek to achieve a proper purpose?; (ii) is there a rational connection between the purpose of the law and the means used to achieve that purpose?; (iii) are there any less restrictive, but equally effective, means available to achieve the purpose of the law?; and (iv) is the law proportional *stricto sensu*, or does it adequately balance social benefits and harms?

In *Om Kumar*,[91] a case concerning whether punishments imposed by disciplinary authorities could be reconsidered, the Supreme Court engaged in a lengthy discussion on proportionality review, concluding that it is frequently applied both to legislation and administrative action.[92] However, it is interesting to note the Court's understanding of proportionality:

> By 'proportionality', we mean the question whether, while regulating exercise of fundamental rights, the appropriate or least restrictive choice of measures has

[87] *Jitendra Kumar* (n 4) [17], [42].

[88] David Beatty, *The Ultimate Rule of Law* (Oxford University Press, 2004) 163; MP Jain, *Indian Constitutional Law*, 5th edn (Wadhwa 2008) 983; Barak (n 74) 200–01.

[89] For a fuller argument, see Chintan Chandrachud, 'Proportionality, Judicial Reasoning and the Indian Supreme Court' (2016) *Anti-Discrimination Law Review* (forthcoming).

[90] Stone Sweet and Mathews (n 80) 75.

[91] *Om Kumar v Union of India* AIR 2000 SC 3689.

[92] Ibid, [27]–[72].

> been made by the legislature or the administrator so as to achieve the object of the legislation or the purpose of the administrative order, as the case may be. Under the principle, the Court will see that the legislature and the administrative authority 'maintain a proper balance between the adverse effects which the legislation or the administrative order may have on the rights, liberties or interests of persons keeping in mind the purpose which they were intended to serve'.[93]

This passage expounds upon the Court's restrictive understanding of proportionality review, which was limited to components (iii) and (iv), ie necessity and balancing. It turns out, therefore, that the Court did apply some components of the proportionality analysis under reasonableness review, although this does not seem to be the case in substantive legitimate expectation cases. There is a difference between applying each of the four components of the proportionality test in all cases, and applying only some components of the test in some cases.[94] In fact, the conflation of proportionality review with one of its components is not a mistake that is unique to the Indian Supreme Court.[95] The confusion, to some extent, stems from the fact that the fourth component of the proportionality structure above is itself referred to as proportionality, albeit distinguished from the structure as a whole by being described as proportionality *stricto sensu* or 'in the narrow sense'.

The even more skeptical reading of *Om Kumar* is that although the Court referred to proportionality review, by inquiring into whether the punishments were 'shockingly disproportionate', the Court applied *Wednesbury* reasonableness in disguise.[96] This formulation was followed in subsequent cases. For instance, the question before the Court in a 2007 case[97] was whether a penalty imposed on employees of a public sector bank for going on strike was justified. Applying its version of the 'proportionality' test, the Court held that it would reconsider the punishment only if it was 'grossly excessive, disproportionately high or unduly harsh'.[98] Thus, while the Court has embraced the *language* of proportionality review in many such rights cases, in *substantive* terms, it has continued to apply *Wednesbury*-style light

[93] Ibid, [28].

[94] Chandrachud (n 89).

[95] See Madhav Khosla, 'Proportionality: An Assault on Human Rights?: A Reply' (2010) 8 *International Journal of Constitutional Law* 298, 305 (explaining how some scholars limit proportionality to balancing). See also Vicki Jackson, 'Constitutional Law in an Age of Proportionality' (2015) 124 *Harvard Law Review* 3094, 3157 ('"proportionality as such" is the last in a sequence of inquiries and therefore is part of a more structured decisional process than "all things considered" balancing').

[96] Abhinav Chandrachud, '*Wednesbury* Reformulated: Proportionality and the Supreme Court of India' (2013) 13 *Oxford University Commonwealth Law Journal* 191.

[97] *Management of Coimbatore District Central Co-operative Bank v Secretary, Coimbatore District Central Co-operative Bank Employees Association* (2007) 4 SCC 669.

[98] Ibid, [15].

touch review.[99] This means that shifting from *Wednesbury* review to proportionality review in substantive legitimate expectations cases, as some Supreme Court cases have predicted, is unlikely to transform the fiction of substantive legitimate expectations into fact.

This discussion also gives us occasion to think more deeply about the trajectory of the doctrine of substantive legitimate expectations in India. As with proportionality review, why is it that the Court has embraced the language of substantive legitimate expectations without its substance? There are two explanations. The first is that, while the Court is conscious of establishing itself as a 'progressive' player in the global marketplace of rights adjudication,[100] it is genuinely skeptical about the idea of protecting substantive legitimate expectations. It is hardly self-evident that protecting substantive legitimate expectations forms an essential ingredient of promoting the rule of law.[101] Further, as the Court has itself noted on many occasions, recognising substantive legitimate expectations can involve major collateral costs. It was this kind of rationale that prompted the Supreme Court, in *Umadevi*, to entirely exclude the application of the doctrine in employment cases.

The more benign explanation is that having been trained in the British tradition which was antithetical to a review of executive policy or practice on the merits, the judges are still influenced by some of the pre-*Coughlan* cases which declined to enforce legitimate expectations in substance, as opposed to procedurally. This explanation fits well with the Court's frequent citation of *Quin*, which (probably aside from *Lam*)[102] is often looked upon as *Coughlan's* bête noire in the legitimate expectations world. There is certainly some truth to both explanations, although one would imagine that the first explanation would retain a more long-term influence than the second. Under the second explanation, the doctrine might change with the arrival of a new generation of judges who may be more receptive to cases such as *Coughlan*,[103] *Bibi*[104] and *Nadarajah*.[105]

[99] Chandrachud (n 96).

[100] See Nuno Garoupa and Tom Ginsburg, *Judicial Reputation: A Comparative Theory* (University of Chicago Press, 2015) 171.

[101] Matthew Groves, 'Substantive Legitimate Expectations in Australian Administrative Law' (2008) 32 *Melbourne University Law Review* 470, 506–11.

[102] *Re Minister for Immigration and Multicultural and Indigenous Affairs; ex parte Lam* (2003) 214 CLR 1 (2003) 214 CLR 1.

[103] *Coughlan* (n 26).

[104] *R (Bibi) v Newham London Borough Council* [2002] 1 WLR 237. This explanation would imply that there is a doctrinal 'lag effect' in operation.

[105] *Nadarajah* (n 81).

THE FAILURE OF SUBSTANTIVE LEGITIMATE EXPECTATIONS CLAIMS IN PRACTICE

Thus far, I have argued that the proverbial rules of the game have been designed and developed in a way that makes it extremely difficult for substantive legitimate expectations claims to succeed. The analysis would remain incomplete, however, without examining whether these rules have actually closed the door to legitimate expectations claims in practice. If claimants were routinely, or for that matter even occasionally, securing judgments enforcing their substantive legitimate expectations, it would be an overstatement to describe the doctrine as fictitious.

Of the 34 Supreme Court cases in which substantive legitimate expectations were discussed in any detail decided between 1992 and 2012 that I examined,[106] the Court did not substantively enforce a legitimate expectation in a single case. This conclusion is uncontestable in many of the cases, where the Court rejected the claim outright. Other cases turned out on closer examination not to be substantive legitimate expectation cases at all.

[106] *Srinivasa Theatre* (n 37) (no substantive legitimate expectation); *Navjyoti Housing Society v Union of India* AIR 1993 SC 155 (procedural protection of substantive legitimate expectation); *Food Corporation of India* (n 11) (no substantive legitimate expectation); *Union Territory of Chandigarh* (n 55) (no substantive legitimate expectation); *Hindustan Development Corporation* (n 12) (no substantive legitimate expectation); *Madras City Wine Merchants* (n 79) (no substantive legitimate expectation); *Assistant Excise Commissioner v Issac Peter* (1994) 4 SCC 104 (no substantive legitimate expectation); *PTR Exports* (n 49) (no substantive legitimate expectation); *Mahudeswaran* (n 79) (no substantive legitimate expectation); *Raghunathan* (n 2) (no substantive legitimate expectation); *MP Oil Extraction v State of Madhya Pradesh* AIR 1998 SC 145 (substantive legitimate expectations used as a shield); *Punjab Communications* (n 3) (no substantive legitimate expectation); *State of West Bengal* (n 11) (no substantive legitimate expectation); *International Trading Co* (n 68) (no substantive legitimate expectation); *JP Bansal v State of Rajasthan* AIR 2003 SC 1405 (no substantive legitimate expectation); *Chanchal Goyal* (n 27) (no substantive legitimate expectation); *Howrah Municipal Corporation* (n 77) (no substantive legitimate expectation); *Hira Tikkoo* (n 78) (no substantive legitimate expectation); *Bannari Amman Sugars* (n 17) (no final opinion expressed); *Umadevi* (n 28) (no substantive legitimate expectation); *Ram Pravesh* (n 38) (no substantive legitimate expectation); *Ramamurthy* (n 36) (no substantive legitimate expectation); *Kuldeep Singh* (n 27) (no substantive legitimate expectation); *Confederation of Ex Servicemen v Union of India* AIR 2006 SC 2945 (no substantive legitimate expectation); *Ashoka Smokeless Coal* (n 83) (no final opinion expressed); *Southern Petrochemical v Electricity Inspector* AIR 2007 SC 1984 (substantive legitimate expectation as a means of subsidiary support for the decision); *UP Gram Panchayat* (n 32) (no substantive legitimate expectation); *Jitendra Kumar* (n 4) (no substantive legitimate expectation); *Dayanand* (n 5) (no substantive legitimate expectation); *Sethi Auto Service* (n 5) (no substantive legitimate expectation); *CSIR v Ramesh Agarwal* (n 19) (no substantive legitimate expectation); *Global Energy v CERC* AIR 2009 SC 3194 (procedural legitimate expectation recognised); *State of Haryana v Jagdish* AIR 2010 SC 1690 (substantive legitimate expectation as a means of subsidiary support for the decision); *Monnet Ispat* (n 6) (no substantive legitimate expectation).

Let us consider some examples, beginning with the most difficult case. *Navjyoti Housing Society*[107] was one of the early cases to consider the doctrine of substantive legitimate expectations at some length. The case involved a claim by housing societies that a change in policy for the allotment of land violated their right to priority over the land. The High Court set aside the new policy, and ordered the allotment of land based on the old one. This decision was later affirmed by the Supreme Court.

Initially, *Navjyoti Housing Society* looks like a straightforward case of the enforcement of a substantive legitimate expectation but it was in fact a case involving the *procedural* protection of legitimate expectations. The Supreme Court's judgment consistently emphasises that the authority should have offered the societies an opportunity to be heard before defeating their legitimate expectations:

> In the aforesaid facts, the Group Housing Societies were entitled to 'legitimate expectation' of following consistent past practice in the matter of allotment, even though they may not have any legal right in private law to receive such treatment. The existence of 'legitimate expectation' may have a number of different consequences and one of such consequences is that the authority ought not to act to defeat the 'legitimate expectation' without some overriding reason of public policy to justify its doing so. *In a case of 'legitimate expectation' if the authority proposes to defeat a person's 'legitimate expectation' it should afford him an opportunity to make representations in the matter* (emphasis added).[108]

The Court also explained that it was 'only desirable' for the state authority to inform the society of proposed changes by way of public notice, and give them an opportunity to be heard.[109] Therefore, the breach was not occasioned by the denial of the substantive right, but by the failure to give the claimants a fair hearing.

In *MP Oil Extraction*,[110] the state Government of Madhya Pradesh had entered into agreements with two companies for the sale of 'sal' seeds. Two other companies challenged the validity of these agreements on the basis of hostile discrimination. The Court relied on the substantive legitimate expectations of the companies that were parties to the agreement while upholding the state Government's decision to enter into the agreement.[111] In this case, since the Government complied with the promise given to the companies and *third party companies* challenged the decision, substantive legitimate expectations were relied upon as a shield rather than a sword. This is unexceptionable, since many of the concerns punctuating the doctrine

[107] *Navjyoti Housing Society* (n 106).
[108] *Navjyoti Housing Society* (n 106) [15].
[109] *Navjyoti Housing Society* (n 106) [16].
[110] *MP Oil Extraction* (n 106).
[111] *MP Oil Extraction* (n 106) [44].

(such as the lack of institutional competence and judicial interference in policy-making) only apply to the reliance on substantive legitimate expectations as a sword, rather than a shield.

In another case,[112] a claimant who was exempted by statute from the payment of electricity consumption tax, argued that the exemption should continue to apply after a change of statute. The Court enthusiastically observed that the doctrine of substantive legitimate expectations applied to the case. However, it went on to explain that the new statute itself contained a 'savings' clause entitling the claimant to continue to benefit from the exemption. The legislature, therefore, had 'acknowledged that right to be existing in the appellants'.[113] This decision is therefore best classified as a straightforward case of illegality, where the Government denied the claimant its statutory entitlement.

To take a final example, in *Jagdish*[114] the question was whether a prisoner fell within the ambit of a remission policy applicable on the date of his conviction, or the policy applicable on the date of consideration of his case for premature release. The prisoner sought the benefit of the policy on the date of his conviction. Although the Court mentioned, in passing, that the prisoner had a substantive legitimate expectation to the benefit of the old policy,[115] its decision rested on the fact that the old policy was made in exercise of the powers conferred by the Constitution. Thus, it would trump the later policy, which was made pursuant to ordinary legislation. Substantive legitimate expectations were not, therefore, necessary for the Court's decision and at best, formed a means of subsidiary support for the decision.

All of these cases suggest that the common law developed by the courts has produced exactly the effect that we might have predicted—marginalising the role of substantive legitimate expectations into irrelevance. Even in cases where the Court has drawn upon substantive legitimate expectations, it has done so only as a means of subsidiary support for claims based on surer grounds.

CONCLUSION

Although the Supreme Court has frequently declared that the doctrine of substantive legitimate expectations is formally part of the law, a closer

112 *Southern Petrochemical Industries* (n 106).
113 *Southern Petrochemical Industries* (n 106) [145].
114 *Jagdish* (n 106).
115 *Jagdish* (n 106) [41].

examination of the Court's case law suggests that the doctrine is fictitious.[116] The common law rules concerning substantive legitimate expectations have emerged, and evolved, in a way that makes it increasingly difficult for claims to succeed. From the very beginning, the Court has been loath to recognise the emergence of a jurisdiction to enforce the legitimate expectation of a substantive right or interest. The doctrine has been categorically rejected in public employment cases.

Substantive legitimate expectations can be dislodged by establishing 'public interest' or 'good faith' requirements that have, in practice, been fairly easy to satisfy. The grounds for dislodging expectations are tested on *Wednesbury* unreasonableness standards, although a formal shift to proportionality is unlikely to dramatically alter the landscape. The numbers confirm what the doctrine insinuates: it is remarkably difficult to find any cases in which substantive legitimate expectations have been successfully vindicated in the Supreme Court.

The Court's typical response is well captured by a 2006 case in which retired military servicemen and their families claimed a substantive legitimate expectation to medical benefits.[117] Acknowledging that the doctrine had an 'important place' in the law relating to judicial review, the Court said that it was 'not impressed by the argument'.[118] The fictitious existence of the doctrine of substantive legitimate expectations continues.

[116] This chapter has focused on the protection of substantive legitimate expectations in the Indian Supreme Court. Although the Supreme Court is not the primary site for the protection of substantive legitimate expectations, it is certainly the most important one.

[117] *Confederation of Ex Servicemen* (n 106).

[118] *Confederation of Ex Servicemen* (n 106) [21].

12

Contrasting Responses to the 'Coughlan *Moment': Legitimate Expectations in Hong Kong and Singapore*

SWATI JHAVERI

INTRODUCTION

THE DOCTRINE OF procedural legitimate expectations has long been a part of the jurisprudence in both Hong Kong and Singapore, but it is only relatively recently that either has had to contend with the issue of substantive legitimate expectations. This push to recognise substantive legitimate expectations follows the prompt to do so from landmark cases like *R v North and East Devon Health Authority; ex parte Coughlan*[1] in the English context. Although *Coughlan* was a significant motivator for the developments in Singapore and Hong Kong, the law has evolved differently. In Hong Kong, legitimate expectations are generally enforced either as a relevant consideration, or protected only at the procedural level. In Singapore, the High Court has recently suggested that the time may be approaching to recognise legitimate expectations substantively and in a much more far reaching way than in the post-*Coughlan* era in England.[2] This chapter examines how the courts of Singapore and Hong Kong have each adopted their own approach to recognising substantive legitimate expectations, both of which are at odds with both *Coughlan* and the post-*Coughlan* development of the law in England. This chapter considers the '*Coughlan*' moment, the inception point of the contemporary doctrine of substantive legitimate expectations, in both jurisdictions and the contemporary

[1] *R v North and East Devon Health Authority; ex parte Coughlan* [2001] QB 213.

[2] Embodied in *R v Education Secretary; ex parte Begbie* [2000] 1 WLR 1115; *R v London Borough Council of Newham; ex parte Bibi and Al-Nashed* [2001] EWCA Civ 607; and *R (Nadarajah) v Secretary of State for the Home Department* [2005] EWCA Civ 1363.

trajectory of the law on substantive legitimate expectations in each jurisdiction. It will examine how the two jurisdictions have dealt with the typical questions relating to the various parts of the 'anatomy' of a substantive legitimate expectation. In discussing the many internal features of the doctrine, this chapter will highlight the ways in which both jurisdictions have departed from *Coughlan* on most of these questions. It will then discuss issues that will need to be resolved on these aspects of substantive legitimate expectations in both jurisdictions.

THE '*COUGHLAN* MOMENT': HONG KONG

Prior to *Ng Siu Tung v Director of Immigration*,[3] the leading case on substantive legitimate expectations in Hong Kong, the focus of legitimate expectation cases had been mainly the assertion and enforcement of procedural rights. Alternatively, in cases dealing with substantive legitimate expectations, the courts did not extensively discuss the contours of the doctrine as it was to be applied in Hong Kong. Accordingly, the Court of Final Appeal in *Ng Siu Tung* was able to craft the doctrine in Hong Kong relatively free from precedent-based encumbrances, by looking at the trajectory of the law and the related academic discussion in the United Kingdom. In contrast with Singapore, it did not look further afield to other jurisdictions.

The case concerned the complex right of abode issue in Hong Kong. On 1 July 1997, the Basic Law (the mini-constitution of Hong Kong), came into effect. Article 24(2)(3) granted permanent resident status and the right of abode to Chinese nationals born outside of Hong Kong to permanent residents of Hong Kong who were also Chinese nationals. On the same day, the Government introduced legislation in the form of the *Immigration (Amendment) No 2 Ordinance (No 122 of 1997)* to clarify that Article 24(2)(3) was limited to those who were born after at least one of their parents had already obtained status as a Hong Kong permanent resident. The idea was to clarify that it excluded those children born to Chinese citizens at a time when they had not yet obtained the permanent resident status which they later obtained. Additional amending legislation, which applied retrospectively, introduced a scheme for the verification of claims for permanent residence under Art 24 of the Basic Law,[4] including a requirement for the applicant to hold a particular permit.[5]

A number of Mainland-born children sought to challenge the constitutionality of both Amendment Ordinances. As there was a large number

[3] *Ng Siu Tung v Director of Immigration* (2002) 5 HKCFAR 1.
[4] *Immigration (Amendment) (No 3) Ordinance (No 124 of 1997).*
[5] Art 22(4).

of applicants (approximately 5000, all of whom applied for legal aid), a group of applicants were chosen as informal 'test cases'.[6] The Court of Final Appeal held both Ordinances were unconstitutional for contravening Article 24 of the Basic Law.[7] Following these judgments, in a constitutionally controversial move,[8] the Standing Committee of the National People's Congress (NPCSC) issued an 'interpretation' of Article 24 of the Basic Law which had the effect of reversing the Court's judgments.[9] The NPCSC's interpretation was expressed so as not to affect those who had obtained right of abode under the judgments of the Court of Final Appeal in relevant cases. The Government of the Hong Kong SAR then also announced that it would allow persons who had arrived in Hong Kong between 1 July 1997 and the date of the judgments in the Court of Final Appeal cases and who had claimed right of abode to have their status as permanent residents resolved in accordance with the judgments in those cases (the 'Concession Policy'). The Government sought to depart from the Concession Policy, either by issuing or refusing to revoke existing removal orders. A preliminary issue in challenging this was determining who had the benefit of the judgments and could avail themselves of the Concession Policy. This involved a diverse group from within the original 5000 cases who had varying degrees of connection to the various executive actions and legislative documents in play. While these applicants did not formally join in the proceedings, they wanted to be treated the same as those who had, in line with the Concession Policy. More important, for present purposes, was the issue of whether and how far the Concession Policy bound the Government and how far the legitimate expectations of those concerned prevented the Government from departing from the Concession Policy.

The applicants raised several arguments in support of a legitimate expectation that they would be treated the same as the litigants in the relevant Court of Final Appeal cases. First, the Government had made general public statements before, during and after the litigation to the effect that it would comply with any judicial ruling, would not seek an interpretation from the NPCSC and did not consider it necessary for each and every legally aided person to commence proceedings and incur costs beyond the

[6] Since there is no formal mechanism for litigation test cases in Hong Kong, no formal orders were made.

[7] *Ng Ka Ling v Director of Immigration* (1999) 2 HKCFAR 4 (in the case of Ordinance No 2) and *Chan Kam Nga v Director of Immigration* (1999) 2 HKCFAR 82 (in the case of Ordinance No 3).

[8] See MM Chan, HL Fu and Y Ghai (eds), *Hong Kong's Constitutional Debate: Conflict Over Interpretation* (Hong Kong University Press, 2000).

[9] The Court of Final Appeal later held that the NPCSC's interpretation was a valid and binding interpretation of Articles 22(4) and 24(2)(3) of the Basic Law and that it bound HKSAR courts: *Lau Kong Yung v Director of Immigration* (1999) 2 HKCFAR 300.

representative cases. Second, representations were made to individual applicants by the Legal Aid Department and the Department of Immigration. For example, the Legal Aid Department wrote letters to individual applicants for legal aid informing them that they did not need to commence proceedings and the Immigration Department, in responding to inquiries on right of abode, responded that litigation was ongoing and applications cannot be processed, which the applicants took to mean that they did not need to take any steps to lodge a claim until the court case had been finally determined. The applicants argued that this induced them not to take the action (by commencing proceedings) which would have provided them with protection under Article 158(3), whereby an interpretation of the NPCSC does not affect judgments previously rendered. Third, statements and conduct of judges and counsel during the course of litigation in the two cases reflected the fact that everyone treated those cases as test cases, representative of parties not formally joined. The applicants said that this engendered the expectation that they would receive the same treatment as the parties in the two cases.

The Court of Final Appeal first needed to determine whether review was possible on the basis of the doctrine of substantive legitimate expectations and, if so, the parameters for such review. It held that the doctrine was part of administrative law in Hong Kong (seemingly on the basis that the doctrine as espoused in *Coughlan* was not disputed, even if it had not yet been expressly affirmed by the House of Lords).[10] The Court understood the doctrine as:

> recognis[ing] that, in the absence of any overriding reason of law or policy excluding its operation, situations may arise in which persons may have a legitimate expectation of a substantive outcome or benefit, in which event failing to honour the expectation may, in particular circumstances, result in such unfairness to individuals as to amount to an abuse of power justifying intervention by the court. Generally speaking, a legitimate expectation arises as a result of a promise, representation, practice or policy made, adopted or announced by or on behalf of government or a public authority.[11]

However, the Court of Final Appeal put its own gloss on the doctrine as it would apply in Hong Kong, making the central point that, while the adoption of an alternative policy does not absolve governments of the duty 'to take account of a legitimate expectation', governments must be free to change their policy.[12] This tweak to the original *Coughlan* formulation

[10] See now *R v Secretary of State for the Home Department; ex parte Hindley* [2001] 1 AC 410, 419, 421 (Lord Hobhouse); *R (Lumba) v Secretary of State for the Home Department* [2012] 1 AC 245, 275 (Lord Dyson); 343 (Lord Phillips).

[11] *Ng Siu Tung* (n 3) [92].

[12] *Ng Siu Tung* (n 3) [93].

was largely influenced by the Court's consideration of the post-*Coughlan* evolution of the doctrine of substantive legitimate expectations.[13] The Court noted that, *inter alia*, *Bibi* had stated as principle that, if the decision-maker fails to properly take into account an expectation, the decision can be quashed for failure to take into account relevant considerations and the court can mandate the decision-maker to exercise his discretion by taking it into account. The generally accepted[14] caveat to this principle is that the decision will only be quashed where the failure to take a legitimate expectation into account materially affected the final decision.[15] The Court of Final Appeal was comfortable with this reading of the doctrine on the basis that it better respected the doctrine of the separation of powers and accorded more with legislative intent by ultimately leaving the decision to be made by the body who was vested with the power in the first instance under legislation.[16]

The reliance on *Bibi* distinguishes the Hong Kong approach in *Ng Siu Tung* from the Singapore position. It is clear in the discussion below that, in devising the doctrine of substantive legitimate expectations in Singapore, the High Court did not consider cases like *Bibi*. It is worth nothing that in his partial dissent, Bokhary PJ was prepared to entertain the idea of the substantive enforcement of expectations,[17] for example if the Director of Immigration decided, after taking account of the legitimate expectations, to depart from them. In this scenario, a court would be free to enforce the expectation substantively. For Bokhary PJ, such a decision would depend on the applicable standard of review.[18]

The Court of Final Appeal went on to discuss particular doctrinal aspects of legitimate expectations. It specified that to be 'legitimate', an expectation would have to be reasonable in light of all the relevant conduct, to stipulate what the applicants would be entitled to expect and be based on clear and unambiguous statements. In the case of the latter, where a representation, statement or policy is capable of having competing reasonable interpretations, the court can only assess whether the interpretation adopted by the Government was reasonable to the *Wednesbury*[19] standard (the original high threshold). In this respect, the Court took the view that, with the exception of some of the general public statements by the government and

[13] Particularly *Bibi* (n 2).

[14] See M Elliott and R Thomas, *Public Law*, 2nd edn (Oxford University Press, 2014) 462–63.

[15] *Ng Siu Tung* (n 3) [98].

[16] *Ng Siu Tung* (n 3) [99].

[17] *Ng Siu Tung* (n 3) [352].

[18] See section entitled 'Standard of Review for Departures from Legitimate Expectations' below.

[19] *Associated Provincial Picture Houses Ltd v Wednesbury Corporation* [1948] 1 KB 223.

the general reply to applicants by the Immigration Department, the other statements, representations and conduct in all of the above categories were capable of giving rise to a legitimate expectation. The strongest of these were the specific representations made by departments, like the Legal Aid Department, that the applicants did not need to commence further proceedings. The Court of Final Appeal left open the question of whether or not detrimental reliance would be required for this ground of review, but did say that it may be a relevant (but still not a required) factor when considering the 'enforcement' of general versus specific representations applied to a very large, innominate class of persons. In his partial dissent, Bokhary PJ denied that detrimental reliance is generally required.[20]

The Court of Final Appeal then turned its attention to the Government's departure from the expectations. The Government's complex argument stated that immediately after the Court of Final Appeal's judgments (which had declared the various schemes unconstitutional, making them null and void), the Department of Immigration had been operating without guidelines on how to process the various applications for residency and right of abode. It therefore had to suspend the processing of applications. The Court recognised that the Director of Immigration still had the power at this point to develop a procedure that would give effect to the applicants' expectations and was not contrary to law. The Government, however, argued that this position changed once the NPCSC issued its interpretation of Articles 22(4) and 24(3)(2) of the Basic Law. That interpretation revived the previously unconstitutional schemes, thus removing the Director of Immigration's power to allow applications for residency and right of abode to applicants who did not comply with those previously unconstitutional schemes. The Government was therefore obliged by law as it stood post the NPCSC interpretation, to depart from the legitimate expectations, which were now contrary to law. As the Court of Final Appeal put it, 'there cannot be a legitimate expectation that the law will not be changed'.[21]

The applicants continued to argue that, although this may have meant that the Director of Immigration could not give full recognition to their expectations (by allowing them to remain notwithstanding they did not comply with the various Immigration Ordinances as revived by the NPCSC's interpretation), a partial recognition of the expectation remained possible. This could have been in the form of the Director's exercise of various discretions available under the Immigration Ordinance, which would have allowed them to enter and reside in Hong Kong, albeit without the same residency and right of abode status as would be applicable through a

[20] *Ng Siu Tung* (n 3) [358]–[359]
[21] *Ng Siu Tung* (n 3) [119].

'full' enforcement of the expectation. The Court of Final Appeal recognised that the partial recognition allowing one to reside is different to providing a right of abode and qualitatively reduced protection of the expectation but saw this as a necessary evil, given that a full recognition would be *ultra vires*.[22] The applicants submitted that the discretion was wide enough for the Director to consider the circumstances giving rise to the legitimate expectation. The Court of Final Appeal accepted this argument, rejecting the Government's argument that the discretion was circumscribed by the Immigration Amendment Ordinances. The Court held that in exercising this discretion, the Government was under a duty, grounded in the ideas of good administration and the duty to act fairly, to take into account legitimate expectations that arise as long as they are consistent with the statutory scheme. Accordingly, the discretion cannot be used as a backdoor for letting in applicants who failed to meet the requirements of the law, but is permissible in exceptional cases. Therefore, only those applicants who had a legitimate expectation as a result of specific representations would have been able to benefit from the discretion.

To allow all within the large group who relied on the general representations to benefit in this way would have undermined the statutory scheme of the Immigration Ordinance. The legitimate expectation of those relying on the general representations would have been protected by the requirement that they be treated even-handedly. Further, even if the Director of Immigration had considered their case in the same manner as others within that large class of persons, he would have been entitled to reach the conclusion that their expectations could have been overridden by the force of the immigration policy which forms the basis of the Immigration Ordinance. The applicants who had specific representations made to them by the Legal Aid Department were different, being a distinct class to whom direct communications were made. It is hard to imagine that recognising these claims as a matter of discretion would undermine the statutory scheme.

The final argument raised by the Government was that the decisions should not be quashed because, even after taking into account the relevant considerations, it would have reached the same decision in light of the overwhelming policy reasons in favour of rejecting the various applications. The Court rejected this in the case of the specific representations. The substantive unfairness to them in light of the specific inducement to them did not justify the holding that the Director of Immigration would have reached the same decision. Thus, the removal orders for the applicants with legitimate expectations as a result of specific representations were quashed.

[22] *Ng Siu Tung* (n 3) [143].

THE '*COUGHLAN* MOMENT': SINGAPORE

Position before *Chiu Teng*

Generally, judicial review of the substance of decisions in Singapore has developed far less expansively than in Hong Kong which, for example, has adopted varying thresholds of irrationality review and utilises proportionality review.[23] Unlike in Hong Kong, the grounds of judicial review relating to the substance of executive decisions have been fixed in Singapore for a significant period of time as illegality and irrationality. Adherence to separation of powers principles has meant that the courts have been reluctant to review the content of decisions outside of irrationality which has been used sparingly and with a high threshold for an applicant to overcome.[24] The courts have also rejected proportionality as a ground for judicial review.[25] In this way, the High Court's decision in *Chiu Teng*[26] to recognise the doctrine of substantive legitimate expectations as a separate ground of judicial review was ground-breaking. Prior to *Chiu Teng*, the courts trod carefully[27] and appeared reluctant to recognise the doctrine explicitly.

As with Hong Kong, there was little discussion of substantive legitimate expectations in Singapore prior to *Chiu Teng*. Three cases discussed (albeit not in great detail) the possibility of recognising the doctrine of substantive legitimate expectations:[28] *UDL Marine (Singapore) Pte Ltd v Jurong Town Corp*,[29] *Borissik Svetlana v Urban Redevelopment Authority*[30] and *Yong Vui Kong v AG*.[31] In *UDL*, the applicant applied for a renewal of its lease which was refused by the landlord, a public statutory board. The applicant

[23] See S Jhaveri, M Ramsden and A Scully-Hill, *Administrative Law in Hong Kong*, 2nd edn (LexisNexis, 2013) Chs 11–14.

[24] See eg *Manjit Singh s/o Kirpal Singh v AG* [2013] 4 SLR 483 [7]—'the *Wednesbury* test sets a high bar'. See also *Chee Siok Chin v Minister for Home Affairs* [2006] 1 SLR(R) 582 [125]—the standard of unreasonableness 'is from a jurisprudential perspective, pragmatically fixed at a very high level'. The threshold has been maintained at a high standard akin to the original threshold proposed in *Wednesbury* (n 19).

[25] See, for example, *Chan Hiang Leng Colin v Minister for Information and the Arts* [1996] 1 SLR (R) 294 [38]–[47] and *Chng Suan Tze v Minister of Home Affairs* [1989] MLJ 89 and [1988] 2 SLR 525, [108]–[121].

[26] *Chiu Teng@Kallang Pte Ltd v Singapore Land Authority* [2013] SGHC 262 ('*Chiu Teng*')

[27] Former Chief Justice Chan Sek Keong, 'Judicial Review—From Angst to Empathy' (2010) 22 *Singapore Academy of Law Journal* 469, 478. See eg *Re Siah Mooi Guat* [1988] 2 SLR(R); *Borissik Svetlana v Urban Redevelopment Authority* [2009] 4 SLR(R) 92; HC and *UDL Marine (Singapore) Pte Ltd v Jurong Town Corp* [2011] 3 SLR 94; cf *Abdul Nasir bin Amer Hamsah v Public Prosecutor* [1997] SGCA 38.

[28] A number of cases had already dealt with the issue of procedural legitimate expectations, eg *Re Siah Mooi Guat* (n 27).

[29] *UDL Marine* (n 27).

[30] *Borissik Svetlana* (n 27).

[31] *Yong Vui Kong v AG* [2011] 2 SLR 1189.

argued this was in breach of a legitimate expectation and sought to assert both a procedural and a substantive outcome. The applicant did not obtain leave for judicial review on the basis that, as a private contractual matter, the case did not raise any public law issues. Justice Lai Siu Chiu observed that it was unlikely the doctrine of substantive legitimate expectations was part of Singapore administrative law, largely because public interest notions would compete with the enforcement of a legitimate expectation, but also because enforcement of legitimate expectations would clash with the public law rule preventing fetters on discretion. In *Borissik*, the applicant sought to challenge a refusal of planning permission to construct a house by the Urban Redevelopment Authority. Leave for judicial review was refused on the basis that the applicant had not yet exhausted all remedies available to her under planning law. However, Justice Tan Lee Meng observed that, in any event, there did not appear to be any promise or representation that the applicant could substantiate as the foundation for a legitimate expectation. He highlighted the conditions for the existence of such an expectation, including the need for a clear and unambiguous statement made to an identifiable class of persons but it appears he had in mind only a procedural expectation, namely that the application for planning permission would be properly considered. Finally, in *Yong Vui Kong*, the applicant argued that he had a legitimate expectation that his application for clemency in relation to his death penalty would be decided by the President of Singapore in his own discretion. The Court of Appeal dealt with this argument briefly on the basis that the Constitution of Singapore specifically stated that the President, in deciding on clemency matters, acts 'on the advice of the Cabinet'[32] and thus there was no room for an argument based on legitimate expectation. In any event, it would be easier to classify the asserted expectation as a procedural versus a substantive one, since it was an expectation as to the process and manner in which his application for clemency would be processed.

Accordingly, in *Chiu Teng*, the Court felt unrestrained by the previous case law which it felt had not considered 'head-on' the issue of recognising the doctrine of substantive legitimate expectations as part of Singaporean administrative law. In contrast to *Ng Siu Tung,* it therefore looked further afield than the UK to also consider the law in Australia, Canada and Hong Kong in devising a doctrine to apply in Singapore. While the Court was influenced by the refusal of Australia and Canada to recognise the doctrine of *substantive* legitimate expectations, those jurisdictions did not have any impact on the way the Court eventually developed that doctrine.

[32] Art 22P(1), Constitution of the Republic of Singapore (1985 Rev Ed, 1999 Reprint).

Facts and Decision: *Chiu Teng*

The applicant was a property developer which had acquired two plots of land. Land usage policy in Singapore provides that leases specify the permitted uses of the land as well as the maximum gross floor area for these permissible uses as conditions of the lease. A payment, known as the 'differential premium' (DP), is payable for lifting these title restrictions. The Singapore Land Authority (SLA) calculates the DP.

The applicant argued that it had a legitimate expectation in the way the DP would be calculated because of information available from the SLA's circulars to developers and the SLA's website. The circulars and website stated that the DP would be calculated based on a Table of Development Charge Rates (DC Table) published by the Urban Redevelopment Authority. The DC Table rates are based on a rate set for different categories of land use in different geographical areas in Singapore. Transactional prices of land for the preceding six-month period are used to calculate the rates based on an average of such prices in any particular geographical sector. The alternative mode of calculation is a spot valuation system based on the *actual* value of land in a locality at the time of assessment.

The applicant sought to have the title restrictions lifted to redevelop the land. The DP was calculated by way of a spot valuation at SGD44 million and not on the basis of the DC Table.[33] The SLA explained that this was necessary for a proper discharge of the state's statutory functions, including to realise the full value of any land of which it is disposing. It pointed to legislation which states that the SLA's function and duty is 'to optimise land resources'.[34]

Following a survey of the law in Singapore and other jurisdictions, the Court found there was a sufficient basis for recognising the doctrine of legitimate expectations and protecting such expectations substantively. The Court rejected the argument that this runs counter to the doctrine of separation of powers:

> [t]he upholding of legitimate expectations is eminently within the powers of the judiciary ... in deciding whether a legitimate expectation ought to be upheld, the court must remember that there are concerns and interests larger than the private expectation of an individual ... If there is a public interest which overrides the expectation, then the expectation ought not to be given effect to. In this way, I believe the judiciary can fulfil its constitutional role [to verify not only that the powers asserted accord with the substantive law created by Parliament but also that the manner in which they are exercised confirms with the standards of

[33] The applicant's own calculation based on the DC Table was approximately SGD11 million—a vastly different amount from that calculated by the SLA.

[34] *Singapore Land Authority Act (Cap 301, 2002 Rev Ed)* s 6(1)(a).

fairness which Parliament must have intended] without arrogating to itself the unconstitutional position of being a super-legislature or a super-executive.[35]

The Court went on to highlight the requirements needed to recognise and enforce legitimate expectations:

(i) An unequivocal and unqualified representation made by someone with proper authority to the applicant or a class of persons to which the applicant belongs. If the representation is open to multiple interpretations, then the interpretation used by the public authority will be adopted. This differs from Hong Kong, where courts utilise the irrationality ground of review to test the authority's interpretation before accepting it.[36]

(ii) Reasonable and detrimental reliance on the representation by the applicant. The applicant's reliance may be disqualified if s/he knew the representation was made in error or suspected it was and chose not to clarify the situation. It would similarly be disqualified if there was an opportunity to enquire about the situation and the applicant did not do so. Again, this differs from Hong Kong, where reliance is not a requirement for establishing a legitimate expectation.

(iii) Even if there is such a representation and reliance, the court will not enforce the expectation if the public authority can show an overriding national or public interest which justifies the frustration of the applicant's expectation.[37]

The Court also indicated that it would not enforce the expectation if to do so would result in a breach of the law or the state's international obligations (giving effect to the idea that they will not enforce *ultra vires* legitimate expectations) or if it would infringe the rights of a third party.

In applying these requirements to the facts of the case, the Court found in favour of the respondent. First, the SLA's website explicitly stated that the SLA made no representations. Second, although the SLA circulars were addressed to a specific class of persons which included the applicant, it was not reasonable for the developer to have relied solely on the SLA's circulars. There had been a similar situation in the market recently and so there was sufficient market evidence to indicate that the DP for the land may not be assessed according to the DC Table.[38] Similar reasoning is used in the context of concepts like estoppel, upon which the High Court observed that the enforcement of legitimate expectations in private law is founded.[39]

[35] *Chiu Teng* (n 26) [113].
[36] See section entitled '"The *Coughlan* Moment": Hong Kong' above.
[37] *Chiu Teng* (n 26) [119].
[38] *Chiu Teng* (n 26) [120]–[129].
[39] *Chiu Teng* (n 26) [113]; cf *R (Reprotech (Pebsham) Ltd) v East Sussex County Council* [2003] 1 WLR 348 [35] (Lord Hoffmann).

In any event, the Court held that any legitimate expectation would be overridden by the SLA's statutory duty to optimise land resources and to 'have regard to efficiency and economy and to the social, industrial and commercial and economic needs of Singapore'.[40] This public interest trumped the financial interests of a corporation like the applicant. The Court held that the state's finances would suffer more than the applicant's if the SLA were:

> to make an exception for this case and not apply its unpublished policy relating to directly-alienated State land to the Land here. The overriding public interest must therefore prevail over the financial interests of a commercial enterprise like the applicant in this case.[41]

ISSUES TO BE RESOLVED

The ways in which both Singapore and Hong Kong have chosen to craft their own versions of the doctrine of substantive legitimate expectations have drawn inspiration from England but departed in distinct ways from the English position. This could be due to the particular vision of the role of the judiciary. Thus, in *Ng Siu Tung*, the Court of Final Appeal preferred the *Bibi* formulation of the doctrine as it better respected the doctrine of the separation of powers. In Singapore, the Court took a different interpretation of the doctrine, preferring substantive enforcement of legitimate expectation, as a better protector of the doctrine of separation of powers.

There are many questions about how the ground of review should evolve. This chapter draws attention to some of the key unresolved areas in both jurisdictions. In Hong Kong, there have been a significant number of cases post-*Ng Siu Tung* that provide guidance. However, in Singapore there have been no cases discussing the doctrine post-*Chiu Teng*.[42] This, of course, does not mean that the doctrine is in a stable state in Singapore. It is possible, given that *Chiu Teng* is only a High Court decision, that an appellate

[40] *Singapore Land Authority Act, Cap 301, 2002 Rev Ed* ss 6(1)(a) and 6(2)(a).

[41] *Chiu Teng* (n 26) [130]; cf *Coughlan* (above n 1) [83]–[89].

[42] See also K Yam and B Tai, 'The Advent of Substantive Legitimate Expectations in Hong Kong: Two Competing Visions' [2002] *Public Law* 688; Z Chen, 'Substantive Legitimate Expectations in Singapore Administrative Law' (2014) 26 *Singapore Academy of Law Journal* 237; C Tay, 'Substantive Legitimate Expectations: The Singapore Reception' (2014) 26 *Singapore Academy of Law Journal* 609; and S Jhaveri, 'The Doctrine of Substantive Legitimate Expectations: The Significance of Chiu Teng@Kallang Pte Ltd v Singapore Land Authority' [2016] *Public Law* 1 for a further discussion of some of the issues discussed in this section. The Singapore Court of Appeal has yet to affirm or overrule the application of the doctrine in Chiu Teng: they stopped short of doing so in the recent case of *SGB Starkstrom Pte Ltd v Commissioner for Labour* [2016] SGCA 27. This was on the basis that the doctrine was, in any event, not applicable in the present case (at para 42 per Menon CJ).

court will seek to revert back to the pre-*Chiu Teng* position or, conversely, broaden the scope of the doctrine further. Therefore, we need to consider the major open threads of legal development in both jurisdictions.

Foundations of Substantive Legitimate Expectations

The courts in both *Ng Siu Tung* and *Chiu Teng* did not undertake a detailed normative discussion of why administrative law should protect legitimate expectations created by administrative decisions substantively. For example, *Chiu Teng* talked generally about the importance of fairness and good public administration:

> It seems to me that in this area, public law has already absorbed what is useful from the *moral values* which underlie the private law concept of estoppel and the time has come for it to stand upon its own two feet … *The doctrine will apply in circumstances where the change or proposed change of policy is held to be unfair or an abuse of power* … But these ills are expressed in very general terms; and it is notorious (and obvious) that the ascertainment of what is or is not fair depends on the circumstances of the case (emphasis added).[43]

It briefly discussed the need for the protection of the reliance and expectation interests of citizens under public law in the same way that they are protected in private law.[44] Similarly, the majority in *Ng Siu Tung* briefly discussed the need to advance fairness and prevent an abuse of power.[45] However, without a further elaboration, these vague and broad notions of 'moral values', 'fairness' or 'abuse of power' could undermine the utility of the doctrine.[46] Judges need a normative compass to guide their application of key aspects of the doctrine. Similarly, administrators need a conceptual guide to structure their discretion, ascribe weight to the expectation and make decisions that are consistent with the doctrine. In particular, it is difficult for either a court or administrators to strike the balance between expectations on one hand and the public interest (the final stage of deciding whether to enforce a substantive legitimate expectation) on the other. For this balance to be struck, it is important to understand the 'values' that inform each side of the scale. From an administrator's perspective particularly, without more explanation it is difficult to understand why their decision to pursue a particular policy goal would be an 'abuse of power' provided it complies with the existing grounds of review (illegality, irrationality and procedural fairness).

[43] *Chiu Teng* (n 26) [81] and [35].
[44] *Chiu Teng* (n 26) [105]–[109].
[45] See text accompanying n 12 above; cf the view expressed in the partial dissent of Bokhary PJ that the doctrine of legitimate expectation is founded on the ideas of trust and faith in the administration, *Ng Siu Tung* (n 3) [349].
[46] See *Bibi* (n 2) [18]; *Nadarajah* (n 2) [67].

This balance needs to be struck. As recognised in *Coughlan itself*, the court has 'to reconcile ... [the] continuing need to initiate and respond to change with the legitimate ... expectations of citizens ... who have relied, and have been justified in relying, on a current policy or an extant promise.'[47] This tension was echoed in *Bibi*.[48] It is precisely this discussion on the 'choice of priorities' and 'principles' to be followed that is absent in both jurisdictions especially at the final balancing stage. The Court only needed to look to *Coughlan* for a possible elaboration of what it is that triggers the conclusion of 'unfairness' or an 'abuse of power' in cases involving substantive legitimate expectations. The Court there held that the unfairness arises as a result of the administration 'reneging *without adequate justification*, by an otherwise lawful decision, on a lawful promise or practice....' (emphasis added).[49] In *Nadarajah*, Laws LJ later said that:

> The search for principle surely starts with the theme that is current through the legitimate expectation cases ... Where a public authority has issued a promise or adopted a practice which represents how it proposes to act in a given area, the law will require the promise or practice to be honoured *unless there is good reason not to do so*. ... The principle that good administration requires public authorities to be held to their promises would be undermined if the law did not insist that any failure or refusal to comply is objectively justified as a proportionate measure in the circumstances.[50]

The above discussion is just one possible explanation for what constitutes an 'abuse of process' as a foundation for substantively enforcing legitimate expectations. It is also important to note that the force of the normative argument in favour of enforcement is premised on there being a 'promise' made by the administration from which it seeks to resile: the promise adds weight to the normative arguments. This brings up again the issue of whether a substantive legitimate expectation is of equal weight no matter what its source (promise or policy).[51]

There are multiple rationales commonly offered for the substantive protection of legitimate expectations, some of which were adopted, albeit with a very brief discussion, in *Chiu Teng* and *Ng Siu Tung*. These include the principle of legal certainty (stemming from the rule of law), 'fairness', promoting trust in the government, promoting good administration and protecting reliance on the part of the applicant. Although all of the above may be morally forceful in justifying legitimate expectations, they will emphasise different aspects of the anatomy of a legitimate expectation claim as being

[47] *Coughlan* (n 1) [65].
[48] *Bibi* (n 2) [24].
[49] *Coughlan* (n 1) [69].
[50] *Coughlan* (n 1) [68].
[51] See below at section entitled 'Outer Reaches of the Doctrine: General Class of Persons Relying on a General Policy or Representation'.

the normatively relevant or determinative one for the outcome of a case. Depending on which one holds force in a particular jurisdiction, the law may pull in different directions or focus on different aspects of the case in substantively protecting legitimate expectations. The intellectual focus of each case will differ. For example, if the focus is on the reliance of the applicant, then the focus will be on identifying such reliance as a definitive requirement for the establishment of a legitimate expectation. Alternatively, if the focus is on the promotion of good administration, then the focus may be, for example, equally on the rigour and transparency of the reasoning process for departing from an expectation on the part of the administrator. Such process-based values may also fit within a definition of good administration. Thus, it is possible that arguments flowing from the promotion of good administration may arguably be more balanced in favour of the administration which can point to equally strong arguments stemming from the promotion of good administration to depart from an expectation. Whereas, if the focus is on the protection of legal certainty or the reliance interest of the applicant, this may stack the burden higher on the part of the administration to justify 'harming' such a reliance interest or certainty-based objective stemming from the rule of law.

The underlying objective can also influence the remedy provided to the applicant. If it is the protection of a reliance interest, then the focus may need to be on remedying harm to that interest through the substantive enforcement of the expectation. Even if all the administration needs to do is reconsider its decision in light of the expectation, the objective of protecting the reliance interest of an applicant may impose a heavier burden on the administration because it would now need to justify departing from a reliance interest. However, if the objective is the promotion of trust in the administration or good administration, it may be possible to have a more negotiated remedy with a partial correction of that defect through a reconsideration of the applicant using a process that is characteristic of good administration. Thus, the focus of the remedy will not be the applicant as much as it will be remedying the 'defect' in the decision-making part of the process. The two jurisdictions therefore, need further clarity on the normative underpinnings of the doctrine and one that feeds into the rest of the makeup of the doctrine as elaborated on above.

Interpreting Representations

A further talking point in the cases has been how to interpret the representations made to the applicants and, in particular, whether they are sufficiently clear and unambiguous to give rise to a legitimate expectation. As discussed above, Singapore and Hong Kong have taken different paths. In Singapore, if a representation is open to multiple interpretations, the interpretation used by the public authority will be adopted. In Hong Kong, by contrast, the courts utilise the irrationality ground of review to test an authority's interpretation before accepting it. Both approaches possess some degree of deference to the executive's interpretation of the representation.

In *Ng Siu Tung*, Bokhary PJ was more cautious about according the interpretation of the public body any degree of deference, especially where a representation is addressed to a broad and diverse class of persons.[52] Bokhary PJ considered that in such a scenario the court should consider not just the interpretation but the *impact* of the representation, bearing in mind the 'touchstone' of fairness governing the doctrine of legitimate expectations. In talking about 'impact', Bokhary PJ accordingly seemed to incorporate the feature of inducement or trust generated by the representation into the issue of how to judge the expectation-generating potential of the representation. Indeed, recent cases show that Hong Kong courts at least are willing to engage much more with the Government's interpretation of the representation or policy relied on by the applicant as generating a legitimate expectation. Additionally, they do not restrict themselves to doing so only on the basis of *Wednesbury* irrationality as the majority in *Ng Siu Tung* stated would be the case.

This was apparent in *Hong Kong Television Network v Chief Executive in Council*,[53] which concerned whether the Government's historic policy relating to the issuing of television broadcasting licences generated a legitimate expectation. As part of this policy, the Government announced its decision to open up the television market. The Government had stated publicly that, given the broadcasting policy sought to broaden programme choices, encourage innovation, maintain Hong Kong's competitiveness and enhance its position as a regional broadcasting hub, there would be no limit on the number of domestic television licences under the new licensing regime to be introduced under the (then) *Broadcasting Bill*. However, a subsequent Chief Executive stated that there should be a gradual and orderly process to the grant of licences and rejected the applicant's application for a licence, limiting the issue of licences in that cycle to two out of three applicants. The applicant challenged this on the basis that the Government's earlier open market policy had generated a legitimate expectation that its application would not be rejected by reason of a restriction imposed on the number of licences but would be considered on its merits. It is interesting to note at this point that the Court did not just accept the Government's interpretation of the policy, or simply restrict its review to a bare rationality check of the Government's interpretation. The Court instead engaged its own

[52] *Ng Siu Tung* (n 3) [360].
[53] *Hong Kong Television Network v Chief Executive in Council* HCAL 3/2014, 24 April 2015 (Court of First Instance).

observations about the 'correct' interpretation or 'proper construction' of the policy.[54]

Courts in Hong Kong have elsewhere reverted back to the *Ng Siu Tung* position of only testing the rationality or otherwise of the Government's interpretation of the representation. This was the case in *Bullen Christian Anthony v Director of Lands*,[55] where the Court applied *Wednesbury* as the basis for testing the correct interpretation of the representation relating to the confiscation of a boat.

This pair of cases highlights that the courts in Hong Kong are flexible in their utilisation of different standards of review for the interpretation of a representation. However, it is clear that there is no concerted effort thus far to make explicit when they will utilise any particular standard of review. From the subject matter of the two cases discussed above, it is hard to draw any bright line distinctions about when the court will take a stronger approach towards reviewing the interpretation of a representation. For now, the cases just highlight the presence of a differential approach to reviewing the interpretation of a representation for the purposes of deciding whether or not it can give rise to a legitimate expectation. This is to be welcomed: there is no reason why a court should adopt an uncalibrated, blanket approach to evaluating interpretations of a representation. Both *Chiu Teng* and *Ng Siu Tung* take an inflexible position, perhaps because each involved areas traditionally viewed as 'high' policy in which the courts are less involved. However, there is no reason why this particular threshold needs to be adopted in other areas of decision-making. Thus, a 'sliding' scale of review for interpretation would be a positive way in which the law could develop. Indeed, both jurisdictions have existing jurisprudence which recognises the different degrees of involvement for courts depending on the subject-matter of the case at hand.[56]

Outer Reaches of the Doctrine: General Class of Persons Relying on a General Policy or Representation

Thus far, the focus has largely been on situations involving specific representations to a defined class of persons. Indeed, it is important to also note that the force of a significant number of the normative arguments in favour of enforcement of expectations is premised on there being a 'promise' made

[54] Ibid at [58] (Au J).

[55] *Bullen Christian Anthony v Director of Lands* HCAL 25/2013, 16 May 2014.

[56] In Singapore, see eg *Lee Hsien Loong v Review Publishing* [2007] 2 SLR 453 [98] (Sundaresh Menon JC). In Hong Kong, see eg *Sakthavel Prabakar v Secretary for Security* [2005] 1 HKLRD 289 [43] (Andrew Li CJ).

by the administration to an individual or defined class of individuals from which it seeks to resile: the 'promise' or 'representation' adds weight to the normative arguments. This brings up the issue of whether a legitimate expectation will have equal normative weight irrespective of its source. Will an expectation that stems from a specific promise or representation be more persuasive than one asserted by a member of a general class relying on a general policy or practice? It is clear from *Ng Siu Tung* that the beneficiaries of the general representations were in a much weaker position in the final analysis. The public interest in complying with the overall statutory scheme was stronger in the claim against them than against those relying on a specific representation.

This highlights the fact that the different scenarios in which an applicant asserts that a legitimate expectation should be substantively enforced raise a range of different issues that can have an implication on the way that judicial review responds to the expectation. Substantive legitimate expectation situations commonly involve some form of conflict between the need to preserve the position embodied in the expectation and promote equality of treatment, versus the need for flexibility on the part of the Government in departing from it. This clash of values can be resolved in different ways. As Craig recognised, different scenarios raise quite different problems:

> Cases [involving an individualised representation that has been relied on] are normally treated as the strongest. This is because an unequivocal representation carries a particular moral force, and because holding the public body to that representation is less likely to have serious consequences for the administration as a whole. Cases [involving a general norm or policy choice, which an individual has relied on] are, by way of contrast, generally regarded as more ... Different principles of judicial review may, therefore, be appropriate in this type of case.[57]

The cases confirm that recipients of general representations made to an innominate class of persons or who are beneficiaries of a general policy or practice have a higher burden in establishing and enforcing their expectation.[58] The question arises whether an applicant relying on a general representation, practice or policy can ever succeed in establishing and enforcing a legitimate expectation. It appears that for applicants in this category, the courts place a stronger emphasis on the reasonableness of their

[57] Paul Craig, *Administrative Law*, 7th edn (Sweet & Maxwell, 2012) 680. See also *Coughlan* (n 1) [59]; *R (Bhatt Murphy) v The Independent Assessor* [2008] EWCA Civ 755 [46]–[47]; *Paponette v The Attorney-General of Trinidad and Tobago* [2012] 1 AC 1 [28].

[58] See eg *Begbie* (n 2) (applicant was a test case for a group of 1500 people) and *R v Secretary of State for Foreign and Commonwealth Affairs; ex parte Bancoult (No 2)* [2009] 1 AC 453 (the Court found it difficult to recognise and enforce a legitimate expectation in favour of a large group of residents of the Chagos Islands).

expectation and / or the existence of reliance. This practice is established in Hong Kong.[59]

A further inspection, however, reveals that the courts struggle with the imposition of this higher burden on applicants in these broader kinds of cases. It can be argued that the innominate nature of the class should not matter or undermine the claim, especially where it is the Government itself which is responsible for creating the expectation through its representations, as in *Ng Siu Tung*, *Begbie* and *Bancoult*. These cases differ from the scenario where an applicant autonomously relies on a general practice or policy (as in *Chiu Teng*) without reaching out to clarify its application to the applicant. For example, an applicant in Hong Kong was unsuccessful in judicial review proceedings which alleged breach of a substantive legitimate expectation arising from their autonomous reliance on a perceived policy of the Government.[60] However, in the other kind of case, where the Government generates expectations in an innominate class, a court should not reject the claim based only on the number of persons in the class or the fact that it was based on a general practice or policy versus a directed representation. As Yam and Tai have observed:

> If the rule of law, as reflected by legal certainty, is to be a fundamental rationale ... then, unlike the more cautious view in *Coughlan*, there is no reason for making the applicability of the doctrine less likely if a large class of persons is involved. Indeed, the larger the class of people affected, the greater the damage to legal certainty caused by a policy change, potentially leading to disruptions in society. Similarly, if trust in public administration is to be the rationale ... then the force for upholding it is stronger, rather than weaker, with large class of people, for more people may lose faith in government as a result of reneging on government promises.[61]

The courts in Hong Kong have thus sought to include cases involving a general class which relies on a general policy or practice within the doctrine of legitimate expectations. Courts elsewhere also recognise some moral force behind the enforcement of these kinds of cases but have struggled to accept them within the doctrine of legitimate expectations, especially as they may not always involve reliance or even knowledge of the general policy.[62] English courts have recognised the awkward characterisation of such cases as involving a legitimate 'expectation' given that the applicant may not even

[59] See eg *Merchant Navy Officers' Guild v Hong Kong v Director of Marine* [2003] HKCU 229 [41] (Hartmann J). See also M Groves, 'Substantive Legitimate Expectations in Australian Administrative Law' (2008) 32 *Melbourne University Law Review* 470.

[60] *Hong Kong Mobile Television Network Limited v Office of the Communications Authority*, HCAL 39/2014, 29 September 2015 (Court of First Instance). See also *Ho Choi Wan v Hong Kong Housing Authority* [2005] 4 HKLRD 706.

[61] Yam and Tai (n 42) 688.

[62] See eg *R (Rashid) v Home Secretary* [2005] EWCA Civ 744 [25] (Pill LJ), [47] (Dyson LJ).

know of the policy. It is thus odd to say they had an 'expectation'. They have therefore preferred to locate the normative foundation of these cases in the idea of consistency of treatment.[63] Accordingly, the Hong Kong and Singaporean courts must resolve whether and to what extent to recognise claims involving general reliance on a general policy by a member of a general class of persons; whether to require reliance or knowledge on the part of such applicants; and whether to locate these cases within the doctrine of legitimate expectations, as part of the existing grounds of review or as a new doctrine based on equality and consistency of treatment.

Standard of Review for Departures from Legitimate Expectations

In *Chiu Teng*, the Court recognised that enforcement of a substantive legitimate expectation competes with the need for flexibility in the Government's development of policy. The issue was, however, how to strike a balance between the two. In *Coughlan*, the Court rejected a bare rationality test based on *Wednesbury* review in all cases, especially in cases where the initial representation and the subsequent purported departure from the legitimate expectation were both *intra vires* exercises of power, on the basis that such a test would cause the public authority to be the 'judge in its own case, for a decision to prioritise a policy change over legitimate expectations will almost always be rational from where the authority stands, even if objectively it is arbitrary or unfair'.[64] If not rationality, the court has to find another, appropriate standard of review for assessing a departure from an expectation. One option is to use some form of structured proportionality reasoning.[65] Alternatively, the courts could engage in a more open, textured balancing exercise that varies with context. This was the approach preferred in *Chiu Teng*, though consideration of the extent of the balancing was restricted to one paragraph:

> As the SLA has rightfully pointed out, it is under a statutory duty to 'optimise land resources' ... and to 'have regard to efficiency and economy and to the social, industrial and commercial and economic needs of Singapore' in the carrying out of its functions ... Its statutory duty would encompass getting the best returns for the State when it deals with State land. This would in turn benefit the public at large. It is therefore unacceptable in the circumstances here to argue that the State's finances would not suffer as much as the applicant's if the SLA were to

[63] See eg the explanation of *Rashid* in *MA & AA (Afghanistan) v Secretary of State for the Home Department* [2015] 1 WLR 3083 [39]–[42].

[64] *Coughlan* (n 1) [66].

[65] See eg *Nadarajah* (n 2) [67]. See also Janina Boughey, 'Proportionality and Legitimate Expectations', chapter 6 of this volume for a discussion of the relationship between proportionality and legitimate expectations.

> make an exception for this case and not apply its unpublished policy relating to directly-alienated State land to the Land here. The overriding public interest must therefore prevail over the financial interests of a commercial enterprise like the applicant in this case.[66]

This may be because the applicant had a weak expectation in the first place or because the impact on the applicant was only financial, rather than on civil or political rights enshrined in the constitution, causing a court to balance the financial impact on the applicant against the impact on the state. Finally, it may also be because, in the planning context, the public interest is naturally stacked against the applicant.[67] This echoes views elaborated elsewhere about the court's limited role in areas of polycentric decision making, such as planning.[68] It also echoes observations that Singaporean administrative law is currently balanced in favour of communitarian values.[69] This can be contrasted with the observation that English courts 'are gradually feeling their way towards an acceptable balance between the conflicting interests at stake in substantive legitimate expectations cases'.[70] While it is unfair to expect the same level of development in Singapore at this early stage of the development of modern administrative law (as evidenced by the recognition of new grounds such as substantive legitimate expectations), the court could have provided more guidance on how this balancing should operate. This would particularly allow courts to engage properly with this part of the test in order to give due importance to both the substantive legitimate expectation and the public interest.

This raises the question of the relationship between *Wednesbury* review and substantive legitimate expectations, which looks at whether the administration had adequate rationale for departing from a legitimate expectation. Both involve a consideration of the reasons for decision-making. However, as discussed above, Singapore has maintained the threshold of *Wednesbury* review at a high and deferential level,[71] whereas it appears with substantive legitimate expectation that the courts may be more involved in their review of the Government's reasons for action. Indeed, the burden of proof is different: with *Wednesbury* it is on the applicant to explain the 'irrationality' of the administration's decision-making, whereas with substantive legitimate expectations the burden is on the Government to rationalise departure from the legitimate expectation.

[66] *Chiu Teng* (n 3) [130]. See Craig (n 57) 690–91.

[67] See eg *R (Reprotech (Pebsham) Ltd) v East Sussex CC* [2002] UKHL 8.

[68] *R (Alconbury) v Environment Secretary* [2001] UKHL 23; *Lee Hsien Loong* (n 56) per Sundaresh Menon JC (as he then was) at [998](b).

[69] See eg LA Thio, 'Law and the Administrative State' in Kevin YL Tan (ed), *Singapore Legal System* (Singapore University Press, 1999) 14.

[70] I Steele, 'Substantive Legitimate Expectations: Striking the Right Balance?' (2005) 121 *Law Quarterly Review* 300, 300.

[71] See above (n 24).

This can be compared with the position in Hong Kong, where (as discussed above), the courts will not enforce a legitimate expectation but merely mandate its consideration. The issue of how the courts will assess a government's consideration of, and subsequent departure from, an expectation is, however, left open. This is because in *Ng Siu Tung* itself the Government had not even considered the expectation, having formed the view it was *ultra vires*. The Court asked it to make a fresh decision and consider whether to exercise the discretion under the Immigration Ordinance to allow the applicants to remain, albeit without right of abode. The issue was only discussed thoroughly by Bokhary PJ, who was prepared to entertain the idea of the substantive enforcement of expectations[72] if the Director of Immigration had decided (after taking account of the legitimate expectations) to depart from it and if the court thought the departure was not satisfactory. It is clear, post *Ng Siu Tung*, that the courts will also review the adequacy of the reasons for not respecting the legitimate expectation.[73] The court's satisfaction as to departure from the legitimate expectation would depend on the applicable standard of review. Bokhary PJ discussed various options, including *Wednesbury* review (with the various thresholds attached to this ground), review on the basis of proportionality and the more open-ended balancing of fairness and the public interest as done in the Singapore context.

This issue was further discussed in *Re Thomas Lai*.[74] The case concerned a change in government land policy which meant that the applicant's village would eventually become part of a country park. This would restrict development on his land in line with the country park policy of land usage. The Court eventually found that there was sufficient evidence to suggest that the Government had adequately considered the legitimate expectation and the issue was the standard of review to be applied to the Government's refusal to give effect to it. The Court recognised the proposals put forward by Bokhary PJ in his partial dissent but eventually held that it did not need to decide on the proposed standard of review because the applicant's case would fail on both *Wednesbury* irrationality and proportionality review. This was due to the fact that the policy was notified to a large and general class of persons; the polycentric nature of land planning policy and resulting expectation (which required a lighter touch and more deferential review on the part of the Court); and the fact that the change in policy would not lead to a complete prohibition on the development of land by the applicant.

Both jurisdictions have significant issues to resolve in relation to their standard of review. This issue will inevitably require definitive resolution in

[72] Above *Immigration Ordinance* (n 4) at [352].
[73] See *Re Thomas Lai*, HCAL 150/2013, 28 February 2014 (Court of First Instance).
[74] Ibid.

future cases where an applicant makes the argument that they were dealt with in a unfair way in the *manner* in which the legitimate expectation was taken into account by the decision-maker (in the Hong Kong context) or in relation to the fact that their expectation outweighs the counter public interest (in the Singaporean context, which was not heavily argued in *Chiu Teng*). In this respect, reverting back to a bare rationality review would be a retrogressive and aberrational approach given the general desire to move to a stronger substantive review in both contexts.

Enforcing Legitimate Expectations

The final broad issue for both jurisdictions to resolve, concerns the mode of enforcing the legitimate expectations. As discussed above, the doctrine ultimately involves balancing the interests of the individual against the broader public interest. The courts in common law jurisdictions have devised a number of enforcement tools to strike this balance. For example, in some jurisdictions (like Hong Kong), the legitimate expectation is protected by redefining it as a relevant consideration that must be taken into account by administrators before they make a policy decision. In others, it is actually 'enforced' through prerogative remedies such as an order which quashes the original decision and requires the administration to make a fresh decision that complies with the legitimate expectation.[75] It is possible, as the Court hinted in *Ng Siu Tung*, that courts may also recognise a partial protection of the substantive component of the expectation. In other scenarios, the legitimate expectation is protected procedurally: for example, the applicant is given a hearing before departure from a legitimate expectation that a particular decision will be made in relation to them is allowed.[76] In this way, the administration is bound to different degrees by the expectation.

In *Chiu Teng*, by concluding that an expectation can be protected by giving effect to the substantive legitimate expectation, the Court followed the high water mark decision of *Coughlan* but did not consider the way the law developed subsequently. *Coughlan* applied certiorari to quash a decision that ran contrary to a legitimate expectation, effectively giving substantive effect to that expectation. This remedial response was qualified in later cases, most notably in *Bibi*, on the basis that a declaration of substantive benefit would inappropriately encroach upon executive power. Accordingly, in *Bibi* the legitimate expectation was substantively enforced but only as a relevant consideration that the executive was mandated to consider.

[75] See *Coughlan* (n 1).

[76] See *Schmidt v Secretary of State for Home Affairs* [1969] 2 Ch 149; *R (on the Application of Zeqiri) v Secretary of State for the Home Department* [2001] EWCA Civ 342.

However, in *Bibi*, the Court said there was almost a presumption in favour of giving effect to the legitimate expectation when the matter was reconsidered by the local authority.[77]

This echoes the views of the Court of Final Appeal in *Ng Siu Tung* and the approach of the Hong Kong courts in subsequent cases in their examination of the reasons for departing from the expectation.[78] It has been suggested elsewhere that the courts should not substantively enforce legitimate expectations, as this sits uncomfortably with 'the accepted principle of judicial deference based on the concept of relative institutional competence',[79] but should consider using either monetary relief[80] or enforcing the expectation as a relevant consideration. However, as Tay recognised, the latter may risk undermining the applicant's interest as the administration is free to determine the weight it ascribes to the expectation. The way in which the relevant consideration-type review was used in *Ng Siu Tung* provides some comfort from this criticism: the Court was not deferential but directed that the legitimate expectation must be accorded substantial weight in the decision-making. This is especially true as *Ng Siu Tung* imposed an onerous obligation on the Director to provide reasons for his failure to comply with the legitimate expectation.

It will be necessary in the future to consider these remedial nuances fully. At this stage in the law's development, remedial flexibility may be preferable, with the court retaining various options in how it should enforce an expectation. For example, the Court of Final Appeal in *Ng Siu Tung* ascribed weight to the expectation in order to avoid the relevant considerations approach undermining the efficacy of the legitimate expectation.[81] The need for some remedial flexibility could reflect the different ways in which it is possible to strike a balance between the applicant and the respondent. For example, it may be the case that a countervailing public interest is compelling enough to deny full protection via substantive enforcement of a legitimate expectation but not compelling enough to deny *any* relief. In such a situation, it may be possible to protect the applicant's interest, albeit to a lesser degree, for example by enforcing the legitimate expectation as a relevant consideration and perhaps even ascribing a weight to it to prevent it being readily overridden by a competing public interest, as in *Ng Siu Tung*. This sliding scale of remedies would also be useful in differentiating the different circumstances: does a legitimate expectation based on an express promise require stronger substantive protection, versus one based

[77] *Bibi* (n 2) [58]–[59].
[78] See *Hong Kong Television Network* (n 53) and *Re Thomas Lai* (n 73).
[79] See Tay (n 42) 641–42.
[80] See Steele (n 70) on this difficult issue.
[81] *Ng Siu Tung* (n 3).

on a general practice or policy which may require protection as a relevant consideration.

CONCLUSION

The doctrine of legitimate expectations and their substantive enforcement are now part of the administrative law landscape in both Hong Kong and Singapore. However, there is significant room to develop and clarify the scope, focus and foundations of the doctrine. These are necessary avenues for development: it will make the difference between whether governments will respond to the doctrine of substantive legitimate expectations by acknowledging the need to take special account of individuals caught between changes in policy and create exceptions for them to the policy or defensively by preventing legitimate expectations from arising. The law operates fluidly in both jurisdictions. A significant number of issues have yet to be tested in the courts. For example, the courts have not had to confront situations where:

(i) they cannot even engage with the question of whether there is a legitimate expectation because the situation involves high policy;[82]
(ii) the precise scope of 'detrimental' reliance where it is required or relevant; and
(iii) the issue of clashing illegalities, namely between fettering discretion through the enforcement of a substantive legitimate expectation and the 'illegality' of departing from the expectation. Legitimate expectation cases can involve multiple clashing manifestations of illegality or *ultra vires*: the initial representation or policy may not be enforced for being *ultra vires*;[83] the need to enforce an expectation, while based on an *intra vires* representation, may be *ultra vires* in the form of a fetter on discretion and conversely the failure to enforce it may amount to an illegality or abuse of power. These varying forms and degrees of illegality may overtime require the creation of a 'hierarchy' of illegality: for example, an initial illegality in the form of an *ultra vires*

[82] *Wheeler v Office of the Prime Minister* [2008] EWHC 1409 (potential breach of an expectation of a referendum before the ratification of the EU's Treaty of Lisbon); *R v Environment Secretary; ex parte Hammersmith and Fulham LBC* [1991] 1 AC 521 (which would involve the Court making decisions on what constituted sensible budgets for a local authority); cf *R v Home Secretary; ex parte Ahmed and Patel* [1998] INLR 570; *Minister for Immigration v Teoh* (1995) 183 CLR 273; *Chan To Foon v Director of Immigration* [2001] 3 HKLRD 109 (ratification of a convention or treaty is a positive statement that the government will act in accordance with the convention, and that it is 'an adequate foundation for a legitimate expectation, absent statutory or executive indications to the contrary').

[83] cf *Stretch v United Kingdom* (2004) 38 EHRR 12.

representation may trump the type of illegality that stems from not enforcing a legitimate expectation.

There is ample evidence to suggest that the courts take initial illegality in the form of an *ultra vires* representation or policy seriously enough for it be considered a 'trump' in the sense discussed above.[84]

In Singapore, in particular, the doctrine of substantive legitimate expectations marks the first time the courts have accepted substantive review in some strong form.[85] Recently, the former Chief Justice Chan Sek Keong recognised the possibility for more expanded substantive review in the future.[86] The Court in *Chiu Teng*, however, did not look at how substantive legitimate expectations fits in with other forms of substantive review currently accepted in Singapore. In particular, it did not address the fact that the final balancing required between the substantive legitimate expectation and the public interest may involve (albeit embryonically) a similar analytical exercise as proportionality (which has thus far been rejected). This raises the issue of whether judges will be comfortable or experienced in dealing with a more involved substantive ground of review given the general absence of such review in the administrative law landscape. It also highlights a possible conflict: there is no need to give reasons in the context of *Wednesbury* review but there is in the context of the final balancing stage of the doctrine of substantive legitimate expectations. There may also be confusion for litigants (of which ground of review to plead) and for judges (of which ground of review to apply).[87] While Hong Kong has more developed jurisprudence in the area of the review of the substance or content of decisions, its outer boundaries remain unsettled. In particular, the courts will need to revisit some of the 'hardline' boundaries drawn in the *Ng Siu Tung* case, including the possibility of substantive enforcement of expectations and revisiting the interpretation of a representation adopted by the executive.

[84] See eg *Dragon House Investment Ltd v Secretary for Transport* [2005] 4 HKLRD 480; *Yook Tong Electric Co Ltd v Commissioner for Transport*, HCAL 94/2002, 7 February 2003 (Court of First Instance); *Re Thomas Lai* (n 73).

[85] See above nn 26 and 27 on the state of substantive review in Singapore.

[86] See above *Re Siah Mooi Guat* (n 27) at [25], [27]. See also Thio (n 69) 749.

[87] Concerns raised in *Begbie* (n 2) 1131.

13

Legitimate Expectations in Canada: Soft Law and Tax Administration

SAS ANSARI AND LORNE SOSSIN

THIS CHAPTER EXAMINES the relationship between legitimate expectations and soft law. In what circumstances can an agency's guidelines create law—or at least legally enforceable expectations? At first glance, the answer would appear obvious. The key reason for developing soft law is to provide guidance and transparency as to the process (and sometimes the substance) of administrative action. Soft law by its nature gives rise to expectations. Whether those expectations, in turn, give rise to legal effects is decidedly less clear. In fact, this question has vexed Canadian administrative law. Nowhere are questions of soft law[1] and legitimate expectations more salient than in the context of tax administration.

We canvass the relationship between legitimate expectations and soft law in the context of Canadian tax administration. The analysis proceeds in three parts. In the first part, we consider the important roles of soft law in a tax administration system premised on self-assessment. Within this analysis, we list and describe six sources of soft law in the tax administration context. In the second part, we explore the development of the doctrine of legitimate expectations in Canada, and the implications of the Supreme Court of Canada's (SCC) most considered treatment of soft law and legitimate expectations in *Agraira v Canada*.[2] The third part of the chapter analyses

[1] Soft law is the generally recognised term for official instruments of various forms which are non-binding and seek to guide, clarify or affect administrative action. Soft law is most often distinguished from 'hard law' such as statutes and regulations which are binding and set out legally enforceable standards, duties and powers. Another term for guidelines is 'interposed law', which Professor William Twining differentiated from 'soft law' in his keynote lecture at the 2014 Osgoode Forum, 10 May 2014, in Toronto, Ontario. He defined interposed law as including the 'descriptions of law that tax administrators develop and that come between the tax code and the practice of tax administration by administrators'. The importance of this 'interposed law' was highlighted by reference to a hypothetical investor who, in making investment decisions, would analyse the risks/benefits of the investment not only on the 'state law' but also the very important 'interposed laws' that are of practical importance.

[2] *Agraira v Canada* [2013] 2 SCR 559 ('*Agraira*').

when (and pursuant to which principles) soft law in the tax administration context (eg information circular, interpretation bulletin, or advance judgment) may give rise to a legitimate expectation.

We conclude that Canadian administrative law has only begun to grapple with legitimate expectations, and that its development in the context of soft law represents an important catalyst for sorting out a more coherent and transparent framework for the review of administrative action.

SOFT LAW AND TAX ADMINISTRATION

The Canada Revenue Agency (CRA) is a large administrative agency[3] that performs various functions, including both 'judicial rights-determining functions' and 'administrative rights determining functions',[4] in pursuit of the administration and enforcement of the *Income Tax Act* (*ITA*).[5] The *ITA* is 'complex'[6] and 'convoluted',[7] and is filled with provisions that are ambiguous and unclear.[8] The CRA recognises the lack of clarity in the *ITA*.[9] The words of Justice Learned Hand are quite appropriate in describing the complexity of tax law:[10]

> The words of such an act as the Income Tax, for example, merely dance before my eyes in a meaningless procession: cross-reference to cross-reference, exception

[3] The CRA is properly considered an administrative agency, separate from the Minister of Revenue. From its start in 1867 as the Department of Customs and the Department of Inland Revenue (*The Customs Act* 30–31 Vict c 6 and *The Inland Revenue Act*, 30–31 Vict c 8), the tax administration agency was renamed and reformed a number of times. In response to increased criticism of the potential political nature of having taxes administered by an elected official, the Government of Canada created a federal agency that, since 2005, has been called the Canada Revenue Agency. The CRA is headed by a Commissioner of Revenue who is authorised by the Minister of Revenue to exercise the Minister's powers. However, the Minister continues to play a role and has (in law) the power to direct the Commissioner to exercise any powers, duties, or functions.

[4] These phrases, referring to the various functions that administrative bodies can perform, are taken from the four-part classification in Ron Ellis, *Unjust by Design: Canada' Administrative Justice System* (University of British Colombia Press, 2013).

[5] *Income Tax Act*, RSC 1985 c 1 (5th Supp) at subsection 220(1).

[6] See eg, *Weaver v The Queen* 2008 FCA 238 [11], [18].

[7] See eg, *Boulay v The Queen* 2003 TCC 96 [7].

[8] Canadian courts have repeatedly referred to the *ITA* in these terms and have noted that many of the *ITA*'s provisions are 'ambiguous or unclear' (see eg, *Canada v Brelco Drilling Ltd*, [1999] 4 FC 35). The Supreme Court of Canada, in *65302 British Colombia Ltd v Canada* [1999] 2 SEC 804 [51], described the *ITA* as 'the most detailed, complex, and comprehensive statutes in [Canada's] legislative inventory'.

[9] See eg the statements of CRA officials in a meeting of tax officials outlying the customer service approach to tax administration (quoted in Lorne Sossin, 'The Politics of Discretion: Toward a Critical Theory of Public Administration' (1993) 36 *Canadian Public Administration* 364, 387–88).

[10] Learned Hand, 'Eulogy of Thomas Walter Swan' (1947) 57 *Yale Law Journal* 167, 169. Although referring to the US income tax law, the comments are apt when describing most tax statutes.

> upon exception—couched in abstract terms that offer no handle to seize hold of—leave in my mind only a confused sense of some vitally important, but successfully concealed, purport, which it is my duty to extract, but which is within my power, if at all, only after the most inordinate expenditure of time.

Complexity is increased by tax law's secondary-law nature.[11] Tax law must take the legal world (which gives legal significance to real-world events and actions, on which tax law then operates) as it finds it. Unless the *ITA* expressly or by necessary implication modifies the legal terrain, tax law only applies after the other laws have exerted their effects. This is a daunting task even for seasoned tax lawyers. Not surprisingly, taxpayers often do not understand the tax consequences of their choices and life-events. In recognition of this complexity and the reality of inherent uncertainties in statutory interpretation, the Mintz Committee recommended that taxpayers and the Minister be allowed to enter into compromise settlements on the basis of litigation risk.[12]

This complexity could be significantly reduced, if not resolved, by applying professional expertise (lawyers, accountants, etc)[13] but for the fact that, in order to function as designed, Canada's income tax system must (at least passively) engage with over 26 million individual taxpayers annually.[14] The majority of taxpayers have no legal or tax experience or training and cannot afford to retain tax experts (nor should they be required to within the context of a self-assessing system). The onus of correctly interpreting the law, identifying legally significant facts, and applying the law to these facts—coming up with the correct amount of tax owing—is on the taxpayer.[15] Where the taxpayer fails at this, s/he may face interest charges[16] and (both criminal and non-criminal) penalties,[17] possibly exceeding the taxpayer's

[11] See eg the SCC decision in *Will-Kare Paving & Contracting Ltd v Canada* [2000] 1 SCR 915, where the Court stated that the *ITA* does not operate in a vacuum, and that legal characterisation of the broader commercial relationships and law affect the operation and effect of the *ITA*.

[12] Canada, *Report of the Technical Committee on Business Taxation* (Department of Finance, 1998).

[13] Of course, these professionals do not always agree, inter- and intra-professions, as to the meaning and effect of all of the provisions of the *ITA* (and other areas of law).

[14] CRA statistics for the 2013 tax year, available online at www.cra-arc.gc.ca/gncy/stts/itsa-sipr/2013/menu-eng.html accessed on 1 March 2016.

[15] Tax administration using a self-assessment process has been described as 'the ultimate delegation of decision making in an income tax system, because it allows the taxpayer to control to the greatest degree possible the process of determining their tax liability'. See Michael Walpole, 'Ethics and Integrity in Tax Administration' (12 September 2009) UNSW Law Research Paper No 2009-33, 1, available online at http://ssrn.com/abstract=1474100.

[16] *ITA* s 161.

[17] The penalty provisions in the *ITA* include: s 162—failure to file annual returns; s 163—false statements and omissions; s 188.1—penalties for charities; and s 227—failure to deduct and withhold as required.

tax liability.[18] CRA employees who judge and analyse taxpayers' tax returns are faced with the same lack of certainty and clarity in interpreting and applying the complex and convoluted provisions of the *ITA*, often with little more expertise and education than most taxpayers.[19]

One policy of tax legislation is the creation of tax law that is 'certain, predictable and fair, so that taxpayers can intelligently order their affairs'.[20] Meeting this policy goal in a 'self-assessment system, which requires individuals without legal training to work through a complex series of provisions [...] for which maximum guidance is necessary'[21] is in part achieved through the creation and distribution of detailed guidelines.[22] The CRA, in order to serve its various functions, 'distills from the statutory text the particulars of the legislator's policy intentions, and drafts and "enacts" the directive and the rules and regulations necessary to give effect to those particulars'.[23] These agency-created documents, referred herein collectively as 'guidelines', are the focus of this chapter.[24]

This soft law is used in the course of giving effect to the statutory rights granted and obligations imposed by the *ITA*.[25] They guide the decisions of various CRA employees involved in determining the existence of and the outcome of disputes between taxpayers and the state that arise in the ordinary course of administrating the *ITA*. They are also heavily employed by lawyers and tax professionals in providing services to taxpayers, and are used by taxpayers themselves to make sense of the Canadian income tax

[18] The *ITA* contains complex provisions for penalties that apply in a variety of circumstances. For example see John Sorensen, Michael Belz and Shiri Trop, 'Non-Criminal Penalties under the Income Tax Act' in *2013 Ontario Tax Conference* (Canadian Tax Foundation, 2013) 12:1.

[19] Many positions within the CRA require no legal or tax education, eg the CRA's advertisement for a 'Tax Services Agent', whose duties include responding 'to business enquiries related to registrations, payroll deductions, GST/HST, self-employment, and corporate income tax', are only required to have education that is a 'secondary school diploma' or equivalent: www.cra-arc.gc.ca careers section, notice accessed 30 July 2014. A copy of the job notice is on file with the authors.

[20] *Canada Trustco Mortgage Co v Canada* 2005 SCC 54 [42].

[21] *British Colombia Ltd v Canada* (n 8) [57].

[22] The *ITA* in PDF form is 3,236 pages long and the Regulations take up another 1,645 pages. The text of the four sections dealing with 'Income and Loss from an Office or Employment', the simplest of the provisions in the *ITA*, covers 50 of those pages. The CRA has issued a number of guidelines to deal with these four sections, totaling another 50 pages of explanations covering only small portions of those four sections. These four sections do not cover other sources of income, investment income, excluded amounts, deductions, credits, or other matters commonly encountered by most taxpayers.

[23] See Ellis (n 4) 135 where such functions are said to be performed by the 'policy and legislative department' of the 'portfolio ministry' of the executive branch of government.

[24] The first such publication by Canada Revenue (as it then was) was in 1970, and consisted of two series of publications: 'Information Circulars' and 'Interpretation Bulletins'.

[25] The TCC in *Dunlap v The Queen* 52 DTC 2053, held that the 'principal purpose of the bulletins is to inform the public of policies which the [Minister] has adopted for the administration of legislation as broad and complex as the *Income Tax Act*'.

system. This is why soft law plays as crucial a role in the smooth functioning of a self-assessment system, the exercise of discretion by CRA officials, and the compliance efforts of taxpayers.

Guidelines and the Integrity of the Tax System

Canada's self-assessment system relieves the tax authority of the duties normally imposed on assessors freeing up resources for administration and enforcement.[26] This is not without cost. A self-assessment system provides greater opportunities for tax avoidance and evasion, undermining the tax base and reducing government revenues.[27] Tax avoidance and evasion increase where, *inter alia*,[28,29] the tax system is perceived as being unfair.[30] In a self-assessment system, 'fairness and even handedness by the tax authority are required to encourage integrity among taxpayers', and perceptions of unfair treatment by the tax authority have an 'important influence on future levels of tax evasion'.[31]

The importance of taxpayer trust within a self-assessment system, and the effects of perceptions of fairness, is well recognised by the Canadian Government and courts.[32] In an increasingly complex and changing legal landscape, actors ought to be able to rely on law with some certainty.[33] Where the law involves administrative discretion,[34] is complex, or is otherwise uncertain, the public will have difficulty in predicting how discretion will

[26] Michael Walpole, 'Ethics and Integrity in Tax Administration' in Surviving Challenges, Seizing Opportunities, Inland Revenue Board Malaysia, Malaysia, presented at National Tax Conference, Kuala Lumpur, 4–5 August 2009 at p 10, available online at http://ssrn.com/abstract=1474100.

[27] Vito Tanzi and Parthasarathi Shome, 'A Primer on Tax Evasion' (Dec, 1993) 40:4 Staff Papers—International Monetary Fund 807, 810.

[28] Ibid, 819. See also James Alm, Isabel Sanchez, and Ana de Juan, *Economic and Noneconomic Factors in Tax Compliance* (Blackwell Publishing, 1995) Vol 48(1), 3–18.

[29] Robert Halperin and Joseph Tzur, 'Tax Evasion and the Low Penalty, Low Audit Rate Phenomenon' (1990) 9 *Journal of Accounting and Public Policy* 179, 179.

[30] Michael Walpole, 'Ethics and Integrity in Tax Administration' (12 September 2009) UNSW Law Research Paper No 2009–33 at pp 12–13, available online at http://ssrn.com/abstract=1474100. See also Soren Schønberg, *Legitimate Expectations in Administrative Law* (Oxford University Press, 2000).

[31] Walpole (n 30) 13.

[32] For example, in the Federal Court of Appeal in *Hawkes v The Queen* [1997] 2 CTC 133 (FCA) [7], Strayer JA observed that tax administrators must avoid conduct that damages the perception of the 'system as fair, equitable, and reasonable in application'.

[33] See Schønberg (n 30) 9.

[34] In the income tax context, discretion may be discretion expressly granted by the *ITA*, may be implied in the implementation of public polices, may materialise in the interpretation given to unclear or ambiguous provisions, or may be implicit in the everyday interactions of tax administrators with taxpayers. See Lorne Sossin, 'The Politics of Discretion' (1993) *Canadian Public Administration* 36:3, 364, 384.

be exercised or the law will be interpreted and applied.[35] Clearly worded and easy to understand representations by public authorities will, in cases of ambiguity, serve to guide an individual's actions and decisions.[36] Therefore, how the law treats soft law may undermine taxpayers' perceptions of fairness.[37] For example, the failure of courts to allow into evidence such things as government policy concerning the application of certain rules of evidence of the treatment of similar taxpayers is seen as having a negative effect.[38]

Soft Law and Tax

There are a large number of tax guidelines that could be considered for the purposes of this analysis. The authority for developing soft law is not expressly found in the *ITA*, but is implied by provisions empowering the Minister to administer the *ITA*. A small subset of these sources of soft law includes:

(i) Income Tax Folios ('ITF');
(ii) Income Tax Information Circulars ('IC');
(iii) Income Tax Interpretation Bulletins ('IT');
(iv) Income Tax Technical News ('ITTN');
(v) Tax Guides and Pamphlets; and
(vi) Advanced Income Tax Rulings ('ATR').[39]

There are other publications that are publicly available even if designed for use by expert specialists rather than members of the public. This category includes the CRA Appeals Manual, and other statements and communications by the CRA (both written and oral, and formal and informal).[40] Relevant statements and publications could also include those made by the Department of Finance (for example comfort letters, news releases, tax bulletins, technical papers).

[35] See Schønberg (n 30) 14.

[36] Schønberg (n 30) 29. Schønberg saw this as fundamental to the Rule of Law (at 13).

[37] See Revenue Canada, *Ensuring Fair Customs and Revenue Administration in Canada: A Discussion Paper on Progress and Innovation to Comment* (Revenue Canada, 1998) at foreword.

[38] A Meghji and S Sieker, 'A Contest of Unequals: Recent Developments in Tax Litigation' in *Report of the Proceedings of the Forty-Ninth Tax Conference*, 1997 Tax Conference (Canadian Tax Foundation, 1998) 11:1, 11:22.

[39] See Benjamin Alarie, Kalmen Datt, Adrian Sawyer and Greg Weeks, 'Advance Tax Rulings in Perspective: A Theoretical and Comparative Analysis' (2014) 21 *New Zealand Journal of Taxation Law and Policy* 362; *Woon v MNR* [1950] CTC 263 (Ex Ct).

[40] These documents are obtained and made publicly available by private entities though freedom of information requests.

Of the above, ITFs and ICs are intended for use by both taxpayers and tax professionals, ITTNs and ITs are intended for tax professionals, Tax Guides and Pamphlets are intended for taxpayers and the general public,[41] and ATRs are applicable to specific transactions. Despite the distinction in use, all of them are written in clear language and appear easy to understand/apply by taxpayers without recourse to tax professionals. ITFs,[42] ITTNs, and ITs are subject to general notices that appear to be aimed at limiting the reasonableness of replying on the information they contain, often referring the reader back to the ITA, Regulations, and relevant cases. ICs are not subject to a general notice, though specific ICs contain statements as to when they do and do not apply, including that they are not meant to replace the spirit or intent of legislation.[43] Tax Guides and Pamphlets and ATRs do not contain any notices, but ATRs are issued to taxpayers and are considered by the CRA to be binding only for that one taxpayer and only within the facts detailed. Despite the various notices, the wording of which is different in the various soft-law instruments, given the complexity of income tax law and the vast volume of 'incomprehensible' text in the statute and regulations, we would suggest that reliance may be necessarily invited by the simple act of making available more accessible and understandable descriptions of the law.

In light of the range of sources of soft law in the context of tax administration, discussed above, how should the legal effects of these instruments be understood? Are instruments intended for use by tax professionals to be considered as giving rise to greater/lesser expectation than those intended for taxpayers? Are instruments which are not publicly circulated (but which are not secret either) be considered to create greater/lesser expectation than those posted on the CRA website? Given the disclaimers that routinely accompany all these instruments, to the effect that none of them 'replace the law', should they give rise to legal consequences? Is a taxpayer who relies on the content of these instruments to his/her detriment within his/her rights to seek a remedy on the basis an expectation has been frustrated?

In order to answer these fundamental questions, it is necessary review the treatment of legitimate expectation in Canadian administrative law.

[41] Guides are often accompanied with forms and directions on how to fill out and file those forms.

[42] ITFs state that they are updated when interpretations change or major developments occur, leading a reader to trust that the information is current. ITFs also expressly state that the folio chapters can be relied upon as an accurate summary of the CRA's interpretation of the law—see for example the first paragraph in the Medical Expense Tax Credit Folio—S1-F1-C1, available online at www.cra-arc.gc.ca/tx/tchncl/ncmtx/fls/s1/f1/s1-f1-c1-eng.html.

[43] See for example paragraphs 3 to 5 in IC12-1, 'GST/HST Compliance Refund Holds', available online at www.cra-arc.gc.ca/E/pub/tp/ic12-1/ic12-1-12e.pdf; IC00-1R4 [7].

LEGITIMATE EXPECTATIONS AND SOFT LAW

Soft law can be described both by what it is and what it is not.[44] In the first (descriptive) sense, soft law includes a wide range of instruments, from guidelines to circulars, policy statements to protocols, which influence a decision-making process. All of the CRA guidelines outlined above qualify as soft law (at least on this standard). In the second (legal) sense, soft law refers to any rules which affect decision-making but are by design or definition non-binding, and so not 'law'. In the Canadian context, 'hard law' would represent all statutory provisions and rules emanating from instruments delegated by statutes to be binding (eg regulations, by-laws, etc). Hard law, in other words, is what authorises CRA officials, on behalf of the Minister, to make decisions. Soft law represents everything else that shapes the resulting exercise of the discretion created by hard law.

Because the CRA itself promulgates the guidelines discussed above, is it reasonable for taxpayers and tax preparers to expect the CRA to rely and make decisions based on their contents? This question is not as straightforward as it sounds. The guidelines themselves make apparent that they are not intended to replace the law. How can officials be held accountable for applying or not applying non-binding instruments? However, it appears to be unfair for those interacting with CRA officials to be given information about how the CRA will interpret and apply the *ITA* if those officials can disregard the information at any time for any reason. Further, the CRA does not treat these different instruments alike. While ITTNs are simply informational, the ITs are clearly intended to disclose how certain matters are likely to be approached by the CRA. ITFs appear to be hybrid instruments which inform and advise. Tax administration needs a spectrum of legal relevance rather than an on/off switch that would simply create or not create legally relevant expectations.

Legitimate Expectations and the Supreme Court of Canada

Canada lacks a detailed conceptual framework for the application of legitimate expectations.[45] The very first detailed discussion of legitimate

[44] See F Houle and L Sossin, 'Tribunals and Guidelines: Exploring the Relationships between Fairness and Legitimacy in Administrative Decision-Making' (2006) 46 *Canadian Public Administration* 283.

[45] For a notable exception, see David Wright, 'Rethinking the Doctrine of Legitimate Expectations in Canadian Administrative Law' (1997) 35 *Osgoode Hall Law Journal* 139. For an example of a more systematic approach in the UK setting, see Adam Perry and Farrah Ahmed, 'The Coherence of the Doctrine of Legitimate Expectations' (2014) 73 *Cambridge Law Journal* 61.

expectations by the SCC took place in *Martineau* in the context of soft law.[46] In that decision, the majority of the Court provided a closer analysis of the duty to act fairly based on the English fairness doctrine. An inmate in a federal penitentiary challenged a conviction for a disciplinary offence relying in part on departures from a Commissioner's Directive providing procedural safeguards/rights. The majority referred to Lord Denning's decision in *Schmidt*,[47] where the doctrine of legitimate expectations was first introduced in English law.

In discussing the role and effect of 'fairness', the majority stated that 'natural justice and fairness are principles of judicial process deemed by the common law to be annexed to legislation, with a view to bringing statutory provisions in conformity with the common law requirements of justice'.[48] The majority held that, between the poles of 'purely ministerial decisions' on board policy grounds that attract no procedural protection and judicial-like functions that attract substantial procedural safeguards,[49] there exists 'a myriad decision-making processes with a flexible gradation of procedural fairness through the administrative spectrum'.[50] Dealing specifically with the application of the Commissioner's Directives, the majority stated that the courts are not concerned with:

> breaches of the prison rules, but whether there has been a breach of the duty to act fairly in all circumstances, ... the rules are of some importance in determining [the question of fairness] as [they are] an indication of the views of the prison authorities as to the degree of procedural protection to be extended to inmates.[51]

The Court attempted to bring together Canadian and English principles in *Old St Boniface*,[52] a case arising in the disparate setting of municipal re-zoning. The majority discussed the appellant's argument based on 'a legitimate expectation of consultation' created by the 'conduct of the Committee'.[53] The majority stated that the English principle merely extends the reach of the rules of natural justice and procedural fairness to give 'a party affected by the decision of a public official an opportunity to make representations in circumstances in which there otherwise would be no such opportunity'.[54] Legitimate expectation was grounded in the 'conduct of a

[46] *Martineau v Matsqui Disciplinary Bd* [1980] 1 SCR 603 ('*Martineau*').
[47] *Schmidt v Secretary of State for Home Affairs* [1969] 2 Ch 149 (CA).
[48] *Martineau* (n 46) 627.
[49] *Martineau* (n 46) 628–29.
[50] *Martineau* (n 46) 628.
[51] *Martineau* (n 46) 630.
[52] *Old St Boniface Residents Assn Inc v Winnipeg (City)* [1990] 3 SCR 1170 ('*Old St Boniface*').
[53] Ibid, 1203.
[54] Ibid, 1204.

public official [that lead] a party [...] to believe that his or her rights would not be affected without consultation'.[55] The majority concluded that, even if there was a legitimate expectation, it would not replace the elaborate statutory scheme with another process of consultation. Some commentators believe that this decision excluded the possibility of substantive legitimate expectations in Canada,[56] while others believe that it left that possibility open.[57]

The SCC in *Reference Re Canada Assistance Plan (BC)* (*CAP*) appeared to resolve the ambiguity regarding legitimate expectations created by *Old St Boniface*.[58] This was an appeal from a British Colombia Court of Appeal decision that extended the reach of the legitimate expectations doctrine by restricting the Federal Government Executive's ability to introduce a Bill into Parliament (aimed at reducing a budget deficit) in breach of an agreement between the Federal and Provincial Governments. The Supreme Court found that the Government had abided by the agreement and, since the agreement's funding formula referred to the statute, it could be validly amended by statute. In dealing with the doctrine of legitimate expectations, the Court referred to *Old St Boniface*, and then drew a distinction between the procedural right to be consulted and the substantive right to give consent. The Court concluded that the creation of substantive rights through the doctrine of legitimate expectations is not supported in Canadian or English cases. The doctrine was said to be part of the rules of procedural fairness, and where it is applicable, it can create additional rights to make representations or to be consulted. The Court concluded that legitimate expectations could not operate to fetter the decision following the representation or consultation. Further, the rules of procedural fairness do not bind a body 'exercising purely legislative functions'.[59] In other words, one government could not bind future governments by making promises about legislation or policy.

In *Baker*,[60] the Court attempted to embed legitimate expectations in the broader duty of fairness and invoked it as one of five non-exhaustive and non-hierarchal 'factors' a court should consider in determining the degree of fairness owed in a particular context. The Court addressed legitimate expectations in the context of soft law in this analysis and held that the

[55] Ibid.

[56] Geneviève Cartier, 'A "Mullanian" Approach to the Doctrine of Legitimate Expectations: Real Questions and Promising Answers' in Grant Huscroft, Michael Taggart, and David J Mullan (eds), *Inside and Outside Canadian Administrative Law: Essays in Honour of David Mullan* (University of Toronto Press, 2006) 189–90.

[57] Wright (n 45) 167.

[58] *Reference Re Canada Assistance Plan (BC)* [1991] 2 SCR 525 ('*CAP*').

[59] Ibid.

[60] *Baker v Canada (Minister of Citizenship and Immigration)* [1999] 2 SCR 817 ('*Baker*').

failure of the decision-maker to follow the applicable guideline or applicable international covenants and agreements did not render the exercise of discretion unfair.[61]

The Court dealt with the legal effect of the publicly available guidelines. Here, the Immigration Manual used by immigration officers provided various criteria and considerations to be assessed in exercising their discretion. In *obiter*, the Court outlined the doctrine for purposes of determining the content of the duty of fairness. After confirming that a legitimate expectation 'does not create substantive rights',[62] and distinguishing the 'object of the expectation from its legal effects',[63] the Court stated that:

> a legitimate expectation that a certain procedure will be followed [means that] this procedure will be required by the duty of fairness ... [and] a legitimate expectation that a certain result will be reached [...] may require more extensive procedural rights than would otherwise be accorded.[64]

The Court clarified that the doctrine is based on the principle that 'it will generally be unfair for [administrative decision-makers] to act in contravention of representations as to procedure, or to backtrack on substantive promises without according significant procedural rights'.[65]

For the Court in *Baker*, the guidelines related more to the substantive review of the reasonableness of the Immigration Officer's exercise of discretion. The Court held that 'the guidelines are a useful indicator of what constitutes a reasonable interpretation of the power conferred by the provision, and the fact that this decision was contrary to the directives is of great help in assessing whether the decision was an unreasonable exercise' of discretion.[66] Even the discretion to make a decision that is wholly a matter of judgment is granted within certain boundaries. Such a decision must be made 'following an approach that respects [the purpose of the discretion and the values it advances]'.[67] In this case, the guidelines reflected the proper approach (which also incorporated the approach set out in an international convention to which Canada was a signatory) and the decision's inconsistency with the guideline and the international convention led to the conclusion that the decision was unreasonable.

Subsequently, the Court explored whether a finding of unreasonableness could flow from promissory estoppel if a promise by a decision-maker gives

[61] Ibid [29].
[62] Ibid [26].
[63] Cartier (n 56) 190.
[64] *Baker* (n 60) [26].
[65] *Baker* (n 60) [26].
[66] *Baker* (n 60) [72].
[67] *Baker* (n 60) [74].

rise to detrimental reliance. In *Mount Sinai*,[68] a government official committed to a process resulting in the relocation of a hospital and then reneged on its approval for the relocation. The majority of the SCC held that it was unnecessary to decide whether a legitimate expectation was created by the Government's representations, and allowed the appeal based upon its interpretation of the applicable statute. Writing for the majority of the Court, Bastarache J held that the Minister was bound by the prior commitment as the initial exercise of the relevant discretion.[69] At that point, the Court held the discretion was, in effect, exhausted, and the subsequent attempt to reverse the decision on the relocation was not authorised and not valid.[70]

Binnie J, in a concurring decision with which McLachlin CJ agreed, concluded that the Minister's decision was 'patently unreasonable [... and] reached by a process that was demonstrably unfair' and, therefore, an abuse of discretion.[71] The respondents were found to have worked closely with the regulators for a long time, developing a 'web of understandings and incremental arrangements with the concurrence indeed the encouragement of successive Ministers'.[72] Binnie J concluded that, where representations are detrimentally relied upon, an estoppel will operate unless a statute or an overriding public interest dictates a contrary result.[73] Alternatively, an unreasonable[74] decision may be quashed and, absent an overriding public interest to the contrary, mandamus might then issue to compel the decision-maker to exercise his or her discretion afresh and according to law.[75]

The minority addressed the respondent's argument that legitimate expectations can give substantive results where the result is not contrary to law and is otherwise within the power of the Minister. While the respondent argued that the doctrine was evolving,[76] the minority noted that there is a difference between the Canadian and English contexts. In England, it was stated that the doctrine of legitimate expectations 'performs a number of functions that in Canada are kept distinct'.[77] The doctrine of legitimate expectations in England was seen as having developed into

[68] *Mount Sinai Hospital Centre v Quebec (Minister of Health and Social Services)* 2001 SCC 41 ('*Mount Sinai*').
[69] Ibid, [90].
[70] Ibid, [100].
[71] Ibid, [66].
[72] Ibid, [8].
[73] Ibid, [16].
[74] The minority referred to a 'patently unreasonable' decision, but this standard was later fused with the 'reasonable' standard in *Dunsmuir v New Brunswick* 2008 SCC 9 [45].
[75] *Mount Sinai* (n 68) [16].
[76] Relying on a number of international and Canadian decisions: *Sous-ministre du Revenu du Québec v Transport Lessard (1976) Ltée* [1985] RDJ 502; *Gingras v Canada* [1990] 2 FC 68 (TD), and *Bloomfield v Saskatchewan (Minister of Health)* [1986] SJ No 675 (QL) (QB).
[77] *Mount Sinai* (n 68) [24].

> a comprehensive code that embraced the full gamut of administrative relief from procedural fairness at the low end through 'enhanced' procedural fairness based on conduct, thence onwards to estoppel (though it is not to be called that) including substantive relief at the high end.[78]

The high end of relief was seen as an inappropriate intervention in government policy in Canada, absent a challenge under the *Canadian Charter of Rights and Freedoms*.[79]

The minority stated that the doctrine of legitimate expectations looks to the public authority's clear, unambiguous, and unqualified conduct in exercising power, and requires that the expectation does not conflict with the authority's statutory jurisdiction.[80] Unlike estoppel, legitimate expectations do not require the person to show awareness of, reliance on, or detriment resulting from the relied on conduct.[81] This is because the focus of legitimate expectations is the promotion of 'regularity, predictability, and certainty in government's dealing with the public'.[82] The minority felt that the decision in *CAP*, referring to *Old St Boniface*, closed the door on substantive relief, but also stated that if 'the Court is to give substantive relief, more demanding conditions precedent must be fulfilled than are presently required by the doctrine of legitimate expectation'.[83]

One limitation on the legitimate expectations doctrine is that purely ministerial decisions on broad grounds of public policy will not typically afford any procedural protections.[84] Another limitation is that a public body exercising legislative functions is only liable to judicial supervision as a result of a successful *Charter* challenge.[85]

[78] *Mount Sinai* (n 68) [26].

[79] *Canadian Charter of Rights and Freedoms*, Part I of the Constitution Act, 1982, being Schedule B to the Canada Act 1982 (UK), 1982, c 11.

[80] *Mount Sinai* (n 68) [29].

[81] *Mount Sinai* (n 68) [30]. Note, however, that in *Coughlan*, Lord Woolf implied that reliance may be a necessary element; see *R v North and East Devon Health Authority: ex parte Coughlan* [2001] 1 QB 213. Note also that in *Minister for Immigration and Ethnic Affairs v Teoh* [1995] HCA 20, the High Court of Australia held that actual reliance was unnecessary.

[82] *Mount Sinai* (n 68) [30], citing with approval SA de Smith, H Woolf and J Jowell, *Judicial Review of Administrative Action*, 5th edn (Sweet and Maxwell, 1995) 417. The editors state that adding estoppel-type requirements to legitimate expectations would 'involve unfair discrimination between those who were and were not aware of the representation and would benefit the well-informed or well-advised [and] would also encourage undesirable administrative practice by too readily relieving decision-makers of the normal consequences of their actions' (at 426).

[83] *Mount Sinai* (n 68) [32].

[84] An attack on such decisions must be based on abuse of discretion: Mount Sinai (n 68), [33].

[85] Mount Sinai (n 68) [34].

Legitimate expectations have also sometimes been labelled to emphasise 'reasonableness' rather than 'legitimacy'.[86] In *Moreau*,[87] for example, it was argued that the applicant had a 'reasonable expectation' that inquiry findings into her conduct as a judge would not result in her dismissal and that she would continue in her role after the impugned action. There is nothing in the facts relied on to locate the basis of these 'reasonable expectations' in 'clear, unambiguous, and unqualified' representations or conduct of the decision-maker. The SCC did not inquire whether there were any legitimate expectations on the basis of which relief was sought, but simply held that 'the doctrine of reasonable expectations does not create substantive rights, and does not fetter the discretion of a statutory decision-maker'.[88] The doctrine was stated only to create and apply to procedural rights, and then only when 'a party affected by an administrative decision can establish a legitimate expectation that a certain procedure would be followed'.[89]

A number of SCC decisions refer to the doctrine of legitimate expectations in passing. In *Mackin*,[90] dealing with the status of supernumerary judges, the Court did not find that a legitimate expectation had been established, but went on to note that even if one had, the doctrine does not apply to purely legislative functions and does not 'operate to entitle the [person] to a substantive as opposed to procedural remedy'.[91]

In *CUPE*,[92] the Court was called upon to determine what factors were relevant and irrelevant to a particular exercise of discretion by the Minister of Labour to appoint interest arbitrators, and looked to the history of the legislation to identify its purpose.[93] The majority held that 'the conditions precedent to the application of the doctrine [of legitimate expectations] were not established in this case'[94] but nonetheless commented on the reach of the doctrine. The majority described legitimate expectations as 'an extension of the rules of natural justice and procedural fairness' that considers the conduct of an administrative decision-maker in the exercise of a discretionary power including 'established practices, conduct or representations' that can be characterised as clear and has in fact produced reasonable expectations of procedure or a certain benefit.[95] The question of 'legitimacy' arises

[86] See Greg Weeks, 'What Can We Legitimately Expect from the State?' in chapter 7 of this volume.

[87] *Moreau-Bérubé v New Brunswick (Judicial Council)* 2002 SCC 11 ('*Moreau*').

[88] Ibid, [78].

[89] Ibid.

[90] *Mackin v New Brunswick (Minister of Finance)* 2002 SCC 13 ('*Mackin*').

[91] Ibid, [162].

[92] *CUPE v Ontario (Minister of Labour)* 2003 SCC 29 ('*CUPE*').

[93] Ibid, [110].

[94] Ibid, [133].

[95] Ibid, [131].

when looking to whether or not the expectations conflict with a statutory duty.[96] In the result, the majority characterised past practices in the appointment of arbitrators as an implied requirement of the appointment power and the Minister, by failing to adhere to those practices, reached a patently unreasonable decision.

In *Mavi*,[97] the SCC considered the decision of Ontario to adopt certain procedures in light of federal statutory requirements, including whether Ontario had behaved reasonably or had fettered its discretion. The Court held that the legislation left Ontario with a measure of discretion, and that the procedure adopted by Ontario was compatible with the statute[98] without conflicting with the intended scope of the discretion.[99] The importance of policy as a guide to civil servants was recognised by the Court, as was the Minister's entitlement to set policy within legal limits.[100] The Court stated that, in order to give rise to legitimate expectations, representations have to be within the scope of the decision-maker's authority. Reliance was held not to be required.[101]

The most recent[102] and most potentially far-reaching discussion of legitimate expectations by the SCC is that in *Agraira*,[103] which relates specifically to soft law. This unanimous judgment of a seven-member Court was concerned with a Minister's discretionary decision, required to be exercised after considering the 'national interest'.[104] The appellant argued that the Minister took an excessively narrow view of the phrase 'national interest', and failed to meet a legitimate expectation that certain procedures would be followed and certain factors taken into account.[105]

While a staff briefing note indicated the petition should be granted, the Minister denied relief. The lower court had held that the Minister's reasons did not address the questions listed in the guidelines or factors identified by the courts as relevant. The SCC considered the reasonableness of the Minister's decision and referred to the guidelines as part of the reasonableness

[96] Ibid, [131].
[97] *Canada v Mavi* 2011 SCC 30 ('*Mavi*').
[98] Ibid, [44].
[99] Ibid, [65].
[100] Ibid, [66].
[101] Ibid, [68].
[102] See *Kanthasamy v Canada (Citizenship and Immigration)* 2015 SCC 61, where the majority of the Court reiterated that guidelines, though useful, are not legally binding and are not intended to be exhaustive or restrictive. The Court concluded that a discretionary decision-maker who limited the criteria to be considered only to those set out in the Ministry guidelines acted unreasonably.
[103] The issues related to the doctrine of legitimate expectations were considered to be incidental to the central issue of whether the Federal Court of Appeal (FCA) chose the correct standard of review and applied it properly: *Agraira* [2013] 2 SCR 559 [3], [47].
[104] Relief could be granted where the person 'satisfies the Minister that their presence in Canada would not be detrimental to the national interest': ibid [42].
[105] Ibid, [2].

assessment.[106] The Court stated that, rather than being a fixed code, the guidelines contained 'a set of factors, which appeared to be relevant and reasonable' for the exercise of the particular discretion.[107] The Minister was not required to apply them formulaically, but they should have 'guided the exercise of his discretion and assisted in framing a fair administrative process for such applications' and, as such, assisted the Court in understanding the Minister's 'implied interpretation of the "national interest"'.[108]

The doctrine of legitimate expectations was stated to be a 'particular face of procedural fairness' that can work to expand the procedural protections otherwise available.[109] Legitimate expectations cannot give rise to substantive rights; courts are limited to granting only procedural relief.[110] In *Agraira*, the Court held that the guidelines, which were publicly available, met the threshold requirements to give rise to a legitimate expectation.[111] The Court stated that in this case the expectation was fulfilled.[112] With regard to relevant factors outlined in the guidelines, the Court was of the opinion that where the guideline (irrespective of its source) is employed by the decision-maker in the making of the decision or in obtaining guidance for the exercise of discretion, and where the guideline is a relatively comprehensive code with respect to the decision of the exercise of discretion, then the factors listed must be considered.

Agraira has been influential in Canadian courts,[113] though only a handful of decisions have relied on it to resolve matters related to legitimate expectations and the (mis)use of guidelines by administrative decision-makers.[114] Of these decisions, only two have considered the substantive effect that guidelines can have when reviewing the reasonableness of an administrative decision-maker's exercise of discretion.[115] In *Pushparasa*, the Federal Court

[106] Guidelines can serve at least two distinct purposes. One is to inform the reasonableness analysis of a discretionary decision; the other is to determine whether the process was fair or not. Here, the broader context of the statutory provision 'includes the Guidelines' which, although not law 'in the strict sense', are 'a useful indicator of what constitutes a reasonable interpretation' of the particular provision: ibid [85].

[107] *Agraira* (n 103) [60].

[108] *Agraira* (n 103) [60].

[109] *Agraira* (n 103) [94].

[110] *Agraira* (n 103) [97].

[111] *Agraira* (n 103) [98].

[112] *Agraira* (n 103) [101].

[113] As at 1 January 2016, *Agraira* had been cited in over 300 cases.

[114] The majority of the decisions cited *Agraira* when dealing with (i) standard of review analysis, (ii) reasonableness of decisions, (iii) sufficiency of reasons, (iv) humanitarian and compassionate ground considerations under *Immigration and Refugee Protection Act*, (v) presumptions of consistent expression in statutes and modern rule of statutory interpretation, or (vi) a court of appeal's role when reviewing JR decision of lower court.

[115] *Frankie's Burgers Lougheed Inc v Canada (Employment and Social Development)* 2015 FC 27 ('*Frankie's*') and *Pushparasa v Canada (Citizenship and Immigration)* 2015 FC 828 ('*Pushparasa*').

(FC) stated that guidelines are useful in assisting the exercises of discretion (inherent in the decision), and may 'frame an administrative process for it to be reasonable and thus fair'.[116] In *Frankie's*, the FC stated that broad, flexible adherence to guidelines set out in *Agraira* has 'many public benefits', including 'increased administrative efficiency, reduced backlogs, decreased scope for arbitrariness and increased certainty and predictability'.[117] Published guidelines were held to 'serve the useful role of giving rise to legitimate expectations regarding the assessment frameworks that will be followed by a public agency', and can serve as a useful indicator of what constitutes a reasonable interpretation of legislation.[118]

Summary of Principles of Legitimate Expectations in Canada

A claimant may have a legitimate expectation to a particular procedure,[119] to have certain criteria considered as relevant,[120] or to a particular substantive outcome.[121] However, one cannot have a legitimate expectation that certain criteria, not made express by pronouncements or conduct of the decision-maker, will not be considered.[122]

Legitimate expectations are generated by a public body's clear, unambiguous and unqualified conduct.[123] The conduct that can give rise to a legitimate expectation includes established practices, actions, or representations (oral or written, specific or general) of the public authority,[124] or a closely related public authority whose guidelines are used in making the decision or guide the exercise of discretion.[125] Also, to give rise to a legitimate expectation, the conduct must be within the scope of the decision-maker's statutory authority.[126] These are objective criteria. Finally, there is no requirement of awareness of, or detrimental reliance on, the conduct by the claimant.[127]

[116] *Pushparasa*, ibid [27].
[117] *Frankie's* (n 115) [94].
[118] *Frankie's* (n 115) [94]–[95].
[119] *Martineau* (n 46), *Old St Boniface* (n 52); *CAP* (n 58); *CUPE* (n 91); *Agraira* (n 102); *Baker* (n 60); and *Mount Sinai* (n 68).
[120] This is not strictly part of the legitimate expectations doctrine, though it is very closely related. The courts have considered conduct that would give rise to legitimate expectations as part of the reasonableness analysis of the decision on judicial review. See *Baker* (n 60). However, the SCC in *Agraira* (n 102), considered factors that would allow a claimant to have a legitimate expectation as to factors to be considered as set out in guidelines.
[121] *Baker* (n 60); *Agraira* (n 103).
[122] *Agraira* (n 103).
[123] *Mount Sinai* (n 68) (Binnie J); *Moreau* (n 87); *CUPE* (n 92).
[124] *CUPE* (n 92); and *Agraira* (n 102).
[125] *Agraira* (n 103).
[126] *Mavi* (n 97).
[127] *Mount Sinai* (n 68) (Binnie J); and *Mavi* (n 97).

As an extension of the rules of procedural fairness,[128] legitimate expectations may both extend procedural protections beyond what the circumstances may otherwise require,[129] and determine what procedures the duty of fairness requires in any circumstances.[130] The conduct of the administrative decision-maker is useful to the courts as an indicator of fairness since it represents the expert administrator's view of what constitutes fair procedure in the circumstances.[131] Legitimate expectations relate both to procedural and substantive accountability for decision-making, but result in only procedural remedies.

Although the SCC has stated that legitimate expectations only give rise to procedural protection, there is a range of substantive legal effects that flow from legitimate expectations. As part of the Court's application of the proper standard of review, the analysis of reasonableness under administrative law appears closely linked to its legitimate expectation reasoning. For example, in *Baker*, the Court justified its finding that the decision-maker had acted unreasonably in part because she failed to consider the applicable guideline. In this way, while legitimate expectations have developed in Canada as a procedural doctrine, the doctrine's analytic roots appear to be shared with substantive forms of review.[132]

LEGITIMATE EXPECTATIONS IN THE TAX ADMINISTRATION CONTEXT

Having explored the sources of soft law in the Canadian tax administration context and the development of legitimate expectations in Canadian administrative law, we now return to explore what impact, if any, legitimate expectations may have in arguably the richest setting of soft law in the Canadian legal system.

Courts' Current Treatment of CRA Soft Law

There are no SCC decisions that deal with the doctrine of legitimate expectations in the tax administration context. We will however briefly examine some Federal Court of Appeal (FCA) and Tax Court of Canada (TCC)

[128] *Old St Boniface* (n 52); *CAP* (n 58); *CUPE* (n 91); and *Agraira* (n 103).
[129] *Old St Boniface* (n 52); *CAP* (n 58); *CUPE* (n 92); and *Agraira* (n 103).
[130] *Baker* (n 60).
[131] *Martineau* (n 46). See also *Baker* (n 60).
[132] *Baker* (n 60); and *Agraira* (n 103).

decisions.[133] The FCA has consistently held that 'policy guidelines do not create legitimate expectations of substantive rights',[134] and has classified taxpayers' request to have the Minister review the matter in accordance with CRA policies and publications as 'a substantive right, in procedural language'.[135] CRA publications and materials have no legal force and are not determinative.[136] Taxpayers cannot rely on CRA publications and other administrative positions, and cannot rely on express promises or views expressed to another taxpayer in advance tax rulings (despite the CRA's position and consistent practice of regarding such rulings as binding as between the CRA and that particular taxpayer).[137]

This body of law, however, pre-dates the most recent developments in the legitimate expectations doctrine and soft law, particularly the Supreme Court's decision in *Agraira*. Older judicial statements about income taxation may also be vestiges of a time where taxation was viewed merely as confiscation of private property by the state—an attitude that, until quite recently, prompted the courts to interpret tax legislation narrowly and strictly as legislation designed to impose penalties. The assumptions and attitudes that underlie an approach holding tax law as 'unique' warrant critical re-examination in light of the change in the role that income taxation plays in modern, welfare democracies.

Legitimate expectations in the tax setting are framed by a legal context in which each assessment of each individual's tax liability in each year is considered afresh. In *Ludmer*[138] the Federal Court confirmed that a tax authority was not bound by a concession made in one year to have to make the same concession in other years even if there was no change in law.[139] In other words, by applying the law to a person's tax liability one way in one year, no legitimate expectation is created on which that person can rely to suggest that similar approaches are taken in the future. This is because the tax authority is authorised to assess each individual taxation year independently,[140] making an assessment conclusive only for the year to which it

[133] Although the SCC has not addressed legitimate expectations in the context of tax administration, it has held that CRA's administrative guidelines are 'not determinative but are entitled to weight and can be an "important factor" in case of doubt about the meaning of legislation': *Nowegijick v R* [1983] 1 SCR 29 [28].

[134] *Oberlander v Canada (AG)* 2004 FCA 213.

[135] *Johnston Canyon Co Ltd v Canada (AG)* 2009 FCA 219 [32].

[136] See *Nowegijick* (n 133).

[137] See *Woon v MNR* (n 39). The authors have not encountered any recent decisions in respect to such rulings, likely due to the CRA's administrative practice.

[138] *Ludmer v Canada* [1995] 2 FC 3 (FCA) ('*Ludmer*').

[139] Ibid, citing *Admiral Investment Ltd v MNR* [1967] 2 Ex CR 308.

[140] See *Ludmer* (n 138). A limited amount of certainty is provided by the time limitations the *ITA* places on the Minister's power to assess, additionally assess, or reassess a taxpayer.

applies, and allowing the tax authority to take a different view in a different year.[141] So long as these inconsistent assessments are issued in good faith and are supported by the law, the courts will not interfere.

Aside from this case specific approach, the doctrine of legitimate expectations is treated the same way in tax administration as in the SCC decisions. Just as estoppel generally cannot lie with respect to an opinion or interpretation of the law,[142] and cannot lie where it is invoked to prevent the exercise of a statutory duty or the application of law,[143] legitimate expectations cannot compel a particular application of the *Income Tax Act*.[144] Rather, guidelines issued by the CRA are held to reflect government policy as to the meaning and scope of the legislation.[145] The Courts have viewed the interpretation of the Act as their responsibility, and that government policy as reflected in soft law cannot bind that interpretive role.[146] On this basis, the FCA has stated that the Minister is not bound in the present or the future by CRA's guidelines.[147] However, a taxpayer may use the CRA's guidelines to support an argument that the interpretation in the guidelines is correct.[148] In this sense, soft law in this context has legal relevance, even if not enforceable per se. Can soft law by itself ground an argument of unreasonableness or unfairness? The short answer in Canada now appears to be affirmative on both fronts. That said, the circumstances in which guidelines or other forms of soft law play a role in legal consequences remains to be fully explored.

For example, in the voluntary disclosure programme, which uses the discretion of the Minister to waive interest and penalties, several cases have held the Minister to the conditions for and the substantive relief promised in the applicable Information Circular. In *Karia*,[149] the FC held that although Information Circulars are not delegated legislation and have no force of law

[141] *ITA* s 152(8).

[142] *Ludmer* (n 138), citing *Stickel v MNR* [1972] FC 672, 681. See also *JP Morgan Asset Management (Canada) Inc v Canada (National Revenue)* 2012 FC 651 [76] (information bulletins of the CRA do not create estoppels).

[143] *Ludmer* (n 138), citing *Canada (Minister of Employment and Immigration) v Lidder* [1992] 2 FC 621 (CA) 625: 'common sense would dictate that one cannot fail to apply the law due to the misstatement, the negligence or simply the misrepresentation of a government worker'.

[144] *Ludmer* (n 138).

[145] *Ludmer* (n 138), citing *Vaillancourt v Deputy MNR* [1991] 3 FC 663 (CA) 674.

[146] Unlike in the UK, where a taxpayer is limited to an appeal on a point of law only, in Canada a taxpayer may appeal to the TCC and challenge both the facts and the law in a full trial (see *Ludmer* (n 138)).

[147] *Ludmer* (n 138). See *Stickel v MNR* [1972] FCJ no 53, reviewed on other ground by the FCA in 72 DTC 6178 (FCA), subsequently affirmed by SCC in 74 DTC 6269 (SCC); see also *MNR v Inland Industries* [1971] SCJ 145.

[148] *Ludmer* (n 138), citing *Vaillancourt* (n 145) 674. See also *Harel v The Deputy Minister of Revenue in the Province of Quebec,* [1978] 1 SCR 851 and *R v Nowegijick* [1983] SCJ o 5, 83 DTC 5041 (SCC).

[149] *Karia v Canada (MNR)* 2005 FC 639 ('*Karia*'). *Karia* was never appealed but was followed in *Wong v Canada (National Revenue)* 2007 FC 628.

'as such', promissory estoppel would operate to prevent the Minister with the necessary lawful authority from exercising discretion contrary to the promise contained in the Information Circular.[150] Where the requirements for estoppel have not been met, the FC has held that Information Circulars are not binding on the Minister in the exercise of discretion.[151] Further, guidelines have been held to be relevant in assessing the reasonableness of the Minister's decision when exercising discretionary powers.[152] Whatever the role of guidelines in setting out relevant considerations the weight to be assigned to the relevant and competing factors, within a range of reasonable outcomes, is for the decision-maker alone.[153]

The TCC held in *Wollenberg*, in reference to the provisions that set a taxpayer's liability rather than those which deal with tax administration, that:

> what Parliament has decreed shall be the rules applicable in determining what is payable by way of tax under the provisions of the Act is paramount and cannot be repealed or amended in any manner by whatever Revenue Canada may choose to publish by way of Tax Guides, Interpretation Bulletins, or otherwise.[154]

In the context of the substantive tax provisions, such publications have some limited legal consequences.[155] Where a provision is ambiguous, such that there is doubt as to its meaning, guidelines are 'entitled to weight' and can be an 'important factor' in the process of proper interpretation.[156] However, courts have refused to simply rely on administrative practice when provisions are unclear.[157] Where a policy contradicts the wording of the provision or otherwise takes a position not supported by the legislation, it can be of no help.[158] Administrative practice has an asymmetrical operation which can

[150] *Karia* (n 149) [7]–[9].

[151] See eg *Brown v Canada (Customs and Revenue Agency)* 2005 FC 1639 [27] (Information Circulars 'cannot exclude all other valid and relevant reasons for which the Minister might exercise his discretionary authority or refuse to do so').

[152] See *Telfer v Canada (Canada Revenue Agency)* 2008 FC 218 [13], citing *Jim's Pizza (1980) Ltd v Canada (Revenue Agency)* 2007 FC 782 (Minister's discretionary power to waive interest). This decision was overturned on appeal, 2009 FCA 23, on the basis that the decision was not unreasonable.

[153] *Canada v Telfer* 2009 FCA 23.

[154] *Wollenberg v MNR* 84 DTC 1055 (TCC) ('*Wollenberg*'). See also *Gallant v The Queen* 2013 TCC 119 (taxpayer used CRA forms required to be submitted with his return to calculate a deduction greater than what the Act allowed; held that it was unfair to require the taxpayer to perform calculations according to the form and then assess on a different basis, but the appeal was dismissed because estoppel could not operate to stop the application of the law).

[155] *Wollenberg* (n 154).

[156] *Wollenberg* (n 154). See also *Harel v Québec (Deputy Minister of Revenue)* [1978] 1 SCR 851.

[157] *Brelco Drilling Ltd v The Queen* 98 DTC 1422 (TCC) 430.

[158] *Wollenberg* (n 154). This is linked to the doctrine of fettering of discretion by an administrative decision-maker.

be used to resolve doubt in favour of the taxpayer, but not in favour of the administrative decision-maker that formulated the guideline.[159]

CRA Guidelines and the *Agraira* Criteria

In *Agraira*, the SCC held that in order for guidelines to be able to give rise to legitimate expectations, the guidelines must be:

(1) publicly available;
(2) used to make a decision or guide an exercise of discretion; and
(3) a 'relatively' comprehensive code with respect to making that decision or exercising that discretion.

Of the six CRA guidelines described in the first part of this chapter, which would meet all three conditions?

The first criterion is that the guidelines be publicly available, but the Court did not say that the agency that created the guidelines must make them publicly available, that they must have been intended for the public, or that they be available to the person seeking to rely on them. All six CRA guidelines are publicly available: Folios, ITs, ICs, ITTN, and Tax Guides and Pamphlets are all made available to and are intended to be consulted by the public. ATRs, however, are not publicly available, though members of the public may access them through access to Information legislation.[160] If ATRs are publicly available for the purposes of the *Agraira* analysis, then almost all government guidelines would qualify provided that someone has at some point requested and been granted access to them.

The second criterion is that the guidelines are used by the decision-maker in making a decision or for the purpose of guiding an exercise of discretion. This criterion appears to be more challenging in respect to the six guidelines discussed. On the surface, none of the six are expressly stated to be used to guide decisions or exercises of discretion, since the staff manuals are expected to be used by CRA decision-makers.[161] However, when looking at the content of the internal staff manuals and comparing them to the guidelines considered in this chapter, the substantive content of the two are for all intents and purposes identical. Also, quite often, the manuals refer

[159] See *Canadian Occidental US Petroleum Corp v Canada* [2001] TCJ No 112 (QL) [30].

[160] As with the various manuals that CRA employees use to make decisions and exercise power every day, ATRs are only available to a section of the public that has paid for access through a commercial publisher.

[161] There are a number of manuals that are used by CRA employees, eg the Appeals Branch Reference Materials include the *Taxpayer Relief Reference Guide* which is intended to be a 'complete and up-to-date guidelines on how to apply the taxpayer relief provisions' and 'easy-to-use reference that has information you need to process taxpayer requests'.

the CRA employee to outside sources, including: ICs; Guidelines and Pamphlets; ITs; ATRs; and ITTN. The only type of guideline referred to in this chapter that is not mentioned in the CRA employee manuals are the Folios, likely because they are too recent to have been incorporated explicitly into the manuals.[162] Therefore, all six guidelines would likely meet this criterion, given their incorporation into the employee manuals used by CRA employees in making decisions or exercising discretion.

The third criterion, that the guideline be a relatively comprehensive code with respect to that decision or that exercise of discretion, will likely be satisfied given that each of the six guidelines, at least with respect to the matters they do address within the topics they are geared towards, is relatively complete. This analysis must, however, be made on a guideline-by-guideline basis.

In light of the *Agraira* criteria and the context of CRA soft law, lower court rulings suggesting there is no legal obligation on CRA officials to consider guidelines is now suspect. Indeed, it may well be that areas of law with dense and long-standing uses of soft law, like tax administration, will lead Canada's doctrine of legitimate expectations in new directions.

CONCLUSIONS

This chapter has canvassed the evolution of the Canadian legitimate expectations doctrine with specific reference to soft law in the income tax context. We have used a representative sample of soft law instruments to show how the criteria developed by the Supreme Court of Canada might alter the way in which those guidelines are understood from the perspective of legitimate expectations. Where once these instruments were seen as not giving rise to procedural or substantive rights to have guidelines considered or followed, there now appears to be good reason to rethink the legal implications of soft law. In this way, we have attempted to grapple both with the legal principles explored by Canadian courts and the administrative realities in which those principles must resonate.

The development of legitimate expectations cannot be isolated from a broader trend moving towards a greater 'ethos of justification' in the administrative state and administrative justice. Chief Justice McLachlin described this trend in the following terms:

> [S]ocieties governed by the Rule of Law are marked by a certain ethos of justification. In a democratic society, this may well be the general characteristic of the Rule

[162] All Folios refer to ITs and ITTNs that they replace, so it can reasonably be assumed that where a reference is to an IT or ITTN that has been replaced by a Folio, the CRA employee will look to the Folio for guidance.

> of Law within which the more specific ideals ... are subsumed ....Where a society is marked by a culture of justification, an exercise of public power is only appropriate where it can be justified to citizens in terms of rationality and fairness ... The Rule of Law, in short, can speak in several voices so long as the resulting chorus echoes its underlying values of rationality and fairness (emphasis added).[163]

An 'ethos of justification' includes the idea that 'arbitrary state action [is] impermissible' such that 'the exercise of power must be [...] justifiable and justified' so that citizens see,[164] through the fog of government action, the 'underlying values of rationality and fairness'.[165] In Canadian administrative law, procedural fairness, substantive review for reasonableness or correctness (depending on the standard of review), and monitoring of jurisdiction together serve to advance and promote a culture of justification.[166]

The intersection of soft law and legitimate expectations can advance the project of justification in several ways. Specifically, by recognising that soft law can give rise to legitimate expectations, the Supreme Court has opened up new avenues for enhancing the transparency and accountability of administrative action. At least in the circumstances confirmed in *Agraira* (but perhaps more broadly), guidelines of the kind discussed in this chapter in relation to tax administration can give rise to enforceable expectations. Soft law and legitimate expectations provide a framework for ensuring greater consistency and coherence in the exercise of discretion—and where it can be justified, also ensure transparency if and when administrative decision-makers depart from guidelines and other policy instruments.

Legitimate expectations invite greater attentiveness to context in the review of administrative action. Administrative bodies come in all manner of configurations of powers, duties, obligations, purposes and roles. They combine, in various ways, administrative, investigatory, and judicial roles in pursuit of efficient, effective, and even-handed implementation of government goals. Given this variety, courts should consider a number of factors when considering the legal effect to be given to soft law instruments. While it is premature to describe exhaustively the scope and nature of these factors, the goal of advancing the 'ethos of justification' suggests at least some

[163] Chief Justice McLachlin, 'The Roles of Administrative Tribunals and Courts in Maintaining the Rule of Law' (1999) 12 *Canadian Journal of Administrative Law and Practice* 171, 174.

[164] CES Ned Franks, 'To Prorogue or not to Prorogue: Did the Governor General Make the Right Decision' in Peter H Russel and Lorne Sossin (eds), *Parliamentary Democracy in Crisis* (University of Toronto Press, 2009).

[165] *Wollenberg* (n 154).

[166] See David Dyzenhaus, 'The Politics of Deference: Judicial Review and Democracy' in Michael Taggart (ed), *The Province of Administrative Law* (Hart Publishing, 1997) 279. See also D Dyzenhaus and E Fox-Decent, 'Rethinking the Process/Substance Distinction: Baker v. Canada' (2001) 51 *University of Toronto Law Journal* 193.

of these considerations. For example, where the legislation applies to the general public, a vulnerable sub-group of the public, where it applies irrespective of deliberate action by the person, where the statute is complex or voluminous, where the words conferring the discretionary power are general or broad, where the nature of the discretion is punitive or relieving, and where the consequences of mistakes can have significant effects on the person's daily life, soft law instruments are more likely to be useful, consulted, and relied on. They ought therefore to be given greater consideration by courts when the guideline supports or favours the private person's position or interest. Further, where the instrument sets out a procedure to be followed and the conditions under which discretionary power will be exercised, guidelines ought to be given greater weight.

While the potential of legitimate expectations in relation to soft law is significant, as demonstrated by the setting of tax administration, considerable uncertainty remains. The sharp distinction drawn in Canadian administrative law between the procedural and substantive implications of legitimate expectations is difficult to sustain. The analysis of relevant factors in the legitimate expectations analysis in the context of soft law remains largely undeveloped. In our view, the importance and variability of soft law in the administrative state will continue to drive the development of legitimate expectations. Canadian administrative law is poised to develop a more coherent and transparent doctrine of legitimate expectations. At the same time, a richer understanding of legitimate expectations can serve as a vital catalyst for sorting out the place of soft law within broader rule of law commitments.

14

Legitimate Expectations in Australia: Overtaken by Formalism and Pragmatism

MATTHEW GROVES*

INTRODUCTION

THE LEGITIMATE EXPECTATION has a long, chequered place in Australian public law and now appears to have passed into history after its most recent consideration by the High Court of Australia. But as with so much of Australian public law, the closer one looks, the less clear things become. This chapter will argue that the legitimate expectation has declined to the point of extinction in Australia because the High Court has shifted focus to more practical questions about fairness that subsume legitimate expectations within a wider and avowedly procedural conception of fairness. That approach is partly founded on constitutional principles which preclude a substantive approach to legitimate expectations. Australian principles governing the separation and protection of judicial power have led the High Court to develop a conception of judicial review that draws a sharp distinction between process and merit. Questions of legality or process lie at the heart of judicial power. Questions of merit lie clearly beyond it. This basic division has led Australian courts to reject substantive legitimate expectations as constitutional heresy but the supposedly clear constitutional lines do not explain the rejection by Australian courts of the procedural conception of legitimate expectations. That issue is influenced as much by the practical, structural conception of Australia's administrative law system as by the doctrines fashioned as the constitutional level. For that reason, a brief sketch of that structure is useful.

* Thanks are due to Greg Weeks for helpful comments.

THE FORMATION AND REFORMATION OF AUSTRALIAN ADMINISTRATIVE LAW

The adoption in Australia of a written constitution within a federal system marked a significant break with the UK heritage upon which Australia's legal system was founded. One feature of the new Australian system that remained in fairly close alignment with the UK legal system was the odd place occupied by tribunals. The Australian Constitution created and entrenched a court of final jurisdiction—the High Court of Australia—but in keeping with the British approach, tribunals were neither expressly mentioned in the Constitution nor used in any systematic way by Australian governments. An early focus of constitutional litigation did, however, lay the foundation for the evolution of a particular conception of tribunals.[1] This occurred in the early cases which considered the constitutional status of specialist bodies, most notably the Industrial Relations Commission, which were not courts in the strict sense. These bodies proliferated in the years after the Australian Constitution was adopted, so much attention was given to their constitutional status and whether they met the strict requirements governing courts that exercised judicial power. A steady run of such cases established some key principles, notably that only courts could exercise judicial power and so there could not be a 'third class of courts' which were neither federal nor state courts in the true sense.[2] Another step precluded the issue of advisory opinions by courts because such rulings lacked a hallmark of judicial power, which is to settle real or live controversies.[3] These cases gave rise to notions of what courts could and could not do, at least in a strict constitutional sense, which culminated in the two interrelated principles established by the High Court in the *Boilermakers'* case.[4] The first was that federal legislation can only invest judicial powers in a body that meets all the constitutional requirements of a court. The second and related principle precluded legislation which invested non-judicial functions in courts. There are hazy details around the edges of these principles,[5] though their central thread clearly

[1] For a long time, the High Court was not the final court of appeal because that function was vested in the Privy Council. Appeals to the Privy Council were only finally abolished with the enactment of the *Australia Acts 1986*, although the influence of the Privy Council in constitutional cases, and public law more generally, had waned much earlier.

[2] *New South Wales v Commonwealth* (1915) 20 CLR 54, 62 (Griffith CJ).

[3] *Re Judiciary and Navigation Acts* (1921) 29 CLR 357, 364.

[4] *R v Kirby; ex parte Boilermakers' Society of Australia* (1956) 94 CLR 254, affirmed *Attorney-General (Cth) v The Queen* (1959) 95 CLR 529 (PC). The High Court decision was reached by a narrow majority of four of the seven judges but was unanimously accepted as settled beyond question in later cases such as *Gould v Brown* (1998) 193 CLR 346. Its correctness has often been speculated upon but the *Boilermakers'* principle is most unlikely ever to be overturned by the High Court.

[5] One source of confusion is the so-called 'chameleon doctrine' by which the character of a function (as either judicial or non-judicial) gains much of its character from the particular

underpinned the dramatic reformation of Australian administrative law in the 1970s. That central thread was the notion that the Constitution dictated what courts and non-judicial bodies could and could not do.[6]

These basic constitutional parameters underpinned the radical reforms to Australian administrative law that commended in the 1970s and eventually spread to the States and Territories.[7] Those reforms included the introduction of statutory judicial review, an Ombudsman and freedom of information legislation.[8] Perhaps the most radical reform was the creation of a specialist administrative review tribunal—the Administrative Appeals Tribunal (AAT).[9] The simplified review offered by this new tribunal complimented the new, simplified process of statutory judicial review. The radical aspects of the AAT lay in the scope of its jurisdiction and its unique remedial powers.[10] The AAT originally had jurisdiction to review decisions made under 30 or so statutes but this has since grown to almost 500.

The exceptional width of that jurisdiction was matched by the equally novel nature of the merits review power exercised by the AAT. The tribunal was entitled to 'exercise all the powers and discretions that are conferred' on the original decision-maker, so that it could affirm, set aside, vary or entirely remake the decision under review.[11] The latter two powers provided an external review tribunal with the radical power to make or remake a decision, though the legislation gave no clear indication how that novel power was to be exercised. The nature of that jurisdiction was crafted slowly through the cases and gave rise to several striking innovations. A central one was the notion that the AAT 'stands in the shoes' of the original decision-maker,[12] and is able to make the correct or preferable

context of the relevant legislation. Another is that the High Court has conceded that judicial power is simply not capable of precise or exhaustive definition.

[6] These various rules are neither unique to the Australian Constitution nor ones that cannot be useful elsewhere. See, eg, *Ferguson v Attorney-General of Trinidad and Tobago* [2016] UKPC 2 [14]–[35] where the Privy Council drew upon Australian, British and European cases to determine domestic constitutional issues about the *Constitution of Trinidad and Tobago*.

[7] They also gained attention in other common law jurisdictions. The changes were described as 'an awesome leap towards changing [the] whole legal structure with regard to public administration' in Law Reform Commission of Canada, *Seventh Annual Report* (1977–78) 14.

[8] The respective statutes were the *Administrative Decisions (Judicial Review) Act 1977* (Cth), *Ombudsman Act 1976* (Cth) and *Freedom of Information Act 1982* (Cth). An important related reform was the creation of the Federal Court of Australia to hear claims under the judicial review legislation and hear appeals from the AAT.

[9] Created by the *Administrative Appeals Tribunal Act 1975* (Cth).

[10] The creation of a tribunal of general review jurisdiction was a clear rejection of the contrary view reached in the Franks Report: *Report of the Commonwealth Administrative Review Committee* (Parl Paper 114/1971) ('the *Kerr Committee Report*') paras 142–43.

[11] *Administrative Appeals Tribunal Act 1975* (Cth) s 43(1). This provision enables the AAT to remit the decision under review to the original decision maker but is rarely used for that purpose.

[12] An expression that originated for the AAT in *Morris v Repatriation Commission* (1991) 30 FCR 453, 460; *Nation v Repatriation Commission (No 2)* (1994) 37 ALD 63, 68.

decision.[13] This concept was one of 'merits review', in which the AAT would decide the right or most appropriate decision by reference to the material before it.[14] This open textured approach enabled the AAT to reach a different decision than the original decision-maker simply because it thought a different exercise of a discretion was preferable, or that the law could and should be applied differently.[15] The independent status of the AAT enabled it to depart from any applicable government policy.[16] These various elements have yielded a coherent and distinct understanding of the character of merits review and made it clearly different from judicial review.[17]

The High Court did not finally endorse these various aspects of merits review until more than 30 years after the AAT was established.[18] That delay was mainly because no suitable case had presented itself to the High Court but perhaps also because the Court had devoted its attention to developing its judicial review jurisdiction. In a series of decisions, the High Court explained the various consequences of the separation of powers upon both the scope of judicial review and the specific role of the courts within it. The key modern case was *Attorney-General (NSW) v Quin*,[19] which occurred 15 years after the AAT was established. The leading judgment was given by Brennan J, who essentially transposed the approach devised in *Marbury v Madison*[20] for judicial review of legislation to review of administrative action.[21] This conception of judicial review was founded on existing

[13] The first iteration of the phrase was 'right or preferable', used by Brennan J in *Re Becker and Minister for Immigration and Ethnic Affairs* (1977) 1 ALD 158, 162. The adjustment to 'correct or preferable' is traced to the Full Court of the Federal Court in *Drake v Minister for Immigration and Ethnic Affairs* (1979) 2 ALD 60, 68 and also when the case was remitted to the AAT in *Drake v Minister for Immigration and Ethnic Affairs (No 2)* (1979) 2 ALD 634. This concept was also mentioned (though not clearly defined) in the *Kerr Committee Report*, para 58.

[14] There is no presumption that the decision under review is correct: *Collins v Minister for Immigration and Ethnic Affairs* (1981) 4 ALD 198, 202.

[15] These possibilities were suggested by the first President of the AAT: Gerard Brennan, 'Anatomy of an Administrative Decision' (1980) 9 *Sydney Law Review* 1, 4–5.

[16] A possibility signalled by Brennan J in *Drake* (n 13). His Honour was also clear about the general inadvisability of the AAT ignoring government policy in favour of its own.

[17] It is for this reason that Australian law can fend off the criticism of Lord Sumption in *R (Lord Carlile of Berriew QC) v Secretary of State for the Home Department* [2015] AC 945 [30] that 'it has never been sufficiently clear what kind of inquiries a "merits review" embraces'. His Lordship need only follow the trail of lamingtons to doctrinal enlightenment from Australia.

[18] *Shi v Migration Agents Registration Authority* (2008) 235 CLR 286, 307 [72] (Kirby J), 315 [100] (Hayne and Heydon JJ), 327 [140]–[142] (Crennan J, Kiefel J agreeing on this point).

[19] *Attorney-General (NSW) v Quin* (1990) 170 CLR 1.

[20] *Marbury v Madison* 1 Cranch 137; 5 US 137 (1803).

[21] A current member of the High Court suggested that Brennan J 'appropriated' the words of Marshall CJ in *Marbury*: Stephen Gageler, 'The Constitutional Dimension' in Matthew Groves (ed), *Modern Australian Administrative Law* (Cambridge University Press, 2014) 170.

separation of powers principles but hardened them with a clear demarcation of power and functions for both the executive and judiciary. The courts, and the courts alone, could determine the lawfulness of administrative actions and decisions but they could go no further. Courts could not consider the fairness or correctness of administrative decisions because any 'merits of administrative action, to the extent that they can be distinguished from legality, are for the repository of the relevant power and, subject to political control, for the repository alone'.[22] The extent to which the courts could consider notions of substantive fairness were governed by the limits of judicial review, which Brennan J explained did 'not go beyond the declaration and enforcing of the law which determines the limits and governs the exercise of the repository's power'.[23] He cautioned that if, in the exercise of this jurisdiction, 'the court avoids administrative injustice or error, so be it; but the court has no jurisdiction simply to cure administrative injustice or error'.[24]

This approach became orthodox.[25] The broad boundaries that Brennan J identified placed clear limits on the nature and scope of review but also served to fortify the role of the courts in their exercise of supervisory jurisdiction in the face of strident legislative incursions, whether by privative clauses of astonishing width[26] or crudely disguised as procedural limits.[27] These were impermissible by reason of the reciprocal nature of the protections in the Constitution. Just as courts could not venture outside their constitutionally demarcated territory, the legislature could intrude into that terrain. The conception of judicial review Brennan J posed was a relatively formalist one that places clear limits on the scope and content of review. Some limits identified in later cases were explained partly by reference to the existence and jurisdiction of the AAT. The courts have, for example, relied on the AAT as a reason why a legislative intention to grant jurisdiction to the courts over questions of fact and policy is unlikely in judicial review legislation,[28] and why the grant of broad discretionary powers may

[22] *Quin* (n 19) 36. Brennan J earlier alluded to such a view in *Church of Scientology v Woodward* (1982) 154 CLR 25, 70.

[23] *Quin* (n 19) 36.

[24] *Quin* (n 19) 36.

[25] See, eg, *SZBEL v Minister for Immigration and Multicultural and Indigenous Affairs* (2006) 228 CLR 152, 160 [25]. Speaking extra-judicially, one recently retired High Court judge referred to this as the 'root principle that informs' Australian judicial review: Kenneth Hayne, 'Deference—An Australian Perspective' [2011] *Public Law* 75, 77.

[26] The landmark case was *Plaintiff S157/2202 v Commonwealth* (2003) 213 CLR 476, where the High Court effectively signalled that privative clauses could have no real effect to the extent that they infringe on the Court's s 75(v) jurisdiction.

[27] *Bodruddaza v Minister for Immigration and Multicultural Affairs* (2007) 228 CLR 651 (inflexible time limits on lodging judicial review application held invalid).

[28] *Australian Broadcasting Tribunal v Bond* (1990) 170 CLR 321, 341 (Mason CJ).

be difficult to impeach on constitutional grounds.[29] These particular limits led Professor Cane to argue that, but for the AAT, Australian judicial review might have evolved quite differently and developed innovative and substantive grounds encompassing all the territory now taken by merits review.[30] That argument is questionable but it is almost certain that the development of the notion of 'correct or preferable' as the guiding principle of merits review has removed the need for Australian courts to consider importing the Canadian approach of variable standards in judicial review. That is because the 'correctness' standard within Canadian judicial review has effectively been assigned to the AAT in Australia.[31]

For the purposes of an analysis of legitimate expectations, several points can be drawn from the origin and consequences of the many individual limits on Australian judicial review. The first is the often neglected point that Brennan J exercised as much influence on the evolution of merits review in his role as the first President of the AAT as he did on judicial review in his role as a Justice of the High Court. In these different roles, he sketched broad principles on the doctrinal basis and functional nature of different avenues of review. His Honour's position on each was surely informed by his experience in the other.[32]

The Australian conception of judicial review can be criticised for its formalism and remedial limitations but those problems are completely cast aside in merits review. What cannot be done in judicial review typically can be done in merits review, and vice versa. A second and closely related point can be made about the remedial powers of the AAT, most notably that a key part of its review jurisdiction is to exercise the power and discretions conferred upon the original decision-maker.[33] This unique power neatly side-steps a recurring criticism made in other jurisdictions of the substantive approach to legitimate expectations, which is that courts tacitly seize

[29] *Cunliffe v Commonwealth* (1994) 182 CLR 272 (Mason CJ), 303 (Brennan J).

[30] Peter Cane, 'Merits Review and Judicial Review—The AAT as Trojan Horse' (2000) 28 *Federal Law Review* 213, 243 and 'The Making of Australian Administrative Law' (2003) 24 *Australian Bar Review* 114, 123–24.

[31] I put aside the peculiar Australian obsession with 'jurisdictional facts' and the pretence that the identification and review of such facts by courts has not evolved from a limited and pragmatic exception to the general refusal of courts to review fact findings in judicial review into a wider and unprincipled rule by which Australian courts now undertake a form of correctness review. An attempt to draw coherence from the cases is made in Mark Aronson and Matthew Groves, *Judicial Review of Administrative Action*, 5th edn (Thomson Reuters, 2013) 235–45.

[32] Brennan J had considerable experience in judicial review prior to his appointment to the High Court because his Presidency of the AAT was accompanied by appointment to the Federal Court of Australia.

[33] A similar power is given to some of the state equivalents of the AAT. See, eg, *Victorian Civil and Administrative Tribunal 1998* (Vic) s 51(1)(a); *State Administrative Tribunal Act 2004* (WA) s 29(1).

control of the discretionary powers granted to administrative officials. That function is performed in Australia by the AAT which, importantly, does so with express parliamentary sanction.

A third important point is the unique power of the AAT over the use of government policy. The AAT is obliged to consider any applicable government policy but the wide ranging nature of merits review enables the AAT to consider for itself the precise weight it should give that policy and even whether the merits of the case might require the policy to not be applied.[34] The AAT can thus enter what Brennan J described as the 'lush fields of policy' because 'it is armed with authority to apply whatever policy it thinks appropriate'.[35] A final, often overlooked, aspect of the role of the AAT is the statutory nature of its review jurisdiction. The AAT is a creature of statute and can only gain review jurisdiction when it is expressly conferred by statute.[36]

The overall impact of these considerations is far reaching. They relieve Australian courts of the need to engage with questions of substantive fairness, which often lie at the heart of controversial legitimate expectation cases, because those matters can be dealt with by the AAT. Governments can hardly complain when the AAT or its State equivalents do so because the power to grant or withhold merits review jurisdiction lies with them.[37] The constant criticism levelled against the doctrine of substantive legitimate expectations—that it cloaks a significant extension of judicial power—cannot be levelled at the AAT because it can only act when expressly granted jurisdiction by the legislature. Perhaps the most important consequence is the very nature of merits review. It is ultimately a fact-based approach through which the AAT reaches what it regards as the best decision according to the evidence before it.[38] This evidence-based approach is not ultimately legal in character and therefore avoids the tortured attempts to discern a clear legal principle for the process of determining substantive legitimate expectations which occurred in cases such as *Coughlan*.[39] That principle in Australia is not a vague legal one of judicial review but a fact-based and contextual one that is central to tribunal review.

[34] *Drake* (n 13).

[35] Sir Gerard Brennan, 'Purpose and Scope of Judicial Review' (1986) 2 *Australian Bar Review* 93, 110–11.

[36] *Administrative Appeals Tribunal Act 1975* (Cth) s 25(1) provides that any statute 'may' provide for review by the AAT of decisions made under that statute. The permissive nature of this language means that the legislature retains an absolute discretion to confer (or not confer) merits review jurisdiction as it may wish.

[37] This possibility is consistent with the wider constitutional reality that 'What Parliament gives, Parliament may take away provided that it does so consistently with the Constitution': *Ferguson* (n 6) [36].

[38] Importantly, this usually turns on the evidence before the AAT, not the decision-maker, and that allows new evidence to be marshalled for the AAT: *Shi* (n 18).

[39] *R v North and East Devon Health Authority; ex parte Coughlan* [2001] 1 QB 213.

THE LEGITIMATE EXPECTATION AND THE GROWTH OF THE DUTY TO ACT FAIRLY IN AUSTRALIA

As the duty to act fairly expanded in Australian law in the wake of *Ridge v Baldwin*,[40] there was a long and often overly complex run of cases that wrestled with questions about the scope of the duty to observe the requirements of natural justice. Many cases after *Ridge* took a narrow approach,[41] but the legitimate expectation was often used in such cases to expand the reach of fairness. Its use depended on now discarded distinctions between the interests held by people affected by the administrative process, notably one between people who had a benefit and those who wanted one. This approach was frequently used in cases involving the renewal of a benefit, as opposed to an initial application. Such cases presumed a clear distinction between 'application cases' (where the grant of some new benefit or advantage was sought), 'forfeiture cases' (where an existing benefit or advantage was ended or adversely changed) and the intermediate category of 'expectation cases' (where there was an expectation that what was sought would be granted).[42] These distinctions were crucial in *FAI Insurances Ltd v Winneke,*[43] where the High Court held that a claim to renew approval of an existing licence to participate as an insurer in a lucrative scheme of government-approved compensation was an 'expectation case' and was thus protected by natural justice. The categorisation of the case as one of expectation was important because several judges held that natural justice would not normally require a hearing of an initial application of the insurance company.[44]

Cases like *FAI* were exceptional and even use of the legitimate expectation in these was criticised by some Australian judges. Barwick CJ reasoned that 'legitimate' meant the concept added 'little, if anything, to the concept of a right'.[45] That criticism was quickly rejected by the Privy Council, which held that 'legitimate' meant 'reasonable', which enabled the concept to encompass 'expectations which go beyond enforceable legal rights, provided they had some reasonable basis'.[46] Although that particular issue was

[40] *Ridge v Baldwin* [1964] AC 40. The step taken in that case (to discard the requirement to act judicially as a criterion of the duty to act fairly) was adopted by the High Court in *Banks v Transport Regulation Board (Vic)* (1968) 119 CLR 222.

[41] See, eg, *Salemi v McKellar (No 2)* (1977) 137 CLR 396 (ministerial power of deportation held not subject to natural justice because it was broad and unfettered and its exercise did not affect a right or expectation of a potential deportee).

[42] *McInnes v Onslow-Fane* [1978] 1 WLR 1520, 1528–29.

[43] *FAI Insurances Ltd v Winneke* (1982) 151 CLR 342.

[44] Ibid, 360–61 (Mason J), 376–77 (Aickin J), 394 (Wilson J).

[45] *Salemi* (n 41) 404.

[46] *Attorney-General of Hong Kong v Ng Yuen Shiu* [1983] 2 AC 629, 636. The High Court endorsed that view many times: *Kioa v West* (1985) 159 CLR 550, 563 (Gibbs CJ), 583 (Mason J); *Minister of State for Immigration and Ethnic Affairs v Teoh* (1995) 183 CLR 273, 291 (Mason CJ and Deane J), 302 (Toohey J), 313–34 (McHugh J); *Re Minister for Immigration*

settled, many Australian judges expressed doubts about the inexact and malleable nature of the legitimate expectation.[47] These doubts are notable because they arose almost from the very first use of the concept in Australian law.

The legitimate expectation featured heavily in the key case of *Kioa v West*,[48] where the duty to observe the requirements of fairness was strengthened when the High Court essentially accepted that fairness was presumed to apply unless clearly excluded by applicable legislation. This and other cases also expanded the range of interests to which fairness applied in their adoption of increasingly wide forms of affectation. On closer inspection, the continued life of the legitimate expectation was not due to such principled reasons. The concept seemed to continue simply because many of the cases that widened the scope of natural justice continued to refer to decisions and actions that could adversely affect 'rights, interests or legitimate expectations'.[49] The obvious contradiction of such language was that it continued the apparent distinction between rights, interests and legitimate expectations but did so as part of an approach so broad that it did not require these finer distinctions. Brennan J reasoned:

> the expansion of the scope of objects properly sought by invoking the notion of legitimate expectation can be attained in any event within the orthodox framework of administrative law … A person who entertains a legitimate expectation is, ex hypothesi, a person whose interests are so affected.[50]

Sir Anthony Mason doubted this approach because it presumed an expanded conception of 'interests' could effectively cover all of the issues to which fairness should apply, such as the 'renewal' or 'revocation' cases.[51] The High Court took a different view in the *Offshore Processing Case*,[52] where the

and Multicultural and Indigenous Affairs; Ex parte Lam (2003) 214 CLR 1, 12–13 (Gleeson CJ), 20 (McHugh and Gummow JJ).

[47] See, eg, *Heatley v Tasmanian Racing and Gaming Commission* (1977) 137 CLR 487, 509 (Aickin J); *FAI Insurances* (n 43) 394 (Wilson J); *McCrae v Attorney-General (NSW)* (1987) 9 NSWLR 268, 276 (Kirby P); *Minister for Immigration, Local Government and Ethnic Affairs v Kurtovic* (1990) 21 FCR 193, 225 (Gummow J); *Haoucher v Minister for Immigration and Ethnic Affairs* (1990) 169 CLR 648, 651–52 (Deane J); *Quin* (n 19) 54 (Dawson J), 67 (Toohey J).

[48] *Kioa v West* (n 46). The case was also notable for an apparent conflict between Mason and Brennan JJ on the ultimate source of natural justice. The former appeared to favour the common law, while the latter focused more on statute. The High Court eventually adopted a fusion of the two: Aronson and Groves (n 31) 408–12.

[49] See, eg, *Annetts v McCann* (1990) 170 CLR 596, 598 (Mason CJ, Deane and McHugh JJ); *Ainsworth v Criminal Justice Commission* (1992) 175 CLR 564, 576 (Mason CJ, Dawson, Toohey and Gaudron JJ).

[50] *Quin* (n 19) 40.

[51] Sir Anthony Mason, 'Procedural Fairness: Its Development and Continuing Role of Legitimate Expectation' (2005) *Australian Journal of Administrative Law* 103, 106.

[52] *Offshore Processing Case* (2010) 243 CLR 319.

Government sought to characterise claims that procedural fairness should apply to the odd regime to determine applications for refugee status from people who had not reached Australian shores as ones involving the exercise of a discretionary power to confer a 'right'.[53] The High Court unanimously rejected such a narrow conception of the claim, holding that a broad approach should be taken to both the interests to which procedural fairness applies and the means by which those interests may be affected. The Court noted that earlier cases had clearly expanded fairness beyond a narrow view of 'rights' to a wider conception that encompassed 'interests or legitimate expectations' and included 'the exercise of a power which affects a right or privilege'.[54] The consequence of this reasoning, the High Court made clear, was that the central task is 'to identify the rights and interests affected'.[55] The failure to mention legitimate expectations at this point was surely no accident. If the requirements of fairness apply in general to the exercise of public or government power that impacts upon rights and interests in a broadly conceived sense, the scope of that duty subsumes and consumes whatever might be protected by legitimate expectations.[56] The failure to mention legitimate expectations was also explicable for another reason. The *Offshore Processing Case* was yet another migration decision of the High Court about the asylum process. The complex legislation and associated administrative arrangements are typically drafted in harsh terms designed to stymie applications as much as possible. Any talk of expectations in this environment is fanciful at best. Government ministers and their officials do their best to destroy the hopes of claimants and use one-sided legislation and policies to pursue that goal. Against that background, the High Court's focus on power rather than expectations was apt.

THE HIGH WATERMARK OF LEGITIMATE EXPECTATIONS IN AUSTRALIA[57]

The recognition of legitimate expectations reached its peak in Australia in *Minister of State for Immigration and Ethnic Affairs v Teoh*.[58] The Minister decided to deport Teoh because of his criminal convictions.

[53] Applications for asylum determination are different for those who arrive in Australia territory but not onto the mainland, as they are deemed to be 'offshore' applicants: Michelle Foster and Jason Popjoy, 'A Failed Case of Legal Exceptionalism? Refugee Status Determination in Australia's "Excised" Territory' (2011) 23 *International Journal of Refugee Law* 583.

[54] Ibid, 352–53.

[55] Ibid, 353.

[56] This view was raised in earlier cases. See, eg, *Haoucher* (n 47) 653 (Deane J).

[57] *Teoh* was described as the 'high watermark' of legitimate expectations by Callinan J in *Lam* (n 46) 46.

[58] *Teoh* (n 46).

The Minister's delegate conceded that the Teoh family faced a 'very bleak and difficult future' but concluded that this was outweighed by Mr Teoh's criminal record. The High Court overturned that decision because the delegate had not treated the best interests of Teoh's children as 'a primary consideration' as required under the United Nations *Convention on the Rights of the Child*. The delegate was not obliged to consider or observe the Convention because it had not been incorporated into Australian law by domestic legislation. The gap was instead filled by novel use of the legitimate expectation. Mason CJ, Deane and Toohey JJ held that ratification of the Convention created a legitimate expectation that administrative officials would observe, or at least consider, its terms. Before making a decision inconsistent with that expectation, the delegate was required to give Teoh notice and a sufficient opportunity to argue against that course.[59] Fairness required that chance be given even though Teoh had clearly had an 'opportunity to provide whatever material he wished' in support of his claims.[60]

The majority in *Teoh* essentially used the legitimate expectation to give a level, and form of content, to procedural fairness that was novel on several counts. One was the finding that it was irrelevant that Teoh neither knew of the Convention nor expected officials to honour its terms because the principles governing legitimate expectations did not require their claimants to 'personally entertain the expectation'.[61] Toohey J explained that '[T]he matter is to be assessed objectively, in terms of what expectation might reasonably be engendered by any undertaking that the authority in question has given.'[62]

This reasoning disguised the artificiality of an expectation that assumed ratification of a treaty by the Executive to be not simply a platitudinous statement but a solemn statement by the Executive to the Australian public of how seriously it regarded this important international document.[63] It also gave the act of ratification novel consequences, and enabled legitimate expectations to arise from a surprising new source not recognised in earlier cases. Those cases had accepted legitimate expectations arising from a range of sources, including undertakings and representations,[64] policy

[59] *Teoh* (n 46) 291–92 (Mason CJ and Deane J), 302–03 (Toohey J).

[60] *Teoh* (n 46) 299 (Toohey J).

[61] *Teoh* (n 46) 291 (Mason CJ and Deane J). This point was critical to the case at hand because Teoh was plainly unaware of the Convention until it was raised by his lawyers in the Federal Court: 298.

[62] *Teoh* (n 46) 301.

[63] *Teoh* (n 46) 287 (Mason CJ and Deane J), 302 (Toohey J).

[64] See, eg, *R v Liverpool Corp; ex parte Liverpool Taxi Fleet Operators Assoc* [1972] 2 QB 299; *Ng Yuen Shiu* (n 46); and *Cole v Cunningham* (1983) 49 ALR 123; *Century Metals and Mining NL v Yeomans* (1989) 40 FCR 564. Such cases after *Teoh* include: *Minister for Aboriginal and Torres Strait Islander Affairs v Western Australia* (1996) 67 FCR 40;

statements,[65] rules,[66] and regular official practice.[67] As McHugh J rightly noted in his dissent, the ratification of an international instrument was a novel addition to these more settled sources.[68] McHugh J also railed against the 'almost comic' notion that people could claim an expectation arising from a source they knew nothing of. His Honour reasoned that the means by which the majority suggested that expectation could be defeated was equally illogical because it would require officials to inform affected people that the official 'does not intend to apply a rule that the decision-maker cannot be required to apply, has not been asked or given an undertaking to apply, and of which the person affected by the decision has no knowledge'.[69]

For a time, the odd consequence given to the ratified but unincorporated treaty was the focus of attention. Several attempts were made by the Commonwealth Parliament to pass legislation intended to reverse the effect of *Teoh*.[70] A parliamentary committee canvassed the possibility that Australia could withdraw from the Convention, so that it could re-enter with a reservation to overcome *Teoh*.[71] Considerable attention was also given to the suggestion of Mason CJ and Deane J that 'executive indications to the contrary' could preclude ratification of a treaty providing the basis of a

and *Carey v Field* (2002) 122 FCR 538, 556–57 (statement as to procedure to be followed before withdrawing tax public ruling). Not every undertaking sufficed. See, eg, *Martincevic v Commonwealth* [2007] FCAFC 164 [51]–[52] (no reasonable basis for expecting to be advised outcome of request for an extension before final decision made).

[65] *Kurtovic* (n 47) 226–27; *Haoucher* (n 47). Such cases after *Teoh* include: *One.Tel v Deputy Commissioner of Taxation* (2000) 171 ALR 227, 241–46; *Pilbara Aboriginal Land Council Aboriginal Corp Inc v Minister for Aboriginal & Torres Strait Islander Affairs* (2000) 103 FCR 539, 553–54 (general statement of procedures to be followed); and *Dighton v State of South Australia* (2000) 78 SASR 1, 19; *Country Energy v Williams* [2005] NSWCA 318 [103] (legitimate expectation cannot arise from judicial decision but can from a policy based upon a lawful understanding of the decision); and *Anderson v Lismore City Council* (2011) 185 LGERA 239 (legitimate expectation arising from council policy that it would not sell the house of a pensioner for arrears absent exceptional circumstances).

[66] cf *Muin v Refugee Review Tribunal* (2002) 190 ALR 601 [124]–[125], [269] (no legitimate expectation arose from internal practice direction which only paraphrased common law fairness requirements).

[67] See, eg, *Council of Civil Service Unions v Minister for the Civil Service* [1985] AC 374; *CUPE v Ontario (Minister of Labour)* (2003) 226 DLR (4th) 193 (SCC); *Anderson v Director General of the Department of Environment and Conservation* (2006) 144 LGERA 43 [142]–[154].

[68] *Teoh* (n 46) 312–13. He also noted that the reasoning in *Teoh* allowed hitherto unknown consequences to flow from ratification of an international instrument.

[69] *Teoh* (n 46) 314.

[70] In the form of the *Administrative Decisions (Effect of International Instruments) Bill*, which was presented to the federal parliament in 1995, 1997 and 1999. Only South Australia enacted such legislation: *Administrative Decisions (Effect of International Instruments) Act 1995* (SA).

[71] Parliament of Australia, Joint Standing Committee on Treaties, 'United Nations Convention on the Rights of the Child' (17th Report, 1998) 65–66.

legitimate expectation.[72] Governments of all persuasions issued statements attempting to exploit that possibility.[73] The effectiveness of those statements was questioned but never decisively tested.[74] It was most likely that one aspect of the debate would cancel the other out, in the sense that ratification and effect accorded to it in *Teoh* would point towards the creation of a legitimate expectation but the strong and clear executive statements to the contrary would leave no doubt as to the intended effect from the view of the executive.[75]

THE DECLINE OF THE LEGITIMATE EXPECTATION IN AUSTRALIA

The heated debate caused by *Teoh* was largely ended by *Re Minister for Immigration and Multicultural and Indigenous Affairs; ex parte Lam.*[76] In *Lam*, the Department asked the applicant for the contact details of his children's carers, saying it wished to contact them to assess the applicant's relationship with his children and the possible effects on them of the cancellation of his visa. The applicant had already supplied that information, together with a letter from the carer, but did so again. The carer was not contacted before the applicant's visa was cancelled, nor was the applicant told that the department no longer wished to contact the carer. The applicant argued this denied his legitimate expectation that the department would do as it had said but, importantly, did not suggest he would have submitted further material or argument had he known the carer would not be contacted. The High Court held there was no breach of natural justice because the failure to adhere to the department's statement had no possible effect on the fairness of the process.[77]

[72] *Teoh* (n 46) 291.

[73] Joint Statement by the Minister for Foreign Affairs, and the Attorney-General, 10 May 1995. A similar statement was issued by the subsequent conservative government: Joint Statement by the Minister for Foreign Affairs and the Attorney-General, 25 February 1997. Ministers in South and Western Australia made similar statements: Leslie Katz, 'A Teoh FAQ' (1998) 16 *Australian Institute of Administrative Law Forum* 1, 6.

[74] Margaret Allars, 'One Small Step for Legal Doctrine, One Giant Leap Towards Integrity in Government: Teoh's Case and the Internationalisation of Administrative Law' (1995) 17 *Sydney Law Review* 204, 239–41.

[75] Perhaps fairness might have even required that such complex and circular reasoning *not* be disclosed to affected people.

[76] *Lam* (n 46).

[77] *Lam* (n 46) 9, 13–14 (Gleeson CJ), 34–45 (McHugh and Gummow JJ), 36–39 (Hayne J), 48–49 (Callinan J). The disappointment of an expectation was also found not to result in unfairness in *Untan v Minister for Immigration and Multicultural and Indigenous Affairs* [2003] FCAFC 69. That case was similar to *Lam* because the alleged unfairness (an expectation that further comments would be made by the wife in response to the possible deportation of her husband) was found to have been overcome by her many earlier dealings with officials.

The High Court doubted central elements of *Teoh* but did not formally overrule the decision.[78] Several judges questioned whether legitimate expectations could arise from the ratification of treaties. McHugh and Gummow JJ strongly doubted whether ratification of a treaty alone could provide a secure basis to impose restrictions or requirements upon the executive or its officials in their exercise of discretionary powers.[79] Callinan J voiced similar concerns and questioned whether the recognition of a legitimate expectation upon a treaty, particularly in the absence of any consequential legislation, was consistent with the separation of powers.[80]

Lam revealed concerns about the legitimate expectation beyond the problems presented by their foundation in ratification of treaties. McHugh and Gummow JJ suggested that the concept served a useful role in evolution and expansion of the duty to observe the requirements of natural justice but now had 'limited utility'.[81] Hayne and Callinan JJ also accepted that concept should have a limited role and be applied with caution.[82] McHugh, Gummow and Hayne JJ also doubted the utility of the term legitimate expectation in a disjunctive sense, by expressing caution about precisely what might be expected and how and by whom it was said to be expected.[83] Callinan J similarly reasoned that the term legitimate expectation was 'an unfortunate one, and apt to mislead'.[84] To some extent these remarks were unremarkable because, as noted above, the legitimate expectation has been doubted in these ways almost as long as it has been used in Australia.

The different judgments in *Lam* contained little common ground beyond such criticisms. Callinan J, for example, held that legitimate expectation should be a subjective device, essentially limited to cases where there was either an actual expectation or could be a 'reasonable inference' that a claimant had or was likely to have consciously considered the matter.[85] McHugh

[78] *Lam* (n 46) 28–34 (McHugh and Gummow JJ), 37–38 (Hayne J), 45–49 (Callinan J). Gleeson CJ expressed no clear view on *Teoh*. The failure to overrule *Teoh* was partly because the parties did not make its status a direct point of contention but also because *Lam* was not heard by all seven members of the High Court (which, by settled practice, would have been required to overrule a relatively recent decision of the Court). It is clear, however, that the *Lam* Court demolished *Teoh* so far it was provided authority on legitimate expectations. See Michael Taggart, '"Australian Exceptionalism" in Judicial Review' (2008) 36 *Federal Law Review* 1, 17.

[79] *Lam* (n 46) 31–34. This important qualification of *Teoh* is not mentioned by UK courts when referring to the case. See eg, *R (on the application of SG) v Secretary of State for Work and Pensions* [2015] 1 WLR 1449, [243]–[245] (Lord Kerr).

[80] McHugh and Gummow JJ thought recognition of such legitimate expectations involved judicial overreach: *Lam* (n 46) 33–34. Callinan J saw the problem as one of executive overreach: 48. Hayne J appeared mindful of these views but expressed no clear opinion: 122.

[81] *Lam* (n 46) 16.

[82] *Lam* (n 46) 38 (Hayne J), 45–48 (Callinan J). Callinan J doubted the concept more openly when he queried its very 'invention': 45.

[83] *Lam* (n 46) 20 (McHugh and Gummow JJ), 38 (Hayne J).

[84] *Lam* (n 46) 45.

[85] *Lam* (n 46) 47.

and Gummow JJ accepted that expectations might be determined by a more objective approach and held that claimants of a legitimate expectation need not prove they had turned their mind to the issue 'in the present case'.[86] Gleeson CJ and Hayne J expressed no view on this point.

The High Court appeared to reach greater common ground about the manner in which expectations might affect the content of procedural fairness. This aspect of the case aligns with earlier Australian ones that had used the legitimate expectation as a functional device to determine the content rather than existence of the duty to be fair.[87] *Lam* took the additional step of accepting that the circumstances of a case which could affect the requirements of fairness included any expectations held by those to whom a duty of fairness was owed. The differing views expressed by the High Court suggest that such expectations need not, and perhaps ought not, be labelled under the more technical and loaded term of 'legitimate expectations'. This interpretation of *Lam* flows from the finding by all members of the Court that any claim of a denial of procedural fairness failed because the failure of the Department to contact the carer of his children had made no difference to the applicant's case.[88] All members of the Court accepted that the legitimate expectation might retain a role in determining the content of procedural fairness but cautioned that the concept did not trump the traditional test of 'fairness'.[89] The clear point was that the legitimate expectation was a means rather than an end and perhaps its time as a useful device to determine aspects of fairness had passed. The explanation of this shift by Gleeson CJ has been very influential. He explained: 'Fairness is not an abstract concept. It is essentially practical. Whether one talks in terms of procedural fairness or natural justice, the concern of the law is to avoid practical injustice'.[90] That 'practical focus' is notable for the absence of any mention of the legitimate expectation, which is in keeping with Gleeson CJ's shift of attention from the source or disappointment of any possible expectation to the overall effect of an official's conduct. The Chief Justice explained that:

> what must be demonstrated is unfairness, not merely departure from a representation. Not every departure from a stated intention necessarily involves unfairness, even if it defeats an expectation ... In a context such as the present, where there is already an obligation to extend procedural fairness, the creation of an expectation may bear upon the practical content of that obligation. But it does not supplant

[86] *Lam* (n 46) 31. Their Honours clearly did not intend to endorse an entirely objective 'reasonable expectation' because they cited English authority doubting that possibility: *Council of Civil Service Unions* (n 67), 408–49.

[87] *Haoucher* (n 47) 672 (Gaudron J).

[88] *Lam* (n 46) 12–14 (Gleeson CJ), 34–35 (McHugh and Gummow JJ), 38–39 (Hayne J), 48–49 (Callinan J).

[89] *Lam* (n 46) 9, 12–13 (Gleeson CJ), 27–28, 34 (McHugh and Gummow JJ), 35–37 (Hayne J), 48–49 (Callinan J).

[90] *Lam* (n 46) 14.

> the obligation. The ultimate question remains whether there has been unfairness; not whether an expectation has been disappointed (footnote omitted).[91]

This reasoning was fatal to Lam because he could easily show that a representation made by officials was not honoured but not what difference that had made. The result would have been different if Lam had shown what further material he would or could have led if the representation was honoured, but such a case would be a clear denial of natural justice that could be established without use of legitimate expectations.[92]

Lam also suggested that there needed to be some sort of detrimental reliance on a representation by the applicant, though not necessarily in every case.[93] For example, a failure to comply with an announced policy of inviting a person to attend an oral hearing could still affect the opportunity of a person who was unaware of the policy, but would have accepted such an invitation.[94] These and similar issues would be best determined by the approach suggested by Gleeson CJ, which focuses upon the more practical question of whether unfairness did or might have occurred, rather than the more abstract questions which attach to legitimate expectations or reliance.

Lam signalled a turning point when those doubts were adopted by a majority of the High Court to endorse a greatly reduced role for the doctrine.[95] *Lam* made clear that obstacles lie in the path of the substantive legitimate expectation and also signalled a narrower role for the procedural legitimate expectation in three related ways. First, the term 'legitimate expectation' requires cautious use, to avoid confusion about what is sought and why.[96] Second, legitimate expectation does not trump the ordinary 'fairness' test for the content of procedural fairness.[97] Third, a disappointed expectation does not bear on 'fairness' if it could not have adversely affected an individual's opportunity to be heard.[98]

[91] *Lam* (n 46) 12–13.

[92] As occurred in other cases around the time of *Lam*. See, eg, *Re Refugee Review Tribunal; ex parte Aala* (2000) 204 CLR 82; *Muin* (n 65); *NABC v Minister for Immigration and Multicultural and Indigenous Affairs* (2003) 135 FCR 282.

[93] The High Court later confirmed that proof of reliance is not necessary to establish a denial of natural justice: *Applicant NAFF of 2002 v Minister for Immigration and Multicultural and Indigenous Affairs* (2004) 221 CLR 1.

[94] Another example is the failure of a council to observe its policy that a statutory power to sell houses of ratepayers would not be exercised against pensioners, absent exceptional circumstances. Pensioners could rightly assume that policy would be followed or they would get notice of, and a chance to put their views, when the council thought the case was exceptional: *Anderson* (n 65).

[95] *Lam* (n 46) 16, 20, 27–28, 34–35 (McHugh and Gummow JJ) and 45–48 (Callinan J). Hayne J also seriously questioned the utility of the doctrine: 37–38.

[96] *Lam* (n 46) 20 (McHugh and Gummow JJ), 37–38 (Hayne J), 45–46 (Callinan J).

[97] *Lam* (n 46) 9, 12–13 (Gleeson CJ), 27–28, 34 (McHugh and Gummow JJ), 35–36 (Hayne J), 48–49 (Callinan J). See also *WABZ v Minister for Immigration and Multicultural and Indigenous Affairs* (2004) 134 FCR 271, 295 (French and Lee JJ), 306 (Hill J).

[98] *Lam* (n 46) 12–14 (Gleeson CJ), 34–35 (McHugh and Gummow JJ), 38–39 (Hayne J), 48–49 (Callinan J).

Kirby J, who did not preside in *Lam*, suggested that nothing in *Lam* obliges abandonment of legitimate expectations as an analytic tool but he conceded that the utility of the doctrine was 'now somewhat limited'.[99] Professor Aronson similarly noted that *Lam* shifted focus from legitimate expectations to 'more straightforward talk of "reasonable assumptions"'.[100] It followed that:

> The focus should be on whether the decision-maker's conduct in making and then breaching the expectation was fair in the circumstances. Of course, there will usually be no unfairness if the subject was adequately forewarned of the decision-maker's change of course. However, *Lam's* bottom line was that it is not *necessarily* a breach of natural justice to disappoint the expectation without prior warning. The focus must remain on whether the departure from the promised conduct was unfair in the circumstances ... (emphasis in original)[101]

The Full Court of the Federal Court echoed that view in *SZSSJ*,[102] when it noted that *Lam* marked a move away from heavy reliance on the legitimate expectation 'as a useful tool of analysis' so that focus 'has now shifted instead to whether departure from a representation might render the process unfair'.[103] According to this view, the impact of *Lam* was that it 'simply pivots the underlying analytic jurisprudence away from a doctrinal reliance upon legitimate expectation towards an examination of the fairness of the process'.[104]

That focus was indeed shifted to the wider fairness of the process when the High Court last considered legitimate expectations in yet another migration case, which essentially signalled the practical end of even its procedural variant. The applicant in *WZARH*[105] claimed refugee status and was interviewed by an independent review officer. That first officer became unavailable but explained to the applicant that she would undertake a fresh hearing of his claims. A second reviewer instead determined the claim without notifying the applicant. The claim was rejected after the reviewer formed an adverse view of the many specific claims the applicant had made to the first reviewer. The Full Court of the Federal Court held that the failure to alert the applicant to these changes, and also to provide him with either the chance to seek the promised further hearing or otherwise put his further

[99] *Applicant NAFF of 2002* (n 93) 23.

[100] Mark Aronson, 'Private Bodies, Public Power and Soft Law in the High Court (2007) 35 *Federal Law Review* 1, 5.

[101] Ibid.

[102] *SZSSJ v Minister for Immigration and Border Protection* (2015) 234 FCR 1. This issue was not mentioned by the High Court when reversing the Full Federal Court in *Minister for Immigration and Border Protection v SZSSJ* [2016] HCA 29.

[103] Ibid, [91].

[104] Ibid, [92].

[105] *Minister for Immigration and Border Protection v WZARH* (2015) 90 ALJR 25.

views, was a denial of natural justice.[106] The majority judges reached this finding after lengthy use of the legitimate expectation doctrine.[107]

The High Court agreed that natural justice had been denied in several ways. The applicant had no chance to put arguments about how the process should be completed or to seek an oral hearing.[108] He also lost a chance to supplement his earlier submissions. Each of the two judgments given held that, when the hearing process was viewed as a whole, unfairness had clearly occurred. That was not because the promise of the first reviewer led the applicant to expect a further hearing. It was simply that what happened after that was unfair.

These findings were reached without use of legitimate expectations as an analytical tool but each judgment disapproved strongly of the use of the procedural version of the doctrine by the majority in the Full Federal Court. Kiefel, Bell and Keane JJ noted the 'tentative acceptance' then 'rejection' of the doctrine in Australian law and concluded that the legitimate expectation did not provide the basis for deciding either whether fairness applied or what it required in any given case.[109] They reasoned that any reference to legitimate expectations 'may well distract from the real question', which was to ask what was 'required in order to ensure that the decision is made fairly in the circumstances having regard to the legal framework within which the decision is to be made'.[110] The criticisms of Gageler and Gordon JJ were more limited but to much the same effect. Their Honours simply noted that any assessment of the fairness of a process, or the 'practical injustice' that may have arisen, could easily become confused if the legitimate expectation was 'used as a basis for determining the content of procedural fairness'.[111] Focus on the opportunity expected only distracted from 'the true inquiry into the opportunity that a reasonable administrator ought fairly to have given'.[112] The message is clear. Fairness requires an overall assessment of the procedure, to establish whether a hearing or other consideration of a matter was fair or not. The key is not to find a departure from an expectation but to find a departure from fairness.

106 *WZARH v Minister for Immigration and Border Protection* (2014) 230 FCR 230.

107 Ibid, [23]–[29] (Flick and Gleeson JJ).

108 Though it was made clear that fairness did not require an oral hearing in all cases because any such entitlement ultimately depended on context: *WZARH* (n 105) [33] (Kiefel, Bell and Keane JJ), [63] (Gageler and Gordon JJ).

109 *WZARH* (n 105) [28]–[30].

110 *WZARH* (n 105) [30].

111 *WZARH* (n 105) [61].

112 *WZARH* (n 105) [61].

WHY HAS ESTOPPEL NOT PROVIDED AN ALTERNATIVE PATH IN AUSTRALIA?

There will always be haggling over the extent to which public law is or should be influenced by private law, though few would question that estoppel and legitimate expectations occupy one area where similar themes abound in public law and private law concepts. Most would also agree that the time for overt use of private law estoppel in the legitimate expectation cases has largely ceased, though not before estoppel infused and influenced elements of legitimate expectations. The House of Lords conceded as much when it signalled that 'public law had absorbed whatever is useful from the moral values which underlie the private law concept of estoppel and the time has come for it to stand upon its own two feet'.[113] That possible connection was stymied in Australia at a much earlier stage by a decision delivered by a future member of the High Court in *Minister for Immigration, Local Government and Ethic Affairs v Kurtovic.*[114] That case was similar to *Coughlan* because the claimed unfairness also arose after a representation was given to a specific person, rather than the public more generally, and was breached by a later unfavourable decision. Kurtovic was a non-citizen imprisoned for criminal offences whom the relevant Minister ordered to be deported. Kurtovic successfully appealed this decision to the AAT.[115] The Minister begrudgingly accepted that decision but warned Kurtovic that his case would be reconsidered if he committed further criminal offences. A state parole board subsequently wrote to the Minister expressing concern that Kurtovic might reoffend on release. The Minister again decided to deport Kurtovic, based largely on the original convictions but motivated anew by the concerns of the parole board.

The Full Court of the Federal Court accepted that the Minister's failure to notify Kurtovic of the second letter, or provide him with a chance to respond to it, was a clear denial of natural justice.[116] Importantly, however, Kurtovic's claim of estoppel based on the earlier letter failed entirely.[117] That was mainly because the Court held the letter did not make a sufficiently clear or unambiguous promise that another deportation order would not be made unless new circumstances arose. But the Full Court held that,

[113] *R (Reprotech (Pebsham) Ltd) v East Sussex County Council* [2003] 1 WLR 348, 358 [35] (Lord Hoffmann).

[114] *Kurtovic* (n 47).

[115] The availability of merits review against such decisions in Australia has varied over the last 25 years.

[116] *Kurtovic* (n 47) 197 (Neave J), 205 (Ryan J), 222–24 (Gummow J).

[117] The Full Court held the deportation power was exercisable 'from time to time', which meant a fresh decision could be made on the same facts used in the earlier decision: *Kurtovic* (n 47) 196 (Neave J), 201 (Ryan J), 208–14 (Gummow J).

even if the letter had contained such a clear promise, a ruling to find such a promise binding would constitute an impermissible fetter on a statutory power granted to the Minister.[118] Gummow J stressed the distinct nature of public power and the rules against fettering as strong reasons against estoppel in public law, explaining:

> ... in a case of discretion, there is a duty under the statute to exercise a free and unhindered discretion and an estoppel cannot be raised (any more than a contract might be relied upon) to prevent or hinder the exercise of the discretion; the point is that the legislature intends the discretion to be exercised on the basis of a proper understanding of what is require by the statute, and that the repository of the discretion is not to be held to a decision which mistakes or forecloses that understanding.[119]

Gummow J also rejected an attempt to deploy the same facts in an argument that the decision was substantively unfair.[120] The claim was based partly on the apparent inconsistency of the Minister's two decisions which, by implication, was more pronounced because four years lay between each decision. Gummow J made reference to observations of Lord Denning, who thought that estoppel should not be available against the Crown in exercise of its powers 'for the public good, even though this may work some injustice or unfairness to a private individual ...'[121] Lord Denning further suggested that the Crown could be estopped in an exercise of its power that was not proper and 'in circumstances which work injustice or unfairness to the individual without any countervailing benefit for the public...'[122] Gummow J identified 'two fatal objections' to this possibility, which might allow the courts to determine the substantive fairness of administrative action 'by some process of "judicial balancing" between public and private interests'.[123] These were:

> First the question of where the balance lies between competing public and private interests in the exercise of a statutory discretion goes to the merits of the case, and is one for the decision-maker, not the courts, to resolve. Secondly, a conclusion that, a representation or decision is ultra vires, ordinarily will preclude its effectiveness. An ultra vires representation is not a mere factor in favour of which the

[118] *Kurtovic* (n 47) 196 (Neave J), 201 (Ryan J), 207 (Gummow J).

[119] *Kurtovic* (n 47) 210. Ryan and Neave JJ agreed on this point.

[120] This claim argued that the change in the Minister's position was substantively unfair and thus 'contrary to law' within the meaning of *Administrative Decisions (Judicial Review) Act 1977* (Cth) s 5(2)(j), one of the Act's open ended grounds. The other such ground is that a decision is an abuse of power: ss 5(1)(e). I have described these rarely used grounds as a 'dead letter': Matthew Groves, 'Substantive Legitimate Expectations in Australian Administrative Law' (2008) 32 *Melbourne University Law Review* 470, 518.

[121] *Laker Airways Ltd v Department of Trade* [1977] QB 643, 707. These remarks were expressed to include powers under both statute and common law.

[122] Ibid.

[123] *Kurtovic* (n 47) 221.

> scales of judicial balancing might be allowed to swing, but peremptorily forecloses such deliberation.[124]

The first part of this reasoning is directed to estoppel but could easily apply to use of the substantive version of the legitimate expectation because it makes clear that attempts to weigh competing interests in judicial review, whether by the approach adopted in *Coughlan* or somehow in determining a plea of estoppel, can be characterised as merits review. The reference of Gummow J to ultra vires representations suggests that the effect of any representation will be judged according to ultra vires notions of legality and not substantive notions of fairness. That approach clearly precludes any use of expansive conception of fairness that was expounded in *Coughlan*.

This rejection of public law estoppel is now orthodox in Australia,[125] though it was doubted only a few months after *Kurtovic* by Mason CJ in *Quin*.[126] Mason CJ conceded that, as a general rule, estoppel was not available against the exercise of discretionary powers by public agencies. But he was not prepared to:

> ... deny the availability of estoppel against the Executive, arising from conduct amounting to a representation, when holding the Executive to its representation does not significantly hinder the exercise of the discretion in the public interest. And, as the public interest necessarily comprehends an element of justice to the individual, one cannot exclude the possibility that the courts might in some situations grant relief on the basis that a refusal to hold the Executive to a representation by means of estoppel will occasion greater harm to the public interest by causing grave injustice to the individual who acts on the representation than any detriment to that interest that will arise from holding the Executive to its representation and thus narrowing the exercise of the discretion...[127]

It is not hard to see why even this narrow exception to public law estoppel did not take root in Australia. The approach of Mason CJ would require courts to balance any wider public interest against the possible injustice to an individual. Such a process has clear parallels to the balancing exercise adopted in *Coughlan* and would thus encounter the many Australian constitutional obstacles to the administration of such a test by courts performing judicial review. We should also doubt the implicit suggestion of Mason CJ, that estoppel could offer a solution that the existing grounds

[124] *Kurtovic* (n 47).

[125] This is the assessment of Sir Anthony Mason, who suggested there was a brief period when estoppel might have taken root in Australian public law: Sir Anthony Mason, 'Estoppel in Administrative Law' in Matthew Groves (ed), *Law and Government in Australia* (Federation Press, 2005). Other remedies in equity against public authorities are considered in Greg Weeks, 'Estoppel and Public Authorities: Examining the Case for an Equitable Remedy' (2010) 4 *Journal of Equity* 247.

[126] *Quin* (n 19).

[127] *Quin* (n 19) 18–19.

of review could not. If, as in *Kurtovic*, an official sought to resile from an earlier statement or promise and failed to inform the affected person or provide him with a chance to respond, the rules of natural justice would provide a remedy. If notice and such a chance was given, but the views of the affected person were ignored, the relevancy grounds or unreasonableness could be deployed. If, however, notice was given and the response was considered, the grave injustice that so concerned Mason CJ would not exist. The only remaining judicial remedy in Australia would be merits review.[128] From the view of judicial review doctrine, the more immediate effect of the rejection of estoppel against the exercise of public powers is that a conceptual device which might have usefully fostered a doctrinal alternative to substantive legitimate expectations suffered the same fate as that doctrine.

Gummow J returned to this issue in *Lam*, where he and McHugh J categorised the expectation recognised in *Coughlan* as 'akin to an estoppel' and thus inconsistent with the (by then) well settled rejection of estoppel in Australian public law.[129] McHugh and Gummow JJ noted that the focus had shifted in English law from estoppel and its more obvious influences to substantive unfairness and abuse of power.[130] This reasoning was curious on two counts. First, it was unclear whether the palpable dislike of English principles was intended as a criticism of their initial source (connections to estoppel) or their later destination (of more open ended and more normative principles). Second, it did not mention the obvious parallel between the use of estoppel in the UK and legitimate expectations in Australia. Both served as useful conceptual devices during times of great transition in public law and both were no longer useful in their own right.[131]

SUBSTANTIVE ENFORCEMENT OF EXPECTATIONS

During the time when the scope of natural justice widened in Australia, the High Court also rejected substantive enforcement of legitimate expectations on constitutional grounds. The key step was taken long before *Coughlan* in *Quin*,[132] where an expectation was claimed to have arisen from a policy

[128] There could also be exceptional remedies from the executive, such as ex gratia compensation.

[129] *Lam* (n 46) 22 (McHugh and Gummow JJ). The quoted phrase was taken from *R v Devon County Council; ex parte Baker* [1995] 1 All ER 73, 88.

[130] *Lam* (n 46) 22–23.

[131] Though in England, rejection of public law estoppel was explicable by the transfer of its functions to substantive legitimate expectations, and perhaps also the waning influence of Lord Denning who was the chief English proponent of public law estoppel: Greg Weeks, *Soft Law and Public Authorities—Remedies and Reform* (Hart Publishing, 2016) 146–47.

[132] *Quin* (n 19).

for appointments to the newly-created Local Court, which replaced the Magistrates Courts. There was no doubt the policy existed because the Attorney-General had stated it publicly and repeated it in correspondence with Mr Quin and other Stipendiary Magistrates who held positions prior to the creation of the new court. The policy was to consider appointments to the new court only from applications of existing Stipendiary Magistrates. While most members of the old court were appointed to the new one, Quin and four others were not by the time a new Attorney-General changed the policy to allow applications at large.

A majority of the High Court rejected an argument that the remaining magistrates had a legitimate expectation which required they be treated in the same (very favourable) manner as their colleagues. The majority held that any expectation could not be enforced to prevent the new Attorney-General from applying his own (less favourable) policy to the remaining magistrates.[133] The Court accepted that undertakings could lead to the imposition of procedural requirements,[134] which was clearly consistent with the long Australian tradition of a procedural approach to fairness. Even that possibility was unclear in light of the wider lack of agreement about the doctrine which ranged from outright rejection, to doubt, to hesitant support.[135] No member of the High Court gave any solace to those favouring substantive enforcement of legitimate expectations. That was partly due to separation of powers considerations raised in the case at hand, which led the Court to express strong reluctance against the possibility of it undertaking review that would affect or engage judicial appointments.[136] Mason CJ conceded, however, that there could be other areas 'in which substantive protection can be afforded and ordered by the court, without detriment to the public interest'.[137] That interesting possibility has not been explored in later cases, though its very mention points to the limits of the separation of powers as an obstacle to substantive enforcement of expectations. After all, the rule of law could easily be said to require observance of expectations for reasons of consistency and fairness. If so, constitutional considerations would require rather than preclude substantive enforcement.

Subsequent decisions gave no further hope to substantive enforcement of expectations. The best example is *Teoh*, where the High Court took a

[133] *Quin* (n 19) 23–24 (Mason CJ), 41 (Brennan J), 60 (Dawson J). The policy was held lawful.

[134] *Quin* (n 19) 20–21 (Mason CJ), 40 (Brennan J), 55–56 (Dawson J).

[135] Brennan J repeated his rejection of the doctrine: *Quin* (n 19) 34–5. Dawson J accepted the doctrine but held its use within discussion of procedural benefits was 'superfluous and confusing': 55. Mason CJ adopted a procedural conception of legitimate expectations but acknowledged this might not 'necessarily be the same as the procedure which procedural fairness or good administration will demand': 21.

[136] *Quin* (n 19) 18–19 (Mason CJ), 33–34 (Brennan J), 58–59 (Dawson J).

[137] *Quin* (n 19) 23.

novel and expansive approach to the procedural effect of legitimate expectations but pointedly refused to take the additional step of requiring actual compliance with the Convention upon which the expectation was founded.[138] The issue was examined more directly in *Lam,* even though it was not raised by the parties. Gleeson CJ stated that 'the concept of abuse of power, in so far as it may embrace substantive unfairness of the kind considered in *Coughlan*' raised wider constitutional issues that could 'involve large questions as to relations between the executive and judicial branches of government'.[139] McHugh and Gummow JJ affirmed the Court's previous stance against a substantive variant of the doctrine.[140] They also explained the constitutional obstacles that doctrine faced in Australia due to the link that *Coughlan* drew between legitimate expectations and abuse of power. One was that abuse of power in its English sense involved 'judicial supervision of administrative decision-making by the application of certain minimum standards now identified by the English common law. These standards fix upon the quality of the decision-making and thus the merits of the outcome.'[141] That characterisation of *Coughlan* revealed the twin heresies it contains for Australian judicial review—consideration of merits and quality in decision-making.

While McHugh and Gummow JJ conceded that the formalist Australian approach did not necessarily eschew values because it 'may be said that the rule of law reflects values concerned in general terms with abuse of power by the executive and legislative branches of government', they cautioned that 'it would be going much further to give those values an immediate normative operation in applying the Constitution'.[142] McHugh and Gummow JJ then appeared to draw support for their general conclusion by tracing the apparent rejection of substantive legitimate expectations in Canada and New Zealand.[143] The reference to those other jurisdictions was curious. If the particular constitutional structure of Australia is the reason to rejection a new doctrine developed in the different UK context, what is the relevance of the approach in yet more jurisdictions? Why is the adoption of the doctrine in the UK distinguishable but its rejection in Canada and New Zealand of note?

138 *Teoh* (n 46) 290–91 (Mason CJ and Deane J), 299, 302 (Toohey J), 313 (McHugh J).
139 *Teoh* (n 46) 10.
140 *Teoh* (n 46) 21. Callinan J agreed on this issue: 48.
141 *Teoh* (n 46) 23.
142 *Teoh* (n 46) 23.
143 *Teoh* (n 46) 25–27.

CONCLUDING OBSERVATIONS

The apparent demise of the legitimate expectation reveals much about the modern direction of Australian administrative law but also the judicial anxieties which lie underneath much of it. At one level, the High Court's rejection of substantive legitimate expectations illustrates the break between the common law of Australia and the United Kingdom. The High Court rejected the substantive UK approach adopted in *Coughlan* in terms that appeared to channel Dicey. After all, Dicey proclaimed that England need not, perhaps could not, adopt the continental nonsense of European public law when it could gain all it needed, and more, from the common law. European public law was not simply different; it was alien and incompatible with English public law. The High Court of Australia rebuffed English innovations in *Coughlan* for the similar reason that it was infected with the sort of continental nonsense English judges had historically sought to guard against.

Sir Anthony Mason acknowledged those constitutional obstacles a few years after *Lam*, when he conceded that adoption of the English approach would require a 'revolution in Australian judicial thinking'.[144] It is unlikely that Australian courts will undertake a fundamental realignment of the strict conception of the separation of powers they have devised over the last 60 years. It is even more unlikely that the English experience of substantive legitimate expectations could provide a direct catalyst for such a change because *Coughlan* and its progeny have seen English courts become, at least from an Australian view, deeply involved in activities of the executive government. There is no inkling that Australian courts will venture down that path.

But the position of the High Court owes much more to the complex formalism that shapes and distorts Australian public law in equal measure. The strident terms in which the High Court has secured the supervisory jurisdiction of the courts has defined and limited the role of the courts. The benefit of that approach is clear. The strict principles governing the separation and protection judicial power have secured the courts' judicial review jurisdiction against any serious legislative incursion. These principles are now so well settled that they almost certainly exercise more influence in the drafting of legislation, so that restrictions on review that might be considered in other jurisdictions are quickly and quietly explained by government lawyers to their masters as simply unconstitutional. If it is so clear that the basic elements of review can never be narrowed or removed, it is hardly surprising to suggest that governments may abide these limits when considering

[144] Mason (n 51) 108.

legislative or administrative action. The fate of substantive expectations in Australia suggests that the courts are equally mindful of their institutional limits and will not venture beyond the broad doctrinal limits that flow from the constitutional settlement they have fashioned. Observance of these limits by the courts when faced with questions of substantive fairness is made much easier by the existence of tribunals of wide jurisdiction to review the merits or correctness of those limits. If the jurisdiction of tribunals can take account of issues that elsewhere could be considered as ones of legitimate expectations, little has been lost through the slow demise of legitimate expectations in Australia.

Index

www.ingramcontent.com/pod-product-compliance
Ingram Content Group UK Ltd.
Pitfield, Milton Keynes, MK11 3LW, UK
UKHW020133290926
15471UKWH00003B/453

9 781509 929733